DURGA AS MAHISASURAMARDINI

DURGA AS MAHISASURAMARDINI

A Dynamic Myth Of Goddess

Indira S. Aiyar

Foreword By
Ajay Mitra Shastri

GYAN

Published by

Gyan Publishing House
5, Ansari Road
Daryaganj, New Delhi-110002
Phone: 011-47034999, 9811692060
E-mail: books@gyanbooks.com

Distribution Network
gyanbooks.com
India, USA, Canada, UK, Australia, France

ISBN: 978-81-212-0510-8 (HB)

Reprint in India, 2024
First Published, 1997

Printed at: Gyan Press, Delhi.

Durga As Mahisasuramardini: a Dynamic Myth of Goddess
Author: Indira S. Aiyar

To
SHANKAR

CONTENTS

LIST OF PLATES

LIST OF ABBREVIATIONS

ABORI	:	*Annals of the Bhandarkar Oriental Research Institute*
ACI	:	*Ancient Cities of the Indus*
AIOC	:	*All India Oriental Conference*
AIRI	:	*Ananthacharya Indological Research Institute*
Ait.Br.	:	*Aitareya Brāhmaṇa*
ASI	:	*Archaeological Survey of India*
AV	:	*Atharva Veda*
Baud.Gr. Sū.	:	*Baudhāyana Gṛhya Sūtra*
Baud. Śr. Sū.	:	*Baudhāyana Śrauta Sūtra*
Bg.G.	:	*Bhagavat Gītā*
Bhāg.P.	:	*Bhāgavata Purāṇa*
Br.	:	*Brāhmaṇa*
Bṛhad. Up.	:	*Bṛhadāraṇyaka Upaniṣad*
Chānd. Up.	:	*Chāndogya Upaniṣad*
DC	:	*The Divine Consort*
Devī Bhāg.P.	:	*Devī Bhāgavata Purāṇa*
DM	:	*Devī Māhātmya*
Devī P.	:	*Devī Purāṇa*
DHI	:	*Development of Hindu Iconography*
EHI	:	*Elements of Hindu Iconography*
EM	:	*Epic Mythology*
ERE	:	*Encyclopaedia of Religion and Ethics*
GS	:	*Gṛhya Sūtra*
HV	:	*Harivaṁśa*
IC	:	*Indian Culture*
IHQ	:	*Indian Historical Quarterly*
IMG	:	*Indian Mother Goddess*
IVC	:	*Indus Valley Culture*
JAOS	:	*Journal of the American Oriental Society*
JBBRAS	:	*Journal of the Bombay Branch of the Royal Asiatic Society*
JBORS	:	*Journal of the Bihar and Orissa Research Society*
JISOA	:	*Journal of the Indian Society of Oriental Art*
JRASB	:	*Journal of the Royal Asiatic Society of Bengal*
JRAS	:	*Journal of the Royal Asiatic Society of Great Britain and Ireland*

L.P.	:	*Liṅga Purāṇa*
Mbh.	:	*Mahābhārata*
Mait. Saṁ.	:	*Maitrāyaṇī Saṁhitā*
Mārk.P.	:	*Mārkaṇḍeya Purāṇa*
MR	:	*The Modern Review*
Muṇḍ. Up.	:	*Muṇḍaka Upaniṣad*
Par.	:	*Parvan*
Rām.	:	*Rāmāyaṇa*
ṚV.	:	*Ṛg Veda*
Saṁ.	:	*Saṁhitā*
Śāṅk GS.	:	*Śāṅkhāyana Gṛhya Sūtra*
Śr. Sū	:	*Śrauta Sūtra*
ŚB; Śat. Br.	:	*Śatapatha Brāhmaṇa*
Taitt.Ār	:	*Taittirīya Āraṇyāka*
Taitt.Br.	:	*Taittirīya Brāhmaṇa*
Taitt.Saṁ.	:	*Taittirīya Saṁhitā*
Up.	:	*Upaniṣad*
VS.; Vāj. Saṁ.	:	*Vājasaneyi Saṁhitā*
YV	:	*Yajur Veda*

FOREWORD

There is no doubt whatsoever that the cult of the Great Goddess, popularly called Mother Goddess, is the oldest form of religious worship in vogue in all primitive societies. Her images, mostly in clay, sometimes baked into terracotta, have been reported from sites of most of the ancient world civilizations right from the earliest palaeolithic times. And India is, perhaps, the only country where the cult not only prevailed from the earliest known times but is also current to this day when most other ancient civilizations appear to have given it up. Her figures, mostly crude and unartistic, have been spotted from most of the pre-Harappan and Harappan sites. That it was a folk-cult not much appreciated by the sophisticated social classes is evident from the reticence of the Vedic *saṃhitās*, most probably coeval in point of time with the pre-Harappan and Harappan culture, about her. When compared to the rather derogatory remarks in a few Ṛg Vedic hymns about some other sectaries, their silence about the Mother Goddess worshippers may be taken to suggest an indifference, perhaps deliberate, in view of their wide diffusion. However, in somewhat later times, the cult was found to be irresistible in view of its great popularity among the masses whose feelings could just not be ignored for long. The epic and Purāṇic literature meant to cater to the needs and aspirations of all the social classes did not only take cognisance of her but recorded popular myths and legends and brought her into relationship with some of the most prominent divinities like Vishṇu and Śiva, especially the latter. She came to be called Durgā and regarded as the spouse of Śiva. She had various forms for different purposes, one of the most prominent of them being the 'Buffalo-trampler' *(Mahiṣa-mardinī)* who is greatly eulogised and adored in the Devī-Māhātmya, a part of the *Mārkaṇḍeya-Purāṇa* studied independently. Her worship was, and still is, very popular in various parts of India, especially the eastern one. She is represented in art variously and it is possible to trace the development of her iconography by carefully seeing her images chronologically.

In addition to her, there were other goddesses, major or minor, worshipped popularly among different sections of the people or in different regions who came to be aligned with her or treated as her various emanations. They were, generally speaking, called 'mothers' *(mātaraḥ)* or 'mother-group' *(mātṛ-gaṇa)*. They were regarded as universal mothers *(viśvasya mātaraḥ)* and associated with various principal gods and treated as their female energies created from their bodies for helping Caṇḍikā, the same as Kālī or Mahiṣa-mardinī, in the destruction of the demons. The number of the Mātṛkās was not fixed but was slightly later crystallised as seven. In art we find them represented separately as well as together. Their earliest collective representation is to be found during the Kushāṇa period at Mathurā or thereabouts where in some reliefs (Mathurā Museum Nos. F. 38 and 126) they are shown 'without any distinguishing vehicles, faces or attributes'. Later, during the same period, various kinds of distinctive marks made their appearance. Thus, a relief in the Mathurā Museum (No. 552) depicts seven divine mothers in a row, each holding a child in the left arm: the first, with three heads (fourth back one could not be shown in a relief) and holding a ladle in her right hand and riding a swan is Brāhmī; Māheśvarī carries a trident and stands against her mount bull; Kaumārī holds a *śakti* (spear) and has a peacock mount; Vaisṇavī carries a *gadā* (mace) and is shown kneeling against here mount *garuḍa*; Vārāhī has a broken staff and a buffalo for her mount; Indrāṇī held an object, perhaps a *vajra* (thunderbolt) and an elephant for her vehicle; and lastly Cāmuṇḍā, is recognised by her *pretā-vāhana*, garland of skulls *(muṇḍa-mālā)*, emaciated body and sunken belly. These are flanked by Vīrabhadra and Gaṇapati on the right and left respectively. These goddesses are obviously the female energies of the gods whose emblems are used for them.

These early artistic representations of the mother goddesses are later reflected in the textual canonisation of their iconography during the Gupta age. The concept of the Seven Mothers *(Sapta-mātṛkās)* became so widespread that in the seventh century the Chālukyas of Badami regarded themselves as nurtured by them *(sapta-mātribhirabhivardhitānām)*. The number of mother goddesses, though generally crystallised at seven, was fluctuating as shown by the art evidence. It was quite natural in view of the accommodative and assimilative spirit of our forefathers and the multiplicity of mother goddesses worshipped popularly in every nook and corner of India from the earliest times. Later, they were reckoned as 8, 9, 12 and up to 64. They were also called *Yoginīs* whose official number got crystallised at sixty-four and their hypaethral shrines have been found at Bheraghat, Ranipur-Jharial, Mitauli and Dudahi. They had their own distinctive mode of worship called *maṇḍala-krama* developed and had their own priests well-versed in this mode. It is to be noted in this context that all the 64-Yoginī temples are circular *(maṇḍala)* in plan. Most of the villages in South India have temples dedicated to the mother goddess called variously. However, all these differently forms or emanations of the same Mother Goddess are called Durgā, Pārvatī or Mahiṣamardinī (this is indeed a description of her role) and are associated generally with Śiva. In fact, they fulfil a psychological necessity. And the creation of goddesses goes on in India, and Santoshī Mātā is a gift of the latter half of the twentieth century.

Although a few works on the goddess cult, including the Mahiṣa-mardinī have been recently published, the present work by Dr. Indira S. Aiyar is undoubtedly the most acceptable and of a pioneering nature inasmuch as it dwells upon the history of the cult including the concept of myth-making in a comprehensive manner. Its very important plus point is the stress on the interdependence of socio-economic-religious life. I am happy to commend the book, which substantially represents her doctoral dissertation approved for its Ph. D. degree by the University of Bombay in 1991, to all serious students of early Indian religious history and congratulate her on this scholarly work.

'Prachi'
23, Vidya Vihar
Rana Pratap Nagar
Nagpur-440 022

Ajay Mitra Shastri

PREFACE

The cult of the mother goddess has an unbroken history in the Hindu religious ethos. The cult's origin in the world's religious history is in the hoary past, and its diffusion ranges over a very wide area as seen from archaeological remains.

The pastoral Aryans settled towards an agricultural mode of living, changing their religious requirements, as they pressed eastwards into India. The Goddess cult must have provided the required ritual needed for agricultural fertility and fecundity. The Goddess Durgā as Śākambharī fulfilled such a need. She is elected and established as the Great Goddess, in the myths relating to her fights with the Asuras. She is exalted in her role as Mahiṣāsuramardinī. The mythic aspect of this episode has not received sufficient attention. The myth's relevance is also important, studied against the socio-historical background. Psychology supplies the reasons behind an ambivalent Goddess. Set against this background, the mythology of Mahiṣāsuramardinī has been adjudged, treating the myth from the viewpoints of the theories on Myth and Symbolism as set forth by Western scholars. The present volume was originally presented to the Bombay University for the doctoral dissertation.

I would like to express my gratitude to all those scholars, friends and well wishers who have lended me a helping hand in the completion of this study.

My special thanks are due to Prof. Y.S. Walimbe, who as my guiding teacher had introduced me to the subject of Myth and Symbolism, affording a fresh approach to the subject, sharpening my perception of the myth.

I express my deep gratitude to Prof. Ajay Mitra Shastri for encouraging me in the first place to publish the dissertation and now readily agreeing to write the Foreword.

I wish to thank Prof. K.K.A. Venkatachari, the Founder Director of Ananthacharya Indological Research Institute, Mumbai, for his encouragement.

It is with pleasure and gratitude that I acknowledge my family's supportive attitude and encouragement, but for which this study would not have been possible. My thanks are also due to their sincere help in the innumerable areas while putting together this work.

Some of the photographic plates I have reproduced are from the following sources:

1. Tattvaloka (Mumbai) : Plates No. 9-13 and 20-28
2. Ms. Pavetri Kumari Shivram: 29-35 (from her unpublished M.A. dissertation, 1987, M.S. University, Baroda);
3. Ms. Carmel Berkson: No. 17

I thank them for their timely assistance. The rest of the photographs are from the personal collection of my husband Mr. Shankar Aiyar.

Last but not least my sincere thanks are due to the Directors and Editors of Gyan Publishing House for their sincere interest and involvement while bringing out this book.

INTRODUCTION

Myths are rich in symbolism, and more so the Hindu myths. The best example is the Goddess myth, scintillating in its varied imageries, the facets throwing up myriads of meanings, each according to the level of perception of the viewer. The depth of perception is sensitized and our view brought into sharper focus, if we understood what a myth is, the meaning of its contents and its function.

In the myth of the Goddess as Mahiṣāsuramardinī the concept of the female principle becomes the Supreme Being, and the Aryan gods welcome her as such[1]. Folk traditions get absorbed and remodelled by the Big Tradition. This fascinating aspect induced me to make an in-depth study of the subject.

The role of the Goddess as Mahiṣāsuramardinī gets mentioned in the epic in some late stutis. This gets elaborated in the Purāṇas, but is given an extended treatment in the *Devī Māhātmya* (DM.) section, a late addition to the *Mārkaṇḍeya Purāṇa*. The DM has been dated to the early 5th centurty A.D., though this concept of the Goddess is seen to be of the 2nd or 3rd centuries B.C., as seen from the iconographic representations of the period. This again would date the myth further back in time, since iconographic representations concretise mythic ideas much later.

Taking the DM as a Purāṇa[2], there are innumerable opinions on the meaning and function of myths[3]. Though myths were held in contempt by earlier scholars, they have grown steadily in importance, and in recent years have been elevated to the status of a discipline pursued by scholars of psychology, anthropology, sociology, and, not in the least, by the historico-religious school. The DM can be interpreted in almost all the ways as put forth by the theorists. The latest is the structural theory propounded by Claude Lévi-Strauss. This theory stands undemolished yet, because no later opinion has offered a more acceptable viewpoint. The theory has some shortcomings, specially as related to myths belonging to sophisticated cultures. Lévi-Strauss himself acknowledged its suitability to totemic, primitive societies. Further, he says each version of a myth is important, and for a weighty assessment of a myth, not only the versions in the Bigger and Smaller Traditions, but all over the world similar groups of myths should be collected and scrutinised to understand the significance of a particular detail. In Indian myths, access to local versions would entail an enormous amount of time and resources which ruled out any such consideration.

Majority opinion of scholars has been that the most suitable method for adjudging Indian myths is the text-historical, or, the historico-religious method. This method involves tracing the possible origin of a concept to its earliest literary mention. This being the Vedas, an attempt has been made to situate the concept in the epithets involving the Goddess, and her fierce, or benign counterparts.

The concept of a group of Mothers seems more ancient than that of a single goddess. Cāmuṇḍā and Kālī also could have grown from this background. These goddesses have folk origins, and they are Sanskritised in the epic. Durgā's origin and affinity to the folk ethos cannot be glossed over, and upto the 7th and 8th centuries A.D., this fierce aspect of the goddess is mentioned in the literature of the period. Village goddesses, a peculiarity of the religious tradition of South, and the myths pertaining to them show the slow haul our myth has taken to be Sanskritised. Since autochthonous cults have had a great influence on the Aryan religion, folk cults could contain the seed for our myth. In the epic, Brahminisation of the Goddess is set in motion which task is accomplished in the Purāṇas.

Myths are seen as symbols themselves, not merely translating symbols into language. Man is termed homo symbolicum, and all his activities are representations of his symbolic thinking. To assess the Mahiṣāsuramardinī myth, symbols from Jung's and Cassirer's viewpoint are discussed. Scholars have stressed the multivalency of religious symbols, and hence of myths.

The valency of a myth is enhanced if the proper socio-cultural context is taken into account. Removed from this context, the myth may lose much of its meaning as intended by its composers. Further, would the stature of the Goddess reflect the position of women of that society? How to explain the anomalous position of women as compared to the supremacy voluntarily acceded to the Goddess by the Aryan gods? How is it that man has tended to deify motherhood but tries to 'control' the single female? Is this attitude reflected in his religious mores ? Why should the human mind always propitiate the polarities contained in the female principle as a deity? Who were the Asuras, and their leader Mahiṣa, and what is their background? These and such other allied questions are tackled in the ensuing chapters of this study.

The current approach is an attempt to strike a balance between Western and Indian (i.e. Purāṇic) traditions and present a holistic study of the myth. A lot of work has been done on the Goddess Durgā, and her various myths, but little attention has been paid to the Mahiṣāsuramardinī myth. The DM itself has been interpreted by a few recent scholars. Ritual significance has always caught the fancy of scholars, and innumerable interpretations have been written on the ritual aspect of the text. Very little work has been attempted on symbolism and myth aspect of this motif. This attempt hopes to fill such a lacuna.

Since the DM is ritually important, it has enjoyed independent status as a myth, not merely as an appendage to a bigger Purāṇa. There are plenty of editions of the text and translations of the DM. In fact, there are translations of the text into European languages, the earliest being 1788 AD.[4] The main text used here is the one published by Ramakrishna Mutt, Madras, with translation (Tamil), and notes by Aṇṇā, 1982. The verses are numbered with reference to the DM. text, and does not follow that of the *Mārkaṇḍeya Purāṇa*.

The Śākta and Tantric aspects of the goddess cult did not seem relevant to the study of the mythic aspects of the Mahiṣāsuramardinī motif. And, a study of Tantrism would entail a deep study of the ritual aspects of the cult, which is beyond the purview of this work.

To understand and appreciate the Devī myth better, a basic study of the views of Western scholars on myth and its meaning is attempted in the first chapter.

REFERENCES

1. According to recent consensus of views the words 'Aryan' and 'Dravidian' denote cultures, rather than races. Opinions are in a flux about the nature of the IV culture. Since this study is about the Goddess cult per se, the nomenclatures 'Aryan' and 'Dravidian' are kept on the traditional lines for the sake of convenience, and to show the difference in their religious approach.

2. Ch. V. Sn Purāṇas
3. Cf. Ch. I.
4. Coburn-*Devī Māhātmya : The Chrystallisation of the Goddess Tradition,* p. 52.

Chapter I
STUDY OF MYTH AND ITS MEANING

The word 'Myth' had a very poor connotation once. It was considered a 'disease of the mind'. Since then scholars of various disciplines like anthropology, archaeology, religion, etc. have realised the importance of myths and their role in assessing a race. A fairly recent opinion has discovered that the components of myths may be amenable to resolution as algebraic equations. In between these two opinions, there are as many views as there are studies on myths. These varied definitions are cited below as an introduction and to show the wide range of opinions the study has elicited.

White studying these opinions it is worth remembering that no single theory was found applicable universally, or was proved infallible. A few definitions may have fitted a few more cultures than others, but that was all. Further, myths are multivalent. As would be seen in this study, Indian myths are amenable to be interpreted in many ways. No single theory should be exclusively applied to the myths. Dogmatism would result only in a forced and artificial interpretation.

A Short Résumé of the Opinions

1. Etymologists emphasized the root meaning of the names of the characters in a myth.
2. Frazer was the first who saw a connection between myth and ritual.
3. It was thought that natural forces were personified as the

heroes of myths.

4. Euhemerists saw the heroes mythicised as gods.
5. The evolutionist theory saw the development in myths as a stage in the evolution of man.
6. Archaeologists put heavy emphasis on lithic evidence to support their theory on myths.
7. Totemism was emphasised by certain anthropologists.
8. Allied to this was the classificatory theory advanced by French anthropologists.
9. History was seen enshrined in myths.
10. A marxist slant was given by some historians.
11. The historico-religious scholars tended to overemphasise the historical uniformity in myths, belaboured by Frazer in his later works.
12. Indian mythologists, along with the ancient Greeks, saw a ritual connection in their myths. The Indians resorted to *Ākhyānas*, for historicity, and *Sthalapurāṇas* to establish a ritual connection.
13. Myths were seen to contain morals to shape our lives.
14. Psychologists similarly emphasised the psychic contents of myths. Symbolism in myths, as a theory leaned on this.
15. If content was important in a myth, its function was seen as the sole meaning. This was a major step for anthropologists, and, later, function was taken as equally important for myth as its contents. Diachronic and synchronic study of myths were undertaken.
16. Primitives were thought to come out with myths under a sudden heavy emotional stress. But this theory was later amended. Primitive mind was seen to think out solutions for problems garbed in mythic binaries. This theory owed much to the scholarship of linguists.
17. The etiological theory sees causation in myths.
18. The text-historical method of tracing the possible origin of a myth to earlier texts has been recommended by a majority of scholars as the most viable theory and best suited to Indian myths. In the present study, this method has been followed in the main, backed by the psychological theory. But, wherever any theory could be used in the assessment of the Goddess myth, this has been pointed

out.

A more detailed assessment of these theories, with Indian examples wherever possible to support the relevant viewpoint follows. The limitation any particular theory imposes on a broader judgement has also been pointed out.

In Ancient Greece, according to Herodotus, Homer and Hesiod are said to have given form to the gods and settled their function. While scrutinizing the myths, Homer found ritualistic connections to them, especially the mystery myths. But both saw euhemeristic reasons for the myths. Euhemeros, a Sicilian, living in the latter half of the fourth century B.C., travelled extensively, and set forth the theory that all gods were deified men. Thus, this theory saw historic background to myths.

Max Müller set forth the philological approach to the myths of the Indo-European genre. But he also felt that myths were the result of 'disease of language', "a dark shadow which language throws upon thought"[1]. In ancient myths of India and Greece, gods were shown to have human weaknesses. This was termed as mythical pathology.

The philological approach to myths was refuted fully by the anthropologists, who studied them later. Scholars who emphasise symbolism in myths have also refuted Max Müller's above view. Myth-making is the fundamental activity of the primitive. To name it as a disease is an incorrect interpretation.

James Frazer has wielded an enormous influence on the study of myths. His main contention was that myths were similar over a very wide area of the world, irrespective of the type of culture, civilised or primitive. He started the trends of the evolutionists that myths were similar where the societies also were similarly placed in evolution. He collected an enormous number of myths to prove this fact.[2] Further, he found that myths were irrevocably aligned with rituals. This idea was enthusiastically taken up by many others including Jane Harrison and it continued to show its influence upto Malinowski.

Criticism

Myths should not be viewed narrowly that they are associated with rituals, or worse still that they originate from rituals. Biblical scholars like E.O. James tried to evaluate myths this way. This connection with rituals was used to explain myths in the Near East, especially the Hebraic ones. Mythical rites have also been described by Frazer as a mimetic action, or, sympathetic magic in Frazer's words. They become the thing they mimic in the immediacy of time and place[3].

Frazer is seen as the proto-structuralist[4]. Like Lévi-Strauss, he also did not have any first-hand knowledge of the societies he studied. He endeavoured to compare human psychology by comparing details of human culture from all over the world. Whereas Lévi-Strauss considered the primitives as capable of discursive thinking, Frazer thought them quite inferior. Both Lévi-Strauss and Frazer dropped facts that did not suit their theory, or tried tortuous arguments to fit these to their theories. Scholars following the Euhemerist theory see Frazer as their leader in this field.[5] Frazer was inclined towards this view but this theory does not fit all myths universally.

Frazer has stated that mythical and scientific thoughts have the same quest for reality. Myth is a combination of the real and the poetic. If it did not have an element of truth in it , it would have no base to stand on and would collapse. But myth like science does not seek to answer any questions. It is the outcome of a dynamic, emotional thought process with a logic of its own.

Some scholars saw *Powers of Nature* transformed as mythical heroes. Alfred Hillebrandt[6] was a follower of this theory. He also believed that geographical conditions had a great effect on the formation of myths. Vṛtra was seen as an Armenian god, connected with snow and ice. Indra released the waters of the rivers in winter with thunderstorms.[7]

Creation of myths is a constant process, never inactive even for a moment. It changes a traditional format of a deity or it discards out-dated deities. There are many reasons for this. Psychology forms an important reason. Fear or pleasure that impresses on the mind, gives rise to gods and demons. Myths are woven around these figures. All human experiences are thus changed to myths and the experiences, according as they are good or bad, are turned to gods or demons. The basic images are changed according to the cultural and religious ethos of a country. Many other factors also may be instrumental in the formation of myths. These may be : diffusion due to migration, climate, and the creative genius of a particular poet or composer, whose influence could be far-reaching. The climate and the environment also have an influence on the religion and culture of a people. This has been relied on by scholars like Payne[8], to explain the cruel nature of the goddess Kālī. Discarding earlier opinions of etymological derivations of myths, it was felt that meanings of the names of a god are too general to rely on. Sometimes etymology in a god's name could even lead to misunderstanding of a myth. Unlike the evolutionists, lower mythology is seen not as a lower stage in the religious evolution of a people, but it is a separate chapter in the religious history. Geographic reasons are thought necessary to find the origin of a Vedic deity, since demons and gods freely exchange places in the ṚgVeda. The complicated evolution of myths is seen as the result of the interaction between the internal and external laws of a culture.

Astral Origins of Myths

The school which tried to reach for the original home of myths reached farther than India, into Babylonia. Astral origins were further added because the Babylonian myths were about heavenly bodies and those people were the first astronomers. The philological or etymological explainers of myths received a fillip from Usner who explained the Greek gods thus.[9] Amongst Indian scholars, Tilak and a few others have relied on the slender astrological evidence to date the origin of a myth.[10]

The evolutionists envisaged that any change in a myth or a religion was only a part of a change in the total scheme of civilization. Tylor and Morgan who were the protagonists of this theory stated that this change was predetermined[11]. Andrew Lang saw myths as symbolising the world around us.[12] The adherents to this approach were mostly anthropologists, and this theory replaced the philological approach started by Max Müller. Their concept of myths was that from any given point in the evolution of cultures, either progress or regress was made by man. The higher mythologies are seen to have been developed by inspired poets from the material contained in a race, comparatively untouched by outside cultures. The myths which are loosely got together and contain no elevating thoughts to distinguish them are said to be the outcome of a degradation of the cultivated class. Further, in certain cases, primitive tribal lore was seen to be akin to Greek myths. This was particularly so in the case of gods, Indian or Greek, when they showed excessive human weaknesses, or according to Lang, an irrational behaviour. The German scholars, Schelling and William Schmidt, along with Lang, tried to philosophise mythical intuition as starting from local representations of god-head, as, for instance, 'this stone', 'this brook', etc.[13] Tylor added to this the part played by the collective unconscious.

The evolutionists stated that the myths reflected the mental condition of a society. Since myths of savage imagination are there in cultured societies like those of the Aryans and the Greeks, a historical condition of the human intellect is seen as the cause for this stage of myths.[14] The human mind is constrained to work in a particular way, whatever the culture, because of certain unity of human thought.[15] This is supported by James.[16] According to this scholar, similar themes like gods versus demons, cosmogony, etc. occur all over the world. This is not due to the diffusion of culture. But, it is due to a stage in the evolution in the religion and culture of the people.

By emphasising the similarity in mythic minds in diverse cultures, primitive, or advanced, they opened themselves up for criticism. The functionalists pointed out their ignoring the connection of myths with rituals, and overtook them with their theory.

Functionalist Theory

The pioneer of this theory is Bronislaw Malinowski. He studied one small community of Trobrianders in an island in Melanesia for four years. Births, marriages and deaths were recorded along with the islanders' rituals. By this method, he showed the 'function' of myths in a community.

Frazer first showed the intimate relationship between myths and ritual, which was later followed by Malinowski, Lord Raglan, Hocart and others.[17] Religious tenets are spun out into stories, according to Malinowski. The power of religion in its rites, places of worship, its icons, a11 revivify memories of past acts of grace. These also influence the morality of the society. The most important concept of religion is how it is lived. A myth is a part of a religion. Therefore, its position on how it shapes society has to be considered; that is, its function has to be adjudged. Thus, a myth is defined by its function. Its function is ritualistic. It acts as a charter for social order and a pattern for moral behaviour. This is called functional anthropology. Social anthropologists like Robertson Smith, Durkheim, Hubert Morse, Radcliffe Brown and others emphasized the social aspect of religion, and that social aspects of myths also should be studied. Thus, the functional approach deals with the relevance of myths in society, and leads towards the cultural approach to myths. The narrative value of a myth is important as it imbeds the moral conduct of man, and binds a contract between him and god.[18] Thus, the primary function of myths is neither to explain anything, nor to recall any historic event, or, to express fantasies. This view emphasises the social aspect of myths. The functional approach gives an insight into the function of myths in society. The functionalists thought that a change in myths and religion was a cultural means towards social cohesion. Thus, the religious change was slow, but was contained always in the larger functioning whole of the society.[19] Any myth that ignores rituals is, according to Malinowsky,[20] not a myth at all, but an oldwives' tale, and it is barren.

Myths establish the patterns of behaviour, since they reach for their model the primeval period. They also support ancient magical rituals.[21] Further, it is thought that since myths provide the rules for rituals and moral behaviour, the function of myths is not to explain, or, recount past history.[22] Primitive myths are living faiths. They work on the already existing folktales of the tribes and magic is the bridge between folk-tales and myths. Main myths always recount the primeval miracle of magic.[23] Malinowsky studied only primitive myths. He felt that these myths would answer the social and cultural queries that are not clear in the higher myths. Myths of higher cultures are found not relevant today, because they are not 'lived out' today. Primitive myths are alive, and are not just symbolic. They are the expressions of the tribe's intellectual explanation to metaphysical questions. Myths perform a cultural function by establishing a precedent for the golden age. If ritually followed, the ancient golden age can be established now. They should be studied for their significance today in social and cultural contexts. The function of myths is to strengthen tradition and validate it by connecting it to primordial time. Being a bridge between the past and the present, myths represent a continuity of culture.

Social Contribution of Myths

Malinowski contributed in no small measure towards understanding myths. According to him, myths justified institutions and customs in a society. This brought into importance the social contribution of myths, and their relevance in society. But, Malinowski concentrated on tribal myths alone, presuming that the study of these alone was sufficient. He emphasized that only those myths justifying custom, etc. were the relevant ones. And, he over-emphasised the ritual connection of myths, disregarded the historical background to myths, opined they were neither aetiological, nor symbolic. They are a reality lived, and therefore not symbolic, and they do not explain anything but state the superiority of a god, therefore, they are not aetiological. Just as Malinowski thought that a people without a knowledge of writing could not have discursive thinking, Levy Bruhl thought that the primitive mind thought only emotionally.[24] He later amended this opinion. This has been disproved by the structuralists. Because a group of people did not possess written history, history as a whole was ignored by the functionalists in studying myths. Myths can become meaningful only if studied against a socio-cultural background. The ambiguity of cultural symbols should be unravelled both by historians, as well as sociologists. A myth is even called the speech of history.[25] According to the structuralists, history is a continuation of myths. History fulfils the same function now that myths did in an illiterate society. Myths ensured the safe preservation of the past and the present for the future, and an understanding of the past also comes from the present perspective of the past. Thus, a synchronic study in the present, of a tribe's culture without understanding its past history and its action on the culture is of little use.[26]

Criticism

Malinowski's statement that there are myths which only validate customs and institutions was an overstatement. The Greek myths for example do not come under this category at all. Similar opinion is that myths deal with sacred subjects or with rituals. This again can be overruled as there are a number of myths which are classified under originating myths. These usually treat with some economic or cultural inventions. For the Trobrianders, myth was part and parcel of their lives and they acted their myths in rituals. This led to the erroneous conclusion that all myths perforce must be connected with rituals. Durkheim and Joan Harrison were of the opinion that myth is the narration in words, while ritual is the same thing acted or performed.[27] Myth and ritual might occur together and have identical motive, because they are able to channelise aggression and diffuse anxiety of people, and thus satisfy a particular need of society. It might be better stated that where myths are closely associated with rituals, they may imply a common origin which arose out of the psychic needs of a community.

Myth and Ritual

That myths are inseparable from rituals has been reiterated with emphasis by many scholars. Indeed, one of the classifications of myths is that they are an explanatory work on rituals. Whether myths belong to primitive or cultured societies, a connection does exist at least in the case of some myths, with rituals. This relationship, though, is neither universal nor obligatory as some scholars are wont to opine.

One opinion is that to get to the original nucleus of a myth, one way is to weed out all the poetic accretions, get rid of all unaesthetic narrations and obtain the original form of the deity, as well as his myths which will be laid bare.[28] If the rituals are studied, we may get to know the form of the deity worshipped in the myth. Rituals are not so much concerned with the idea behind the deity, as with his person itself, seen to exist in the myths.

To understand the mythic figures of most of the epics, a clear understanding of the religion of the pre-epic period should be gained, if it is available. But it is not always possible to trace the origin of the epic deities to the Vedas, because progress has not always been in a straight line. Nothing may have been recorded in the existing literature. The myths of the epics might have been well-known to the authors of the Brāhmaṇas, and the Upaniṣads. But their priorities were different, and therefore they may have paid scant attention to these myths.

Vedic gods' names are derived from appellatives. It is almost impossible to differentiate the different phases of growth in the mythology. Though the Brahmins stood above folklore; they were not away from them, and were also influenced by them. Vedic mythology is thus not a system but a conglomeration of different elements, which includes those of the autochthonous peoples. Another difficulty in interpreting Vedic mythology was, the gods underwent reinterpretation as the Aryans moved to the interior regions towards the tropical plains. Though the methods of interpreting myths differ with people, one way of studying the Vedic myths may be through its ritual literature. Some rituals like the *Soma* sacrifice may have been assimilated from an older popular belief.[29] The mythology of the ṚgVeda seems thus never a finished product, but seems constantly in a flux. Vedas seem a vast magical treatise expressed symbolically.[30] The images have a ritual significance. The most common myth in the ṚgVeda seems to be the cosmogonic myth. All myths of creation or cosmogonic myths are connected with assuring success of a beginning of sexual or cultural life. They narrate order emerging from chaos.[31]

Difference between the Vedic and the Brāhmaṇa Myths

In the Vedic period, the conflict was between the gods and the demons. Virtuous men doing sacrifices were prevented by demons and the humans were protected and assisted by the gods. In the Brāhmaṇas, the mythic period of "then" was re-enacted ritually to bring back the good times. In the later Brāhmaṇa and Upaniṣadic periods, myths were written from the view point of the Brahmins who considered themselves gods. Gods now disliked virtuous men or demons, who would compete with them for the limited quantity of power, immortality, and heaven. Thus the opposition between gods and demons was applied between gods and excessively virtuous men.

The different ethical attitudes of gods are reflected in the cosmologies of the two periods. In the earlier period, heaven and earth were separated or joined by intervening either. The gods in heaven and men on earth transacted business, with the demons outside this parameter. In the Purāṇic period, the two worlds were heaven and hell separated by the axis mundi, *Sumeru*. The gods fought the demons and also men-ascetics (by guile).[32]

Even the structuralists have agreed that, irrespective of whichever was the original, both myth and ritual are very similar to each other. But, it is not right to judge a particular myth as a standard format and assess myths all over the world accordingly.

It may be wrong to rigidly classify myths as sacred or explanatory of rituals, etc., it is opined, because myths are traditional tales, and men do not react the same way to emotional stimuli, like birth, sex, war, death, etc.[33] This might not be right, because the mode of expression may differ according as the culture varies, but the mythopoeic mind is said to be the same the world over. But confining myths always in association with rituals shows no logic.

One opinion is that, if a people in a myth-making stage of religion come across a ritual or custom which seems anamolous they try to explain it by inventing a myth for it, and thus the myth usually follows the ritual.[34] Some myths may show an apparent disconnection with rituals. But a closer examination may reveal that it does explain some ritual, or, ceremonies. Such contributors to the evolutionist theory also reiterate that at least in primitive societies, since the savage is a man of action than of theories and words, he prefers to act out his emotions, and myths are composed later to justify such actions. Mythologies may be the dramatic representation of the emotional needs of the primitive mind. As time passes, the primitive attempts to classify and find a moral basis to the stories. There are many similar points between myths of cultured societies like the Greeks and the Indians, and those of the primitives like the aborigines of Australia, the natives of Africa and the Amerindians. Another origin is seen in the relationship between myths and rituals. A dance by an individual of a tribe in ecstasy is noticed by other tribe members and copied. The original meaning is lost with each copying and a myth is composed to explain it. Wars and hunts are mimed to return to the ancient sacred time. Some myths are born to explain such rituals and not vice versa.[35] Ritual myths are those without reciting which no rites can be performed. By reciting a myth, one leaves the profane time and enters the sacred time. Just as Homer and Hesiod modified Greek myths, Hindu myths were expanded and rewritten by Hindu ritualists. In Greece, people lost faith in what the gods did, but believed in the gods. Hesiod and the Upaniṣadic thinkers went one step further reaching to the origin of myths. They regressed to the ancient sacred period not by ritual, but by thought. The primitive myths are concerned with how the gods created. On the other hand, the Indo-European myths deal with what happened to the gods and not what they created. The adventures of the Indian Great Goddess, or those of Zeus or Ba, a1 made popular mythology more interesting.

Many ills are cured by reciting a myth, because in mythical time recreation of the world took place. By reciting the myth, the world is created again as of yore, and the ills are washed off. Critical situations can be warded off by the recitation of a myth, and irremediable situations could also be corrected. Some myths, like for instance the cosmogonic myth, can be recited to overcome despondency due to sterility, sickness, defeat in war, etc. These situations can be reversed by the recitation of the myth. One can achieve inspiration for poesy, and the aged and the decrepit can gain hope from such recitations. This means that the myth is multivalent, that is, it is valid on several levels. Most primitive myths are cosmogonic, creation myths, whereas only some myths of the more evolved societies deal with cosmogony. In Indian myths, one of the *Pañcalakṣaṇas* is cosmogony, and thus this subject becomes an obligatory additive. The *Devī Māhātmya*, starts with the Madhu-Kaiṭabha episode which is a creation myth. Cosmogony myths are recited for agricultural ferility also. The primitive tribes who act out these myths are extensively covered in Eliade's *Myth And Reality*, pp. 43-47.

Thus, myths are sacred and true, because they deal with supernatural beings. They give the history of how some new facts emerged, in culture, society or religion. They are the paradigms of all human acts. Myths should be known, not just read, because thus one gains knowledge of the events and through this power one is able to manipulate the particular events to suit the needs. Thus myths justify the creation and the existence of humans.

For the anthropologist, the whole myth is important in all its aspects; but, to understand a culture fully, a deep knowledge of the rituals and the techniques should be gained. It has even been stated that myths are about rituals.[36] Tylor, and Andrew Lang, the evolutionists, felt that all societies had similar myths irrespective of whether the people were civilized or primitive. This view ignored the function of myths and their connection with rituals. In myths of rituals, once rationalisation occurs, and doubts arise, rituals are discontinued, and the myths die out. James[37] feels strongly that myths can be understood only when the cult is supported by archaeological evidence and the two together are studied. Rituals generate myths, it is true, but sometimes myths generate rituals. Again, not all myths are formed from rituals. Sumerian and Mesopotamian myths have no connection with rituals, it has been proved. The former myths were concerned with agriculture and fertility, while those of the latter dealt with the relationship between God and men. There are a few Greek myths which are associated with rituals but do not originate from rituals. Those myths of Greece which emphasize fertility and associated rituals like transvestism, etc., may have originated from rituals. If those elements are removed from the myths, the myths sound disjointed.[38]

A recent Indian scholar[39] has dealt with the origin of such goddesses like Aditi, Mātaṅgī, Lajjā Gaurī, Ambuvācī, and others on the basis of the *sthalapurāṇas*. *Sthalapurāṇas* contain local versions of the history of the place as well as myths concerning the icon and rituals associated with it.

Historical Interpretation

Religious historians feel equally strongly for their interpretation of myths. The religious historian is moved to consider not only the phenomenon of the religious symbol, but also the history in which it is embedded. Though myths are interpreted by psychologists, anthropologists, and sociologists, all striving to interpret myths strictly from their points of view, the historico-religious view seems the only true approach, and one's rewards are rich if one is not swayed by the views of other disciplines[40]. Further, religious experience buried in history becomes history itself, the historical moment coming into existence due to the impact of culture and society on the religious experience. Myths are viewed as records of beliefs, and some facts may be imbedded in them, to obtain which, the historian has to sift carefully through the material.[41] There has been vast movements of legends geographically, all over the country. Some of these are also found in Tamil and Sanskrit literature and in the Buddhist *Jātaka* tales. The best definition of a myth is that it is sacred history, and its characters are true. It tells of a reality that took place in the original time. It is real, because it deals with the things that exist today, and also because supernatural beings enact it.

Myths have in them embedded historical consciousness. It is the view of society turned onto itself. So it is authentic.[42] The period of myths or when they are said to have taken place could be located as *proto chronos*, because gods are said to have been its participants and supernatural events are said to have taken place. Myths explained some social or religious changes. To give credibility, in successive generations, the whole format was changed or fresh material added to make the myths relevant to the particular period. The myths sometimes changed so much that the original was transformed beyond recognition. If a myth retained such a form, then it lost its credibility. Complicated explanations were needed to explain obscure contents.

Myths are built around two constituents: The agent of action and the purpose of action. Whatever the culture, myths try to draw morals and teach through their actions. Primitive tribes prefer to listen to myths with morals. Myths are narrations of a very remote period, preserving and thus giving importance to a particular event. They are thus a prototype of history, containing a people's past as they saw it. They may not be accurate in their description of history, but from them the values of a society may be gleaned. At rituals, the *Ākhyānas* in the *Purāṇas* were recited. These preserved the genealogies of kings' dynasties. As such they were the preservers of history. Such myths also contained elemental or archetypal characters, themes, and symbols.[43]

If Greek myths are uniquely different from Near Eastern myths in this that fertility in myths is never presented as separate from rituals, the unique difference of Indian myths from those of the Near East and Greece is that abstract ideas are embedded in them. The concept of *Ādityas* (releasers), and *Dānavas* (restrainers) carries on as *'sat'*, *'asat'*, which later gets fully developed in the *Upaniṣads*. The ideas contained in the Hindu myths become more explicit in the later myths, but are seen to be implicit even in the Vedic myths.[44] Fertility and sex are approbated, but destruction is necessary. Worldly affairs are secondary in importance, and the whole pattern of the cosmos, taken together, is of prime importance. Gods are definitely superior, Reality is one only, and shades of it are unacceptable. There is a very small portion of Indian mythology which has originated from rituals. There is a contemplative and abstract streak running through all its myths. An examination of the ṚgVedic hymns shows that they were composed to celebrate certain historical events. Mythopoeisation grew when the Aryans made a religion out of these events. This was achieved by symbolism and the change of meanings of certain words. The myths relating to the conflict between the gods and demons are said to be about historic events. When, with prejudice, the enemies were spoken of as evil, the asuras[45] came to stand for evil when the Aryans commemorated these events. The victories of Indra were hymned. These were recited and the original feat re-enacted. Thus, history is seen to be changed into religion. Human functionaries as well as powers of nature in the Aryan versus Asura conflict were intermingled in the Vedic religion. Human functionaries at first were said to have been assigned powers of nature, and both mentioned in their combined attributes, in the beginning. These attributes were so confused that myths had to be invented to make sense.[46]

The agricultural and urban societies of the Near East and the Middle Eastern Asian countries have myths of the battle between gods and demons. This is seen as symbolising the restoration of order in the world, by the victorious deity and chaos is annihilated. This fight of a god with one or many demons is a recurrent myth amongst the Mesopotamians, Hittites and the Egyptians. This is the myth about the fight between Marduk and Tiamat, Tesup and the serpent Illuyankas, or between the two serpents Re and Apophis.[47] Seen thus, it is not surprising that an agricultural country like India was preoccupied with battles between gods and demons, even in the Vedic myths.

Lévi-Strauss states[48] that in a modern society history fulfils the same function which myths used to do for primitive societies. In fact, history is the continuation of myths. Myth is the language of history.[49] This also might be one of the reasons why cultures different in space and time have similar themes.

Primitive myths, more than any others, contain in them ideas of political, social and cultural set-up as well as technocratic and religious changes. Myths are seen as the treasure-house of history deposited by the primitive or early cultures.[50] They allow the listener to interpret them according to his understanding. The primitive man projected into the mythological past, when he wanted to understand the origin of things. In myths, the first attempts were made to give chronology to occurrences, and genealogy and history to the gods. But a point to remember is that time in mythologies is one undifferentiated unity of the past, present and future.

Indian myths, i.e., the Purāṇas are said not to be come under any classification, or specific analysis. Structural as well as other classifications have been attempted, but, the myths were too complicated to come under any such simplistic single theory. The viable method approved by many scholars has been the text-historical method. Under this method, the origin is traced to possible .early mentions. This includes also an evaluation of symbols. Again, there should be no arbitrary value judgement of symbols.

Social and Cultural Function of Myths

In the nineteenth century, the word 'myth' was given the meaning 'fiction', or 'illusion'. Now we understand the word as a true story which is valuable as a true mirror of a society, its culture, and religion. The study of myths gives us an understanding of the society and the culture of the period, and helps us to understand also the contemporaneous societies, if the myths were still in use. Since myths are sacred (some are cosmogonic) stories, they are true, and relate realities. Myths are recited only at a particular time and place, unlike folktales which can be recited as entertainment at any time or place.[51] Ethnologists, anthropologists, and historians of religions now understand the word myth as it was intended to be understood by the primitive, as 'sacred' and 'true'. To understand man and his culture, the various expressions of his thought process should be studied. Mythology is one such expression. Other facets are language, religion, science, and art. All these are complementary to each other, and not exclusive. The fundamentals of a myth are said to arise not from nature but from society.[52] Myths may be said to elevate man, because they took place in the sacred time and transport the reciter to that period. Culture originates and evolves due to the intuition of a privileged few. Society is constantly enriched by the values and meanings discovered in the myths, formed through the inspiration of a few mytho-poets. The function of myths though is not to guarantee 'goodness' or morality, but it gives models for men to follow, and it gives meaning to the world. But, Malinowski felt that a myth's functional importance lies in its capacity to take care of the morality of the people. This is not borne out by the human and animal sacrifices engendered in mythic rituals and the practice of sexual orgies, cannibalism, head-hunting and all such sanguinary rites enjoined in myths. It also codifies belief and provides guidelines of behaviour for men. Myths teach man that there is something transcendent beyond the mundane, either a world peopled by gods, or the manes. They help man rise above himself and partake of the world of gods.

The recital of cosmogonic myths takes the human back to the period before creation; and re-creation, that is, order is reinstated from chaos. When thinking becomes rational, instead of physically enacting regression into order, man does so in his mind, and goes back to the original period when there was not even thought. This is the womb of creation itself, as it is stated in the Upaniṣads. In the post Upaniṣadic period again, that is in the Purāṇas, the creation myth is to justify the transcendental supremacy of the sectarian deity. The return to order is narrated to show the superiority of the Goddess, as in the *Devī Māhātmya.*

The composer of the myth goes into the past to get a solution to the present-day problems. Thus, his myth gets form and content. The myth not only becomes for the composer and his people meaningful, but it assigns meaning to itself and its surroundings. This is relevant more to the tribal myths. In mythology, there is no questioning. There is only going back to original time. And it endeavours to return the world to that primordial Time when the world was in the 'original' period and everything was perfect.[53] The real function of myths is not to present an objective picture of the world, but man's understanding of himself, and of the world he lives in. Deep and profound religious experience may find emotional outlet only in myths, and, following it, in rituals.

Myths are said to be impersonal, and governed by the idiosyncracies of a culture.[54] As a culture evolves, also its concept of the deity changes. Thus, mythic consciousness, which throws up images of these deities, does not merely reflect a certain social structure but is itself one of the factors that creates social consciousness. The relationship or the identity of the microcosm within man to the macrocosm outside him is realized by the stages of mythical images and concepts. Since myths are a study of men by men, anthropologists are helped by studying them. Man is the subject of their study but he imprints the environment by his experiences. The dilemma of such a situation of the subject and the object of the study being the same is immensely helped by the study of myths. The content of a myth is important, irrespective of its function. The structuralists have helped the anthropologists by their suggestion that myths should be studied not only as a representation of a society, but also as a social representation of its culture. Cultural values are transmitted through myths.

Some scholars criticise the sociological interpretation of myths.[55] Society notices only abnormal events or things and weaves myths about them. They do not make myths about common-place occurrences. In our assessment of myths, caution is necessary, in What we do not attribute absurd sociological reasons for them.

Myths serve as metaphors for human situations.[56] Since myths relate what happened to men, they should be treated as facts, and not fiction.

The main collection of Hindu myths is in the Purāṇas. These are compiled by the Brahmins, sectarian in outlook. Thus, some of them degenerate into diatribes. Some others, on the other hand, rise to an inspired level of poetry. Myths unlike popular opinion, are said to present only problems, never solutions. If we try to force a solution from a myth then we only twist its meaning to suit our purpose. Myths try to help men overcome pessimism about their affairs or life, by providing consolation and comfort to them. Purāṇas are seen[57] as a result of the pessimistic philosophy of the Upaniṣads confronting the orgiastic primitive Tantrism. Myths started to take the vocabulary of philosophy, but arrived at a solution by discarding dry philosophy, and taking emotionally satisfying coarse rituals.

James[58] states that archaeology renders great help in adjudging myths. In the Near Eastern religions, like Judaism, Christianity, Zoroastrianism, Hinduism and Islam, documentary evidence exists regarding myths and rituals. But since myths grow out of religious cults and beliefs, archaeological evidence of the cults proves to be of assistance in evaluating myths.

Classificatory Theory

Every mythology is fundamentally a classification of ideas, but growing from religious beliefs, not scientific enquiry. Classification is an essential feature of developed mythologies and have exerted a great influence on the evolution of religious beliefs.

This has contributed vastly in the evolution of Indian henotheism towards monotheism, as each god classified according to his capacity earlier merges with or overlaps others. Myths are said to be the result of a confusion of ideas in the minds of undeveloped beings. When the rich figures in mythologies complete their growth, myths about them cease, and they give way to one Supreme God. The classification of things arose because men thought of themselves in grouped classes, and applied this same idea to other things.[59] Inherent in the classificatory division, myths fell divided into two opposing groups. The most influential of these polarities was the sacred/profane grouping. The structuralist theory also stands on binarial opposites. Further, primitive groups divided themselves into a totemist classification. Many myths, Greek as well as Indian, can be seen to easily fall under the classificatory analysis. As social affinities weaken, discursive thinking comes into prominence, and scientific classification follows.

Attempts have been made to find allegorical meanings of theoretical and moral truths in myths. But this has not been successful. This is because the basis of myths is emotional and not intellectual. Primitive myths have coherence of feeling not of intellectual reasoning. The primitive man feels a solidarity of life and feels one with the surroundings.

Myth and Magic

Magic according to Frazer was followed by religion. This cannot be accepted. We have no proof in any religion when magic collapsed and when religion took over. Man thought that he could control nature through magic. When the objective was dangerous, the magical ritual became elaborate and myth resulted.

Psychological Assessment

Psychoanalysts should not pronounce arbitrary judgements in assessing a myth or a godhead, unless the judgement is corroborated by an enrichment in the devotee's life. If an evaluation hurts a devotee, then such an assessment is valueless. His evaluation should be cautious. Psychology had neglected religion, and Jung had also come under criticism. But, lately religious symbolism has been given due emphasis in the psycho-analytical study of myths.

The Mother-Goddess worship is said to belong to a period in the psychological evolution of people, wherein sexual awareness has not arisen yet, as in the pre-Oedipal stage, and the ego is dependant on the protective mother.[60] According to this theory, Goddess worship belongs to a regressive stage, and identifying the ego with the Mother may result in self-castration or cutting off one's own head and offering it ritually.

Psychology could probe into the motivating force in the unconscious, which gave rise to the myth. But history shold provide the context of the myth. Interpretation of myths, unrelated to this context is futile. Psychoanalytical studies of myths have come a long way since Freud. They allow multiple interpretations of myths.

Myths and dreams are very similar in characteristics to the extent that they have been termed the dreams of the masses.[61] Symbols according to Freud and Jung are static subjects that bear some indirect reference outside themselves. Dreams do tend to be symbolic much of the time. The psychoanalysis of dreams has helped in evaluating myths. Dreams are said to provide models for myths. Certain myths are certainly derived from dreams. But it cannot be generalized and stated that all myths are so derived. Myths use cultural norms explicitly. They are a "controlled projection of the unconscious"[62], later worked on by the conscious mind to suit the needs of the community and its cultural demands. Lévi-Strauss feels that [63] the study of myths may not reveal sociological or ethnographic facts. But it leads us towards an understanding of the contents of the unconscious, which gives rise to such images. This shows the influence of psychologists on this theory. Freud nominated the idea that myths are symbols thrown up from the subconscious. But he attributed myths to the infantile thinking of the psyche. Jung amended this and said that it was the mature thinking of the psyche.[64] Stated simply, it meant that all human beings possess certain inborn tendencies to form certain general symbols. These symbols manifest themselves through the unconscious mind as myths, dreams, delusions and folktales. That myths and dreams have a common origin, that is, the collective unconscious, is not statistically proved. Therefore it has been refuted since by Western scholars.

The best argument of Jung is the concept of archetypes, that arises out of our unconscious, instinctively. Though Jung did not substantiate this statistically, later science has proved the power of instinct in living things. Freud's opinion in psychoanalysis, that man thinks of his pre-natal period as sheer bliss like paradise, and returning psychologically to that period helps cure a lot of childhood traumas, has a parallel in myths also. Man tries to return to the pre-creation period, and thus returns to the blissful period. Thus, myths allow not individuals but whole communities to regress in time. Myths arise from the undeveloped soul-life of a race, and dreams are an individual's myths.[65] The difference between psychology and myths is that the former takes the individual psyche back to the state in the womb, that is, before creation and the latter takes the whole community to that position. Both are for the purpose of healing or mending the psyche.[66]

The stage of myth-making is a necessary stage of our consciousness. It is not an invention. It is a series of stages, and its contents are polytheism. Each stage is experienced by the human consciousness successively and lived by it.[67] According to Cassirer, mythic imagination materialises in forms and images. Primitive man is said to live his experiences of the outside world, and myth is the outcome of an intense excitement in this encounter. Mythic forms are not clear cut, because whatever catches the emotions ofthe primitie, rouses it to a pitch by fear, and hope shapes the myths. The subject is holy. This may not hold good for non-religious myths. Anthropologist Boas founded the theory that myths are the outcome of wish-fulfilment. This may be relevant only to a part of folk-tales and myths, similar to the theory that myths and rituals have the same origin. Myths are collective in the sense that they are not only traditional but also individualistic because they are personal. There is no free choice of a people in their mythical conceptions. The mythical consciousness of a people is said to seize them by force as it were. The contents of such a consciousness are pre-historic and buried in the depths of our unconscious. Jung's collective unconscious was stated as a necessity to primitive myths by Durkheim. But this was rejected by his follower and nephew, Mauss. Mauss stated that the particular pattern of behaviour of an individual is necessitated by social forces embedded in the concrete patterns of life, as rules and norms. Therefore, the social patterns of a tribal or a primitive, or even a modern community, are neither the sum total of individual behaviour, nor the result of a 'collective' mind imposed on them, but are the result of each individual's experience of the general social pattern within the ego's consciousness[68].

Many Amerindian tribes state that their myths arise from their dreams. This gave rise to the theory of the tribal unconscious of Freud and Jung, which is that it is common and inherited in humanity. For the primitive tribes, who do not distinguish between dream and waking states, and for whom dreams are so important that they colour or shape their daily lives, the Jungian statement might be true, but not for culturally developed people, who tend not to give importance to dreams or tend to forget them. Man honours his own libido in the mythic image, transferring into the image or the symbol an empirical object. If man is prevented from thus expressing his inner wishes, these then turn into a psychological malaise. Since Jung's archetypes are a unique contribution to the study and assessment of myths, Jung's theory on myths, as archetypal images given form by the conscious is given below.

The Archetypes

The archetypes arise spontaneously not governed by language, tradition or migration, and may arise at any time or place without any reason. When the archetype throws up an image into the consciousness, the latter gives it form by filling it by drawing from its experience. Therefore, the form does not exist for the image, till it arrives at the conscious level. The mother archetype throws an image into the conscious from the unconscious, from where some event or events force it up. The mother image thrown up can be of an infinite variety. It could be the concrete type like the personal mother relationships as for example, mother, grandmother, etc. It could be a mother image like the goddess figures. The goddess figure again could be a mother figure, benign, or a punishing figure, or the ideal personified as the goddess like the country, university, etc. It could also be associated with chthonic places like caves, water in wells, etc., and also in abstract figures like the *maṇḍalas*. Evil figures are Moira (fate), Nirṛti, Kālī, and such others. For the Western mind the ambivalence of the goddess figure could not be tolerated. Good was separated from evil; God was in heaven, and the devil in hell. For the Indian mind, our knowledge was intuitive and we could accept with equanimity ambivalence in goddess figures. Man becomes the spouse-consort or the child to the goddess. But woman can easily identify herself with the goddess figure. Since the archetype belongs not to the individual psyche but to the collective we may put it that the mother-goddess image represents the pre-conscious mother aspect of the collective psyche.

It is a psychological fact[69] that the mother image cannot be exactly represented anyhow else other than the empirical 'mother' idea. The mythological mother concept may not be the exact copy of the empirical mother idea. This is because the former's origin is supernatural, her feats and life extraordinary, never like a human mother. In fact, she may have no children of her own, but as a mythical figure, the whole world is her children. (Pārvatī, the spousified goddess has no naturally born children, but her devotees approach her as her children). Her deeds are miraculous or monstrous. Because of these facts unrelated to human figures, it is necessary to tabulate her under the 'mother motif'.

Jung's Opinions on Myths

Myths are the psychic life of the primitive. He cannot live without them, any more than the modern society can do without industries, etc. They not only represent, but they are the psychic life of the primitive. Myths are not invented by the primitive. He experiences them. They are the revelations from the pre-conscious psyche. They are not allegories about physical happenings. Myths result when the conscious receives images from the unconscious and fills them according to its empirical experiences. The psyche contains all images that are thrown up in myths. Thus, myths are the psychic phenomena that reveal the nature of the soul. Distinguishing how myths are not allegories, Jung says that allegory is a paraphrase of the conscious content, whereas the symbol (represented in myths), is the expression of the content of the unconscious[70]. The archetype, existing in the unconscious of the psyche, in primitive psychology, is called 'representations collectives', and, in the field of comparative religion, it is called 'categories of the imagination'.

As mentioned earlier, symbolism in religion, and theories on myths have profited enormously from Jung's contribution of archetypes to psychology. Recent evaluations on myths have taken as their base the 'collective unconscious' and images thrown up from it, in their reasoned arguments in their theories.

Zimmer agrees with Jung when discussing Indian myths[71]. Indian myths are not the outcome of individual experience, but are due to the images thrown out from the collective unconscious. The are renewed and reshaped according to the needs of the successive generations. The myths are multivalent in their meaning; thus they satisfy the individual needs of the devotee. Their varied meanings are made apparent by meditating on their inner significance. The events and episodes in the myths percolate down to the psyche, salving it and helping it in its progress. These myths resist definition and classification. They are thought to be more archaic than the Greek myths, which where polished by later day's poetic genius, and mythical anomalies were given modern ex-planations. But we must remember that Indian myths were also given a new meaning by the ritualists. Indian myths glow with their multifaceted collective unconscious of a variegated culture.[72]

Sometimes, the psychological assessment of myths is carried too far. The myths of Rāma Dāśarathi and Kṛṣṇa are said to contain the heroes, Oedipal complexes.[73]

Fantasy and dislocation, that is, mythical logic, which we judge to be illogical and arbitrary, could have arisen out of the collective unconscious, or from the individual story teller's imagination, or from the ideas of the supernatural (since myths do deal with the supernatural elements). But Hindu myths are an exception to most of these suggestions.

Religion and Myth

There is such a close connection between myth and religion, that there can never be a hard and fast rule as to when myth ends and when religion begins. In the history of religious development both have been inextricably mingled with each other. Religion might be flowing smoothly out of the former because, higher thoughts contained in a rudimentary form in myths later find expression in religion. Dealing with the nature of myth and religion as forms of human expression it was felt[74] that myths take forms out of the unevolved and the unanalytic mind of the primitive, since only the primitive 'feels' sympathy for the world. This would not explain myths of evolved races; the mind of the primitive has been proved to be capable of analysis. Myths and religion arise due to a passionate response to the world, and they are the outcome of intense feeling. This again is not true of all myths. Some myths do not arise due to high emotions. As to the source of myths, they could have the same source as religion, because they deal with gods and also form a part of religion. This theory of the same source for myth and religion is also not feasible as it is not universally applicable.

Cassirer agrees with Jung that myths arise from the common mythical consciousness. Myth is an expression arising from the universal and common energy of humans. It is a uniform thought underlying the varied expressions in the surrounding material world. Behind the diverse mythical forms, there is only one mythical consciousness. This is expressed in constantly changing forms, never confined in rigid, final forms. This is as it should be, for, otherwise, religion would be bereft of mythical interpretations, and remain barren. Sometimes, in the evolution of myths, their forms may develop further or the myth may itself be abandoned or completely changed.

The three Stages in Cultural Development

The three stages in cultural development are as follows: The first stage is the primitive stage of consciousness, of beliefs in fantasies, and fictitious concepts. This is also the theological stage. Here man's desires and ideas are transformed into demons and gods. The second stage is theoretical knowledge and enquiry based on the scientific view of reality. Man now has the ability for abstract concepts. The third and the last stage is the complete spiritual domination of reality. Man distinguishes between his inner and outer worlds and he confines his thinking to the facts existing in these. Each stage eliminates the earlier one as he progresses. Both myth and religion spring from their own world of spiritual soil. They never abandon this at any stage of their development. Their origin and motives are unique. In mythology, the mythic image is, in the beginning, no different from the material world. Myth is said to start from mimetic dance. The mime and the image it conveys are fused in one. When slowly a differentiation begins to occur between the real and the mimed, religion may be said to have started its influence. As the mythical consciousness is deeply probed, religious consciousness is seen to be inseparably enmeshed into it. Religion is at this stage meaningless if bereft of mythical contents. As religious thought evolves, our understanding distinguishes between form and content and recognises symbols as different from its contents. All over the world, at different periods, religion comes to terms with mythical images, and resets simultaneously its relationship to the empirical world. Each religion comes to terms with the empirical world in its own way, depending on its own historical and spiritual character. At this stage, objective reality is still not detached from the mythical, imaginative world, and the attitude of a people towards myth necessarily reflects its attitude towards existence. An ideal religion would necessarily degrade mythology and denigrate it, as it applies a similar critical view to the material world. If we want to understand the universal system of human culture, first, we have to go back to our myths and try and grasp their meaning, because myth is the original direction of the human spirit. It is an independent area of expression of man's consciousness.

Division of time and space is done by mythical consciousness not by noticing the fluctuations in these, but by dividing these into the sacred and the profane. When a spiritual crisis occurs in the consciousness as a whole, man's intuition attempts to divide this into different strata of meaning. The first division contains the germs of mythical thoughts which will be determined and dominated by them. The domination is not so much by mythical thinking as by mythical feeling and intuition. Astonishment and terror create a spiritual awareness in the consciousness and this gives rise to the fascinosum and tremendum of the sacred. That which is holy mythically need not be ethically pure. This is the reason for the rituals of human sacrifice and such other allied rites. The division of the sacred and the profane starts from the most primitive beliefs in magic and continues upto the ethical religions.

Myth Incapable of Ideation

Mythical forms do not present themselves in the mind suddenly and fully formed. They appear in the intuitive process of consciousness. This is no simple process. Myriads of sensory perceptions are converted into spiritual units by subtle nuances of processes. There is no representation of a thing in myth, but it *is* that. Therefore it is that myth cognises by translating its truth into action, since it is incapable of ideation. The ideas of myths, irrespective of belonging to the most primitive or the most sophisticated stage of culture, are transformed into gods and devils, of purely magical worldview or the highest spiritual experience. There is no passive contemplation in myths. To understand mythical forms, one has to reach behind its objective configurations and understand the dynamism which pulsated in the mythical consciousness. Thus any mythical form would be barren, if the thought which formed it, does not reach back into intuition.

Magic with its confused multiplicity of demons and forces filling the world is the lowest form of myth. This tries to unify the forces into some semblence of organisation. As magic rises higher in the spiritual thinking and the demons turn into gods, each with a history and efficacy, myth assigns a hierarchy to these forces and makes the world intelligible. A similarity unifies disparate things because of the magical characteristics they possess. The worship of nature gods may not be of the personification of forces, but of an objectivization of mythical thoughts. This shows an advanced stage of objectivization. This primordial force of mythical imagination is still alive in folk-tales. From this stage the 'I' starts differentiating itself from the spirits of nature and passes from the stage of emotion to a stage of action, examples of which are the fertility cults of agriculture. At the next stage, these bonds between nature and man take new shapes in his tutelary gods and deities. Action is divided into disparate functions and each assigned to a god.

Man removes the mythical powers from inside him and projects them as gods outside him. They develop into cult heroes, who cease to be mere powers of nature, but become a figure of salvation shedding light and power. This is the expression of 'I' consciousness. Religion is not the outcome of culture but religion gives rise to culture, as for example, domestication of animals could have arisen from totemism. The sign of freeing subjectivity on the road towards religious evolution is when 'I' and the world come to grip with each other, and the figures of gods separate as well as bind them together. From the figures of gods rise a single supreme figure of a god as the creator. The figure of god is the outcome of the mythical ideas of relationship between man and god. But this relationship is concretely expressed in the cult. The mythical motif can be shown not to proceed from a physical entity, but from an activity of man. Thus, a repetitive process is given mythical imagery and is shown as a reflection of a temporal thing. This action comes first, and the mythical explanation comes later. The cult it is which forms the foundation of the myth. When cult develops further, sacrifice becomes its centre. Man recognises god as superior to himself who cannot be compelled by magic but can be propitiated by sacrifice and prayer.

Binding the gap between Ethics and Reality

Some myths, not all, arise to bridge the gap between ethics and reality. As for instance, a mythical mother cannot be impregnated carnally, but only spiritually. Thus some myths find a fitting solution to dilemmas. Religion with its mythical images allays our fears about the world and offers assurance and sympathy through its symbols. Though the symbol may not be meaningful from the empirical standpoint, it nevertheless is psychologically true. As such it is the greatest human achievement. Figures like Kālī, Hecate, etc., are the result of the archetypal images thrown up by the unconscious which the conscious from its empirical experience transforms. These are positive in their influence and are socially helpful. The *Devī Māhātmya* as well as the latter day Devī poems like the *maṅgal* poems are an attempt to synthesize diachronic events with a synchronic structure. Opposites could exist simultaneously in the divine plane, and there is no contradiction, since these images are thrown up from the unconscious. If the god is infinite, the manifestations of him are out of līlā. His representations may be experienced by the world, like disease, death, etc., but he is present even when these manifestations are absent. Mythic symbols resolve any contradiction that might exist in religious ideas. Malignant, gruesome rites or narrowly materialistic conceptions may be transformed into mythical symbols. The main point to remember while adjudging a myth is not to let our own background of religion and culture colour our evaluation.

Myths and Fantasy

Myths start from fantasy. But this fantasising instinct may lie dormant for a long while. Myths start from quite unintentional processes, but culminate in significant forms. A god may be given identity by a symbol, a ritual may show how to obtain his favour, but it is mythology which describes his origin and adventures in his evolution that fixes his character. It is well said that "divinities are born of ritual, but theologies spring from myth".[75] Myth shows a conflict between human and trans-human powers. It shows negative and hostile powers challenging, and finally being defeated and killed. Myths do not distort the world but try to find a reconciliation between irreconcilable opposites. Since it deals with the world or is cosmic in its interests, and is not the outcome of subjective poetic fantasy, the general lay-out of a myth tends to fall into a systematized format, say, for example, the Hegelian thesis, antithesis and synthesis.

But, in Hindu myths, there can be no lasting and permanent solution to the contradictions, that is, no Hegelian synthesis is offered for the antithesis. The contradictions in the myths are held in a temporary state of a compromise, till they break away and re-emerge in another myth as opposites. Aesthetic satisfaction is also afforded in these moments, frozen out of a constant flux.[76] By such a refusal to force a synthesis on apparent contradictions, the Hindu might be underlining his idea of a world where all ideas are present simultaneously, at all levels. No single concept exists to the exclusion of all others. These contradictions and variety are the true charm of these myths, teaching us in the process, to savour each minute dissention for its own sake and in its own scale.

The fantasies which give rise to myths have a rich symbolism. They thus give rise to a number of variations. Thus, a single god will accomplish feats of incompatible qualities, or, the same feat is ascribed to different gods, as for example, Mahiṣa killed by both Durgā and Skanda. Myths which stand the test of time are those that withstand both poetic fancy and the influence of local versions. Myth is a symbolic concept of a supreme form of life and these symbols help men to reorient themselves, through religion, in the cosmos. Myths are the transformed thoughts from the cosmic fund of ideas.[77] This is another way of putting Jung's collective unconscious. Further, according to this author, a poetic capacity is not necessary to compose myths. Philosophy and discursive thinking may overcome myths, but an universally valid poetic and religious intuition will again triumph with yet another myth. James[78] states erroneously that the primitive mind does not think of the origin of the world and does not dwell on the antique period namely the mythopoeic time, and that they are only concerned with their problems of daily living. Primitives are concerned with explaining not only how they and their world were created, but they try explaining the origins of customs, institutions, etc. Secondly, he states that myths dwindle into folk-tales when the culture breaks up. But, when a culture breaks up, the same myth may transform into a new form to satisfy the present pressures. Further, if the myth is true for all times, then it remains unaltered whatever cataclysmic experiences th· community undergoes. Unless and until the ideology behind a cultural or a religious institution is understood, the significance of the mythology of that culture would remain elusive, according to Dumezil.[79]

If myths are found to have the weakness of inconsistency, this weakness is in the viewer not in the myth itself. Myths might have varied formats but they follow fixed laws and provide a stable view of events as history, if we knew how to sift truth.[80] At every step, myths follow a steady fundamental law, showing their inner consistency and cohesion: Myths are of a religious nature and they are a type of mental therapy for people suffering from anxieties.[81] Since man partakes of the numina, when he recites or participates in myths, he is liberated from personal anxieties. It is the role of the religious symbol to give a meaning to the life of man. To understand man's past and present, we must study his myths. In Hindu myths, metaphysical thoughts have developed out of mythological imagery.[82] Great mythologies do make it clear to man that he is face to face with numen. The word myth might be viewed as an ambiguous term, but they contain a particular type of a story, traditional, about gods and demons, and their battles. Though they seem set in their plot, they are yet amenable to improvisation.

Error and evil are necessary not only for humans but also for the cosmos. Even though, as for instance, Mahiṣa stands for *tāmasic* (negative) qualities, he renders a great service to the world. There are five interpretations of evil in mythology: (1) It might be the mark of an angry god; (2) In the constant fight between good and evil in this world, there might be a temporary superiority of evil; (3) It might be as a punishment for evil people; (4) It might be god's will even though the people involved are not wholly evil; and, (5) Neither God nor man is responsible. God acts as a physician who is not responsible for the breakout of the epidemic, but he helps cure it.[83]

Cassirer's Contribution

Cassirer spent more time and thought on the philosophy of myth, than anyone else. He also subscribed to the view that symbols are thrown up from the collective unconscious. He has suggested,[84] that, between the receptor and the effector systems, man has created a system of symbols linking those two. Man understands his surroundings and his place in it, by the use of symbols. Symbolism plays such an important role in his life that he may be called animal symbolicum instead of animal rationale. Religious symbols may change, but the underlying principle, the symbolic activity, remains the same.

Cassirer has advocated that myths do not represent symbolic thinking, but are symbols themselves. The form of a myth could be understood better by studying its expression and the type of consciousness that produces a genre of myths; and not by going into its source or function. But, this would depend on the type of myths one is considering. Lévi-Strauss bases his structure of myths on the Hegelian thesis, antithesis, and synthesis. Both Lévi-Strauss and Cassirer arrived at the structure of myths by studying the development of the structure of language. For Cassirer, it was the symbolic expression leading to the structure; for Lévi-Strauss it was the reverse with structure being of primary importance leading to the symbolic aspect. But both followed Kant in their assumption that, by means of the transcendental form, the human spirit constructs the physical world. Cassirer's 'basic mythical configurations' underlying the structural form of myths may be analogised with Jung's 'collective unconscious'.

Each part of a mythology is important only when viewed as a whole, and the whole attains meaning and inner truth. The unity in the diverse representations of myths is due to the potency of the sign. A mythical process rises above a mere physical representation of the world of the given things, to the spiritual level. But it does not become fully spiritual because it replaces material images with other images which are still material, but based on magic. But it contains seeds of a spiritual process which will dissolve it in future. The freedom into a fully spiritual world would be achieved only when the mythical images are fully understood and thus one rises above them.

Function of a Name

The function of a name, according to this scholar, is not to exhaustively describe a concrete situation, but to denote, or describe one facet of a whole gamut. Out of a multiplicity of sense data and images the mind receives, it selects those few which conceptualise certain experiences in the concrete world. This is the first view of the world or a situation. Therefore, it is not a negative, but a positive selection, when a peculiar name is brought up from these centres of our experience by conscious intellectual effort.

Mythical thought is traditional by nature, because its objective is to grant sanctity to human life, by anchoring to the Original Past. This makes it unalterable in its content or form. But we have seen that the strength of myths is their ability to alter their content and/or form to suit the particular necessity of a community. Myth and science cannot stand comparison, because they are two different entities. Myths will dissolve into nothingness the moment we apply a strict scientific enquiry to them. But we would be nearer to judging comparable entities, if we were to compare the thought process of a myth with that of science. The mythical world is not the outcome of any sudden chance occurrence. It has its own laws which it follows in all its numerous manifestations[85]. This is against Levy-Bruhl's theory of myths as sudden eruptions when the mind thinks emotionally, though he himself later amended this opinion. Myths deal with poetry, not logic; but, even poetry has its own logic.

Freud believed that symbols have a broad universal meaning. This idea has been found to have relevance in its application to myths. Jung said myths are not invented, but were experienced, and are the original revelations of a pre-conscious psyche.[86] Jung also said that mythological motifs produced by the archetype have many implications. Cassirer believed that myths and religious fantasies are created by the expression of symbols and are concentrated with meanings and emotions. There are thus many similarities between Jung and Cassirer.

Cassirer thus thought,[87] that myths have no other references, other than themselves, and that people thought of symbols rather than in terms of symbols. That the primitives have a special mentality filled with potent magical associations and random imags utterly devoid of any logic is an excessive view. The opinion of Lévi-Strauss seems more balanced in this regard. He discovered that the primitives do possess a capacity for conceptual thinking. That the mind (primitive's) in a high state of excitement expresses symbols as gods or demons seems conjectural, and lacks proof. The total rejection by Cassirer of all intellectual component in mythical images is not tenable. Both Freud and Levi-Strauss have emphasised that the images are expressed from the unconscious and this should not be ruled out. Cassirer recognised that the important principle of a myth is dynamic, not static. Yet, when he discusses mythical imagination, he talks of the levels of meaning of the static symbol, not of the dynamic. Cassirer's positive contribution to the study of mythical forms is his emphasis on their emotional nature.

Myths arise from static symbols with dynamic potentialities.[88] This has more acceptability than the theory of Jung and Cassirer. Myths have significance only if they make use of one or more special symbols, and each of these symbols signifies some important and complex emotion or intuition which cannot otherwise be expressed. But, many myths have dynamic symbols having an allegorical and complex meaning. It implies the transposition of whole episodes on to different emotional or semantic levels. Myths like dreams have an enormous range of mode and area of symbolic meanings.

Symbols and Myths

Many other scholars have expressed their views on symbols as connected with myths. A few of these are given below.

One of the earliest and therefore the most original views was held by Bachofen. We tend to communicate our inner thoughts in symbolic forms. In our struggle against the odds in the world, we try to relate to some superhuman entity through myths, rituals and prayers. Symbols in myths are invested with special powers. They are valid for truths for varying levels. In symbolic pictures or icons, it is made up of various component elements. This might be seen in the iconography of Mahiṣāsuramardinī, which is composed of Devī, her vāhana, the gaṇas who assist her and Mahiṣa. But, this symbol to be understood has to be conveyed in words, or, in an icon, where the meaning is presented all at once. But, its interpretation goes on all the time in many variations. Thus, the mind thinks in symbols which are transformed into myths and are explained in words. A myth[89] is the exegesis of the symbol. A symbol stands for a unified thought, whereas a myth depicts this in outward and discrete images. Myths and symbols fulfil the need raised by the weakness of language to express fully the intuition of man. Speech tries to bring the infinite into finite understanding, whereas symbol takes us far beyond the finite world into the realm of the infinite. Myths contain the earliest memories of history. History provides the content and religion the form for myths.

Jung felt that symbols are used to express concepts which are not comprehended by us fully. His opinions have already been dealt with in the earlier section.

Kerenyi,[90] states that if the symbol in the myth is archaic, it goes deep into the psyche and, losing its individuality, or distinguishing marks, it becomes a part of the universal unconscious. If the symbols are from an enlightened or an evolved state, it loses its universality and becomes an individuated mark of the psyche. If it evolves further, and rises into the conscious, then the conscious will project imags which it can explain allegorically.

Eliade says that symbolism by itself would not make much sense, unless the overall socio-religious context is also taken into account. Symbols point beyond themselves, opening up levels of meanings in the human mind and in the thing they symbolise, otherwise impossible to unravel or understand. Symbols are compared not to reduce them to a common ground, but to enrich the study with the variations on a theme. All studies in religion should involve a study in symbolism. All efforts should be made to grasp the symbolism behind religious facts. This does not mean that symbols should be reduced to a common factor. On the other hand, such a study would imply integration. Some symbols appear due to historical reasons. Such symbols would have diffused along with the advancement of technology and culture. For example, agriculture homologised to the sex act, could not have taken place earlier than the discovery of agriculture. Symbols depend on precise historical events. Psychology tells us that even when we lose the significance of a symbol, it delivers its message and fulfils its function.

The first stage of symbolism is when the symbol literally becomes what it signifies, as for example, seen in the tree which is the cosmos.

Symbols reveal certain facts of the universe which otherwise would not be apparent. To the primitive, all symbols are religious, and, to their mind, nature and symbol are inseparable. This connection is rendered sacred by intuition[91]. Symbols have the capacity to be simultaneously multivalent on different levels and this is evident on the plane of immediate experience. Since they have this inbuilt levels of meanings in them, they are capable of structurally uniting many realities into a single symbol. This teaches man the Unity of the Universe and his part in it. Thus they have existential relevance. That is, they point to a truth which has relevance to human existence. The most important role they play is that they mediate between paradoxes, which gives an insight into the ultimate reality, which as mentioned earlier would not be otherwise expressible. Religious symbols are relevant to human activity in the present and also gives meaning to existence. It gives, in other words, a cosmic reference to the individual's existence.

If, at a certain period in history, a religious symbol expresses clearly a certain transcendental meaning, it can be surmised that this meaning was held in it in obscurity, earlier than this period. Further, to decipher a symbol we should take into account not only its meanings, but also its context.[92]

Myths are expressed in symbols. But, symbols after all are of a mediating nature, by virtue of which, they obscure what they try to reveal. Symbol tries to signify things greater than itself or of a graver import than that it purports to signify. Myths are impersonal and are governed by the idiosyncracies of a culture. Myths are symbolic. The meaning of true symbolism is multivalent. There is a certain looseness in interpreting myths. Myths also try to portray reality by analogy. They most usually present themes in metaphors. It has been found that aborigines try to understand a thing by comparing it to a known similar object. Symbols are multivalent and therefore also are myths. This being so, myths can be interpreted in any number of ways. It also is the reason why there can be no monolithic theory to explain myths. Myths (unlike dreams) are impersonal or, non-individualistc. They belong to a whole tribe. Culture determines the specific character and the structure of myths, and their meaning also depends on the culture. Cultural symbols change in their values constantly and get reintegrated back into society. Thus a myth's format is never set. It changes with change in society and its needs.

Symbols can be variously interpreted. This itself should caution us in rushing to classify a myth by any one arbitrary theory. It is not the myth that is important in evaluations, but the symbols. The problem of evaluation lies with the subject itself, like the symbols, not the method. Symbols are abstract. Society transforms and uses them to suit their particular context. According to Chakrabarti,[93] only psychoanalysis and the historical method used together can give any meaningful adjudgement to symbols and myths. These are the storehouses of the culture of mankind.

Personal symbolism is entrenched in dreams, whereas cultural symbolism is contained in myths. Therefore, there is a distinction between myths and dreams. Culture is the determining or the colouring factor of myths. As such, cultural symbols (i.e., myths) are constantly changing, re-integrating and re-evaluating the cultural norms into themselves. Therefore, myths are never completed. Each generation adds its own values into it, and thus myths are in a constant flux. In myths, there are metaphysics, and planes of the sacred, cosmic, and profane present. They are able to exist so because of the flexible symbolism which changes in value as the ethos changes. In Hindu myths of the Purāṇas, Tantrism and Bhakti lent their valorization.

Before referring to Lévi-Strauss, whose structural study of myths (with a few drawbacks,) has been an important contribution to the study of myths, a few more opinions are considered.

Aetiological Myths

Aetiological myths sanctified cult spots and raised the ritual sanctity of a cult in a new region. Sthalapurāṇa performed this function. This was true of Hebraic myths also. Myths of origin according to James[94] were primarily aetiological. But this was not to satisfy the curiosity of the whys and hows of custom. It was more to validate the existing custom by placing it in the original, that is the sacred time. Poetry, philosophy and psychology, all of these, may possess elements of a myth. But a myth is separate from all these. That the primitives possessed a mythopoeic mind is a fallacy according to James. They do not lack logic but have a different evaluation in the relationship between the sacred and the profane. Ritual and myth were two facets of the same sacramental activity of validating through dramatic activity a relationship between the sacred and the profane. Myth had to be a symbolic representation of the Ultimate. However, the latter was conceived, as it mediated between the hostile and benign forces, surrounding our existence. If there is any contradiction significant in the myth itself, and there is no resolution, then, at least, the myth brings up the contradiction and lets us face it. Admission of failure to resolve conflicts in myths itself is an important characteristic of myths. Mythology thus has also the facility to disguise failure. As against James' opinion, myths are felt by the mythopoet,[95] and they exert an enormous influence on the listeners. In this, they differ from folk-tales, fables, fairytales, etc. Myths appeal to the faithful, but they do not stand critical examination for validity. Myths are of complex character. They are a form of poetry, try to bring about the truth they portray, and they validate rituals. Greek myths are classified into three categories.[96] Those that validate rituals; cosmogonic and such sociological ones which explain the origin of a tribe, custom, etc., and, historical myths narrating catastrophes and battles. This could be true of Hindu myths also. Mythologies are compared to nature, in their "permanence, profundity and universality".[97] The tales of gods which they narrate are well known even before their mythologisation, but nevertheless they are amenable to changes. Myths are anomalous in this that their tale is fixed, but is capable of future manipulation; and they are static, but they can be transformed. A myth's form is shaped by artistry, but is influenced by its peculiar contents. Form and contents are very important in the make-up of the whole myth.

Characteristics of Myths

Eliade feels that we try to go back into the perfect and sacred past from the profane present, and thus assure for ourselves perfection in our present condition.[98] He says that, in the sacral myths about the return to origin, they sacralise customs and institutions. But, in secular matters, it is merely recited to fix matters down in tradition and to establish their relevance. There are a few characteristics of myths. (1) They are the history about supernatural beings. (2) This history is true, because it treats with realities, and it is sacred because it deals with supernatural beings. (3) Mostly they deal with the creation of the world, or the origin of a sociological nature. (4) By knowing a myth one knows the origin of things and thus one can control and manipulate things. (5) One attains sacrality as one recites a myth because one is transported to that original time.[99] A myth cannot be defined by any rule other than by itself.[100] Myths are a part of our psyche. Therefore, there should be modern myths. The Marxist communism can be termed one with its just suffering and a classless society, which is the return to paradise type of myths. Germans, during the Second World War, were fed with myths of their superiority as a race.

Myths have two things of note: It is about human behaviour, and it has elements of civilization.[101] There is no break in the continuity between primitive and modern time. Myth in modern times, deals with the human condition as the anxiety of man living in time. Modern Western man has rationalised his thoughts and demythologised his myths. Therefore, his anxieties have no recourse in myths and turn to neuroses. Modernism has hurt man's psyche. He has lost his spiritual values and he is paying the price for the break-up of his moral universe.

Origin of Myths

One cannot say with certainty how myths originated, in preliterate cultures. It is also doubtful whether all myths originated in the same manner. We cannot judge the material of an intuitive nature from our level of literacy, and ratiocination, as this would not bear satisfactory results. Myths could not have originated as simple narratives and it cannot be said that they developed their functional, i.e., validatory, iterative, and such other characteristics later on. Certain myths could have functional origins. Since we do not have proper material at our disposal, it is best to assume that narrative and functional characteristics developed side by side.

Development of Myths

Myths become traditional by being passed from generation to generation. They should possess some extraordinary qualities inherent in them both in content and expression to remain popular. The original recounteur who is anonymous should have possessed these qualities to a great degree. He would also possess a way of singing or reciting them faithfully and still show relevance to that particular society. At each recitation the myth would get further coloured by that particular singer's in novative genius. Thus, changes in minor details would creep in unwittingly. For the myth to become traditional it would be seen that it is not only dependent on the genius and/or limitations of the singer, but also those of the society. These give its narrative and functional standards. Myths could keep changing upto the point when they became traditional.

Classification of Myths

According to function, we can classify the myths in this way: First would be those that are primarily narrative and entertaining. This type is rare. If they are not in praise of a hero or a god, they become folk-tales or legends. It of course follows that, if they are in praise of a hero, they could contain some events in history.

The second type of myths is more common. It comprises those which are recited at regular timings. Certain myths are recited at the solstices of the sun, at the beginning and the end of the rains, or the harvests. By going back into the sacred time when the myths were enacted, the community hopes to reap the results of that golden period. Eliade classifies all myths under this genre. This is too simplistic a view.

There is another type which can also be housed along with the above mentioned myths. These are the charter myths. These give religious sanction to a particular custom, institution, etc., as for example kingship, and succession to the throne. These sometimes may overlap the first class. Eliade has done extensive work in collecting myths from varied cultures from all over the world. He universalises the mythopoeic mind of the primitive and the cultured civilizations, though what he says about the commonness of 'return to the origin' type of myths is true. There are myths which are in praise of a deity, to win his favour for the present period. There are others which lend authority to a custom or institution. There is the *Puruṣa Sūkta* justifying caste classification. The legendary antecedents are narrated for the king's geneology, and thus divinity is conferred on him, or divine approval is attested for his status.

The third and last type is the speculative and explanatory myths. These either try and overlook, or, suppress an insoluble problem; or, try to find a solution between polarities; or, give it a divine background and make an unpalatable solution acceptable. Some elaborate myths try to solve problems of a fundamental or abstract nature. The solution offered, if the problem is insoluble, is mythical. Only when the solution is easy and direct is it stated directly, or shown as an alteration in the custom or an institution. No myth can offer a perfect resolution of a problem. It seemingly solves it or offers a solution. Solution can be offered on four levels: (1) Disguise the problem by a tale which pretends the problem is not there. (2) Offer a Lévi-Straussian type of solution by introducing a mythical factor which reduces polarisation. (3) Bring in impersonal forces in a personalised and understandable form. (4) Bring in different sets of polarities that make the problemless severe. If myths offer a resolution to problems, then their role is speculative.

The speculative and functional character of myths might have arisen gradually from their narrative characteristic. Myths arise to satisfy the needs of a community. Supernatural or unnatural components may be later accretions, integrating the experiences as symbols arising from dreams or the unconscious. This conclusion differs from the one which sees myths as just charters, connected with rituals or about nature, or as an evolution from the reaction to the world of a mythopoeic nature, errupting in symbols pregnant with meaning. But myths of both primitive and cultured societies should be studied in depth, which will show their contribution in shaping those societies and affecting their evolution. For this, ancient myths of civilised societies are well as those myths of the present day primitive societies ar equally important. Myths are about gods and form part of religion. Sometimes they are associated with rituals. They arise from the collective unconscious.

As for the Devī myth, patience is needed to sift the material of the Purāṇas which is vast. Whatever is obtained after this sifting has to be studied with the background of history, social law, etc. The mythology of Devī forms a small part of the Purāṇas. Devī is uniquely Hindu and as the Great Goddess the study of mythology lies at the heart of Hinduism. Whether the study of Devī would help in understanding the wider area of world myths or not, it would be rewarding in itself, if we are able to see the multiple value that her devotees have been seeing in it and we are able to enjoy it as a delighting and many-splendoured myth. To extract the 'meanings' of myths is not a simple task. The first level is the level of the story-teller, i.e., the Ṛṣi. The second is the divine level as understood by scholars of mythologies, where the struggle for power between divine or supernatural beings is depicted. The third is the cosmic level where metaphysical principles are seen in symbolic truths. The final level is the folk-lore level, where we relate to the myth to find parallels in our fears and anxieties and strive to overcome them.

No single level of meaning can be taken as the truest or the most authentic. All are important. Thus the number of meanings that can be read into a good myth is innumerable. These levels are simultaneous and not contiguous. This study does not purport to exhaust all levels of meanings of the myth nor does it emphasize the myth taken as the only important version of the theme.

The image of the supreme Goddess as a flame of non-erotic valour, whose single concern is the annihilation of the demons, but who is courted by the demons for a spouse is the inherent opposition in her make-up. She is born out of the *tejas* of the gods, but creates goddesses out of her own śakti. The image of the Goddess, chaste and sexually provocative, subduing and releasing the enemy, is retained as an ambiguity in myth and icon. If according to Lévi-Strauss 'being in place' is what makes things sacred,[102] Devī put back things in their ordered place and removes demons who are themselves out of place and creates chaos around them.

The paradox of the goddess underlies the various myths and her character as Kālī and Pārvatī provides stark contrast. She is the annhilator and the protector.

Transformation in Myths

The ideas contained in myths have parallels in philosophy and cult. The former is an intellectual elaboration of the cult, and the latter is an emotional one. Myth contains both. It thus lends strength both to the concept and images of deities. When contradictions can be solved, a myth does so intellectually, and where it cannot, it allows the emotion through the cult to find an irrational solution. Hindu myths have an enormous variety. They show poetic imagination and skill. The variations in the myth could also be due to accretions when it was handed down as an oral tradition. The attention to immensely minute details in descriptions in the myth may be due to the Hindu idea of living a moment to its utmost fullness. This is achieved by savouring every detail in descriptions of a particular moment in war, love or beauty. Bhakti is another way in which a solution is obtained for irrationalities in myths. Each time a myth is told, it slakes the thirst of the devotee as he lives in it. The myriad versions are not capable of satisfying the devotee's quest for its innumerable details. The juxta-position of the mundane and the sacred is to make man aware of the sacred moments of life he should savour. A mortal might rise to divine heights or a divinity may lose his superior heights and be hurled down to the mundane level. The variety, repetition, and detail make up the content of the myth.

Many versions of a myth enable one to spot certain variations, or repetitions. These would be very important in ascertaining the true meaning of a myth. Every version adds a particularly important message of the myth. Hence, the necessity of studying all the variations in a myth. Sometimes, the variations are explained in a myth that, because the incident took place in cosmic time, in different periods, the characters were different for each period. There is really no end to variations in mythology. What would outwardly look perfectly symmetrical, would on close scrutiny bring up a minute change in detail. Since the transition can be carried on ad infinitum, from one variant to another, it is very difficult, well-nigh impossible, to break a myth into basic units.

There is a connection between the content of a myth and the problem it tries to solve, which is termed as its unconscious meaning.[103] This relationship may either be presented in a straight-forward way, or, hidden in a transformation of the myth. Transformation of myths could be in its format, varying from myth to myth, or from one area to another, or the time of its action could be changed. The message of a myth could itself change, but it never ceases to exist. There are only two ways in which a myth could die out. It could be historicised or it could be elaborated into fiction.

Myths have several levels of interpretations, and no one level could be used as an only way of interpretation. If there are different versions, they are all later taken together to be adjudged. The myth's position in a group and its area of influence should be kept in view while adjudging it. Further, myths cannot be isolated from folk-tales, arbitrarily, because what is a folk-tale in one area might be transformed as a myth in another area. Repetitions of a theme in other myths tend to emphasize the theme. Amongst the variations would lie the same original theme. Therefore, it is important to consider also transformations of myths. Myths sometimes are borrowed from one culture to another. The new culture's current data of values are superimposed on the old format to meet the societies' present demands. This is a common occurrence in mythologies all over the world. Thus a myth undergoes changes to meet its current cultural needs. Myths like symbols have their own standards in being consistent. If a myth is true in the many interpretations, then it remains popular always. One of the main functions of myth is to authenticate the levels of reality.

According to Lévi-Strauss,[104] the variations in a myth occur due to the binary opposites becoming weak. This happens when there is a change in the cultural or social conditions when a myth travels. The original myth does not make sense unless adapted to local conditions, and thus the myth's structural components change, shuffle and rearrange.

In the Mahiṣāsuramardinī myth, the local variations of the conflict (in Maharashtra, and the South), are between the goddess and her husband, Śiva. In the Brahminical versions, annihilation of the husband cannot be thought of. Even Kālī stands on a quiescent Śiva. She has not killed him. This might have much primitive colouring. This version was changed slowly to have Kālī admiringly watch Śiva dance. Similarly, the buffalo demon was left with erotic sentiments towards the Goddess and was even allowed to leave his body and attain heaven in human form. But he was never exalted to the position of the Goddess' spouse.

Lévi-Strauss, and the Structuralist Theory

Anthropologists like Malinowski followed a functionalist assessment of myths. They felt that myths were merely charters validating social and cultural customs. According to this theory, if one knew the basic drives of a people, one can judge their myths and other socio-cultural manifestations. Lévi-Strauss changed this and shifted the emphasis to the structure of myths as reflecting the structure of the society.

There are three definitions of myths : (1) These are stories of our past, which we know to be false; (2) The theologists define it as statements about inexpressible supernatural events, couched in physical and expressible terms; (3) The anthropologists view it as a sacred tale. There are also three stages in the assessment of myths: First, it was Frazer, along with Durkheim and Tylor who pointed out the importance of the study of myths for anthropology. Secondly, Freud and more particularly Jung, emphasized the unconscious as the field from which myths arise. Thirdly, Lévi-Strauss stressed the structure of myths.

Early anthropologists like Frazer sought to find common or similar things in the myths of the world Lévi-Strauss' contribution to this theory was that universality exists only at the structural level in culture, never at its empirical manifestations. One lone fact, however deeply studied cannot lead to the true meaning of a myth. We have to study by comparing the complete sets of myths from all over the world, never just one myth in isolation.

Structural Theory

Mind naturally functions in structural forms. Experience is also assimilated in structural forms. Man thinks of the time-space continuum as divided into segments classified accordingly. Time is not an agglomerate of events, but is made up of sequential events. This innate habit of compartmentalising an aggregate follows in artificial or man-made things also, like for example, artefacts and myths. These structural forms arise from man's unconscious, and, for this reason, is common to people all over the world. This follows Jung's theory.

Structural analysis of myths entails the breakdown of its components into opposing pairs. Tabulating these pairs may enable one to find the connection between these. The components of pairs of opposites balance one another and their structure can be represented algebraically. We apprehend our surroundings through our senses, and tend to cut up our information into segments. The method of structural analysis is : (1) To classify the subject under study in opposing binaries. (2) To construct a table of possible relationship between them. (3) This table should yield connections which would allow us to understand the binaries. Lévi-Strauss' main concern is with the universal manifestations of the mental processes projected into the social and cultural life of a people. To understand man fully, society and religion, which are the mental projections of the conscious and unconscious processes, must be considered. Myths can be resolved by breaking down their 'elements' into pairs of opposites. This breaking down is the structure of the myth. By elements he means translated words.[105]

Lévi-Strauss' analysis of myths gives eminence to two aspects in their structure: *scheme*. At the back of patent structural forms, lies a conceptual format, and these are linked in pairs of binary *contrasts*.[106] This scheme or schema has pairs of opposites in many layers, existing simultaneously. For example, in the *Devī Māhātmya*, the cosmological level is in the first episode; as well as the conflict of Goddess versus the Demon. The sociological plane is in the contrast of a woman set against a buffalo, personifying evils in society. Religious level would be the ritual of reciting the whole *Māhātmya* as a *śruti*. In the final resolution, according to Lévi-Strauss, the distance between the opposing binaries is said to dissolve. In the *Devī Māhātmya*, the distance is brought to nought, not by resolution but by elimination of one component of the pair.

Lévi-Strauss claims the following:[107] Firstly, the meaning of a myth cannot be searched among its constituent elements, but, in its whole composition. Secondly, a myth's language is unique. Thirdly, its expression is also complex. From these, it is inferred that a myth is made up of constituent elements which are different and complex units.

Though Lévi-Strauss compared the structure and analysis of myths to that of language, he himself later on rejected this analogy, because myths have meanings of varying levels and can be interpreted in any number of ways. Hegel is said to have influenced Lévi-Strauss in the latter's idea of thesis, synthesis and antithesis. The influence of Hegel's philosophy is seen in the dialectic method of resolving the concept of the nature of reality and the way this could be grasped. Hegel emphasized contradiction in language. Marx is more involved with the contradiction in the situation itself. Lévi-Strauss follows the latter in his structural analysis. He is not so much bothered by contradictions in the terms of language, as with the contradictions themselves as envisaged in myths.[108]

The study of myths could be compared to the study of language. Myths make their structure apparent by reiterating the sequence of events. A myth grows continuously till the intuition which sets it on, runs dry. Noticing the differences between the scientific and the primitive mind, and the qualitative difference in the working of the mind in both the cases, Lévi-Strauss avers[109] that the mythic mind is as capable of intellectual thinking as the scientific mind. It is only its application that is different, not its quality.

Lévi-Strauss takes all the different versions of a myth as equally important. But, by version, he means both the version and its interpretation.[110] A myth according to him[111] is multivalent and has complex meanings with relation to other myths of the same type in a group, and, further, with other such similar groups.

Though the field work of Malinowsky is respected and followed even today, his 'functional' theory has fallen by the road. Frazer compiled an immense quantity of similar myths to show an uniform evolution of the human mind. He endeavoured to compare human psychology by comparing details of human culture from all over the world. Lévi-Strauss is not interested in the uniformity of the evolution of the human mind. He contends that the similarities of the human mind exist in the structural level of myths, never as physical facts. His three main points of work are : (1) Kinship theory, (2) The logic of myth, and (3) The theory of primitive classification.

Contribution

Lévi-Strauss' analysis of the structure of a myth reveals a summary of the themes which the myth throws up during analysis. The essence of a myth underlying its themes is revealed in the structural analysis of a myth. But, this type of analysis can never be separated from the meaning of the myth itself. The meaning of a myth is contained partly in the author's own interpretations and partly in the listeners'. Anthropologists must try and understand the cultural ethos of a society and the relevance of the myth to that society, before adjudging a myth. Lévi-Strauss has eminently fulfilled this.

It is again due to Lévi-Strauss that the structure in the contents of a myth has become overt and important. Not merely content with the structural analysis of myths, he further showed that such an analysis has a sociological value. He shows that not only is the structure of the myth dialectical but the relationship between the social and mythical world is also dialectical. That is, a statement in the myth changes the social set-up, which in turn gains a response in the mythical world. This chain reaction is constant. A validation of such a statement is not possible with his myths, because of lack of historical information of the tribes he has covered. Therefore, his task in this direction cannot be said to be fully successful. The effectiveness and the importance of structural analysis can be judged only when it is applied to a rich mythology like the Indian, backed by ethnological statistics. Lévi-Strauss has analysed one Greek Myth, the Oedipus myth, and O'Flaherty ha attempted to analyse the myths of Śiva *(Asceticism And Eroticism In The Myth Of Śiva).*

An analogy between Elliot and Lévi-Strauss is seen in the latter's attempts to explain concepts in myths, as better expressed in material ideas or objects, rather than in abstract concepts, placing them in opposition. This seems as a follow-up of Elliot's methods in his poems though Elliot used the same principle for emotional expressions.[112] Lévi-Strauss used myths to prove his structural theory on thought categories. Myths are clearly the outcome of the mental processes of people. They are the expression of a community as a whole and as such are important. He treats myths as would a structural linguist. He attacks myths with principles similar to a linguist examining an unknown language. By proving that myths have an underlying structure, he applies this principle to all levels of a culture which would show a structured pattern. Since this contribution to the study of myths, their content has become important. Myths or a segment thereof can well be understood, only if their place in the whole culture is connected and the whole picture assessed. The theory that only the social organisations reflect the culture of a tribe has been abandoned due entirely to Lévi-Strauss.

The structural theory is very well suited to adjudge tribal or primitive myths, specially totemistic, according to Lévi-Strauss himself.[113] He was always concerned with primitive totemic communities, and how their social life is reflected in their myths. They use myths to solve their problems. The social components of a tribe are reflected in a myth if the solution to their problem is arrived in a straight forward way, because the components of the myth are also straight forward. If the solution is arrived at in a complicated and obtruse way, then the social components depicted will not relate to the actual set-up, but indeed may even be upside down.[114] He assumes along with Freud that myth is a collective dream. Modern society overlays its myths with sophisticated rationalization. Therefore, to get at the universal logic, the unsophisticated primitive myths are chosen for study as providing the best ground.

Criticism

Structuralists lay emphasis on all versions of a myth, but not on their chronology. Lévi-Strauss criticised functionalists that myths should be studied by themselves (but he himself would resort to analysing them with the culture in mind.)[115] Any myth would lose its meaning if transported away from its soil and culture. Granted that many levels of perceptions are possible in myths, and they, like poems, do not lose the true essence in translations, it is also true that the further we are away from a myth's culture so much is lost in our interpretation. In Indian myths the participants are sometimes confused and want to be enlightened. If myths provide a solution for polarities, then we gain not only an understanding of the solution but also of the polarities themselves.

Primitive myths are said to show an irrational thinking process in them. They seem to proceed from a state of mental infancy.[116] That the primitive has capacity to think in an abstract fashion can be entertained only by an armchair theologian. Universality of a mythic mind is also refuted on the grounds that similar myths are not acceptably universal in diffusion.

The examples of myths are chosen to fit his theory. So long as the theory has not been used to explain all types of myths, its universality has to be taken on faith. Lévi-Strauss assumes that all binary opposites can be algebraically expressed. But in primitive societies, relationships bristle with emotion and taboos, and will not be brought under mathematical logic. This is a more serious weakness in his arguments.

Lévi-Strauss states that myths contain hidden meanings, as messages from the older to the younger generation. He ignores cultural limitations of time and space. He detected a hitherto overlooked quality amongst tribals that they possess an analytical mind and that they find a via media for polar oppositions in their myths. Ricoeur[117] has objected that structural opposition could be applied only to myths of savage societies, and never to civilized ones. It would follow that no single yardstick should be applied in appraising myths. One should be able to apply any or all theories, and not arbitrarily use just one property. Myths after all are a form of human expression and may not come under a narrow classification.

Under Lévi-Strauss' theory, a myth cannot be examined singly. But the whole collection of similar myths have to be taken under consideration. As such there is no significance for a single myth which is a drawback. Each detail should be considered and, if a small detail persists in all the versions, then that is the most important piece in the structure of the myth. The mythologist arranges the facts as he finds them irrespective of their suitability. This is what makes the structuralist theory unsuitable for civilized myths. Binaries of opposites which is the basis of the structuralist theory may work in primitive myths. In civilized myths, the polarities are less, and the myth may rest on a single idea.

Lévi-Strauss tries to overlook the lower nature in men, and sees only the pleasant aspects of human behaviour as necessary in human evolution. There is no involvement in the concrete behaviour of men. He moreover emphasises the form of the myth, and its content is of secondary importance. But, if the content is ignored, the context is lost, and the meaning gets vitiated. He further believes that all myths in all cultures have only one function, namely, that they mediate between contradictions. All myths according to him are speculative, reflecting on problems and trying to resolve them. It is a weakness to view myths as having a single function. He has also not done much fieldwork. He leaves ideas not suited to his theory or twists them to fit his theory.

The Mahiṣāsura Motif

According to Lévi-Strauss, it is in the nature of a myth to provide a logical model capable of overcoming a contradiction. Viewing the Mahiṣāsuramardinī myth in this light, an attempt is made to highlight one prominent contradiction in the myth, and to solve it as seen in the myth.

In the Brahminic, that is the Greater Tradition, all the Purāṇas state that Mahiṣa offered a proposal of marriage to Devī, through his henchmen or himself directly. Devī spurns it and in the fight that ensues she kills him. In the folk-tales from all over India, the version is different. In North India, Bainsasura was a corn god. In Maharashtra, Jogubai that is Yogeśvarī, who is none other than

Durgā, is married to Mhatoba, who is Mahiṣāsura. Satavi another goddess assimilated to Durgā, has near her shrine Mhasoba, that is, Mahiṣa, worshipped in a shrine. In South India, in Andhra Ūrammā, the goddess, has a buffalo dedicated to her, called *Gauḍa-Kona,* husband of the goddess. He is also called *Devara-Potu,* devoted tothe goddess. Before this buffalo is sacrificed to the goddess in the annual festival, another buffalo is chosen and dedicated to her, so that *she does not remain a widow even for a day.* If this is so in Andhra, other similar versions exist in other states. In Karnataka, the folk tradition says the Brahmin girl who was tricked into marriage by a Caṇḍāla is born as Mārī, the goddess worshipped by the lower castes, and her husband was born as the buffalo to be sacrificed every year. The Greater Tradition is accepted as later than the folk-tradition, because the latter is autochthonous, and wielded its influence over the Sanskritised religion.

The Contradiction that the Brahmins Faced

They had to assimilate a goddess whose husband was a buffalo and who was sacrificed to her ritually. The problem was either to remove or supress Mahiṣa. Though Tantrically a supine Śiva under Kālī's feet could be explained and the goddess' victory over her husband covered in metaphysics that Śiva without Śakti was a corpse, they could not accept the fact that the Goddess should kill her husband. The memory of Mahiṣa as the consort of Devī was latent upto Bāṇa's period when his Caṇḍīśatakam shows covertly erotic undertones in the verses. The best answer that could be thought of might have been to incite Mahiṣa to ask for Devī's hand in marriage, with pride and such other Tāmasic qualities. Devī the Aryanised Goddess, spurns the offer and under the invigorating influence of liquor, kills the upstart. Though the Aryan connection of the Goddess was slowly stabilising, the Mahiṣa problem must have been too popular to expunge altogether and this must have been the logical model that Lévi-Strauss states, that overcomes the contradiction inherent in the tale. The motif of the buffalo in folk-tales can only be explained as the victory in the battles between two cults. The buffalo totem must have been defeated by a stronger autochthonous goddess cult. The contenders might have been so powerful, that the buffalo had to be raised to the position of the goddess' consort. When agriculture was established, the buffalo in the local cult variations might have been assimilated to the corn god himself or in an inversion of the myth as an enemy of corn. Ritual in the Greater Tradition also was built around the sacrifice of the animal in the annual harvest pūjā, the Navarātri. Mahiṣa's power was almost cosmic that no existing god could face him in battle. A new Goddess was therefore created.

The structural theory is not well suited to Indian myths. But for an attempt at it, all the local variations of the myth distributed over a vast region should be studied. And to collect this is a gargantuan task, well beyond the means available and the limitations enforced on this study.

To round up, a survey is made to see how the myth fits with the theories mentioned in the beginning of this chapter.

The etymological meaning of Durgā is one who is difficult of access, or one who helps her devotees over inaccessible or dangerous places and situations.

The connection with rituals is the function of the *Māhātmya* itself. Mahiṣa is the personification of drought and Durgā as the autumnal sun annihilates him. This satisfies the theory of natural forces mythicised as the characters in myths.

The evolutionists would see the goddess of the local cults becoming the goddess of a more cultured people.

There are sufficient iconographic evidences of an early period to support the cult from the archaeological point of view.

Totemists would see the victory of one cult over the other as a totemic battle. The classificatory theorists can see innumerable divisions of light versus darkness, deva versus asura, sāttvic versus tāmasic, etc.

The Aryan colonisation of the interior forests and hilly areas was seen in the Brahminisation of the Goddess cult and its extension over a larger area. According to the Marxists, the oppressed classes saw as a panacea for their ills, Devī as their saviour. Foreign parallels could be seen for our myth and historical uniformity was established. The moral of getting out of the binding and blinding fetters of delusion by worshipping the cause of it is explicit in the myth itself. The goddess motif, benign or malignant, satisfies the traumatic needs of the society even today. Symbolism can be read into the myth ad infinitum.

Thus, we see the immense of richness in the Hindu mythic

imagery that it satisfies almost all theories expressed on the subject from the earliest period upto today. This would be one of the major reasons for the popularity of the theme.

With this background on the subject of myths, their form and content, from the viewpoint of the Western scholars, we move on to our myth, Durgā, as Mahiṣāsuramardinī. It has been seen that this myth fits almost all theories on the subject. This is not a denigration of the theories, but an understanding of the richness and grandeur of our myth. Hindu myths are evaluated with a deeper understanding if they are traced to their Ur-texts, that is the Vedic literature. But our understanding is sharpened if we go behind the Devī concept, and go to the hoary past, when her cult originated and spread over vast areas. This is possible only by studying the archaeological remains from the Palaeolithic period to the Indus Valley Culture period, which task is undertaken in the next chapter.

REFERENCES

1. Cassirer, *An Essay on Man*, p. 109.
1a. For a detailed discussion on Indian views on myth Cf Ch V. Sn. Purāṇas 326.
2. Cf. Golden Bough.
3. Cassirer, E., *The Philosophy of Symbolic Forms*, Vol. 2, Mythical Thought, p. 68.
4. Leach, Edmund, *Lévi-Strauss*, p. 8.
5. James, E.O. *Primitive Ritual and Belief*, p. 222.
6. *Vedic Mythology*, Vols. I and II.
7. *Ibid.*, p. 112 ff.
8. *The Śāktas*.
9. Cassirer, E., *The Philosophy of Symbolic Forms*, Vol. 2, p. 18.
10. Also Stella Kramrisch in *the Presence of Siva*.
11. Preston, James. *J, Cult of the Goddess*, p. 92.
12. Custom and Myth; *Myth, Ritual and Religion*, Vols. I and II.
13. Cassirer, E, *op. cit.*, p. 16.
14. Lang, A., *Myth, Ritual and Religions*, Vol. 2, p.11; Vol.1, pp. 4, 5, 38.
15. Mendelson, E.M, *The Uninvited Guest*, p. 124.
16. E.O., *primitive Ritual and Belief*, p. 181.

17. Spence, L, *The Outlines of Mythology*, pp 4-5.
18. Malinowsky, *Sex, Culture and Myths*, pp. 123, 247 ff.
19. Preston James, *Cult of the Goddess* p. 92.
20. *Op. cit.*, pp. 250-54.
21. Malinowsky, *Magic, Science and Religions* **and other** *Essays*. pp. 120-121.
22. Malinowsky, *Sex, Culture and Myths*, pp. 250, 291-92.
23. Malinowsky, *Magic, Science and Religion* **and Other** *Essays*, p. 63.
24. Lévi-Strauss, Claude—*Myth and Meaning*, pp. 15-16.
25. Barthes Roland, *Myth Today;* Quoted in **Chakrabarti**, Kunal, *Myth and its Interpretation*, p. 389.
26. Lévi-Strauss—*Structural Anthropology*, Vol. I., p. 9.
27. Kirk G.S., *Myth :Its Meaning and Function in Ancient and other Cultures*, p. 22.
28. Held, G.J., *The Mahabharata*, pp. 103-4.
29. Hillebrandt, A., *Vedic Mythology*, Vol. I, p.1.
30. Renou Louis, *Religions of Ancient India.*, p. 17.
31. Eliade, M, *The Two and the One*, p. 114.
32. O'Flaherty, W.D., *The Origins of Evil in Hindu Mythology*, pp. 80-81.
33. Kirk, *Myth*, p. 28.
34. James, *Primitive Rituals and Belief*, p. 166 ff.
35. *Ibid.*, pp. 184-86.
36. Frankfort, H. and H.A., *Before Philosophy*, p. 16.
37. James, *Myth and Ritual in the Ancient Near East*, p. 20.
38. Kirk,—*Ibid.*, pp. 12-29.
39. Dhere R. C., *Lajja Gauri*.
40. Eliade, M. Kitagawa, J.M.-G.M., *Methodological Study of Religious Symbolism*, p. 86.
41. Dikshitar, V.R.R.— *Migrations of Legends*, ABORI, Vol. 15, Art. 9, pp. 212-19.
42. Thapar, R, Society and Historical Consciousness in *Situating Indian History*, pp. 355 and 357.
43. Thapar, R., *Origin Myth* pp. 294-95.
44. Kirk, *op. cit.*, p. 211 ff.
45. Shendge, M., *The Civilized Demons*, pp. 49 ff.
46. Shendge, M., *Ibid.*, pp. 309.
47. Eliade, *The Two and the One*, p. 148.
48. *Myth and Meaning*, p. 42.
49. Chakrabarti, Kunal, *Psychoanalytic Approaches to the Study of Ancient Indian Myths*, p. 389.
50. Bachofen J. J., *Myth, Religion and Mother Right*, p. 48.

51. Eliade — *Myth and Reality*, pp. 1-10.
52. Cassirer, E, — *Essay on Man*, p. 79.
53. Keremyi, C.—*Prolegomena*, pp. 6 and 10.
54. Chakrabarti K., *op. cit.*, p. 387.
55. Farnell, L.R.—*The Value and Methods of Mythologic Study*, p. 47.
56. O'Flaherty, W.D., *The Origins of Evil in Hindu Mythology*, p. 9.
57. O'Flaherty, *Ibid*, p. 8.
58. E.O., *Myth and Ritual in the Ancient Near East*, p. 20.
59. Durkheim and Mauss, *Primitive Classification*, p. 82 ff.
60. Dimcock, Edward, C., *A Theology of the Repulsive*, pp. 283-289.
61. Chakrabarti, K., *op. cit.*, p. 384, fn. 2.
62. Chakrabarti, —*Ibid.*, p. 386.
63. Leach, Edmund, Lévi-Strauss, p. 30.
64. *Man And His Symbols*, ed., Jung.
65. Jung, C.G., *Psychology of the Unconscious*, p. xiiiv.
66. Eliade, M., *Myth and Reality*, p. 78.
67. Cassirer., *The Philosophy of Symbolic Forms*, p. 5.
68. Pace, David, *Claude Lévi-Strauss*, p. 149.
69. Jung, C.G.—*Archetypes and the Collective Unconscious*, p. 161, fn. 21.
70. *Ibid.*, p. 5 fn. 10.
71. *Myths and Symbols in Indian Art and Civilization*, pp. 40-41.
72. Zimmer—*Ibid.*, p. 40.
73. Chakrabarti, K., *Op. cit.*, pp. 393-96.
74. Cassirer, E., *Essay On Man.*, p. 30.
75. Langer, S.K.—*Philosophy in a New Key*, p. 138.
76. O'Flaherty—*Asceticism and Eroticism in the Mythology of Siva*, p. 318.
77. Langer, S.K., *Op.cit.*, p. 163.
78. *The Concept of Deity*, p. 16.
79. Eliade —*The Quest*, p. 34.
80. Bachofan. J.J., *Myth, Religion and Mother Right*, p. 176.
81. Jung., *Man and His Symbols*, p. 68.
82. Dandekar, R.N., *Asura Varuna*, ABORI,Vol. XXL, p. 190.
83. Dimcock, E.C., *A Theology of the Repulsive*, p. 201.
84. *An Essay on Man*, p. 24 ff.
85. *The Philosophy of Symbolic Forms*, Vol. I, Language, p. 88.
86. Jung, C.G. and Kerenyi, C.-*Introduction to a Science of Mythology*; pp. 111, and 101.
87. *The Philosophy of Symbolic Forms*, Vol. II, p. 4 ff.
88. Kirk, *Myth.*, p. 279 ff.

89. *Myth Religion and Mother Right*, Preface pp. xxi and xv.
90. *Kerenyi, Prolegomena.*
91. Eliade, *Patterns in Comparative Religion*, p. 268.
92. Eliade —*The Two and the One*, pp. 101, 104, 204, and 206; also *Methodological Remarks on the Study of Religions Symbolism*, pp. 95-104.
93. Kunal, *Psychoanalytic Study of Ancient Indian Myths* p. 402.
94. *Myth and Ritual*, p. 254.
95. Frankfurt H and H.A., *Before Philosophy*, p. 15 ff.
96. Farnell, L.R., *The Value and Methods of Mythological Study*, pp. 46-47.
97. Kerenyi, C., *Prolegomena*, p. 1.
98. *Myth and Reality; Patterns in Comparative Religion.*
99. Eliade, *Myth and Reality* p. 18.
100. Eliade, *Myths, Dreams and Mysteries*, p. 14.
101. *Ibid.*, pp. 24-27.
102. Brubaker, R.L., *The Goddess and the Polarity of the Divine Consort*, p. 204, fn.1.
103. Lévi-Strauss — *Structural Anthropology*, Vol. II, p. 204.
104. Leach, Edmund — *Lévi-Strauss*, p. 41
105. Burridge, K.O.L., *Lévi-Strauss and Myths*, p. 98.
106. Lévi Strauss, *The Story of Asdiwal*, p. 17, fn. 8.
107. *Structural Anthropology*, Vol. I, p. 210.
108. Burridge, K.O.L.— *Lévi-Strauss and Myth*, p. 98.
109. *The Structural Study of Myth*, pp. 229-230.
110. Douglas, Mary, *The Meaning of Myth*, pp. 51 ff.
111. *Structural Anthropology*, Vol. II, p. 65.
112. Yalman, Nur—*The Raw : The Cooked : : Nature : Culture*, p. 71.
113. *Structural Anthropology*, Vol. I. p. 22.
114. Lévi-Strauss—*Structural Anthropology*, Vol. II. p. 173-204.
115. Burridge, *Ibid.*, p. 97.
116. Spence, Lewis—*The Outlines of Mythology*, p. 24.
117. Kirk, *Ibid.*, p. 83.

CHAPTER II
THE CULT OF THE MOTHER GODDESS
(Origin and Diffusion)

The earliest expression given by man to the concept of deity is not the Mother Goddess. But, the area of diffusion of her cult is vast and it has endured through civilizations. Man's imagination has transformed and transmuted the idea of a Mother Goddess according to his individual culture and to suit the requirements of the period. "The depth and intimacy of man's relationship with nature found expression in the ancient symbol of the mother goddess".[1] She moves down in history through kingdoms and culture and her cult changed and adapted to the particular requirement.

According to a historico-cultural school, in the beginning was Urkultur—the Primordial culture, when there was equality of status between man and woman and food was obtained by means of food gathering and hunting of small animals. According to this school,[2] there were two grades of pastoralists. The Aryans belonged to the higher grade, where stock-raising was supplemented by agriculture. Since the people had to lead a hardy out-door life, they were led by men who were of the hero-class, brave, strong and war-like. Since they had to fight against the elements, their gods were personifications of the sky and the elements like rain, storm, wind, etc. The agriculturists, on the other hand, were led culturally by women. Their religion was also chthonic and was concerned with fertility of the Earth Mother, magic, etc.[3] There is a similarity of the Urkultur to some primitive tribal societies like the Australian aborigines, etc. This split into two distinct forms of society: the totemic society in which man was predominant and, the matrilocal and matriarchal societies where woman was important. It was the latter culture which gave rise to the cult of the Mother Goddess; and worship of the Earth Mother also reached its height.

In the Urkultur, since discursive thinking was at the incipient stage, the Supreme Being could be an animal, a male or a female. For the next stage (called *Prima Kulturen*), opinions are divided as to whether matriarchate existed alone and whether woman was supreme at any stage of that civilization such that the Mother Goddess was the only Supreme Being. Importance to women is seen in such institutions as matrilocalism, avunculate, and gynaecocracy, which gave social, juridical and religious importance to woman. But importance does not mean predominance. J.J. Bachofen[4] was of the opinion that the more primordial the people, the more the feminine-nature principle will dominate religious life and woman's social position will be higher. This stands refuted even by primitive tribes of the Australian aborigines and their patriarchism.

Eliade[5] says: "We have no proof that religious structures are created by certain types of civilization or by certain historic moments. All one can say is that the predominance of this or that religious structure is occasioned or favoured by a certain kind of civilization or by a certain historic moment. When we consider religious structure historically, it is their statistical frequency that matter. Civilization, societies and historical moments furnish opportunities for the manifestation or the predominance of these non-temporal structures." He is discussing one aspect of the Mother Goddess, viz., the Earth Mother, but this holds good for the Goddess cult generally. There are reasons of how and why the goddess cult arose and why it held man's imagination, with its power. These questions are answered by psychologists, sociologists and anthropologists. Here we deal with the cult per se.

Origin of the Cult

In archaeology (which is the only record of the period), of the proto-historic period, there is a wide diffusion of the cult objects of the goddess. The origin of the cult is attested to be the Southern Steppes of Russia and the area of diffusion is the Fertile Crescent, i.e., from Crete and Anatolia to the land between the Euphrates and the Tigris bounded on the North by the Caucasus. The period of its development was from the Neolithic to the Christian Era. It influenced all religions of the near East and upto the Indus Valley. It left its imprint on the patriarchal Aryan religion. The only two religions which kept her cult out are those of the Muslims and the Jews.

In the Palaeolithic period when exactly the cult of the Mother Goddess arose is not certain, but it was found in Western Asia, South Russian plains and the Don Valley. The figurines found here were of the female form with explicit delineation of the exaggerated maternal organs. These are supposed to have arrived here, brought by an Asiatic migration called the Gravettian culture (from the word *gravette* a blade-tool) in the Upper Aurignacian period (30,000 BC -10,000 BC) of the Palaeolithic period. The figurines were made of bone, ivory, stone and in bas relief. In Eastern Europe and Western Asia, bone was used. The Venus figurines were 5 cms - 25 cms tall. The celebrated ones are the Venuses of Lespunges, Willendorf (Austria) and Laussel (Dordogne).[6] These figurines were given an ochre-wash. Ochre is the surrogate of blood and therefore stands for fertility and fecundity. The two ends in the progress of civilization—the Khoi-Khoi or the Hottentots worship stones daubed with red earth (as is common amongst Hindus) and at the other end are the Greeks who used it in the Dionysian cults. The exaggerated female organs and a large stomach suggestive of pregnancy were also symbols of fertility and abundance. The exaggerated organs of fertility and motherhood as displayed in these goddess figurines are not just physical organs, but are symbols of the numina in its creative aspect. These are then the divine epiphanies of the Goddess.[7] As it spread to Eastern and Central Europe, the figurines became grosser. The one of Willendorf near Austria is grotesque, though the one at Unter Westernitz in Moravia is more elegant. The figure at Laussel is nude and pregnant and is looking at a bison horn, turning to face it, which she holds in her hand. They have been found at Gargarino and Mezine in Ukraine. At Gargarino, they were found at habitation levels, and therefore they must have been worshipped in the homes. At Mezine, they are highly stylized and decorated with geometric abstractions. One of the patterns is the svastika.[8] These stand for the magico-religious powers of the Mother Goddess. The depiction of spirals in the Ice Age represented the moon as well as feminine fecundity.

Cowrie shells were also used in this period as they resemble the portals of birth. These, along with red-washed Venus Figurines, became symbols of life in mortuary rituals.

Funerary Cults

The earliest specimen of death ritual was found in a Chinese cave 50 kms. from Peking. The head was retained because it was thought to be the seat of potent strength in magico-religious rituals. (This belief persists till today in the Tantrik ritual murders. In medieval India, the skull was an important cult object in the *Kāpālika* and *Kālabhairava* sects). Through a hole in the skull the brain was sucked out and eaten to part-take of its magico-religious qualities. Another Neanderthal skull was found in Italy. It had been given a red wash and placed ceremoniously on animal skulls. Shells surrounded the corpse. These burials belonged to the Palaeolithic and Neolithic periods. In the Palaeolithic era, in the Gravettian and Upper Aurignacian period, man was interested mainly in fertility and propagation. The Magdelanians, who followed them (15000-6000 BC), were interested in the abundance of the hunt.

When hunting gave place to raising of flocks and tilling the soil, the change of seasons was observed. The resurrection of vegetation after its death in winter was connected with human after-life and the two were combined around the 5th millenium. B.C. in the Neolithic and Chalcolithic periods. Venus figurines started reappearing in the Nile Valley, in Mesopotamia at Tell Arpachiyah near Nineveh.

In the Neolithic era, food-gathering gave place to food production. The importance of the female grew; but side by side the role played by the male in procreation began to be recognized. The male's function was not clearly perceived and, therefore, though there was a male god, he played a subordinate role.[9] Paternity was a matter of inference as opposed to maternity which was a matter of observance."[10]

Clay figurines were found in the Mosul District of Northern

Iraq. They belong to a period prior to 4000 B.C. This shows a continuity in the idea of the symbol from palaeolithic time. Some of them are hollow, and may have been used as a vase and some are of the amulet type.

Once the idea of the goddess was fixed in the human mind, she was represented either as a single goddess incorporating within herself all the various functions connected with her cult, or, these functions were distributed amongst separate deities.

The Fertility Cult

The fertility cult of the Mother Goddess was a natural phenomenon in the early stages of the Neolithic era, because man's preoccupation was with fertility and abundance. Even though the cult had spread widely in the Chalcolithic era, in the Neolithic era there were not so many sites. There are a few in Tell Halaf[11] and in Eastern Mediterranean, in Ur and Abu Shahrain, in Uruk (now Erech) in Mesopotamia, and in Iran. In Egypt at Wadien-Natuf, burials of Mesolithic civilization have been discovered. There are two types of burials. One is the inhumation of the body in a bent position and the other is when the skulls alone are buried. Thus the ritual burial of the Palaeolithic period continued right up to this period. These are termed the Netufian burials.

There are two feminine goddess statuettes prior to 6000 B.C. at the oldest city, Jericho. There are also three statuettes of a man, woman and a child with their eyes inlaid with shells. There is an androgynous statuette and one, of a goddess of the terrible aspect.

In recent years, remains of a perfectly laid village with fortifications have been unearthed in the north of Bulgaria, where a ceramic statuette of the Mother Goddess has been discovered of the period 3600-3000 B.C.[12] Clay figurines belonging to the same Bronze Age period of the goddess have been found in Susa. In Russian Turkestan, the figurines have exaggerated breasts and navel, but have no face. In Anatolia, in the southern Turkish coast, the figurines of the Chalcolithic (when both bronze and stone implements were used) period are cruder than those found belonging to the Bronze Age.

Since fertility and the cult of the dead seem to go together, in Hacilar (7000 B.C.), burials of skulls have been found. There are seen three aspects of the Mother Goddess: (1) a young woman (2) a woman giving birth to a bull or a child and (3) an old woman accompanied by a bird of prey. The figures are on relief in wood, sometimes two metres high and also in plaster clay.

At Hacilar,[13] the goddess is seated on a leopard holding a leopard cub in her hand. The goddess is shown in various postures, sometimes accompanied by a child. But by 5200 B.C. the child or the animal accompanying the goddess disappears. The last phase of this culture showed geometric figures on ceramics.

When this culture disappeared, it reappeared in Tell Halaf (a site near the village Arpachiyah near Mosul), where the goddess figures are abundant. There are no written records of the period, but archaeological data occur regularly, though the cult representation varies. For example, the cult of the bull occurring in the Danube valley must have spread from the Near East, but there is no cult of bull sacrifice either in India or in Crete. Mother and child icons, so common in the East, are rare in the Danube area, and are never found near burial sites.

Sumerian Ancient Goddess

In the historic period, with written records, the most ancient goddess is the Sumerian Nammu, "the mother who gave birth to the sky and the earth" and the ancestress who brought forth all the gods.[14] The planetary goddess was Inanna, the Akkadian Ishtar of the later period. She is the goddess of fertility who marries Damuzi. She goes to the netherworld to get sovereignty from her sister Ereshkigal. She dies but is revivified on the condition that she sends somebody to take her place. She sees her husband, the shepherd enjoying his sole sovereignty and in anger sends him down. He is allowed to come upto the world for six months. In the Akkadian version, Ishtar goes down, but since she is the goddess of fertility all life comes to a stand still, till she is allowed to come back for six months. The Sumerian and Akkadian kings, who impersonated Tammuz/Damuzi, enacted a heiros gamos with a priestess acting for the goddess. The appearing and disappearing of vegetation were always felt to be a sign of the period ic creation of the universe. The idea of the heiros gamos of the sky and the earth separated forcibly (by Indra in the Vedic myth) appears in all religions, primitive, tribal, or patriarchal religions of Egypt, Greece and India.

In Anatolia,[15] the figure of a mother goddess, with leopards and a god standing on a bull, may be the forerunner of the Indus

Valley Śiva and the mother goddess. These were found in Catal Hüyük, circa 6000 B.C. There is a continuity between these figures and the Hittite storm god, the statues of Jupiter Dolichenus, worshipped by the Roman soldiers and also of the goddess figure with the Hittite goddess Hebat (Hepatu) and Cybele of the classical period.

In Crete and Continental Greece, the religion was a symbiosis between the Mediterranean substratum and the Indo-European conquerors from the north. As in India, when an urban civilization collapses, it is not extinguished but culturally it regresses into rural and popular forms.The archaeological evidence may not show all that was in the earlier culture. They may exist in a few cultural forms in a few pockets of the tributaries of the indigenous population, the descendants of an earlier culture, who had escaped the first onslaught of the invader.[16] In Crete, a celebrated cave taken over by the Greeks for their Eleusinian mysteries is at Amnisos near Cnossus. This was consecrated to Eilcithyia, a pre-Hellenic goddess of childbirth.

The Hittites were the Indo-Europeans who invaded and occupied Anatolia in the 2nd millenia B.C. They overan the Hurrians of Mesopotamia and Syria and the early inhabitants of Anatolia, the Hattians. The Hittites assimilated the Sumero-Akkadian as well as the Hattian or Hurrian religious traditions. As seen earlier their pantheon was headed by a storm-god and a mother goddess.

Women's Important Position in Farming

Agriculture was mainly a woman's discovery and responsibility. When man's function in procreation was dimly perceived, the furrow as the woman and the plough as the man was the resultant idea. The diffusion of this idea is very wide-spread, and is of primitive intuition. Women's important position in farming in contemporary societies of Nicobar, Borneo, Orinoco Indians, Nias and Ewes in Africa, Jibaros of S. America,[17] is self evident.

The identification of the phallus and the spade has been pointed out linguistically by Przyluski.[18] These notions also lead us to understand Sītā, as the furrow[19], and a goddess of the harvest.[20]

The Earth Mother is slowly expanded into many goddesses, each with one of her qualities. Their character is more sharply delineated than the Earth Mother.

"The turning of the Earth Mother into the Great Goddess of Agriculture is the turning of simple existence into a living drama."[21] The Earth divinities took into themselves many syncretic qualities of Mother Earth, because it is human nature to attribute as many qualities as possible to a favourite divinity. But Mother Earth never lost her character as the Giver of all life, food and, being the womb and tomb of life.

Since high eroticism would be the harbinger of fecundity, rites with agricultural and other fertility characteristics were connected often with hetaerism, nude women are made to run over the fields to invocate rains (in India). Nude or menstruating women were connected with sowing activities in Germany, Finland and Estonia. Woman, fertility, sexuality and nudity are all powerful centres of sacred power, which could be channelized for agricultural abundance.

If the Earth Mother is understood as the source of all life, death and contact with her again is only a renewal of contact with the source of life.

Agricultural and Vegetatal connection with the Mother Goddess will be treated later.

The American Indian tribe of Umatilla will not till the earth because it will hurt the Earth Mother's body.[22] Because she is the Tellus Mater, infants after death are not cremated but buried, i.e., returned to the mother.[23] She is the Ur Mutter—the Primordial Mother. Even in highly evolved cultures, we find statements connecting women with agriculture. Both the Koran, and Nārada commenting on Manu assimilate woman to[24] agriculture. Sexual excesses or heirogamies, like the Oraons of Central India, who do not start agricultural activities till the priest and his wife imitate heirogamy, are made use of in agriculture. Since perfection existed in the original time, they go back to that period and imitate divine heirogamy.

Mother Earth is the womb to which the dead are consigned so that they will return to life revivified by the Mother in their temporary soujourn. Therefore, bodies are buried in a bent fashion or in the embryonic position. Coming closer in time, in the Bronze and Iron Ages, Danish people were buried with ritual offerings.

One such burial has been discovered[25] with a cart and a horse carrying a gilded disc of a fertility cult which later was centred on the earth mother. Bronze neck rings were also found which were used as torques on the statues of the goddess.

The burial urns of Adichanallur[26] contain skeletons in the embryonic position, with bronze figurines of a variety of domestic animals, amongst which is the bison. There is also a Mother Goddess figure made of gold fillet work, and this is likened to the goddess of Minoan-Crete.

Another opinion of this bent position (since Palaeolithic burials) is that the body was tied in this position soon after death and then buried, because of the fear that the dead would harm the living. Ochre-wash was a life-giving agent and, along with artefacts, it helped the spirit make a safe crossing to another world.[27]

The Aegean Goddess was[28] the primary divinity in Crete. She was known as Rhea, also Dictynna and Britomaris. In the Hellenic religious traditions, these became Athena, Aphrodite and Artemis. Further, the Virgin Mary cult or Mariolatory drew its formation from these ancient precedents. Kingship was connected with the goddess cult throughout the Near East and the Eastern Mediterranean,[29] where it was the throne Goddess who was considered to confer royalty on the kings.[30] J.J. Bachofen[31] details the tradition of the Goddess cult connected with throne amongst the Assyrians, Etruscans, Tyrrhenion Lydians, Sabines, Carians, Mysians, Aramaeans, Phoenicians, and Persians. He takes this as a hallmark of a highly advanced culture.

'Cybele' was a Phrygian Goddess of caverns, but she was personified as earth in its primitive and savage state. She was worshipped on the top of the mountains.[32] Marpessos of Mount Ida in Phrygia was the birth place of Cybele. Rhea, the Cretan Mother Goddess, was very early "identified with Cybele, a goddess of the power of nature and arts of cultivation, who was worshipped upon the mountains in Mysia, Fydia and Phrygia".[33] She was associated with a lesser god-Attis, a vegetation deity. This pairing was exactly like Ishtar/Tammuz and Astarte/Adonis. Her statue has a turretted crown, which is an attribute of the Asiatic Mother Goddess.[34] Her throne is flanked by lions. There are a few parallels with the Purāṇic Indian Mother Goddess. Her festivals were marked by orgiastic dances with cymbals and flutes and swords striking shields. Her priests flagellated themselves with whips made up of knuckle-bones. Turkish archaeologists have unearthed a 2nd century B.C. marble statue of 'Kybele' near a Syrian Fortress,[35] under Roman occupation. 'Demeter' was the goddess who seems to have taught cultivation of corn to the Greeks.

The rituals connected with Earth and agriculture have sacrifices at the time of sowing and harvesting. It was human sacrifice in earlier times. In the myth of Creation, there is the sacrifice or violent death of a primeval giant, out of whose flesh and blood the crops and trees were created. By imitating this, the life of the corn is strengthened and it increases the harvest. Regenerated by the cosmic force, the grain is made to live again. Thus, fertility is increased by human or animal sacrifice.[36] The first fruits are also offered as a sacrificial offering.

Sexuality assists fertility of the fields. Ritual prostitution, orgies before sowing (Holi) festival, are all rites to assist the fields to yield more.[37]

For the primitive, when the plant dies, it was assisted to renew itself through magical rituals, through the Great Goddess, and through women as the instrument of the Goddess, and through Eros. The mystery religions like the Eleusinian would not have caught human fancy if they had not been grounded in agricultural rituals which again went back to pre-historic period.

Mystery Cult

Coming back to the Greek goddess, Demeter who played an important role (along with her daughter Kore/Persepone) in the mystery cult, heaped benefits on mortals who worshipped her. She was called 'Thermophoros', i.e., a goddess who gave laws, and, she was also a goddess of marriage. Obviously, her cult has had a great civilizing influence on the Greeks and she must have been a culture Goddess.

The famous Eleusinian Mysteries are vegetation cults. The death, and regeneration of seeds is assimilated with death of mortals and hopes of regeneration. Because of Demeter's connection with agriculture, the cult was popular. The return of Kore from the netherworlds was celebrated in the lesser Eleusinia at Agrai, a suburb of Athens, in the month of February. The Greater Eleusinia was celebrated once every five years in September in

Athens and Eleusis. Here the initiates, after various preliminary ceremonies, underwent esoteric experiences through some rituals enacted as a heirogamy between the priestess and the heirophant (the initiate). The storage of corn in the silos must have been applied to Kore's descent into the netherworld. The corn brought up in September from the silos where they were stored after threshing in June must have been the basis for the mysteries.

A reverse valuation from motherhood to cereals is given by J.J. Bachofen.[38] The Demetrian motherhood as a Mystery of Woman's powers is manifested in the transformation of the seed grain and the reciprocal coming into being, death being the inevitable event, which brings a person to a higher birth.

In the Orphic mysteries, the initiates escaped the wheel of birth and through their union with the mother goddess, emerged as a god. The Mother Goddess mysteries according to Bachofen, are as ancient as matriarchy; wherever matriarchy is found, it is bound up with chthonian religions, whether Eleusinian Mysteries or any other comparable ones. The cultic concepts of matriarchy are the roots and the social forms are the consequences.

Though the Egyptians and the Mesopotamians believed in the cosmic waters (as a male) to be the progenitor of the universe, both had different conceptions of the gods. The Mesopotamians believed in the Great Mother, whereas the Egyptians made the Mother Goddess into the ancient image of the cow and sky, who take in the dead and transform them into starry immortals.[39]

The Hittite goddess of 2000 B.C. bears the Harrian name Hepatu and is mounted on a panther with Teshub, the Storm God, next to her also mounted on a panther. She is in the rock sanctuary of Yasilikaya, two miles from the capital of Asia minor, Boghozköy. She is the earth goddess of fertility eventually known as Ma and developing martial characteristics she became the Roman War Goddess Ma-Bellona. *This is a familiar transformation of a fertility goddess into a war-goddess.* She was the goddess of birth Mama in the Gilgamesh epic.

The Minoan and Mycenean Goddess

She is pictured as a Mountain Goddess, standing between lions. Sometimes as in Crete, her place is taken up by a tree or pillar, as seen on a seal from the Central Palace Sanctuary at

Knossos. She is also associated with the netherworld, around 2400 B.C. She appears here more than a thousand years after she was well established in Arpachiya in Assyria.

Crete was such a powerful centre of the goddess cult that all aspects of her were worshipped. Finally, she was expanded into three goddesses, in Greece, Athena took her snake and bird emblems; Artemis, her wild creatures, forests and streams; and Aphrodite her doves. In the Eastern Mediterranian, she was the goddess of fertility and vegetation, sometimes accompanied by a youthful partner. Her emblems such as snakes, the dove, the double axe, horns of consecration and obese female figurines abound.

In Syria and Palestine the goddess cult is deep rooted.

Anat was a fruitful mother goddess without losing her virginity. She was the consort as well as the sister of Baal. She was the counterpart of Phoenician Ashtarte. She delighted in wars and conflicts and she was called the "Lady of the Mountain".

The Indo-Europeans moving from the Caucasus regions into Iran and thence into India played a major role in the development of the myth of the Mother Goddess in those regions. In Elam and Susa, on the periphery of Iran, Mother Goddess figures have been found.[40] At Susa, she is known as Kirrisha. She may even be the Zoroastrian Goddess Anahita—a goddess of fertility and water. She was worshipped in the form of Ishtar, with prominent breasts, dressed in golden raiments and a crown of stars. She was the mistress of all sexual life and had a retinue of priestesses engaged in ritual prostitution.

No less conspicuous were those forms of the goddess in Baluchistan, in Kulli and Zhob. But, before coming to this, the goddess worshipped as and in stone is dealt with.

Stone, because it was awe inspiring, standing direct and autochthonous, became sacred in the primitive mind. The Great Mother is represented by Cromlechs (by the Khasis of Assam as much as) by the early man.[41] Cromlechs and megaliths were always found near neolithic agricultural lands.[42] Because they were *svayambhū,* auto-genetic, they were believed to help in fertility. They were taken for phalli and connected with the goddess cult.[43]

The three metres high anthropomorphic stone figure of the Mother Goddess found in Udaiyanattam village in South Arcot Dt. Tamil Nadu, is a megalith.[44] It is surrounded by smaller stones.

Another one had been discovered at Mettur. Similar two were also found in Andhra Pradesh. These bear resemblence to the anthropomorphic cult images found in the Gangetic plain. A similar one found in the Madhya Pradesh was identified with the Vedic goddess, Aditi, and was the logos for the Indian art festival held in London. This may throw some light on the diffusion of the Dravidian speaking people. Similar ones belonging to the period of 1700 B.C. have been found in Crete.

The belief in the fertilizing powers of the stone is so great that Athenian women used to slide down a particular stone to be impregnated.[45] In Portugal, touching certain stones, even now, ensures safe delivery for the woman, and, children are walked up megaliths to ensure good health. From simple stones which strike men by their immensity, they have become symbols of the sacred power they contain and by this process they possess the qualities such a sacred power would have.

The goddess as a symbol of fecundity was connected with symbols of the Moon, waters (*tīrtha* and *kuṇḍa*), woman and earth.

The Sky God or gods (when one god divides into many to spread each quality) become sacred because of their association with the Great Mother as the Earth Mother. The thunder, the moon and the rains are the fecundating principles of the Sky God. The moon particularly holds a great importance in fertility rites and it is represented as horns.[46] The connection of the crescent moon with the horn held by the Aurignacian figure in Laussel can be understood as a symbol of fertility.

The importance given to the mother goddess as the Universal Mother is seen in the following two examples. They are of two extremes of culture,[47] civilization, and era. They are purposely juxtaposed to show how, like a child, man has clung to the mother image.

(1) The Universal Mother and the Supreme Deity from the Kagaba people of Columbia in S. America:

"......... Mother of all our seeds, bore us in the beginning of things ..... the mother of all nations. She is the mother of the thunder, the mother of the streams .... and of all things .... She is the mother .... of all our temples and she is the only mother we possess. She alone is the mother of the fire and the sun and the milky way". When the fields are sown the priests chant and the

Kabaga say "Our mother of the growing fields .... To our mother above do we belong".

A Sanskritised version would be
Ya Devī sarvabhūteṣu ...... saṁsthitā/
Namastasyai, namastasyai, namastasyai, namo namaḥ//[48]

(2) The Homeric Hymns xxx : The Earth Mother of All :[49]

"I will sing of well-founded Earth, mother of all .... She feeds all creatures that are in the world .. O queen .... to you it belongs to give means of life to mortal men and take it away. Happy is the man whom you delight to honour. He has all things abundantly ...

Hail mother of the gods .... freely bestow upon me for this my song substance that cheers the heart."

The Kulli Culture in Baluchistan

The next area in the diffusion of the Mother Goddess cult in Baluchistan. Here the centres are Kulli in Southern Baluchistan (with pottery of the Buff ware) and Zhob in the Northern Baluchistan (with the pottery of the red ware type).[50] In Damb Sadaad (Mian Ghundai), on a platform on a high mound with drains, are found mother goddess figurines of the Zhob type as also the Harappan culture type of bull figurines with ovoid marking. Thus, there is contiguity in the cult upto the Indus Valley.

The Kulli figurines have splayed ends, but they stand on a pedestal. Their heads are adorned by cowrie shells. Their faces are eerie-looking. Some figures have two infants in their arms.

Treating the artistry of the Kulli goddess figurines, Guha[51] says that there are two types of depiction of the mother goddess. The Aurignacian specimens have their organs exaggerated. The other type was depicted only with a vestige of organs, but heavily ornamented. Kulli figurines stand between these two extremes. The splayed bottom exhibited by both the Kulli and Zhob types show an earthiness of the Goddess, specially in the aspect of Earth Mother. The figures bear infants in their arms and have almost stark faces showing the combination of life, fertility and death in the goddess.

They seem to serve the same purpose in the cult as in the earlier mentioned sites of Elam, Mesopotamia, Anatolia, Egypt and the Aegean.[52] They are ornamented by what looks like cowrie shells, again a fertility symbol.

In the Kulli Culture there are plenty of clay figurines of animals and mother-goddess representations. The former may have been votive offerings for plentitude in cattle or hunting or just toys. The latter show the popularity of the goddess cult, and must have served as icons in domestic worship. Their faces look like a caricature and with their rounded eyes, beak-like noses they look like "scared hen"![53] As at Harappa, they are not matronly in their figure. They are loaded with necklaces, bangles and bracelets. One figure holds two infants in her arms. The Harappan dancing girl's coiffure is done exactly like the mother-goddess figurines of Kulli and the ornamentation also is similar. In the Zhob culture the figurines are similar to Kulli (i.e. animal and mother goddess figurines) and occur at Sur Jangal, Periano Ghundai, Moghul Ghundai, Kandani and Dabar Kot. The mother-goddess figurines are similar to the Kulli ones in shape, though their necklaces are shown "more schematically" than those on the Kulli ones. Their faces are totally different from the southern culture. Their rounded eyes are set on high foreheads and their heads are covered by high coif or shawl. "The effect is terrifying even in a tiny model not more than 2" high".[54] There are two from Dabar Kot where the face is just a grinning skull. These are "a grim embodiment of the mother-goddess who is also the guardian of the dead —an under world deity concerned alike with the corpse and the seed corn buried beneath the earth".[55]

The fertility motif connected with such an aspect of the goddess is represented by the following models.

In Moghul Ghundai, there was found a phallus carved in stone, and another one in rough pottery at Periano Ghundai. From the latter site was also found a figurine "consisting of an enormously exaggerated female vulva and thighs". Such models found on both banks of the Knob river have no parallel in the Kulli Culture. But analogous models have been found in the Harappan Culture.

Thus, from the above survey of the mother-goddess cult's origin and diffusion, we see an unifying Weltanschauung which underlies the culture and religion of the areas which worshipped her. She was a Great Mother unifying in herself both the positive and negative aspects of the goddess. Proceeding eastwards we arrive at the Indus Valley Civilization known as the Harappan Culture, which is contiguous in the cult, with Baluchistan.

The Harappan Culture

The Harappan Civilization is South Asia's first civilization[56]. Its area was at a conservative estimate three to four times that of Sumer. It was an urban civilization,[57] and the area of control of its culture was triangular, roughly thousand miles.[58] This has been assimilated to Hariyūpa.[59] Its proto history could go back to 5000 B.C., and its origins would be the Indo-Iranian borderlands. The period of its culture was 2300-1700 B.C.[60] Its apogee was around 2300 B.C., co-eval with Sargon of Akkad.[61] They are "found" here as a mature civilization, fully urbanised with a script. The people are supposed to have come (by land area) from Mesopotamia.[62] This civilization has been commented on as egalitarian. But it is also seen as a class society—divided into the exploiting merchant class, not engaged in actual production of goods, and the labour class housed in uniform barracks adjacent to the temple and therefore classified as temple slaves.[63]

The end of the civilization has been attributed to various causes. A few are cited. It was due to: tectonic tilts;[64] improper irrigation practices, denudation of forest lands, rise in the level of the Arabian Sea along the coastline in middle second millenium B.C.;[65] Aryan invasion;[66] climatic changes and invasions;[67] increase in ground water salinity.[68] Some hold the view that the civilization was decimated by the Aryans or the hilltribesmen from Baluchistan, or that the best of the culture, the people themselves, due to weather changes, moved northwards and southwards through Gujarat (Lothal), even down deeper south.

As for deforestation, Stuart Pigott[69] says, "The very fact that kiln-burnt bricks were used so lavishly in the Harappan culture shows that almost unlimited timber must have been available for fuel in the 3rd millenium B.C."

Another opinion is[70] that Vṛtra was the controller of the dams on the Indus system. Uśanas[71] committed perfidy by going over to Indra's side and giving him the thunderbolt (Vajra). Thus Indra was able to defeat Vṛtra, break the dams open and let loose floods on the Harappan civilization. The population which had fled tried to return to their homes and they were decimated by fire.

The Harappans, according to the same author,[72] were no other than the Panca-carsinī of the Ṛg veda (V.86.2) Pancajanāḥ (III.59.1). Also ṚV 1.89.10: Aditiḥ Pancajanāḥ; Sāyana's commentary states that the pancajanāḥ are the four castes with Niṣādas as the fifth; or else, the Gandharvas, Manes, devas, asuras, and rākṣasas. Yāska agrees with the latter opinion.

Further,[73] these people may have been Semetic (that is, the Asuras), Alpine (Gandharvas), Mongolian (Yakṣas and Piśācas) as surmised from the archaeological opinions on the skulls. A.L. Basham supports Fr. Hera's view that these people were Dravidians and their language was the ancestor to Tamil.[74]

These are a mixed race with a predominant mediterranean strain, allied to the proto-Elamites and Sumerians. These are attested by the images of fertility symbols and figurines of female goddesses. (as well as symbolic representations cf Pl. 2.) These occur on seals, clay tablets, and other objects at these sites.[75]

Yoni Stones

There have been many scholars disagreeing on the cult significance of these stones. A modern view[76] is that these stones were used as counter weights for the arm of a shaduf well. These wells are known in India as *lat*, or, *piccolah*. Many scholars have felt these are mere architectural pieces, especially the bigger ones. But the uniformity of style and the large number found would force us to agree with Marshall in his view that these were cult objects. Marshall has said: "It could hardly have been utilitarian nor are they suited for personal ornaments ..... These figures of the Fertility Goddess are particularly significant, because the form of the ring-stones from Taxila to Kosam also calls to mind the peculiar ring-stones from Harappa and Mohenjodaro".[77] Similar ring-stones have been found in large numbers near Mathurā, Basarh, Saṅkiśa, Rajghat, Patna, etc.

There are minor variations amongst these such as dissimilarities in the profusion of ornamentation and sometimes the central perforation is absent. Some of these are of polished sandstone, and most of them belong to the Maurya-Suṅga period.[78] This is again an example of the continuity of religious thought in the human mind.

These symbolic stones wielded a powerful influence on the religion of the later Aryans. Opinions are divided on the amount of influence this culture bore on the Aryan theology, but this would be treated later. Exactly as the Minoan-Mycenean religion with the later Indo-European element influenced Greek Myth and ritual, so also the Aryan culture underwent a change under the influence of the Harappan culture.

Another opinion[79] is that the Indus language was an earlier form, of the Ṛgvedic language. Their language and rites like animal sacrifice and veneration of the pipal tree were later adopted by the Vedic Aryans.

Supporting the Elamite roots of the Harappan culture is a further opinion. Commenting on David M. Alpine's[80] work, Possehl says that there was an ancient Elamo-Dravidian language family which covered all of Southern Iran and extended into the Western portion of South Asia. "The cultural and historical implications of this are enormous".

I. Mahadevan finds an "amazing continuity of the Indian historical tradition" when speaking of the bilingual similarities in the signs of the Indus seals and the Indo-Aryan and Dravidian equivalents.[81]

The Venuses of Gagarino were found at all levels of habitation and therefore it was inferred that they were objects of domestic worship.[82] Similarly the Mother Goddess figurines were also found at all levels of habitation.[83] We may safely assume that these figurines were also objects of daily domestic worship. (cf Pl. 1.)

Religion was the intensifying factor that created and gave form to the Harappan civilization. Mohenjo Daro was the ceremonial centre. But Harappa was the cult centre which is attested by its buildings. The buildings look ritualistic and, just as in Baluchistan, the bull and the Mother Goddess figurines recur.[84] Mackay[85], on the other hand, feels that there are no buildings of harappa or Mohenjo Daro which could be termed sacred. The goddess figurines are heavily ornamented, with a fan-shaped head-dress (cf Pl). This has a cup-like depression on both sides of the head. They have smoke stains in them which further strengthen the idea that these cult icons were worshipped in homes. The goddess' figure is not corpulent like the earlier matronly figurines, but is slim, which leads to the assumption that she may have been a virgin goddess.[86]

In the burial Urn at Adichanallur (cf Pl. 6) there are a number of bronze artefacts, the most numerous of which are the figurines of the buffalo and the dog. The figures of the buffalo date the burial to 4000-5000 B.C. when the animal had been successfully domesticated, but the oxen had not been introduced into the region. The Bronze Mother Goddess figurine found here is corpulent leading to the surmise that she is associated with fertility cults (cf Pl 5). There is gold fillet work exactly like the ones in Minoan-Crete.[87] This might throw a pointer towards the movement of the Harappans.

The burial urns at Cemetry H, upper stratum I in Harappa, have round their neck the painted motif of human forms, interspersed with peacocks, and pipal leaf. The peacock is seen as the totem of the mother Goddess of the river and speech, *Sarasvatī*. With the name Śiti Kaṇṭha, the bird is associated with the gods Rudra-Śiva and Skanda.[88] In some, there are figures of dogs also painted. If the dog could be taken as representing Yama's dog, the peacock as helping the soul in the form of the human figure to cross the river of the dead, then the people could be related to the Ṛgvedic Aryans. But, in South Indian Iron Age burials, the site is oriented towards the south, the direction of *Yama*. Further, it is interesting to find a wrought iron buffalo horn and trident in one burial, both symbols of Mahiṣa and Durgā. [89](cf Pl. 7)

About the goddess[90] figurines of the Harappan Culture Malati J. Shendge[91] states that they are representations of *Uṣas*, though by what method she arrives at this conclusion is not evident, unless the connection is between the Assyrians,[92] and the Aryans, and *Uṣas* is thus deduced. Most of the terracotta representations of the goddess or those on the seals, do not have the exaggerated organs of reproduction like the "Venus" figurines. On the other hand, care is taken in the delineation of the face and elaborate coiffeurs are shown.

Further, the seal where the goddess is associated with trees, with a man holding a sickle, could be a picturisation of a sacrifice, to revivify the sap of the vegetation goddess.

Or she may be kneeling in obeisance to the harvest deity. Amongst the seals which show her in association with vegetation, there is also depicted wild, not domestic animals. She could be a goddess of the forests, mistress of the hunt or animals, instead of a specific goddess of vegetation alone. Whether there were two goddesses associated separately with vegetation and animals, or, whether these were the two facets of the same goddess, it is difficult to surmise. But from the large number of seals found, one could say, she was a very popular goddess, not propitiated by the elite class alone.

The figurines are either given a red wash, or, are in a smoothly polished red slip. The magical potency of the colour red is obvious.

Pupul Jayakar[93] sees in the Harappan religion, similarities with folk tradition as well as the Atharva Veda and some times the Brāhmaṇa ideologies. There are variations of svastika as and mazelike patterns which are oft-repeated decorative motifs. These resemble the auspicious rice flour patterns drawn on the thresholds in Hindu households.[94] The well-known seal of a woman upside down, with her arms on her knees, and a tree issuing out of her womb has two tigers on both her sides. These animals are seen as the guardians of initiation.[95] On the obverse side of this seal is a seated figure with raised arms, while a figure holding a knife and a cup approaches. The script is identical on both sides. This may be taken to depict human sacrifice to appease Earth Mother and beg for fertility and fecundity. This is assimilated with the Ś.B.[96] as well as with ritual killings by the following tribals: the Khonds of Orissa, the Marriahs, the Oraons, the Kalahandis and the Baigas of Central India.

The Aurignacian figures of animals carved on stones in France were cult objects with the purpose of increasing the animals in the hunt. Such a depiction continued down to the Indus Valley, where they are used as seals. This does not necessarily mean that the idea was diffused simultaneously in different areas. But it could be that people using similar artefacts could come to use similar ideas. Their use as seals was that it was taboo to break a cult object and thus access to the contents of the parcel would become automatically forbidden. The seals have come down to the present day, as mere signatures to protect the property. P. Jayakar sees the seals as "the earliest visual expression of the autochthonus peoples of India .... the visual representations of the Atharvan spells, emerging forms that have concretised primordial mysteries, illuminating a living ritual and technology that telescope five thousand years."

The Series of Seals

The amulets and the seals are made of clay, faience, metal and semi-precious stone. The script on the seals is seen as mantras or dhāriṇīs. In the Atharva Veda amulets played an important part. The Indus Valley seals are portable shrines drawing the wearer into a magical area of safety and protection, imbuing him with the powers that lay posited in the incantations written on them. On the other hand, there are opinions that the script, following universal usage, announced the name of the owner, along with his titles, honorifics, etc. The seals were for commercial purposes.[97] "The more important ideograves, judged by their frequency, evolved into traditional symbols of various kinds". Further, the steatite seals imply a system of rank and title.[98] The seal as a method of marking property is of great antiquity and its use is very wide in the Ancient East.[99]

The sun and the moon are never picturized on the seals; only chthonic forms like trees, fish, birds, animals and human figurines appear. The height of man's vision rises only to the top of a tree, no more.[100]

The next motif is the pipal or neem tree. Myths about trees can be classified into the following seven categories: microcosm of stone/tree/altar; image of the cosmos; cosmic theophany; symbol of life and fertility related to the Great Goddess; as the centre of the world (axis mundi); mystical bonds between tree and men, i.e. as repository of the spirits of the ancestor, and finally, as the symbol of the resurrection of vegetation[101]. Almost all of these find their place in Indian vegetation cults. This plant theophany is further developed in the non-Aryan Durgā as she calls herself Śākambharī[102]. The tree reveals the basic theme running through all the above classifications. It represents ritually and physically the living cosmos. The tree was adored for what it stood, never qua tree. There is no such thing as a tree cult. But in the primitive mind, the tree and the underlying symbolism are inseparable. The cosmic tree idea can be found in such diverse religions as Hebraic esoterics, Islam, Finnish and Icelandic folk tales.[103] The Indian pipal tree can be compared to the Babylonian Kiskanu.

The pipal motif was not only used in religious contexts, but also as an art form, used as a decoration on pottery. This motif was widespread not only over the whole Harappan culture area, but outside this area also.[104] This could be taken to indicate the wide political and cultural influence Harappan Civilization had. If as Shendge would like to see it as imported from Assyria, she cannot see how the pipal changed from its Assyrian terebinth.[105]

She further sees it as a symbol of a fertility god. Though the religious significance of the various domestic and wild animals excluding the bull and the cow, depicted on the seals is not clear, there could be no doubt about the religious sentiments behind the seals of half human, half animal figurines.[106]

A series of seals from Harappa and Mohenjo Daro picturize the transformation of the goddess spirit of the tree, merging with a buffalo and further transforming into a tiger made up of śamī leaves.[107] This is seen on seals from Kalibangan also.

This could also be the proto Tiger-mother *(Huligammā)* of South India or the composite animal figures of later Hinduism.[108] In another seal, a goddess (of the tree) is standing, with a worshipper kneeling in supplication in front of her. There are seven female figurines in the foreground, in long pigtails.[109] This is assimilated with Nāgārjuna asking for the power of alchemy to the deity of the As'vatha.[110] The seven figurines are seen as resembling the later Sāt Sahelias of the northern river valleys, the *sapta kannigais* (virgins) of Tamil Nadu and *Sāt asarā*, the seven apsaras of Maharashtra.[111] But they are seen to represent the goddesses of diseases like Sītala and her sisters, "a primitive Indian cult. But since the sex of these seven figurines is indeterminate they have been either designated as the proto saptarṣiṣ or proto sapta màtṛs.[112] The god in the centre is dakṣiṇataḥ-kapardāḥ and the figures are Viṣaṇin of the Ṛgveda. (VII. 18.7).[113]

Comparable to the seal mentioned earlier of the tiger and the pipal tree, is a jaguar in combination with a cosmic tree in Mayan Iconography.[114] The jaguar is a mythical lunar animal. Men connect the tree with their mythological ancestors descended from it.

The Sapta Mātṛs are said to wear peculiar conical hats with long streamers floating from it. A similar corn goddess/Mother Goddess, the Demeter of Mexico is Chicomecoatl. She is the oldest aboriginal goddess, renewing vegetation through sex, goddess of death and the underworld. She has seven snakes adorning her. Dressed in a mantle of snakes, she has jaguar's claws. She is both the goddess of death and fertility.

What is termed transformation is looked at as theriomorphism. A justification for theriomorphism was that the characteristics in an animal. For instance, the fierceness of a lion/tiger, never changed in a genre, whereas the traits in men were not consistently uniform. Therefore, one falls back on animal representations to show certain stable characteristics in a divinity[116]. It was usual to portray only part of an animal as for example, horns, as magical symbols.[117]

There is no lion on Indus Valley seals[118] and no tiger in the hymns of the Ṛgveda. In the Indus Valley, the tiger is not violent, but protective.[119]

Separated by 5000 years, the primitive people living on the banks of the Narmada, depict on an amulet worn by these people, a lady riding a tiger. Both the skirt of the lady and the tiger are formed of leaves. The arms of the lady are tendrils.

Tiger is an archaic symbol of power. In the Hindu tradition, the lady always rides a tiger till in the Brahminic tradition, it is changed to lion. Mackay[120] thinks that the seal of the transformation of the tree spirit into the tiger as a Goddess, depicts proto-Durgā with her vehicle or vāhana, the tiger. Animals 'stood for' their god-doubles and may have contained the germ of the idea of later vāhanas.[121] The association of an animal with a deity is un-Aryan or pre-Aryan; e.g. Skanda with a peacock and Durgā with a lion/ tiger.

There is a seal on which is depicted the conventionalized form of the tree and urus ox projecting from the bottom on both sides upto their necks.[122]

The urus ox is called the humpless bull that was commonplace in Mesopotamia whereas the local variety was the humped Bos Indicus. The latter is less common on the Indus seals. It is not clear whether this was just an art form borrowed from Mesopotamia and Uruk or whether these animals existed in that period and became extinct later.[123] It is shown in profile with two horns superimposed and slanting forward and it is taken for an unicorn. This in a slightly modified form is depicted in Boghazkoy,[124] that is Boghazkai, the Hittite capital in Asia Minor. A further connection is seen between these two animals (which are extinct European wild bison or ox) and the Upaniṣadic two birds sitting on a tree, one partaking of the fruits of the tree and the other looking on. The pipal tree is further termed the tree of cosmic ignorance by the same author. The animals depicted on the seals are thought to have phonetic values, similar to those used in Tantric books.[125]

The treatment of the Harappan culture's religious or cult artefacts would not be complete without touching on the proto-

Śiva seals. This fertility god and the mother goddess figures and their cult must have started from the Iranian high lands and Sumer, and travelling through Baluchistan must have arrived at Harappa.[126] This Śiva-Paśupati with horns and a sprig of flowers or leaves between them is depicted on two seals. He sits in a taut yogic posture. The sprig of vegetation makes him a vegetation and cult deity[127]. The horns of a bull represent the crescent moon and the two horns represent full moon and stand for fertility as well as the Great Goddess.[128] Again the horns on the figurines point to the archaic idea of the horns of consecration.[129] The seal figurine cannot be proto Śiva, it has been contended[130]. Though it is a fertility deity in yogic posture personifying power, it could not be Śiva because Paśupati is said to be the lord of domesticated animals and not wild ones, in the Atharva Veda. This is refuted by Ath. Veda (11.2.5).[131]

From a similar seal in Mesopotamia of the Akkadian period 2330-2130 B.C., it is inferred that the horns stand for divinity and fertility. Of the yoni stones, Srinivasan refutes them and quoting[132] Dr. Michael Jensen she states they are used in astronomical calculations. This was also seen to be Tvaṣṭṛ-Vishvakarman, a craftsman-god of the indigenous population, later adopted by the conquering race. If it had a fourth face hidden from view, it would be Brahmā. The animals surrounding the figure are seen as totems.[133]

Jayakar says, under careful scrutiny there is no sign of three faces, but that he is wearing a mask. Doris Srinivasan also feels that it is a bull's face and the dew-laps are hanging on both sides of the face.[134]

M.J. Shendge feels it is an indigenous culture laid on to an original Asura figure.[135] It is further thought that the two deer at the bottom of the seal are the prototypes of the deer at the bottom of the Sarnath Buddha statue.[136] The idea of a fertility god has come to India from the Tigris Euphrates Valley around the 4th millenium B.C.

In Lepenski Vir, that is on the banks of the Danube on the borders of Yugoslavia and Romania, a burial in yogic pose has been found. The pose has been termed *baddha* or *vajra āsana*. There are sculpted stones near the site, round stones with shallow depression in the middle and Yoni stones with deeper depressions. Some representations are shown in great detail of parturition. They are in yellow sandstone with reddish patches, and the site has been dated to 6000 B.C.[137] In a village in the north of Bulgaria, excavations have revealed goddess figurines of the period between 3600-3000 B.C. In the Daimabad excavations,[138] a clay image of the mother goddess standing on a bull has been found in Inamgaon which attests to the antiquity of the cult of joint worship of Śiva-Pārvatī in Maharashtra.

In another excavation in Gujarat,[139] at Nagwada village, a six-inch tall steatite goddess has been found. She has inlay decorations on her ears and shoulders and may belong to the first half of the third millennium B.C., making her cult in this region even earlier than the Harappan period.

Of the period 100 B.C., on the inside of a silver vase is the embossed form of a figure in Yogic Paśupati pose. He is surrounded by deer, horses, rhinoceros and wild boars. Thus, the religious tradition has continued through cultural changes from food gathering upto Iron Age. Discussing the artistry of the Harappan artefacts, S. Piggott[140] eulogises the rounded form of some of the figurines and states that they show such mature artistry and "unexpected naturalism" that there were doubts about their antiquity. A red sandstone torso of a male from the Harappan site has astonishing similarity to its Kushan successor specially in the delineation of the heavy lines of the abdomen. The bearded bust of a man from Mohenjo Daro is justly famous. Eyes, nipples and shoulder disc are made of inlay work. But since the work is hieratic, it is more rigid than the naturalistic style of Harappan art.

Mother Goddess figure in a cult grouping has been discovered in a cave painting on a hill near the village Kathatiya, about 50 kms. from Bhopal.[141] This is outside the Bhimbetka cave group. The painting is in ochre and black, depicting the Goddess as the central figure, with twenty men dancing on both sides of her in two groups. All of them are ithypallic. This would belong roughly to the period 5000-3000 B.C. (cf. Pl. 8).

There are many traces of links with the latter day Hindu ism:

(a) the figurines of the mother goddesses may be likened to the grāmadevatās of village shrines where a non-Brahmin is a priest "the outcastes who still know the ways of the Gods before the Gods".[142]

(b) Paśupati Śiva on the seal and

(c) the animals which are later carried forward in the base of the Saranath Buddha Statue.

(d) Worship of the phallus, sacred animals and the pipal tree.

Many of the features of modern Hinduism cannot be accounted for by the Aryan religion and may be from the Harappan traditions. "The old faiths die hard; it is even possible that the early historic Hindu society owed more to Harappa than it did to the Sanskrit-speaking invaders".[143] and .... " the way of life which developed in the Indus Valley during the Harappan period, which was subsequently modified and extended during the Iron Age to almost all parts of the subcontinent, and particularly flourished in the alluvial rice-growing plains, to become the source of the common elements in the culture of the different regions, must have been particularly well-suited to the environment that it could have demanded so little modification over so long a period and yet have supported so vast a population: its very success sowing through the centuries the seeds of modern dilemmas".[144]

In this survey of the Goddess cult in Baluchistan and in the Harappan culture area, we find the Mother Goddess not necessarily bound with a young god. She existed in all levels of habitation showing the popularity of her cult. She is shown along with symbolic representations of trees, stones and animals. Rituals of sacrifice pertaining to the negative side of her cult are depicted on seals. We may have no historical proof to account for the break and silence in the period between the Harappan and the Aryan cultures. But through the Vedas, she emerges in the epic to hold her own and in the Purāṇas she rises to majestic heights, and to her original glory. Her cult has as much popularity now as it had during the Indus culture as seen in the tribal representations.

She was the Great Mother, chthonic, and therefore a synthesis of bounty and death, fecundity and destruction, a bountiful mother and a vengeful demanding goddess. This idea pervades all cultures and areas of her cults and undergoes transformations according to the local cultural demands, but, remains basically unchanged.

REFERENCES

1. Frankfort H. and H.A., *Before Philosophy*, p. 245.
2. Eliade, *Myths, Dreams and Mysteries*, p. 176 fn. 1.

3. Bhattacharyya, N.N., IMG, p. 4.
4. *Myth, Religion and Mother Right,* p. 171.
5. *Myths, Dreams and Mysteries,* p. 178
6. Eliade, M, *History of Religious Ideas.*
7. Ch.I. Sn. Symbolism.
8. Eliade, *Patterns in Comparative Religions,* p. 20.
9. James, E. O, *The Cult of the Mother-Goddess,* p. 22.
10. Matriarchy, Article, *Encyclopaedia Brittanica,* Vol. 15, p. 92.
11. James, *Cult of the Mother-Goddess,* p. 26.
12. *The Times of India,* 2-3-80.
13. James, *Op. cit,* p. 46.
14. Eliade, *History of Religious Ideas,* pp. 66-67.
15. *Ibid.,* p. 139.
16. *Ibid.,* p. 130.
17. Eliade, *Patterns in Comparative Religion,* p. 258.
18. Lévi, Sylvan; Przyluski, Jean; and Bloch, Jules-*Pre-Aryan and Pre-Dravidian in India,* Intro, p. xx.
19. *Rām,* I. 66.
20. *Mbh.,* VII. 105. 3. 945.
21. Eliade, *Op. cit,* p. 261.
22. Eliade, *Myths, Dreams and Mysteries* pp. 155-56.
23. *Ibid.,* 166 ff.
24. *Ibid.,* p. 185 fn. 1.
25. Levathes, Louis E—Mysteries of the Bog, *National Geographic,* Vol. 171, no. 3, March 1987.
26. Slater, Gilbert, *The Dravidian Element in Indian Culture,* p. 75.
27. Larousse, *Encyclopaedia of Myths,* p. 7.
28. Farnell, L.R., *The Attributes of God,* p.p. 49-50, calls her Cybele.
29. James, E.O., *Myths, Rituals in Ancient Near East,* p. 102.
30. For Similar Indian Ideas also Under Ch. III section Lakṣmī.
31. *Myths, Religion and Mother right* p. 215.
32. James-*Op.cit,* p. 173.
33. A Dictionary of Classical Antiquities p. 542 quoted in S.K. Dikshit-*The Mother Goddess,* p. 68 fn. 7.
34. Larousse, *Op. cit,* p. 174.
35. *Sunday Standard,* 11-1-81.
36. Eliade, *Patterns in Comparative Religion,* p. 337, ff.
37. Ewe Negroes of W. Africa, China, Greece, Ukrain and Java have one or other of the above forms in their harvest rituals, Ibid., pp. 355-56.

38. *Myth, Religion and Mother Right*, p. 88.
39. Frankfort H. and H.A. *Before Philosophy*, p. 239.
40. James, *Myth and Ritual in the Ancient Near East*, p. 132.
41. Eliade, *Patterns in Comparative Religions*, p. 219.
42. Eliade —*History of Religious Ideas*, p. 121..
43. Dikshit, S.K., *The Mother Goddess*, p. 72.
44. *The Times of India*, 29-7-82.
45. Eliade, *Patterns in Comparative Religions*, p. 224.
46. James, *Cult of the Mother-Goddess*, p. 13.
47. Eliade, *From Primitive to Zen*, p. 16, no. 12.
48. D.M. 5.
49. Eliade, *Op. cit*, p. 55, no. 33.
50. Piggot, S., *Prehistoric India*, p. 72.
51. J.P., Seals and Statuettes of Kulli, *Zhob, Mohenjo Daro and harappa*, p. 5.
52. James, *Myth and Ritual in the Ancient Near East*, p. 107.
53. Piggott, S, *Prehistoric India* p. 105.
54. Piggott, *Ibid.*, p. 127.
55. *Ibid.*
56. Possehl, Gregory L, ed., *Ancient Cities of the Indus*—hereafter referred to as ACI, Intro, p. IX.
57. After the Definition of an Urban Culture by Childe Gordon, V, *The Urban Revolution*, pp 15-17, ACI.
58. Dales, George, F, The Decline of the Harappans, p. 307; ACI.
59. Kosambi, D.D., Origin of Brahmin Gotras, JBBRAS, Vol. 2, Part I, p. 52.
60. Fairservice, Walter. Jr., The Origin, Character and Decline of an Early Civilization, p. 66; ACI.
61. Wheeler, Sir Mortimer, Harappan Chronology and the Rig Veda, p. 289, ACI.
62. Kramer, Samuel, N, The Indus Civilization and Dilmun.: The Sumerian Paradise Land, p. 171; ACI.
63. Chakraborty, Aparajita—The Social Formation of the Indus Society, pp. 2132-33, The Economic and Political Weekly, (XVIII, 50, 1983) cf. also Bhattacharyya, N.N., History of Śākta Religion, p. 13.
64. Dales, G.F., *New Investigations at Mohenjo Daro*, p. 193; Raikes, Robert. L., The End of Ancient Cities of the Indus, p. 303; ACI.
65. Dales, G.F., The Mythical Massacre at Mohenjo Daro, p. 296; ACI
66. Wheeler—*Op. cit.*, p. 292; ACI
67. Singh, Gurdip—The Indus Valley Culture, pp. 236 ff; ACI.
68. Ramaswamy, C., Monsoon Over the Indus Valley during the harappan Period, p. 242, ACI.
69. *Ibid.*

70. Shendge, Malati J., *The Civilized Demons: The Harappans in Ṛgveda*, p. 255.
71. *Ibid.*, p. 282.
72. *Ibid.*, pp. 135/6.
73. *Ibid*, p. 278.
74. *The Times of India*, 7-1-80.
75. Eliade, *The Quest—History and Meaning in Religion*, p. 52.
76. Leshnik, Lawrence, S.—The Harappan "Port" at Lothal: Another View, p. 208; ACI.
77. Quoted by B.C. Sinha, *Hinduism and Symbol worship*, p. 128.
78. Banerjea J.N., *Pauranic and Tāntric Religion*, pp. 110-111.
79. Rao, S.R., Induscript and Language pp. 157-188, ABORI, LXI, 1980.
80. Editor's Introduction, p. 255; ACI.
81. Study of Indus Scripts Through Bilingual Parallels, p. 267; ACI.
82. Eliade, *History of Religions Ideas*, Vol. I., p. 20.
83. James, *Myth and Ritual*, p. 134 fns 100-01.
84. Intro, p. 58; ACI.
85. *Early Indus Civilization*, p. 52.
86. *Ibid.*, p. 58.
87. Slater, Gilbert, *The Dravidian Element in Indian Culture*, p. 75.
88. Kosambi, D.D., *Myth and Reality*, pp. 75-76.
89. Allchin, *Op. cit*, pp. 313-14.
90. Kosambi compares them with Mesopotamian goddess as stated earlier.
91. *The Civilized Demons* p. 195.
92. *Ibid.*, pp. 188-89.
93. *The Earthern Drum*.
94. Allchin, *Op. cit*, p. 313.
95. *The Earthern Drum*, p. 48.
96. 2, 3, 6, 7, *The Earthern Drum.*, p. 48, fn 5.
97. Mahadevan, I, *Op.cit*, p. 262; ACI.
98. Possehl, Editor's Intro., p. 255.
99. Piggott, *Op. cit.*, p. 184.
100. Jayakar, *Op. cit.*, p. 45.
101. Eliade, M, *Patterns in Comparative Religion*, p. 266 ff.
102. D.M. 11. 48-49.
103. Eliade, *Op. cit.*, p. 274.
104. Shendge, *Op. cit.*, p. 190.
105. *Ibid.*, p. 28.
106. Allchin, *Op. cit.*, p. 313.
107. Jayakar, *Op. cit.*, p. 53.

108. Allchin, *Op. cit.*, p. 55.
109. Mackay, *Op. cit.*, plate XVII.
110. Jayakar P., *Op. cit.*, p. 133, fn 20.
111. *Ibid.*, p. 56.
112. Allchin, *Op. cit.*, p. 313.
113. Kosambi, D.D., *Op. cit.*, p. 51.
114. Eliade, *Patterns in Comparative Religion*, p. 164.
115. Neumann, Erich, *The Great Mother*, p. 182.
116. Farnell L.R., *Attributes of God*. p. 23.
117. James, E.O, *Myth and Ritual*, p. 25.
118. Possehl, p. 230; ACI. Mackay, *Op. cit.*, p. 68.
119. Jayakar, *Op. cit.*, p. 58.
120. *Op. cit.*, p. 60.
121. Gonda, J. *Change and Continuity in Indian Religion*, p. 87 fn 99 quoting S. Kramrisch and A.K. Saraswati; cf Ch V, Sn The Vāhana of the Goddess: Lion/Tiger.
122. Mackay, *Op. cit.*, p. 59.
123. Allchin, *Op. cit.*, pp. 306-07.
124. Shendge, M.J., *Ibid.*, p. 191.
125. Mackay, *Op. cit.*, p. 159.
126. James, *Myth and Ritual*, p. 135; also Allchin, *Op. cit.*, p. 311, Supporting Marshall.
127. Mackay, *Op. cit.*, p. 58.
128. Eliade —*Patterns in Comparative Religion*, p. 164.
129. James, *Cult of the Mother* - Goddess, p. 33.
130. Srinivasan, Doris—Unhinging Śiva From the Indus Civilization, p. 77, JRAS, no. 1, 1984.
131. Jayakar, *Op. cit.*, p. 50, and fn 9.
132. *Ibid.*, p. 87, fn 55.
133. Kosambi, Origin of Brahmin Gotras, JBBRAS, Vol. 26, Part I, p. 51.
134. *Ibid.*
135. *Ibid.*, pp. 194-95.
136. Piggott, *Op. cit.*, p. 202.
137. Sankalia, H.D., Lepenski Vir, *Illustrated Weekly of India*, 6-6-1977.
138. *The Times of India*, 28-9-86.
139. *The Times of India*, 31-3-88.
140. *Op. cit* p. 185-86.
141. Personal notes from Shankar. A. Aiyar.
142. Piggott, *Op. cit.*, p. 201.
143. Piggott, *Ibid.*, p. 183.
144. Allchin, *Op. cit.*, p. 332.

CHAPTER - III
VEDIC PERIOD

The Vedic period is taken up next in this study. It is a well-known fact that the Indus Valley Culture had goddess worship, which is not found to any great degree in the early Aryan religion. That there are no goddesses of great stature in the early Vedas itself has been denied by Vertain scholars.[1] If the former view is accepted, then, the influence of the conquered on the conquerors, changing the latter's religion is a necessary corollary. If the latter view, that the goddess cult was existing sufficiently in the early religious texts to grow into a strong cult later, is accepted, then the reason would rest on the only factor that it was the outcome of the change in the Aryans' way of living over a period of time. Both these viewpoints are considered here and it would be seen that both these were contributory factors to the ensuing emergence of the goddess cult. The changing patterns of the Aryans' living, and social and economic structures necessitated accepting some of the fertility cults from the earlier civilization.

J. Gonda[2] prefers to believe that the germ of later Hinduism was contained in the early Aryan religion itself, rather than allocate much credit to the pre-Aryan influence for the later religious beliefs and practices. There is a huge gulf between the assertion that the Vedas are the supreme authority in all religious matters and in the religious practices which are all post-Vedic. If there is harping on the Vedic origin of any religious belief, it just reflects the inner longing for unchanged continuity in the beliefs.[3]

The syncretisation of the Indus Valley religion and that of the Aryans seems a certain fact. Otherwise, it would be difficult to explain certain features like phallic worship, cult of the goddess, asceticism, yoga, etc., in the Aryan religion. In the societal hierarchy also the Indus culture seems to have influenced the Aryans. Otherwise, the rise to power of the Brahmins would be anamolous to the Aryan culture. We need not say that the Indus Valley Culture (IVC hereafter) was exterminated totally or that it was directly from the IV that the religious ideas were assimilated by the Aryans. The IVC could have retired into regression and the ideas preserved in the peripheral, 'popular' settlements which resurged again after the invaders settled further inwards. A similar situation arose in Crete and Continental Greece, with autochthonous Mediterranean substratum and the Indo-European invaders. The beliefs of the original inhabitants are decipherable only through archaeological remains, whereas the 'invaders' ideas can be seen in their literatures of Homer and Hesiod[4]. But the point to remember is, unlike the Vedas, these literature showed the first stages of integration of the conquered.

One opinion is that Mother-right existed in the Ṛgvedic period, when a group of mother was accepted for one child. Uṣas and Agni had sersveral mothers. Skanda-Kārtikeya had seven mothers, who were initially sent to kill him, but who eventually adopted him.[5] The above is interpreted that "a pre-existing matriarchal form of society shows itself through the myth of several mothers jointly giving birth to a god with an equal number of heads or faces. These mothers as representatives of local tribes or gentes, are later replaced by eponymous Brahmin ancestors, the ṛṣis."[6]

The Vedic goddesses had been divided into three classes :[7]

(1) Natural goddesses like Uṣas, Sarasvatī etc.
(2) Abstract ideas: *Puraṁdhī*-plenty, *Iḷā*-nourishment, *Dhiṣaṇā*-Abundance.
(3) Feminine dimunitive added to the god's names-Varuṇānī, Indrāṇī' etc.

Aditi, Sinīvālī, Kuhū, etc., do not come under this classification. These goddesses become powerful soon.

The ṚV.X.63.2. divides the goddesses into three groups, derived from the Great Goddesses: (1) Aditi, (2) Pṛthivī, (3) The waters. There was also a tendency to group similar goddesses and have a prominent goddess as their mother; e.g: Sarasvatī was the mother of floods,[8] Araṇyānī was the mother of forests,[9] Uṣas was a group of light rays.[10]

According to Yāska one classification of the goddesses is :

(1) according to their single or group *(gaṇa)* nature

(2) according to their status i.e., higher if whole Sūktas are addressed to them and lower if only a verse or so in a Sūkta is addressed to them.

(3) according to the idea underlying their personalities, i.e., abstract ideas, natural phenomena, feminine suffixes to gods' names, artificial objects or implements.

P. K. Agrawala[11] has made an exhaustive list dividing them again into three classes.

(1) *Terrestrial*—Which include Nature Goddesses like Pṛthivī, Rātrī, Sarasvatī; Collective or host goddesses; amongst feminine dimunitives added to the gods' names only Agnāyī; personification of abstract ideas; tutelary like Sītā—the furrow, Urvarā—the arable field, etc.; plural of natural phenomena like—Āpah, Nadyaḥ etc;

(2) *Atmospherical*—Lunar goddesses like Sinīvālī, Kuhū, Rākā, Guṅgū, etc;

Abstract personifications: Aditi, Diti, Vāk, Dānu, Ūrvaśī; Tutelary goddesses: Patyā-Svasti, Pṛṣṇī cow (speckled), Saramā (the bitch of Indra and the gods);

Female gender of gods: Indrāṇī, Rodasī (of Rudra), Yamī.

(3) *Celestial*—Eminent nature goddesses: Uṣas, Sūryā, Bṛhaddivā (broad sky);

Abstact ideas personified—Virāj (ruling Principle), Savasī (Might), Saraṇyu (swift), Vṛṣākapāyī (the female Ape), Rāj or Rāt (radiant);

Feminine genders of the gods: Devapatnīh or Gnāḥ-wives of all gods,

Viśve Devīḥ-wives of all gods.

Another opinion[12], was the grammatical gender of the language was one of the reasons for the emergence of feminine divinities, like Vāc and Purandhī. There was also some notion about dividing nature into sexes as for example, river was feminine and ocean was masculine.

The goddesses are said to possess no concrete form, since mostly they were wives of the gods. There is a diversity in their number also. For instance, taking *Indra* as a sample, he has streams as his wives. Sītā and Urvarā are mentioned as his wives, elsewhere. In the VS.28.8.Iḍā, Sarasvatī and Bhāratī are mentioned as his wives.

Another opinion is[13] that goddesses like Durgā, Kālī, Ambikā,

Umā are mentioned very few times. These are tribal goddesses, who were finally absorbed into the Aryan religion as wives of Śiva.

Ambivalence in the Goddess

The goddess has always been invested with both positive and negative characteristics. Sometimes, as in the early Vedic period, different goddesses portray different characteristics, and we had Aditi, a wholly benevolent deity and Nirṛti, who is invested with all the negative characteristics. When a Great Goddess appears who subsumes into herself all the minor goddeses, she necessarily takes upon herself both the beneficent and maleficent qualities. Later, the Bhakti cult and the avatāra concept gave a justification for the ambivalence of the divinities.

The fascination towards deifying the negative aspects in life like death, decay and destruction was natural in the primitive. As much as he was awed by the departure of near ones and other living creatures like animals and plant life, he was reassured by new birth and fresh reappearance of plant life, which he surmised was due to the revivification of the dead by a benevolent but harsh deity.

. The Earth as mother goddess is most associated with this ambivalence. But the Aryans would not connect anything negative to their bountiful mother earth. Therefore, they made Earth a benevolent goddess and the goddess Nirṛti was given those negative aspect, when she was connected with Earth. The survival of the phenomenal world is assured only by the equal mixture of negative and positive characteristics, life and death. For the youthful rejuvenation of life, nature's destructive power is as important as her vivifying creative power. "Indeed the positive power cannot for one moment exist without the negative power. Death then is not the opposite, but the helper of life .... and without it life would give way to nothing".[14]

Light and darkness had impressed themselves on man's mind so deeply that gods and goddesses have been divided into two groups associated with these phenomena. Those connected with light are fair, beautiful and benevolent towards their devotees. The dark ones have all the negative characteristics and they look fierce and are dark-complexioned.[15] This ambivalence can also be expressed as life which is time. This is so in all traditions—*a-mrta, and a-mor, mor-tis.*[16]

In most ancient religions, the primordial mother was ambivalent but she was markedly so in Egypt and India. In Egypt, she was Hathor, Goddess of the eastern sky, and also the cow of the western mountain, the goddess of the dead.[17] The terrifying demoniac aspect of the Goddess is seen at Byblos near Palestine in the feminine statues found there belonging to 4500 B.C.[18] In the early, that is the primitive stage of the cult of the goddess, there is a melding of the positive and negative characteristics, in the same goddess. In the Cretan island where the goddess cult can be traced to the middle of the fourth millenium B.C., she emerges as a well defined figure both as a goddess of fertility as well as the chthonian guardian of the dead. But when the cult spread to the mainland Greece, her attributes were divided between various goddesses.[19] In Crete she was the goddess par excellence, Britomartis or Diktyanna.

Aditi

On the basis that the Phrygians, Hittites and even the Greeks knew goddess worship, it is felt that it is untenable to say that there was no goddess worship in the Vedic period. Aditi occurs in the ṚgVeda about 140 times and in about one hundred passages she is mentioned "incidentally" either alone or with other gods[20]. She is putrakāma, even if she is unbounded and she tikes repeated conception[21]. Her connection with a wide range of ancient religions like Egyptian, Babylonian, Phoenician, South Arabian, etc. is seen. The *Nighaṇṭu* gives Nanā as a synonym for Aditi. This is seen as connected with the Sumerian Nanā, Inannā, Ninā, etc. Nanā is a word for both mother and daughter according to Yāska[22] and Sāyaṇa.[23] This is seen again as a similarity to mother-goddess cults in Uruk and other countries.

The ṚgVedic verse (I.89.10) is:

Aditirdyauraditirantarikṣamaditirmātā sa pitā sa putraḥ/
Viśvedevā Aditiḥ pañcajanā Aditirjātamaditirjanitvam//

Sāyaṇa says:

Evam sakalajagadātmanāditiḥ stūyate/

Searching for origins, as similar to the Iranian goddess Ardvī, both these could be traced to the Erech goddess Nanaia (which was the later Vedic Nanā). The above verse shows her omnipotence. Scholars are divided in their opinion about the derivation of the name and this shows her obscure origins. She is a mother-goddess par excellence. J. Przyluski[24] says: "The Great Goddess is then at the same time the mother of gods and of men; through her the cattle increase and the plants grow. All that has life manifests her power. A figure so majestic soon became the centre of a cult in which all the peoples participated: pastoral and agricultural, nomadic and stationary, barbarian and civilized. Sages' devoted abstraction and the simplest minds could meet in a common sentiment of veneration for a goddess who is the incarnation of our profoundest instincts and symbolises perfectly the unity and immensity of the cosmos."

As the culture changed, the Great Goddess was made into a war-like divinity. Life and death are cyclical and necessary for progress. War was worse than disease, and is the worst of catastrophes, and therefore this was also attributed to the Great Goddess. There was another opinion,[25] that Aditi is not a Great Mother in the true sense, because she has derived her name from the term *Aditeḥ putrāḥ*, "sons of freedom", much as Indra's mother was Śavasī, because he was "son of might", śavasaḥ, or, his wife was Śacī, because he was lord of might, Śacīpati. In the above verse, she is only a reflection of the qualities implicit in a Great Goddess, no more. But V.S. Agrawala,[26] states firmly, quoting many ṚgVedic references[27] to support his statement that this verse is really the true character of a Great Goddess and a Mother Goddess. One cannot ignore the mother aspect in Aditi's make-up and evalute her, because she is as much a Mother as a Goddess.

Aditi and Pṛthivī are seen as powerful goddesses and the contention that the ṚgVeda shows a bias towards gods is refuted[28]. Aditi is Mahī Mātā, the Great Goddess, Guardian of Ṛta[29]. Her origin is shrouded in pre-Vedic religion. Her name is derived to be the negative prefix 'a' with 'diti' and is said to mean 'free' from bondage. The Sanskrit etymology would give the derivation of the name from the root do 'to divide', the negation of which is a fitting appellation for the benevolent Magna Mater.[30]

The name *Aditi* is taken to prove that the name of a god far from being a mere appellation was an essential part of the personality of the God. This can be shown by the explanation in V. S. 9.5 (18.13) where *adīnām* is 'not depressed, cheerful, nobleminded', etc. These may not be accurate as meanings, but explain the idea of the character of Aditi. No doubt the thought was in the poet's mind when he added the appellation Great Mother to the name of Aditi.[31]

Her supremacy is unmatched in the ṚgVeda and this is taken to support the statement that the goddess cult was quite popular in this period. She is the immortal genetrix of all the gods and living forms. She is the mother and creator of all things past, present and future, from whom all things spring and return. She has no negative characteristics in her, which is borne out by ṚV VII. 66.6, though here again she is not supreme by herself, but is addressed along with Mitra and Varuṇa. She is 'what has been' and 'what will be'.[32] Her greatness is because she was capable of expanding and assimilating various characteristics that could be attributed to her. But she obviously was not eclectic enough to survive after this period. She is a great mother standing for universal motherhood and ṛta. In her cosmic character she contains in herself the male counterpart of spouse/son.[33] She stands for the unity of the universe, and represents the whole of it. Her true significance stands in her motherhood—the plenum—void which precedes and is the substratum later of the created, fragmented and limited phenomenal world. Being a goddess, she is again the "intelligence" of the living world, and is the "ground of being". Therefore is she father, mother, and son, everything that has been, and will be. This could be construed as the anticipation of the later brahman-ātman doctrine.[34] She is bi-sexual like the Moon. She is Dyaus and Pṛthvī; she is Mātā and Pitā. She stands for the unity of Sky and Earth.[35] She may be the prototype of the Ardhanārī form of Śiva.[36]

There is also another opinion that Aditi is a vague and amorphous goddess. She must be a very ancient goddess whose nature and function is forgotten even in the ṚgVedic period.[38] Aditi was needed only to mother the Ādityas and she took their characteristics of light and might. The Aryans also patterned their lives according to these divinities. She is said to be a virgin goddess, that is, after Indra's birth. Her virgin godhead could be seen as the Kanyā Kumārī aspect of the later Goddess. The myth states[39] that, after the hero's birth, she should die or get her spouse killed, so that no more conception can take place in that womb. There are other epithets which also point to her virgin status like 'yuvati', 'anarvā', 'apravitā', etc.[40] Śavasī is Indra's mother, identified with Aditi by Sāyaṇa.[41] Ambā, Ambikā and Ambitamā are all names or adjectives as applied to the Mother Goddess. In her macro-cosmic stature, various personifications like Āpaḥ are assimilated with the Goddess. Water personified should not be confused with personification of rivers. They are regarded as the primal cause of creation. Apsarases who live in the waters (literally move in water) are connected with fertility and in later literature are connected with sexual symbolism.

She is also closely connected with concrete aspects of nature like earth, cow, dawn or dyaus-sky. She is the bestower of happiness,[42] well-being,[43] gifts,[44] and longevity.[45] She protects her protegees,[46] answers their prayers,[47] pardons sinners[48] and delivers supplicants from distress.[49] She is the guardian of the inviolable Ṛta[50] and is opposite of Nirṛti. In the post-Vedic period, Aditi becomes the wife of Viṣṇu in the *Vāj. Sam.*,[51] and still later in the Purāṇas she becomes the wife of Kaśyapa. A terra-cotta figurine surmised to be of this goddess has been discovered in the excavation at Hulas village 140 kms. north of Delhi, in the Saharanpur district. She belongs to the first millennium B.C.[52]

Late entrants into the Vedic religion like Śrī-Lakṣmī and Ambikā grow in stature and occupy an important position in the later religion. Obviously, Aditi was not pliable enough to absorb local cult goddesses into her cult. She almost disappears in the Purāṇas or, along with a few other goddesses, gets absorbed into some cult.

Nirṛtti

Nirṛti is the goddess of all negative qualities. She is a personification of only abstract ideas, but these define her character well. She is also assimilated to the earth goddess, in the characteristic of decay, which results in death. This quality can be understood when we remember that a way of treating the dead was internment, and decay and death were mutually connected.

She is responsible for abortion[53]. She has noose and snares like Varuṇa[54]. The *Taitt. Āra.* (1.2.3.) mentions "*viśirṣṇi ghṛdhraśirṣṇim ca apeto nirṛtīm hatha, paribādham sveta kukṣam nijaṅgaṁ.*" This is a headless goddess. She has her prototype in the Inamgaon excavations of the chalcolithic period.[55] For a modern reference, the Warlis of Thana district, worship such a headless goddess called Palghat, associated with fertility and prosperity.[56]

A similar idea of connecting the goddess with death is seen in the funerary scene depicted on a sacrophagus from Hagia Trioda. A bull is sacrificed and its flowing blood is seen sanctifying the earth under which burial had taken place.[57]

Sukumari Bhattacharji[58] sees resemblance between Nirṛti and the Grecian Ker, goddess of death and the Furies in the Eumenides, but finds no connection between them. But, there is a resemblance with the moon, and also witchcraft, and her resemblance to the Roman Lares, god of ancestral spirits is seen, as also her resemblance to the goddess of Germany and Scandinavia Nerthus. The name is also similar to the Sanskrit Nṛtu. Nerthus was connected with the Earth in the capacity of fertility and propagation, and the yearly propitiation held in her honour similar to Durgā pūjā.[59]

Nirṛti is obviously of tribal origin[60] and her characteristics of death, destruction and disease have been taken over by the Purāṇic Kālī, Karālī, Cāmuṇḍā, Chinnamastā, Manasā and such other minor and regional sectarian goddesses[61]. The new Hinduism under the Guptas had to syncretise all the regional goddesses in order to be acceptable to the masses. South Indian images of Māriyammā or Māriyattāḷ are also similar to Nirṛti.

She is of the class of sinister and sinful deities and her colour is black. The animal offered to her is black cow with horns.[62] In the bricks built for the fire altar, black bricks are laid for her. She is the guardian angel of thieves and robbers. Colour plays a very important part in the Indian mythology and the association with night, manes and rain is well brought out in Nirṛti's black. The colour stands for strife.[63] Ass is an offering to Nirṛti.[64] Since there is a connection between asses and Yama, Nirṛti's connection to Yama is seen in the Rāmāyaṇa.[65] In the Mahābhārata,[66] Nairṛta grass is set and the Pāṇḍavas sing praises of yama and Rudra. Thus the connection between the goddess and the gods is seen in the epics. Yamī, the twin-sister of Yama, is also connected with the earth and this is seen as a link between Nirṛti and Yamī.[67] Because Nirṛti and Kuvera have naravāhanas and Śiva was appeased by human sacrifices, again a tenuous resemblance is seen between these deities.[68]

She is Jyeṣthā in the *Baud. GS.*[69] She appeared before Lakṣmī in the churning of the ocean, therefore she is older than Lakṣmī, the Aryan goddess.Her icon also shows her holding a lotus in her hand. So she might have been the goddess of prosperity of the Dravidian or non-Aryan population. In the Lakṣmī pūjā (in Bengal) the pūjā begins only after Alakṣmī is driven out of the sacred precincts, symbolically.[70] Lions are said to be attached to her chariot and tigers follow her. She is married to Adharma, and her children are Mṛtyu, Bhaya, and Mahābhaya; (Terror), in the Mbh. 1.60.52-53.[71]

Pṛthivī

The depth and intimacy of man's relationship with Nature gave rise to the conception of Earth as Mother and a Goddess. A large number of the words for earth have meanings of space or firmness: e.g. pṛthivī- "wide." Etymologically, Sanskrit "go-earth, place" could be assimilated to Zend 'gava', Gothic 'gawi' or 'ganja,—a province, and Greek 'Gaia' or 'Ge'. All these mean earth in the most physical and immediate form. The Grecian Ge was probably pre-Hellenic and she was not given any importance by Homer.[72]

Earth was perceived as an immediate presence bringing forth, nourishing and receiving back, in a constant cycle, and this immediacy in perception of her size, solidarity and abundance gave the primitive man the idea of the earth personified as a goddess.

A Homeric hymn addressed to earth says, " .... Happy the man favoured with thy goodwill! For him the soil of life is rich with harvest; in his fields the flocks thrive, and his house is full of wealth".[73]

The Earth is celebrated along with the Sky God in a heirogamy. She is said to support the sky stretched tautly across herunlike the Egyptian Nut who is the sky spreading over her husband. A similar heirogamy or sacred pairing of the Earth and Sky was existing in Mesopotamia. Earth goddess was praised with heaven Anu, or with Water—Enki, or with Enlil the Storm-god.[74] This idea of cosmic heirogamy is not universal as seen from the religions of Australians, Arctic peoples and the hunting and herding tribes of Northern and Central Asia.[75]

The idea of earth as mother and protectress of children is

widely diffused. Such areas are: China, New Zealand, North India, Amerindian areas, Paraguay, Greece, Rome and in the middle ages Germany, Japan, Caucasus, Hungary, Romania and Scandinavia.[76]

Burial of the dead in the embryonic fashion and the Laws of Manu forbidding children under two to be cremated, but to be buried, are instances which bring out the idea of returning life to the mother, so she may infuse it with fresh life and put it forth again. This simple idea of man's life put back into the earth got a further philosophic explanation in the later Brāhmaṇas, that his vital energy is re-integrated with the elements of the cosmos. "... Thy breath goes away to the winds, thy ear to the points of the compass, thy bones return to the Earth."[77]

As culture evolved, man became pastoral and moved further in to the agricultural stage; and the idea of Earth as a mother changed and Earth became a goddess[78]. In Greece, Gaia was replaced by Demeter.

The ambivalence of Earth, sustaining and nourishing all types of life forms as well as taking them back and enveloping them in her soft bosom to put them forth again, could not be contained in a single goddess. Just as water as the life-giving force is variegated in her many forms of sea, river, rain, etc., so also many goddesses had to be ideated to represent the multi-forms of the Earth goddess. The ambivalence of the Earth goddess as Gaia or Ge is seen in one Homeric hymn addressed to the Earth.

... "To Thee it belongs to give life to mortals and to take it back from them ....".[79] Similarly Aeschylus[80] singing her glory says that she "Gives birth to all beings, feeds them and receives back from them the fertile seed". The negative aspect of Mother Earth is not a termination of life, when the dead are put back into the bosom of the earth. But like germinating seed, it is just a resurgence back into life.[81]

When the Earth was propitiated as a goddess, agricultural rites were performed for different stages in cultivation, though the rites differed according to the places and stages of culture. Bergaigne in his *La Religion Vedique* has said that the Vedic goddesses were merely to provide an antithesis or complement to the gods. Even if this be so, in the Dyaus-Pṛthivī couple, Pṛthivī gains more prominence than Dyaus who soon becomes a deus otiosus.

In the ṚgVeda[83], there is a short single verse dedicated to Pṛthivī. The goddess Earth is here differentiated from the material earth.

"O, Pṛthivī, you bear mountain-piercing tool (or thunder bolt). Rich in torrents, O, Mighty, One, you quicken the earth (*bhūmi*)". She is not only the mother of the plant kingdom, but also of human beings. This is attributed to her along with *Dyaus* in the *ṚgVeda;* but in the *AV.* she alone is given this attribute. She is also requested to be kind to the human beings, she receives back into her bosom and preserves them against decay and *Nirṛti.* There is another passage also where she is invoked to keep away the three *Nirṛtis.*[85] She is pictured as a fertile goddess, giving birth to her ten daughters, the directions,[86] or these daughters are mentioned as ten sisters.[87] Aramati, the genius of piety[88] and devotion similar to the Avestan Spenta-Armaiti is assimilated to the Earth goddess.[89] She is also the Great Cow[90]. The two secondary goddesses connected with the Earth are *Urvarā,* the plough land, and Sītā, the furrow.

But, Pṛthivī is considered as insipid goddess.[91] She is identified with Aditi many times. She was the prototype of the Sāṁkhya Prakṛtī and was later assimilated to Sītā.

Before taking up Pṛthivī in her aspect of agricultural fertility, the following few verses from the *AV.* may sum up the discussion so far:

"Truth, greatness, universal order *(ṛta),* strength, consecration, fervour *(tapas),* spiritual exaltation *(brahman),* the sacrifice, support the earth. May this earth, the mistress of that which was and shall be, prepare for us a broad domain! ...

"The earth whose are the four regions of space upon which food and the tribes of men have arisen, which supports the manifold breathing, moving things, shall afford us cattle and other possession also!

"The serpent, the scorpion with thirsty fangs, that hibernating torpidly lies upon thee; ....

"The earth upon whom day and night jointly, black and bright, have been decreed, the broad earth covered and enveloped in rain, shall kindly place us into every pleasant abode!"[92]

The physico-psychical relationship between man and earth is seen in the following statements:

".... the mystical experience of autochthony, the profound

feeling of having come from the soil, of having been born of the earth in the same way that the Earth, with her inexhaustible fecundity, gives birth to the rocks, rivers, trees and flowers. It is in this sense that autochthony should be understood: ...."

"This kind of cosmo-biological experience rooted man in a mystical solidarity with *the place* which was intense enough to have survived till now in folk-lore and popular traditions".[93]

The discovery of agriculture may have changed the course of history by changing the structure of society. But man learnt firsthand from the seed, the rhythm of life, the sexuality of woman and the hope of rebirth. This harmony, by identification with the cosmos was far more important than the changes in social history.[94] The Earth Goddess ceased to be considered primarily as the goddess of birth alone. She was many-sided personality—the virgin, the bride, and the mother as in Sumero-Akkadian religion. She was *Ninsikil-la* "the pure lady", *Nin-lu ama kalamma,* "the lady who gives birth", "the mother of the land". Before accepting *Enki,* and after becoming his spouse, she is *Dam-gal-nunna* "the great spouse of the prince". She is the goddess of vegetation as manifested on the lush slopes of the mountain and known as "*Nin-hur-sag-ga*".[95] These would bring to our mind the parallels in Kanyā Kumārī, Pārvatī, Durgā as Vindhyavāsinī or Umā Haimavatī. The king with the queen or the priestess celebrated the divine coupling on earth, simulating the heirogamy. This rite was seen to re-establish fecundity on earth, after the winter blight.[96]

Sexual and sacrificial rites performed on fields are rituals enacted to rejuvenate the Earth and make her fertile.[97]

The mother giving birth and the earth putting forth fruits are thought similar. It would be just a step further to draw the conclusion that the mother's fertility would affect the fertility of the earth, through sympathetic magic. (Tantric rites associated with agriculture are thus seen to be earlier than the Tantric texts.) Menstruation was thought to be a factor to assist fertility. Therefore, Earth is seen as mother in many parts of the Deccan and Punjab, Earth-Mother is given rest, during her menstruating period before she starts her productive work. Saturnalian sex orgies are performed to increase earth's fertility. Similarly, women in the nude expose themselves to the earth, are thought to increase the fertility of the earth. Also, women in the nude expose themselves to the sky, during times of drought to help it rain. The sacrality and fertility symbolised by blood is assimilated to vermillion and Hindu women wear a *tilak,* to symbolize fertility. The custom of women denuding themselves as a ritual act prevails in Peru, Chile, New Mexico, Nicaragua, and other Latin American countries. Briffault,[98] says that, "the belief that sexual act assists the promotion of abundant harvest of the earth's fruits and is indeed indispensable to secure it is universal in the lower phase of culture". Manu says,[99] *"Iyam bhūmirhi bhūtānām śāsvatiryonirucyate"* and[100] *"kṣetrabhūtā smṛtā nārī bījabhūtaḥ smṛtaḥ pumān".*

The Masais will not plough the earth because she is their mother and they cannot hurt her body.[101] The Baigas of Central India would sow only in forest regions which had been burnt away by themselves. They would not clear the earth since it would hurt her. The Votyakes and Chermisses also treated Mother Earth with concern taking care not to hurt her.[102] The Amerindian tribe of Umatilla also refused to till the soil because it would hurt the mother and it would be a sin.[103]

In the harvest rites, all over the world, there is an ambivalent attitude with regard to the "harvest-sprit" Either he/she is treated with respect as the corn-spirit or, hated for bringing death to the corn. This is particularly prevalent in Germany, Scotland, amongst the Slavs, the Norwegians, etc.[104]

A divinity of corn and growth became also the divinity of the dead. The diffusion of the mixed cults of fertility and the dead is so wide that there is a symbiosis and synthesis of these in the resulting religion, which has a fuller understanding of man's existence in the universe.[105]

Ritual orgies are performed in the fields for increasing fertility. Such rituals took place in China, Greece, Central American Pipile tribe, Java, Ukraine, etc.[106] Holi is a watered down version and is a simulation of the heiros gamos. It is similar to the Roman Lypercalia, when young men touched females to make them fertile, and, Floralia, when young men ran naked down the streets. These rites also imitate chaos, by ignoring all social norms and therefore make return to creation possible.

Durgā the Great Goddess, was a syncretic divinity of local goddesses and cults, particularly associated with vegetation cults. She is also connected with the chief divinity of the spirits of the dead. The productivity of the Earth is personified as the corn goddess. Durgā, the Purāṇic Great Goddess announced that she will support the earth with life-sustaining vegetables grown out of her own body as Śākambharī.[107] She is worshipped with nava patrikās during Durgā Pūjā.

Kore is seen as the Western counterpart of Kumārī; and Persepone in her many connections with Father, and also, in the aspect of a nature goddess, resembles the Mother-Goddess Durgā of the Purāṇas.[108]

Pṛthivī was later made the wife of Viṣṇu in the Purāṇas and gave up her earthly qualities to Sītā.[109]

UṢAS

The hymns on *Uṣas* are beautiful for their poetic fancy. But *Uṣas* is not a goddess of great stature. She is more etherial than a concrete or a realistic goddess. She is dawn personified and as such may be termed the "creative renewal".[110] Amongst the Vedic goddesses, she is the only one who has no husband. The power of a goddess gets uncontrolled if she is not subdued by marriage and this is the reason why she is repeatedly raped by Indra, and this gets mentioned in the ṚgVeda, and afterwards she is abandoned.

Uṣas is often compared to warriors, and she may be taken as a war-goddess. There is a touch of cruelty in her. She is a Virgin goddess and also infuses fresh life into everything, including vegetation. In all this she may be seen as the prototype of Durgā. She is pictured as dark in the beginning and turns slowly effulgent. This is again seen as Kauśikī emerging from Pārvatī who is left dark and is Kālikā.[111] Though her epithets make her out to be an all-powerful goddess, her stature is less than that of Aditi.

Ambikā

Tryambaka is an epithet of Rudra in the early ṚgVeda.[112] In the Yajur Veda, the word is used to denote the three sisters/ mothers of Rudra. The VS III. 57 requests Rudra to enjoy his allotted portion along with his sister Ambikā-"Eṣa te Rudra bhāgaḥ saha svasrā Ambikayā." The same sentiment is expressed in the Taitt. Br.[113] except that Devī is compared to autumn, "Ityāha śaradvai asya Ambikā svasā tayā vai eṣa hinasti". In the Taitt. Saṁ. (1.8.6.2) in a separate hymn to Ambā, she is told that *Rudra* has been appeased with offering and being pleased he may give prosperity. Ambā or Ambikā is propitiated separately so that she, along with Rudra will bestow prosperity.

avāmba rudramadimahyava devaṁ tryambakaṁ/
yathā naḥ śreyasaḥ karadyathā no vasyasaḥ karadyathā naḥ
paśumataḥ karadyathā no vyavasāyayāt//.

Rudra's connection with the mother-goddess cult is seen in the epithet Tryambaka and the goddess associated with tryambaka is Ambā or Ambikā, which is seen in the Tait. Saṁ. quotation cited above.

In the *VS.*[114] Ambikā and Tryambaka are invoked to give happiness and good husbands for the maidens. Obviously Ambikā and Tryambaka are connected in the fertility cult. It could be that in this śūkta, bhaga signifies yoni. In the Mait. Saṁ.[115] The Autumn is Rudra's yoni, his sister Ambikā.

The main rite of offering sacrificial cakes to the goddess is done at the cross-roads, in the Tryambaka Homa.[116] This shows the popular form of the rites of the mother-goddess cult, which formed an important part of the Tryambaka sacrifice.

Hecate was a mother-goddess of fertility and ghosts; fish and snakes were sacred to her.[117] These associations of the goddess suggest a strong identity with the Indian Mother-Goddess. *Hecate* was also the goddess for increasing cattle, and the goddess of marriage. In the Orphic cult, she occupied the centre of the world as Aphrodite and Gaia. To her, the triple roads or forked road or crossways were dedicated. And sacrifices were performed in her honour. The beasts were usually dogs. She was the goddess of the night and of phantoms. She sends the fear phantom, the Empusa.[118] The similarity with Durgā suggests itself naturally from the above account.

The Mait. Sṁ.[119] *"ambī vai bhaganāmnī, tasmāt tryambakāḥ"*, the goddess' name is suggested as *Bhaga.* In the *Kāṭhaka Saṁhita.* 36.14 this name is changed to Bhagā. This name could be the prototype of Bhagavatī of the Purāṇas. In the apocryphal hymn of the ṚgVeda, the *Rātrī-Durgā Sūkta,* we have Bhagavatī as an epithet of the goddess.

As seen above, *Ambā* or *Ambikā* is the sister or yoni, i.e., mother of *Tryambaka;* besides these, *Ambikā* is also used as a name for the goddess. Though there are other derivatives (ambi, ambī, ambālī, ambālikā, ambayāvī) only these three seem definitely to denote the mother-goddess, and could denote the three aspects of the goddess. It may be surmised that the followers of Tryambaka and Ambikā tried to syncretise their cults in the Yajur Veda Tryambaka rites and its Brāhmaṇa commentaries.

Śrī Lakṣmī

Śrī and Lakṣmī were disparate goddesses in the Veda, but tend to merge into a composite goddess in the Upaniṣadic period. These two concepts are taken up separately.

The word *śrī* is a common noun in the ṚgVeda. Various entities, or abstract quantities, like benefit, advantages, riches, prosperity, well-being, were denoted by the word śrī. With the Maruts the word śrī denotes splendour, beauty and glory. Personifield śrī appears for the first time in the Yajur Veda. Along with Lakṣmī she is the consort of the Cosmic Pūruṣa in the sun.[120] Economic element of wealth and prosperity is meant by the word śrī, not just possession of auspiciousness or beauty.[121] Possession of śrī gives social eminence. The word Śrī came to mean ruling power and majesty. The cushion on the throne was designated śrī. The king is said to be in possession of the embodied power when he sits on it. Vediç mantras are other parts of the throne,[122] Prajāpati, Bṛahaspti, Soma and Varuṇa are its four legs. Prestige is attained by the primitive or early man by the possession of goods which have social or ceremonial value, and not economic value. When many allied words of śrī in various Eurasian languages are studied, the status or prominence of a person is seen in his possession of wealth and prosperity. The use of the word śrī in the Avesta is similar to its usage in the Veda. It is felt that śrī is an attribute in the ṚgVeda and as such is not a pre-Vedic goddess[123]. But other opinions are that she is a pre-Aryan fertility goddess[124]. In ŚB. (11.4.3. 1-18), Śrī is accepted by the Father God and recognised by the ten leading gods. In the ŚB. (14.9.3.8)[125], Śrī is equated in status with Agni, Soma, etc.

In the Yajur Veda, when a man departs to the other world, he is said to have attained śrī.[126] A new concept here is that sacrifice is performed to attain śrī.[127] In the Atharva Veda, the word comes to denote material prosperity. In the Brāhmaṇas also, the same ideas are contained. Here the concept śrī is not used to mean beauty or brilliance. But the meaning widens and Lakṣmī appears as a separate deity, accepting oblations.[128] Alakṣmī and Śrī appear, but with no mutual connection in AV. XII. 5.1. & 5. In the Sāmavidhāna Brāhmaṇa[129], Śrī and Alakṣmī appear in concurrence in two connected performances for obtaining prosperity. This material prosperity is of kṣatra, anna, prajā, etc.[130] In the Upaniṣads and the Śrauta-sūtras, the same concept is carried on. In the S'B., Śrī is opposed to pāpman-"-evil, misfortune, unhappiness, misery, wickedness". Pāpman is connected with mṛtyu—death. Therefore, śrī is connected with life and with entities which would assist in a comfortable existence.[131] Śrī associates with kṣatra "ruling power, whereas it does not have connection with brahman". Rule *(rāṣṭra)* itself is regarded as śrī.[132]

In the DM, the king and the *vaiśya* do severe austerities for a period of three years, at the end of which *Devī* appears before them to grant boons. She grants more than what the king asks for, stability now, and thence, raised to a Manu,[133] whereas the *vaiśya* is shortshrifted in a single *śloka* (24) with brahmajñāna. This partiality may have as its basis the earlier thoughts of Śrī attached to royalty and not to knowledge.

Lakṣmī

The word lakṣmī means a mark, sign, a token" and lakṣman is a sign, good or bad. Both these words are derived from *lakṣ-* "know by means of indicating characteristics."[134] A better interpretation seems to be that *lakṣan* is a token or a mark, which by its outward signs can be perceived by the senses and, lakṣmī, is an object whose presence is evil or auspicious. Bhadralakṣmī occurs in the ṚgVeda once in the tenth book, that the speech of the wise is imprinted by the power of the mind. This is not a lakṣma but an entity of speech of the mind.[135]

In the Veda itself these two i.e., lakṣma and lakṣmī, started merging. Tait. Ār.[136] states that Hrī and Lakṣmī are the two wives of Puruṣa and that Lakṣmī is the deity of prosperity. In the *Mantrabrāhmaṇa* lakṣmaḥ, the manifestation in connection with pāpīlakṣmī is denoted. Thus, no distinction is made between the deity Lakṣmī and her characteristics lakṣmaḥ

AV.[138] speaks of misfortune or Alakṣmī. There is repeated mention of alakṣmī or pāpīlakṣmī.[139]

Several fiendish female beings lalāmī, arātī, araṇi, ṛsyapadī, vṛṣadatī, goṣedhā, vidhamā and vilīdhī are grouped round Lakṣmī and she is their leader[140]. Slowly the auspicious part of Lakṣmī came into prominence and still later she merged with śrī. Without any mutual connection, in the S'B[141]., both are propitiated for fulfilment of wishes, amongst others.

The change from a sign of prosperity in the Vedic age to the prosperity itself[142] in the post-Vedic period is quite comprehensible in that the idea of luck was related to material prosperity and well-being. Further, *Bhāgya*—something "to be divided", "to be shared" also came to mean wealth. *Lakṣmī* is now accepted amongst scholars as a pre-Vedic agricultural deity along with Demeter or Kore of Greece, Isis of Egypt, and Ceres of Rome. Women were associated with agriculture in its early stages, till the plough was discovered, when men took over tilling the land. Therefore, all earlier divinities of agriculture were goddesses.[143]

It has also been mooted that Lakṣmī was the disease of the corn. This was later transferred to a new divinity Alakṣmī and, Lakṣmī retained all the beneficent qualities alone.[144] Laksmī's fickle quality move the minister Sumati of Raja Simha Pallava to berate her, that there were two poisons which emerged during the *amṛtha-manthana Lakṣmī* and *Kālakūṭa*. Of the two *Lakṣmī* is worse because she afflicts and makes miserable many people.[145]

Śrī Sūkta: It is a late khila of the ṚgVeda II. It was such a popular sūkta that the other Vedas also had one of their own. *Sāma Veda*'s is 3.267.5; *Atharva Veda* takes for itself the *Āpastamba sūtra mantra* 4.7.4 and calls it *Srī sūkta.*[146]

In the ṚgVedic sūkta, there are 15 stanzas, the sixteenth one being phalaśruti. The first two stanzas are about Lakṣmī, and the next ten are about Śrī. The last two are about the composite goddess Śrī-Lakṣmī. There are various opinions about the period of its composition. It is concluded that most of it was composed in the Brāhmaṇa period and the last two in the Upaniṣadic period[147], when Śrī and Lakṣmī syncretised into a single goddess. This has the description of Lakṣmī's form. Lakṣmī is differentiated from Alakṣmī.[148] Her affinity to the lotus is stressed.[149] The gajalakṣmī motif is stressed in stanza 3. The gajas symbolise clouds, nāgas meaning both.[150] Nāga could also mean that Lakṣmī was an un-Aryan goddess of the Nāga tribes[151]. The lotus and the water-spraying motifs denote the fertility aspect of the goddess.

She is the Indian Ceres. Gaurī denotes the colour of the ripe corn. Kardama means mud of the rice fields; karṣiṇī means "abounding in dung"; ārdrā means moist. All these epithets show Lakṣmī's agricultural origins, as also her folk antecedants. Śrī-Lakṣmī's connection with lotus is prominent. There is repeated mention of it in this sūkta. Lakṣmī is also called Padmā or Kamalā. There are two possible connotations to this symbolism: Firstly, the lotus flower represents fertility and abundance in creation. It is organic creation at its most vigorous. Cosmic creation is also seen in this symbol. At a different level of meaning, just as the flower floats unconcerned over mire and mud, though rooted in it, so also the goddess, though connected with worldly abundance and prosperity, is unaffected by it and she transcends it and remains same.

Rice is associated with all fertility rituals and worship. Lājahoma performed by the bride in the wedding ceremony is also for prosperity and fertility. Lakṣmī pūjā performed in the South during the Āśvina śukla daśamī is patently a harvest-fertility pūjā where rice, water, coconut and leaves are used. The objective of this pūjā is long life and prosperity for the husband. The Lakṣmī pūjā performed in Coromandel for nine days in September is for the same objective.

In the South East Asian islands, where Hindu influence is seen, there is a very wide-spread diffusion of Śrī-cult connected with rice cultivation.[152]

The śrī of kings and the lakṣmī of merchants, sometimes remained disparate. Śrī is aiśvaryapradhāna (aiśvarya is any successful attempt in this world) and Lakṣmī is saubhāgyapradhāna (welfare and happiness), according to Mbh. 3.37.33.[153] and Rām. 3.46.16. She was a goddess of wealth and therefore the goddess of Vaiśyas in the Buddhist period. Many votive offerings have inscriptions showing this interest in their goddess. Many of their names are compounds of the word śrī.[154]

When Bali defeated Indra, Lakṣmī was so pleased that of her own accord, she went to live with him. When he was banished to the nether regions, he was allowed to come up to the earth for three days, during Diwali, when Lakṣmī also came with him. Hence she was worshipped with rites, and lights were lit to welcome her. This could also be interpreted as the corn-goddess' common disappearance from the earth to the nether world. Bali was a demon of vegetation.[155] Lakṣmī was an non-Aryan divinity of agriculture and fertility. When she returns to the earth worship is offered to her from Bhādrapada to the spring.

Her association with Kubera is seen in the Śrī sūkta itself; ṚV.[156] "upaitu māṁ devasakha kīrtisca maṇinā sahā". Devasakha is Kubera and Maṇibhadra is his treasure. Judging by the coin of the Yaudheyas, it is surmised that Śrī was associated with Kārtikeya.[157] But since Lakṣmī would be a natural choice as an insignia for kings, she may have been depicted (along with the god for victory in wars) on coins by many kings and these could contain also their iṣṭa devatās on the obverse side of their coins. Much reliance need not be placed on proving Lakṣmī's associates numismatically.

The myth in Mbh.[158] of Lakṣmī abandoning the Asuras and joining Indra may point to her aboriginal origin, as a vegetation divinity. She may have suited the Aryan pastorals because, as she reasons herself for her defection they do not feed the cattle well, and they kill them; therefore she is unhappy with them.

Lakṣmī's association with Viṣṇu was a late event in the third or fourth century of the Gupta (early) era. She was associated with various divinities before this. Lakṣmī, and Sarasvatī were made consorts of many gods because of the tendency in the Gupta Age to assign multiple consorts to the major deities.

Her connection with Viṣṇu occurs in the Viṣṇu Purāṇa and also in the Viṣṇudharmottara Purāṇa[160] where of her own accord she goes to Viṣṇu. In the Śānti Parva of the Mbh.[161] Śrī is said to be born from a lotus on Viṣṇu's forehead. This would be to bring her in alignment with Viṣṇu's cult. Judging by these literary evidences and also by the sculptural evidence, it would corroborate the period of bringing Lakṣmī into the vaiṣṇava cult to the early Gupta period, i.e., 3-4th centuries A.D. After this period only, Viṣṇu's icons are represented holding a lotus.

This alignment is in keeping with the social thinking of the period, when woman had no status as a single person, but her status was due to her position as a spouse. Śrī-Lakṣmī retained her popular position because of two characteristics: (1) her submissive role as a wife, which was an ideal in the Hindu male mind and, (2) her role as a goddess of wealth the pursuit of which attracted men of all sects.[162] She was associated with Dharma.[163] and Indra. This connection between Śrī and Dharma may mean that those who live by dharma, may be rewarded with prosperity.

Śrī was appointed to become the wife of the Pāṇḍavas who were really the five Indras.[164] In the Rāmāyaṇa:[165]

"Rāmalakṣmaṇayor madhye Sītā rājati te snuṣā/

Viṣṇuvāsavayormadhye Padmā Śrīriva rūpiṇī//"

shows her connection with *Indra.*

In the late 5th century A.D., Śrī is mentioned as a śakti of Viṣṇu and the latter carries on the functions of creation and destruction through her. She plays a formidable role in the Pāñcarātra speculations as the śakti of Viṣṇu.

Durgā and Lakṣmī are seen to be the two aspects of the same pre-Aryan fertility divinity and were closely related to each other.[166] But Manusmṛti distinguishes in the worship offered to these two deities by a householder. The chasm widens when Lakṣmī is absorbed in the Viṣṇu cult and Durgā into the Śiva cult.

In the present day, Śrī-Lakṣmī is worshipped in images of clay along with that of Gaṇeś'a. Gaṇes'a has a yakṣa type of figure and is also associated with prosperity. This worship may be a remainder from Śrī's earlier connection with Yakṣas.

Sarasvatī

Sarasvatī in the ṚgVeda is a river first and then the river was raised to the stature of a divinity. She was the main local deity of the Aryans living near the river, and she was a "typical local goddess".[167] She is mentioned along with Dṛṣadvatī. On the banks of the Sarasvatī the Aryans performed their religious rites, and developed their culture. This may have been the first place, after they entered India, when they had a stable existence. "In fact, intellectual progress and cultural advances are possible only in a settled society".[168] The change in the lifestyle on the banks of the river must have made a powerful impression on the Aryans.

As a river goddess, since all food is dependent on the river waters, she is associated with fertility and fecundity. The intricacies of the Aryan rituals must have grown on the banks of the Sarasvatī. Therefore, they must have raised the river to a deified status and made her the goddess Vāk, the source of the universe.[169]

Even in the RV, she has been associated with speech, albeit very few times.[170] The Vedas treat Sarasvatī in her three aspects: (1) goddess of speech, conferring wealth on us; (2) as the goddess of the river and, (3) as the river itself.

In Ṛ.V. VII. 96. 1 (Hymn to Various Deities) Sarasvatī is the lordly one among rivers and connected with asuras. This is the only time a female deity is associated with asuras.

> *"bṛhad u gāyise vaco*
> *suryā nadīnāṁ*
> *Sarasvatīm in mahayā suvṛktibhiḥ*
> *Stomair vasiṣṭha rodasī"*

"I wish to sing a high word: (she is) the asuric one among rivers. Magnify indeed Sarasvatī with songs, with praises, O Vasiṣṭha, and the world-halves".[171]

Another opinion is[172] that most scholars, while evaluating Sarasvatī, base their opinions on Yāska, or, Sāyaṇa who classify the goddess either as a personification of a river, or, a goddess of speech. But she is an aerial goddess. She was associated with Vāk only in the later literature, while this connection is seen in the ṚgVeda itself by many. The Ṛk 6.61.2 is really about the goddess, but it has been connected to the river. Ambitama, Nadītama, and, Devitama are all vocatives in the Ṛks, asking for motherly affection for the supplicant. The mother-goddess character is well defined by the epithet ambā. Further there have been contradictory opinions about the Ṛks pertaining to Sarasvatī; whether they mean the goddess, or, just the river. To decide this, the following evaluation is suggested.[173] An atmospheric goddess should possess two characteristics: (1) of pouring rain, and, (2) of the ability to do extraordinary feats *(balakṛti)*. The first characteristic in Sarasvatī is belaboured by the interpreters, to suit their opinion, while the latter is well justified as seen in the episode of the killing of Vṛtra, and the son of Bṛsaya; though[174] there is an opinion that Vṛtra is Bṛsaya's son. Pāvīravi means āyudhavatī, and Sarasvatī definitely possessed the weapon vajra. She is so powerful that even gods approach her on their knees.[175] In the sixth *maṇḍala* of the ṚV, there is a change in the development of this goddess and she becomes a war-goddess feared even by the gods, bringing death to the enemies.[176] That a fecundity deity wields a weapon is quite in keeping with the characteristics of an Indo-European deity. Her Iranian counterpart is Harqaiti. The three characteristics that are delineated about this goddess are: benignity, humidity, and heroism. All these can be easily seen in the Indian goddess also. She is also equivalent to the Indo-European Anāhitā, and the

Roman goddess Freyja.[177]

On the banks of the river, not only Vedic rituals must have been performed, but war-like activities must also have taken place. Divodāsa managed to avenge the defeat of his forefathers by annihilating the Paṇis; a battle with the hostile tribes, Pārāvatas, must have also been fought on the banks, and the defeated tribe while fleeing by crossing the river, must have been swept away by the currents. Hence her epithet Pārāvataghnī.[178]

Sarasvatī is also connected with the manes, "since whatever one thinks with one's mind that one says with one's speech".[179] Sarasvatī is said to be the goddess of prajña, or, dhī-knowledge. But dhī, in the context used with Sarasvatī is used with the meaning 'karma'. Moreover, many other gods (Bhaga, the Maruts, Indra, etc.) are also invoked in the same way, asking to 'inspire', or, to 'protect' dhī (if one takes dhī to mean knowledge).[180] Sarasvatī's connection with the mind and also with abundance (when assimilated with the milch cow), increased her popularity, and, she could give fulness of inspiration (dhī) to compose hymns, and, a step further, she became the goddess of wisdom.[181]

Vāk that is identified with Sarasvatī is also of two types:

(1) the holy Vāk of the sacrifices, i.e., the deified speech, and,

(2) the speech uttered by the gods.

These two fused later, not unnaturally, because the voice of the *Ṛṣis* coincided with that of the gods, or, putting it another way, the latter gave birth to the former. Sarasvatī, who was earlier mantrarūpā Vāk, became, in the Brāhmaṇas, the goddess of speech. One interesting point is, in the YV, Vāk is said to control Sarasvatī.[182]

In the later Vedic religion, Sarasvatī is identified with Vāk, the principle of transcendental Speech, and, she is the goddess presiding over knowledge and all spoken word.[183] In the VS. XIX, she is associated with Indra, Aśvins, etc. In the Sautrāmaṇī rites she is praised for curing Indra and the Aśvins. In the VS. XX. 55, she is mentioned with two other goddesses, Iḍā, and, Bhāratī to complete the triad of goddesses.

In the AV.[184] she along with Sinīvālī is required to bless the womb of the bride with fecundity. The S'B[185] as also Tait. Saṁ.[186] identifies her as Vāk, along with Sinīvālī. She has the powers to give personal wealth,[187] and children; she can soothe ill infants,[188] kill parasitic worms.[189] She is connected with garbhā-dhāna rituals *"garbhaṁ dehi Sinīvālī garbhaṁ dehi Sarasvatī"*,[190] as well as the Saptapadī ceremony of the wedding. All these indicate her position as mother-goddess connected with fertility, birth, and children.

Sarasvatī occasionally accompanies other gods. Since she is connected with material prosperity, she is associated with Pusti, god of abundant nourishment.[192] She is called Puṣṭipatnī. But in the ŚB[193] this quality of hers is transferred to Śrī.

She was coveted by both the Gandharvas and the gods. In ŚB[194] Vāk was given away to the Gandharvas by the gods, in exchange for soma. According to another version, the gods won Vāk with the help of Yajña, and kept her hidden frorn the Asuras, in the fire.[195]

In later mythology, she, as Vāk, or Sarasvatī, is coupled with Brahmā, which is developed from her association with Prajāpati in the Brāhmaṇas. Dakṣa Prajāpati seduces his daughter variously named Uṣas, Dyaus, Pṛthivī, all of whom are only different forms of Aditi[196]. From the association of Sarasvatī with Vāk, it was a natural development of the goddess into Vidyā Devatā. In the Purāṇas, she is associated with the colour white-complexion, dress, and the lotus flower. This choice may be due to the sparkling white waters of the river[197]. She has also been connected with Viṣṇu and held to be his tongue or residing in his mouth.[198] She is also the co-wife of Lakṣmī in some myths. But she represents the spiritual, ascetic, religious values, whereas Lakṣmī stands for the material prosperity. She is identified with thought and speech and therefore with creativity and fine arts. She is extolled as the highest power of the cosmos in her connection with culture. Her vehicle, the swan, shows the purity of the goddess rising above wordly imperfections. Since she is the goddess associated with ascetics, she is not much favoured in domestic worship. Sarasvatī and Sāvitrī appear as nude goddesses in the epic, Purāṇas and Tantras.[199] This is seen as a Purāṇic development of the Vedic goddess Aditi. Sarasvatī is given a guardian of water, Sarasvān,[200] as a son or consort, just as *Dakṣa* is both the father and son of Aditi.[201] This confusion is natural in the development of a mother-goddess, as mentioned earlier.

In the Purāṇas, the word Sarasvatī has been etymologically derived from Sṛ, Saras, to move about, to glide. This describes the movement of words issuing from the mouth, in speech. Later on, she became the deified speech. The secondary meaning of *Saras is* water. Thus Sarasvatī came to denote the river. A step further in her development, she became the goddess presiding over the river. The river deity and the goddess of speech became identical. This development seems similar to that in the Vedas.

In Purāṇic myths she is said to be created by Kṛṣṇa, Rudra, or Brahmā[202] or his spouse *(Matsya and Skanda).* She is the daughter of *Viṣṇu (Skanda Purāṇa)* and his wife (*Bhaviṣya* and *Devī Bhāgavata Purāṇas*). Just as the ṚgVeda speaks of her ghora aspect, the Purāṇas also do so. In the Brahmāṇḍa Purāṇa.,[203] she is one of the nine Mātṛs accompanying Lalitā in her fight with Bhaṇḍāsura. The Vāyu *Purānas.*[204] speaks of her as one with a loud roar-Mahānādā. Iconographically, she has four arms holding vīṇa, akṣamālā and pustaka, dressed in either yellow,[205] or, white[206] garments. Being Brahmāṇī, her vāhana is the same as Brahmā's, the swan. Sometimes though, she is represented on a peacock. As a goddess, Sarasvatī has usually been in a group with Iḷā, and Bhāratī also known as Mahī, and the wives of the gods. The trinity of Sarasvatī, Iḷā, and Bhāratī resembles the Purāṇic Durgā, Lakṣmī, and Sarasvatī. The Vedic trinity are related respectively to atmospheric, terrestrial, and celestial spheres.[207]

Bhāratī

Bhāratī is Mahī, earth.[208] Bharatas must have been the most powerful clan, while the Vedic rituals were growing, when the Aryans were settled on the banks of the river Sarasvatī. Their family goddesses must have been given an honoured position in the divine hierarchy of the Vedas. In the Purāṇas, Bhāratī and Sarasvatī became two names for the same goddess.

Iḷā

Iḷā is food in the ṚgVeda, and Iḷā-Aditi is the source of food.[209] She is often connected with the cow, whose milk and butter, when used as offerings, is represented by the goddess Iḷā. She is "nourishment",[210] and refreshing draught. She is the personification of liquid oblation to the sacrificial fire.[211] She seems to have a resemblance to the Minoan Idaean Mother who derived her name from the mountain Ida in Crete and came to be accepted in Greek mythology. She, like the Indian Irā (or Iḷā, or Iḍā) stands for food and speech. It is surmised[212] that goddess Iḍā spread from India to the Minoan islands. This seems quite probable that, along with commerce, it is natural that religious ideas could spread. For instance, the goddess in Minoa is called Potniai, meaning a mistress.[213] This could be the South Indian goddess of the Pattini cult. The gold fillets found in the Adichanallur burial sites are akin to the ones used in the religious cults in Minoa. These could be the result of the contact due to increasing exchange of trade between the Phoenicians from the south and east, and the Minoans towards the Mediterranian and, perhaps Atlantic shores.[214] Thus exchange and mutual influence were quite possible between distant countries through trade contacts.

Sinīvālī

Sinīvālī is a fertility goddess in the ṚgVeda,[215] and in the AV. In the *Gṛhya sūtras,* she is associated with Garbhādhāna,[216] and Puṁsavana. She is connected with birth-*bahusūvarī.*[217] From passages in the *Saṁhitās* and *Brāhmanas, Sinīvālī* is described as *sukaparda-* with a beautiful knot of hair, *sukurīrā,* which is the same as *sumukuṭa,* that is, having a charming crown; and *svaupaśā*—having lovely limbs[218]. In the AV. 7.4.6. she is called Viṣṇu's consort.[219] She is also said to favour Indra. "*Indram* .... pratīcī" (turning towards Indra).[220] She is invoked for cattle in the Bṛhad. Up.(6.4.19)

In the late Vedic texts she and Anumati become phases of the moon. She is mentioned along with Kuhū, Rākā (and Anumati) also and each of them becomes a phase of the moon. *Kuhū* and *Rākā* are old Austric names for full and new moons and they survived as Vedic goddesses.[221]

Anumati

She was originally conceived to counteract the evil influence of Nirṛti. Later on she was grouped with Sinīvālī, Rākā and Kuhū as a moon goddess. These goddesses are surmised to be stellar goddesses who later evolved into the Kṛttikās, who again became the mothers of Skanda.[222]

Hrī

In the Taitt. Ār., Śrī is replaced by *Hrī* as one of the consorts of *Puruṣa.* "*HrīścaLakṣmīśca patnyau.*"[223] She may have been a popular folk goddess as seen from the Buddhist *Jātaka.*[224]

Puṣṭi

Puṣṭi means abundance and she is equivalent to Sinīvālī[225] and Sarasvatī.[226] As a goddess she appears in the Mānava *Gṛ, Sū.* for the first time.[227]

Bhūti

She is prosperity and appears in the AV.[228] She is invoked in the *Pāraskara* Gṛ. Sū.[229] In the *YV. Bhūti* is said to free a person from the bonds of Nirṛti.[230] There are a few more minor goddesses like Subhadrā (fertility goddess), Pathyā-goddess of bounteous paths and welfare, and Śraddhā-the deified faith.

Sītā

Sītā is the personified goddess of the furrow and as such she is invoked in the ṚV.[231] She is associated with Indra and he is called Urvarāpati in the ṚV.[232] She gains a more concrete personality in the *Sūtras*, most probably because these deal with agriculture. Rituals connected with the furrow are given in the AV.[233] and also in the *Pāraskara* Gṛ. Sū.[234] she is named the wife of Indra. "Indrapatnīmupahvaye Sītām" This sūtra has also a Sītāyajña elaborated in it;[235] also Gobhila GS.;[236] Mānava GS.[237] In the Taitt. Br. she is called Sāvitrī. After the Vrjji confederacy was broken by Magadha and their lands taken over, the idea of State started forming. Distinction was made in different types of land holdings. State owned land given to agriculturists to plough, develop and form villages, was called Sītā.[238]

Māyā

The Asura Goddess: She is a mother-goddess of the Asuras. She goes to the Asuras as an occult power and they win over the *devas.*[239] At a later period Māyā was ascribed negative qualities. As "illusion" she holds a prime position in Sainkhyan and Vedautic philozophy. As a personification of this quality she was identified with Durgā; or, as a daughter of Anṛta and Nṛti (or Nikṛti); mother of Mṛtyu and daughter of Adharma[239a].

She was invoked for protection along with Pṛthivī, Hrī, Aditi-Virāj, Aditi and creation's first creature. In the Jaiminīya Br. the ogress has yoni all over her. Indra kills her by taking the help of Sumitra whom he asks to court the ogress Dīrghajihvī. Later a reversion in the myth occurs and it is Indra, who gets covered by yoni.

In the third cent. B.C., the Qxyrynchus Papyrus[240] recording various mother-goddesses, mentions Maiya of the Gangetic plain. In the ṚV.[241] and Bṛ. Up.[242] Māyā is taken as the Śakti of the God.

Umā

Most forms of the mother-goddesses go back to folk origins like Kālammā and Ellammā. Ellammā is connected to Paraśu Rāma, because the latter's mother, Reṇukā's head is borne on Ellammā's body. Kālī's shrine always has an icon of Paraśu Rāma. The Babylonian word for mother is Ummu, or Umma; the Akkadian is Ummi, and the Dravidian word is Ammā. All these are seen to bear resemblance to each other as well as to the goddess Umā. Her derivation from 'mā' to measure, seems artificial. Similarly the Phrygian mother-goddess is Ammā or Mā. This word is found in old High German, Dravidian Scythian, and other languages[244]. This again can be connected with Ambā, Ambi, or Ambikā. Thus the mother-goddess concept of Umā has a very wide diffusion in her antecedents.

Umā, like Śiva has both positive and negative characteristics.[245] The seven tongues of Agni[246] are: Kālī, Karālī, Manojavā, Sulohitā, Sudhūmṛavarṇā, Sphuliṅginī, and Viśvarucī. There might be two different sets of goddesses brought together in these names, just like Rudra and Agni were syncretised. One set of goddesses would be Umā, Ambikā, Pāravatī, and Haimavatī, being wives of Śiva. The other set would be belonging to Agni, like Kālī, Karālī, etc. Perhaps Gaurī and such others belong to Nirṛti, the goddess of evil.[247]

Umā seems a late addition in the Vedic texts. She appears in the Kena Up. and Taitt. Ār.[248] She occurs in the Jaiminīya Gṛ. Su.[249] and Atharva Pariśiṣṭa.[250] The two names, Umā and Ambikā appearing in the same Gāyatrī of Śiva, naming Śiva as their husband, show the effort at syncretising the goddesses.

Rātri

Rātri is given a complete sūkta in the ṚV.[251] She is the starlit night guiding men safely home and keeping dangers away. It is noteworthy that it is called Durgā stava.[252] Several of the epithets of this goddess are noteworthy—Bhadrā, Bhagavatī, Kṛṣṇā,[253] Śivā,[254] Durgā.[255] The name Durgā may be taken from the AV.[256]

She is here personified as a dark night as opposed to her picturisation as a starlit night of the ṚV. sūkta noted earlier. Since movement might be restricted in a dark night fraught with dangers, the name Durgā could have arisen to mean, either that she was difficult of access, or, that she helped her devotees cross over difficulties.

Śacī

The Purāṇic Śakti could be seen in the word Śacī, the derivation of both being from the word 'śak', to be powerful.[257] There are goddesses made up by adding feminine diminutive 'ṇī' to the god's name. The exception is Śacī, who is distinct from Indrāṇī, and is the śakti of Indra. Śacī, Indra's strength, is said to bestow auspiciousness on the invoker.[258] Elsewhere the goddess' strength is said to support Indra as Dawn is said to support the Sun.[259]

While discussing the Indra-Vṛtra myth, M. Eliade has opined that myths (and therefore the gods) are multivalent, that is, they have simultaneously cosmogonic, naturalistic, and historic valencies. Gonda,[260] has taken the gods as archetypes, or, prototypes whom man tries to understand from the different levels of his experience. It was Rudolf Otto,[261] who felt that Vedic, or for that matter all gods, should be interpreted from the standpoint of the power of the Numina. Numinous is that which arises out of the depths of our consciousness. It reacts with the stimulus from the phenomenal world (natural phenomena) and the experience from our sensory perceptions. Thus natural phenomena and mental forces give rise to opportunities for man to apprehend the hidden power, the numinous, and this may result in personalizing it into a divine form. However, when we interpret the Vedic gods and goddesses, we must remember their multiple valencies and not try simplistic solutions. Structural (the interaction of the macrocosmic and the microcosmic), Jungian psychology (divinities arising from the inner depths of our consciousness), and historic (they arise due to some historical incident)—all these are needed to understand them.

In this brief survey of the Vedic goddesses, it becomes evident that the Vedic religion had goddesses, but, they did not occupy as prominent a position as the gods, in the literature of the period. A similar situation arose in the Greek literature. Homer's *Iliad*, though it reflects the religious beliefs and practices of the period, does not contain a few important ones, such as the cremation of the dead, and any reference to the mother-goddess cult, which from the archaeological evidence is seen to be a powerful factor, due to the Minoan-Mycenean religious influence.[262] Such discrepancies and errors could also have existed in our literary data.

Historical and Sociological Background

When man changed from a food-gatherer to a cultivator, his belief changed from one god to multitudinous gods, each with one attribute. This characteristic is also seen in the Aryans' Vedic goddesses. The indigenous mother-goddess cult could have provided what was lacking in the prosaic heroic religion of the Indo-European/Aryan religion of the ruling classes, with which it was assimilated. For an agricultural and pastoral people, agriculture was of vital importance. The Great Goddess, who was to emerge, held together in herself all the various functions of the cult goddesses, and maternal principle of nature, giving life to the flocks, and to mankind. Aditi was her prototype. It is seen that, just as in the early Vedas, patriarchal gods were prominent, driving the indigenous mother-goddesses underground, the latter re-emerged in the later Saṁhitās and early Brāhmaṇas. The inter-marriage, probably necessitated by exogamous rules must have brought indigenous brides with their own faith, seen from the Xth mandala of the ṚgVeda going on till the Brāhmanas.[263] Nirṛti, Śacī, Mīḍhuṣī, Yamī, Ambikā, Rudrānī, Śrī, Lakṣmī, Sarasvatī or Vāk, emerged as mother goddesses. The Aryans could have been attracted towards an icon-worshipping cult which was aesthetically appealing and personally more satisfying than a grand yajña.

The Aryans had reached the Punjab and the Uttar Pradesh. But between the 7th and 8th centuries B.C. in the southeast Uttar Pradesh and Bihar, non-Vedic religions flourished. Yakṣas, Nāgas and other non-Aryan cults were followed. The social strata was built differently. Merchants flourished and led prosperous and peaceful lives. Artisans and free peasants lived a comparatively trouble-free life and these formed the bulk of the population. Politically old tribal structures were crumbling and were replaced by small principalities, which still retained small portions of the tribal ethnic structure. Aryan religion infiltrated slowly, but was in the process changed in its complexion by indigenous cults.

From 200 B.C. to 500 A.D., with the Bhakti movement and the avatāra concept, Smṛtis with their harsh divisions of caste emerged. Belief in the Trinity of Gods Brahmā Viṣṇu and Śiva, in pūjā also came about. Indigenous gods and goddesses re-emerged in a synceretic movement. There was a transformation in the mythology. The syncretization was between ethnic and cultural amalgamation of the pantheon.

There are four major types of goddesses in the Vedas, according to Lynn Gatwood[264] and these are Diti, Aditi, Pṛthivī, and Uṣas. Diti is seen as a Devī-like goddess (that is independently powerful by herself), and Aditi "who is not Diti" is the Aryan goddess. These two goddesses are seen to represent the racial and caste division, and the conclusion drawn is, that the people who followed Aditi were called Ādityas, Aryans; while those who followed Diti were called the Daityas. Aditi is seen as a prototype of the Spouse-goddess (that is, an insipid goddess who attains and keeps her position due to her marital status). Aditi is rarely invoked alone, but usually with her sons.

Hunting leads to domestication of animals and the society moves from hunting to pastoral, and, thence to agriculture. This leads to a change in the outlook of the people and reflects in their religion. When the Aryans changed from pure pastoralists to partial agriculture, sexual motifs connected with fertility crept into their religion. When they were pastoralists, the form of religion must have been sacrifice of animals. When surplus formed, and trade increased, cattle must have formed the best form of payment and there must have arisen resistance to sacrifice. The class of society also changed. Previously the whole tribe must have shared the produce and had common meals. When surplus arose, this cohesion gave way and a class of elite surplus-holders arose, and laws were formed to suit them and caste was hardened.[265] The indigenous goddesses married to the Aryan gods, brought tribes into the Aryan society, who could increase agricultural production. Thus agricultur-oriented fertility rituals are found in the later Saṁhitās and Brāhmaṇas. Śat. Br. has numerous passages connected with such rites. YV.,[266] also contains such ideas. In the Vāmadevya Sāman of the Chāndogya Up.[267] there is a sex-oriented explanation of yajña. Most of the non-Vedic sex-oriented rituals got absorbed in the Brāhmanic religion. Those that were not thus accepted became the visible tip of the Tantric iceberg.

The caches of copper implements used by the indigenous tribes in north and central India bear mute witness to the invading pastoral Aryans' driving away or subjugating the original inhabitants, and their culture. While the Aryans proceeded eastwards, those who did not oppose them were made Kṣatriyas, while those who did were made Śūdras. Existing tribal organizations were dissolved and new kingdoms were formed. The economy changed, because the expanding Aryans turned agriculturalists and turned vast forest areas into arable land. The Bigger Tradition looked down on the tribes, residing on hilly tracts and forests, who refused to accept the Brahminic laws of government and religion from the period 500 B.C. onwards. When they ignored caste restrictions they were labelled mlecchas, and were outlawed from Aryan culture. This classification included foreign dynasties also. The mleccha rulers got assimilated into the big Tradition by virtue of their status and false genealogy was fixed for them by the priestly class. The indigenous tribes were more subtly assimilated, by absorbing their popular deities into the Aryan religion, particularly the mother goddesses. Vindhyavāsinī was Brahminised as the Great Goddess. This was co-eval with the Śākta and Tantric influence on the Aryan religion. These tribal areas formed a belt between Magadha and the Southern dynasties like the Andhras, and had to be overcome to establish political and commercial contacts and trade routes stabilised with better communication links.[268]

The agricultural Vaiśyas turned to trading, Śūdras became tillers and the most powerful caste, the Brahmins became the biggest land owners.

The nature of a deity generally reflects the values of the social groups and categories that worship it. Conversely, to understand the goddesses, we could study the position of women in this period, which would reflect the religious mores.

Normally, the position of women would improve as the society moved towards cultural advance. But, women had good status in the Vedic period and this deteriorated in the ensuing period. "Let a wife be absolute mistress over her father-in-law over her mother in-law; let her be mistress over her husband's sisters her be mistress over her husband's brothers[269]." This is in contrast to the Laws of Manu with regard to women.[270]

The Princess, Gārgī Vākaknavī was a famous ascetic. ".... the position of women among Indian Aryans progressively changed from one of freedom and influence to one of imperative subjection and effacement. The *Brahmanas* ...... indicate a gradual decline in their position".[271] In this era, women shared in the economic activity of the period, and were equal to men in education, participation in religious and cultural activities, choice of marriage partners, and had a reasonable amount of security in property rights.[272] There was no stigma attached to the single status of women. *Amaju* was the ṚgVedic term for an unmarried woman.[273] Women are held in esteem, if they share in the economic activities of the society, whatever the period. (Women's position in England improved vastly after World War I, when they bore a major share of their country's war-time activities in almost all fields.) The woman of the Vedic period was also a helpmate in the pursuits of her husband.

When the conquerors started marrying into indigenous tribes, freely as seen in the Brāhmaṇas and the epics, these women were aliens to the culture, language and religious practices of their husbands. They were severely restricted in participation in those activities, and as a corollary, the Aryan woman's position also deteriorated. The marriage age of girls was brought down to ensure pure lineage for the men, and to assure the continuity of the lineage for the sake of property rights. Education was not possible under the circumstances and anyhow longer years of tutelage were needed to master the growing intricacies of rituals. By 500 B.C., women's status had become unenviable in the society. But worse was yet to come[274]. Between 200 B.C. and 300 A.D., there were many foreign invasions in the country. The Greeks invaded under Demetrius and Menander (190-150 B.C.), and, Scythians and Parthians came between 100 B.C. to 50 A.D. Nearly half the population in the north upto Patna in Bihar, was decimated, or enslaved and taken away. Under such pressures, the family's purity had to be guarded and women were restricted severely in all fields. Their proprietary rights improved somewhat as compared to the early Vedic Age. But woman was kept subservient and made dependant on her father, brother, husband or sons.

As seen so far, economic, social and political changes took place after the Vedic period, which affected the religious outlook from the period of the Brāhmaṇas and the epics. Religion was changing qualitatively and quantitatively. Qualitatively, Hinduism had to absorb a lot of tribal divinities, when the tribals accepted Aryan suzerainty. Their gods were perforce agricultural divinities ie mother-goddesses.

Quantitatively, Buddhism adopted many Hindu goddesses and expanded into a vast pantheon. Jainism grew more slowly. Vaiṣṇavism and Śaivism adopted quickly, the latter rapidly. All the gods were given goddesses to satisfy mass leanings. Still there was no satisfaction in the pantheon, till Śakti was raised above the trinity of gods and made a Supreme Goddess. The ideologies of religion are said to be objective and too slow to have any impact on society. On the other hand, the religious change in the position of the Goddess cult was a precedent to the altered status of women, which had invidiously started deteriorating in the late Vedic age. Further, when societies face shattering experiences, the existing religious values may collapse altogether, or, more often than not, newer interpretations are given to them and they grow in strength.

REFERENCES

1. Agrawala, P.K., *Goddesses in Ancient India*, Infra.
2. *Change and Continuity in Indian Religion*, p. 13.
3. Gonda, *Ibid.*, p. 9, Intro.
4. Eliade, *History of Religious Ideas*, pp. 128-29.
5. Kosambi, D.D., Origin of Brahmin Gotras, JBBRAS, Vol. 26, Part I, p. 73.
6. *Ibid.*, p. 75.
7. Griswold, Religion of the RgVeda, p. 103 quoted by P.K. Agrawala, *Goddesses in Ancient India*, p. 48.
8. ṚV. VII. 36.6.
9. ṚV. X. 146.6.
10. ṚV. VII 77.2.
11. *Ibid.*, pp. 52-54.
12. Hillebrandt, A, *Vedic Mythology*, Vol. II, pp. 251-52.
13. Bhattacharyya, N.N., IMG, p. 100.
14. Bachofen, J.J., *Myth, Religion and Mother Right*, pp. 33-34.
15. Sharma, P.K., *Sakti Cult in Ancient India*, p. 241.
16. Danielou, Alain, *Hindu Polytheism*, p. 16.
17. Neumann, Erich, *The Great Mother*, p. 219.
18. Eliade, *History of Religious Ideas*, Vol. II, p. 45.

19. James, *Cult of the Mother Goddess*, pp. 128-31.
20. Dikshit, S.K., *The Mother Goddess*, p. 44.
21. ṚV. VI. 67. 4; IX. 74. 5; X .72.8, etc.
22. Nirukta VI. 6.
23. ṚV. IX. 112.3; Dikshit, *Op. cit.*, p. 45 fn. 3.
24. The Great Goddess in India and Iran, p. 417, IHQ, X. 3, Sept. 1934.
25. Keith, A Berridale, The Aśvins and the Great Goddess, pp. 721-26, IC.3. 1936-37
26. Aditi and the Great Goddess, pp. 401-9, IC.4. 1937-38.
27. pp. 402 -5.
28. Agrawala, P.K., *Goddesses in Ancient India*, p. 139.
29. Ṛtāvarī - ṚV. VIII. 25.3.
30. Agrawala, *Op. cit.*, p. 58.
31. Gonda, *Notes on Names and the Name of God in Ancient India*, p. 19.
32. ṚV. 1. 89. 10.
33. Agrawala, P.K., *Op. cit.*, p. 59.
34. Werner, Karel, *Men, Gods and Powers in the Vedic Outlook.*, JRAS, 1982, no. 1, p. 21.
35. ṚV. I. 89. 10; AV. VII. 6. 1; etc.
36. Dikshit, *Op. cit.*, p. 50.
37. Bhattacharji, S., *The Indian Theogony*, p. 160.
38. Bhattacharyya, IMG, p. 94.
39. ṚV. IV. 18. 1-3.
40. Ananda Coomaraswamy, *Elements of Buddhist Iconography*, Cambridge. 1935, p. 272; quoted in Agrawala, P.K. *Op. cit.*, p. 59.
41. ṚV. X. 101. 13.
42. ṚV. V. 51.11; VII. 35.9.
43. ṚV. II.29.3; V.51.14; VI.51.11.
44. ṚV. V.49.3.
45. ṚV. I. 94.16.
46. ṚV. IV.54.6; IV. 55.1; IV.75.12.
47. ṚV. III.54.20; V.46.6.
48. ṚV. II.27.14.
49. ṚV. VIII.25.10; X.36.3; X.39.11.
50. ṚV. VII.66.6.
51. ṚV. XX.XIX.60 - N.N. Bhattacharyya, *History of Śākta Religion*, p. 32, fn.5.
52. Art. by B.S. Padmanabhan in The Hindu 24-7-83.
53. AV. II. 25.I-Agrawala, P.K. - *Op. cit.*, p. 111, fn. 655.
54. AV. XVI. 8.2; XIX. 44.4; VS. XII. 65; *Ibid.*, fn. 657.

55. Dhavalikar, M.K., The First Farmers of Maharashtra, p. 7, also P.K. Agrawala *Ibid.*, fn. 692.
56. Dhavalikar - *Ibid.*, p. 17; cf. also ch. V . Sn. Lajjā Gaurī.
57. James, *Myth and Ritual in the Ancient Near East,* p. 139.
58. *The Indian Theogony* pp. 86-87.
59. Dikshit, *Op. cit.*, pp. 54-55; cf. also Know, Sten - Indo-European Religious Ideas in Ancient India, p. 64; Art. 7, *Annals of the Bhandarkar Institute,* March, 1925 Vol. VI, Part II.
60. Gatwood, Lynn, *Devi and the Spouse Goddess* p. 65.
61. Bhattacharji, *Op. cit.*, p. 85.
62. Agrawala, P. K., *Op. cit.*, p. 111.
63. Hillbrandt, *Vedic Mythology,* Vol. II, p. 15; In Varuṇā's sacrifice black animals are killed.
64. Bhattacharji - *Op. cit.*, p. 84.
65. V. 37.
66. II. 71. 7.
67. Bhattacharji, *Ibid.*, p. 93 ff.
68. *Ibid.*, p. 185.
69. *Ibid.*, p. 162; cf. also ch. IV Sn. Jyeṣṭhā.
70. Bhattacharji, *Ibid.*, p. 90.
71. Danielou, Alain - *Hindu Polytheism,* p. 138.
72. Eliade, *Patterns in Comparative Religion,* p. 239.
73. Eliade, *Ibid.*, p. 245 fn. 2 To Earth 1 ff.
74. Frankfort, H. and H. A., *Before Philosophy,* p. 239.
75. Eliade, *Myths, Dreams and Mysteries,* p. 172.
76. Eliade, *Patterns in Comparative Religion,* pp. 248-49.
77. Ait. Br. ii. 6.13; etc.
78. Weber, Max, *Sociology of Religion,* p. 13.
79. Eliade, *Patterns in Comparative Religion,* p. 239. fn. 2.
80. Choe Phori V. 127-8, fn. 3. *Ibid.*
81. Eliade, *Myths, Dreams and Mysteries,* p. 189.
82. Agrawala, P.K., *Op. cit.*, p. 45.
83. V. 84. 1-3.
84. ṚV. X. 18. 10.
85. ṚV. X. 114. 2-3.
86. ṚV. X. 72. 3-4.
87. ṚV. IX. 91.1; IX. 93.1; III. 29.13.
88. ṚV. VIII. 34.21; VII 42.3; X 64.15.
89. ṚV. V. 43.6; VII. 36.8; X. 92.5.

90. RV. III. 55.14.
91. Gatwood Lynn - *Devi and the Spouse Goddess*, p. 35.
92. Ath. V. XII, 1, Selections, Verses, 1, 4, 46 and 52-tr.; Eliade - *From Primitives to Zen*, pp. 37-40.
93. Eliade, *Myths, Dreams and Mysteries*, pp. 164-65.
94. Eliade, *Patterns in Comparative Religion*, pp. 360-61.
95. James, *Myth and Ritual in the Ancient Near East*, p. 114.
96. Vide, Frazer, James - *The Golden Bough*, Vol. I., p. 353 ff for rites or rituals connected with crops; and rituals of offering the first fruits of the harvest vide, p. 373 ff.
97. Eliade, *Myths, Dreams and Mysteries*, pp. 186-87.
98. *The Mothers*, Vol. III, p. 207 ff.
99. IX. 37.
100. IX. 33.
101. Malinowski, Bronislow, *Magic, Science and Religion and Other Essays*, p. 175.
102. Eliade, *Patterns in Comparative Religion* p. 246.
103. Eliade, *Myths, Dreams and Mystries*, p. 155.
104. Eliade, *Patterns in Comparative Religion*, p. 340.
105. *Ibid.*, p. 353.
106. *Ibid.*, p. 354/5.
107. DM. - 11.49; Matsya p. XCII, 42-43.
108. Dikshit, S.K. - *The Mother Goddess*, p. 50.
109. Bhattacharyya, N. N., *History of the Sākta Religion*, p. 32.
110. Gatwood Lynn, *Op. cit.*, p. 39.
111. DM. V. 86-88.
112. Agrawala, P. K, *Op. cit.*, p. 113.
113. I.6.10, 4-5.
114. III. 606.
115. I. 10.20 - *Śaradvai rudrasya yoniḥ svasāmbikā.*
116. Śat. Br. 2.6.2.4-17. Tait. Br. 1.6, 10; Kāthaka. Saṁ. 36.14; Mait. Saṁ 1.10.20;.and in the Sūtras: Baud. Ś sū - 5.16-17; Āpastamba Ś su.-8.17. 1-18.10; Kātyā Ś. sū5.10.2-21; Lātyāyana, Ś. sū.-5.3.5-11.
117. *A Dictionary of Classical Antiquities*, p. 271, Col. i.; Dikshit, S.K.-*The Mother-Goddess*, p. 50.
118. Jung, C.G. - *Psychology of the Unconscious*, p. 224.
119. 1.10.20.
120. VS.-31.22-Kāṇva 35.22.
121. Gonda, J., *Aspects of Early Viṣṇuism*, p. 185 ff.
122. J.B. 2.25; AiB.8, 12, 13; in Gonda-*Ibid.*, p. 188.

123. Agrawala, P.K., *Op. cit.*, p. 94.
124. Dhal U.N., *Goddess Lakshmi: Origin and Development*, p. 127; Jaiswal, Suvira, *The Origin and Development of Vaiṣṇavism*, p. 90; Gonda, *Op. cit.*, p. 213.
125. Dhal, *Ibid.*
126. Tait. Sam. 7.4.42; Dhal, *Ibid.*, p. 19.
127. Tait. Sam 7.3.7.1.
128. Dhal, *Ibid.*, p.p 32-34.
129. 3.1.3.7. - fn. 368, Agrawala, P. K., *Op. cit.*, p. 96.
130. *Ibid.*, p. 23 ff.
131. Gonda, *Op. cit.*, pp. 186-7
132. S'B.6, 7,3,7.
133. 13.12 and 20-24.
134. Oldenberg in Gonda, *Ibid.*, p. 215.
135. Agrawala, P.K., *Op. cit.*, p. 94.
136. 3.13.2
137. 1; 4; 5-Gonda, *Op. cit.*, p. 217.
138. I. 18; Agrawala P.K., *Op. cit.*, p. 95.
139. AV. VII. 115, 1-4. *Ibid.*
140. AV. I. 18, *Ibid.*
141. *Mādhyandina recension*, 14.9.38; Agrawala, P.K., *Ibid.*, fn. 366.
142. S'B. 8.4.4.11.
143. Jaiswal, *The Origin and Development of Vaiṣṇavism*, pp. 89-90.
144. Dhal, *Op. cit.*, p. 45.
145. Swali, Haridas - Jyesthā - the Ambivalent Goddess, p. 332, JASOB, Vols. 56-59/1981-84.
146. Dhal, *Op. cit.*, p. 48.
147. Dhal, *Ibid.*, p. 56.
148. 5-6 stanzas.
149. 4, 5, 13.
150. Gonda, *Op. cit.*, p. 220.
151. Jaiswal S - *Op. cit.*, p. 90.
152. Gonda examines this aspect exhaustively *Op. cit.*, Pp.220/1
153. Gonda, *Ibid.*, p. 215.
154. Jaiswal, *Op. cit.*, p. 93.
155. Dhal, *Op. cit.*, p. 127.
156. RV. II. 6.7.
157. Jaiswal, *Op. cit.*, p. 98.
158. XII. 221. 79-83.

159. I.9.105; Jaiswal, *Op. cit.*, p. 96.
160. I.41.1, *Ibid.*
161. XII. 59. 13.3.
162. Mbh. 1.60.13.
163. Mbh. 12.218.11 ff.
164. Mbh. 1.189.48.
165. 2.60.13.
166. Dhal, *Op. cit.*, p. 111.
167. Gonda, Pūṣan and Saraswatī, p. 10, Book Review, JRAS, 1986, no. 1, pp. 120-21.
168. Davane, G.V., The Goddess Saraswati in Sanskrit Literature, *Journal of the University of Bombay*, Vol. XXXVII, Oct. 1968; p. 72.
169. ṚV., X. 25.
170. ṚV. 1.3.11; II.3.8; VII.35.11; X.65.13.
171. Tr. Hale, W.E. - *Asura in Early Vedic Religion*, p. 63.
172. Airi, Raghunath - Vāg Vai Sarasvatī, p. 201, AIOC, Varanasi, Oct. 1968.
173. Airi, *Ibid.*, pp. 203-04,
174. *Ibid.*, p. 206.
175. ṚV. II. 41.16.
176. ṚV. VII. 95.4.
177. Airi, *Ibid.*, p. 210, fn. 1.
178. Airi, *Ibid.* pp. 208-9.
179. S'B. 12.9.1.13; ṚV. X 177.2.
180. 7.36.8; *Maruts - 7.36.7; and Indra.-* 8.46.11.
181. Gonda, *Op. cit.*, Ch. 4.
182. VS XVIII. 37.
183. *Vāgvai Śaraswatī Vāk tu Saraswatī;* S'B.2.5.4.6; 3.9.1.7; 7.5.1.31; 11.2.4.9; 12.9.1.13; Tait Br. 1.3.4.5; 3.8.11.2; Gopatha Br. II. 1.20; etc., Ait Br. 3.1; 2.24; 6.7, Agrawala, P.K., *Op. cit.*, p. 89. fn. 215.
184. XIV. 2.15.
185. 6.5.1.9.
186. 2.4.6.2.
187. AV XIX. 31.9-10.
188. AV. VII. 10.1.
189. AV. V. 23.1.
190. AV. V. 25. 1-13.
191. Mānava Gr. Sū. 1.11.18.
192. Tait. Br. 2.5.7.4.
193. 11.4.3.16.

194. 3.2.4.3f.
195. S'B. 3.2.1. 18-23.
196. Dikshit, S.K., *The Mother Goddess*, p. 47.
197. Davane, *Op. cit.*, p. 73.
198. Skand. P. 7.33.96, Kinsley, D, *Hindu Goddesses*, p. 58, fn. 13.
199. Mbh. VI. 23-12.5; Matsya P. 13.51-52; Padma P.V. 17.215, etc., also tantra cudamanī and mahatantra; Dikshit, S.K., *Ibid* p. 47, fn 7.
200. ṚV. VII. 96.4 ff.
201. Kosambi, D.D., *Origin of Brahman Gotras*, p. 74.
202. Brahmavaivarta, Padma and Skanda; Purānic references taken from Gupta, A.S. - Conception of Saraswati in the Purāṇas in Purāṇa IV. 1.
203. IV.7.27.
204. I.23.34.
205. Bhaviṣya P. II.4.47.
206. Skanda P. VII.33.33.
207. Gupta, A.S., *Op. cit.*, p. 57.
208. Agrawala, P.K., *Op . cit.*, p. 65.
209. YV. IX.5; XVIII. 13; AV. VII. 6.4; - Dikshit, *Op. cit.*, p. 48, fn. 2.
210. Gonda, *Aspects of Early Viṣṇuism*, p. 176.
211. Agrawala, P.K., *Op. cit.*, p. 64.
212. Dikshit, *Op. cit.*, p. 78.
213. James, *Myth and Ritual in the Ancient Near East*, p. 102.
214. Slater, Gilbert - *The Dravidian Elements in Indian Culture*, pp. 75-76; cf also Sir John Marshall. *Mohenjo Daro and the Indus Civilisation*, Vol. I, p. 58.
215. ṚV. II. 32.6-8; X. 184.2.
216. Mānava Gr Sū. 2.18.2; Kauśika. S. 35.5; Bṛhad. Up. 6.4.21.; etc; and Mantṛa Br.1.4.7; Agrawala, P.K., *Op. cit.*, fn 509.
217. AV 14.2.15 & 21.
218. YV. XI.56; Kāthaka Saim. XVI.5; Mait. Sam. II.7.5; S'B. VI.5.1.10; and, TS.IV.5.3. Dikshit, S.K., *Op. cit.*, p. 52, fn. 2.
219. Gonda, *Aspects of Early Viṣṇuism*. p. 226.
220. Gonda, *Ibid.*, p. 228.
221. Bhattacharyya, N.N., *History of Śākta Religion*, p. 18.
222. Agrawala, P.K., *Op. cit.*, p. 104.
223. 3.13.2.
224. No. 535 - Agrawala , P.K., *Op. cit.*
225. Taitt. Sam. 2.4.6.2.
226. Taitt. Br. 2.5.7.4 and S'B. 11.4.3.16, Agrawala , P.K., *Op. cit.*, fn 432.
227. 2.13.6.

228. XII. 1.6.3, *Śriyā mā dehi Bhūtyā.*
229. 2.17.9.
230. V.S. XII. 65.
231. IV. 5.7.6
232. VIII. 21.3.
233. III. 17.8-9.
234. 2.17.9.
235. 2.17.1-19.
236. 4.4.28-30.
237. 2.10.7 and Kāthaka G.S. 71.7, Agrawala, P.K., *Op. cit.*, fn. 476.
238. Artha Śāstra II, 1; Jayadissa Jātaka No 513 - Romila, Thapar, *From Lineage to State*, p. 123 fn 14.
239. ṚV VII. 104.34, Agrawala, P.K., *Op. cit.*, p. 121.
239a. Monier Williams, *English Sanskrit Dictionary* 1981. p. 811, col 1.
240. No. 1280, Agrawala, *Ibid.*, p. 122.
241. VI. 47.18.
242. 2.15.19.
243. cf Sn Māyā, *The Special Power of the Asuras*, Infra.
244. Dikshit, *Op. cit.*, p. 59.
245. Hopkins, E.W. - E. M, p. 226.
246. Muṇḍ. Up. 1.2.4.
247. Weber in J. Muir's *Original Sanskrit Texts*, Vol. IV, London, 1863, p. 36 as mentioned in Agrawala, P.K., *Op. cit.*, p. 118, fn. 769.
248. 10.18 *"namo hiraṇyabāhave hiraṇya pataye Ambikā pataye Umāpataye namo namaḥ"*.
249. 2.9.14.
250. 40.4.3.
251. X.127.
252. Stanza 13 - *"Ya imam Durgastavaṁ punyaṁ rātrau sadā paṭheṭ"*.
253. Stanza 3.
254. Stanza 4.
255. Stanza 5.
256. XIX. 50.2 *"no adya pārayati durgāni viśvahā."*
257. Dikshit, *Op. cit.*, p. 50.
258. ṚV. I. 83.3.
259. ṚV. I. 56.4. *Op. cit.*, fn. 248.
260. Some Observations on the Relations Between "Gods" and "Powers" in the Veda, *JRAS*, 1982, no. 1, p. 16, fn. 15.
261. *Ibid.*, pp. 14-15.

262. James, *Myth and Ritual in the Ancient Near East*, p. 289.
263. Bhattacharji, *Op. cit.*, p. 5.
264. *Ibid.*, p. 34.
265. Bhattacharyya, N.N., *Ancient Indian Rituals and Their Social Content*, p. 15.
266. Vāj. Saṁ XXIII. 22-32.
267. II. 1.3.
268. Thaper, R, *Ancient Indian Social History* pp. 166 ff.
269. ṚV. X.85.46.
270. V. 147.148.154.
271. Briffault, Robert, *The Mothers*, Vol. 1, p. 347.
272. Altekar, A.S., *The Position of Women in Hindu Civilization*, pp. 336-39.
273. *Ibid.*, p. 32.
274. *Ibid.*, p. 350.
275. For further details cf. chapters 1, 2, 7 and 9 of Altekar's book cited above.

CHAPTER - IV
THE MATṚS AND KĀLĪ

There are two important features of the goddess cult in India. The wide diffusion of the cult of groups of goddesses, and, the evolution of the cult of the Great Goddess. The former seems earlier and had formed a foundation for the growth of the latter.

References to the Mātṛs in the epic are around 1st century A.D.

There are various groups of goddesses, and the size of the groups vary. In the smaller groups, there is a tighter unity of identity, sometimes even going as far as similarity in names. The larger groups are amorphous, and the members seem to be put together in a haphazard fashion, their only common feature being their sex. These groups further contain benevolent as well as malevolent goddesses and both types have separate rites of pacification and adoration.

The origin of the groups of goddesses seems to be Dakṣa's daughters. The list of these vary in different accounts; but they contain names of well-known goddesses and demonesses, as for example —Śrī, Aditi, Nirṛti, Diti, etc.

Mātṛs

Mātṛs are a group of goddesses with possible non-Brahminic origins. In the Brahminised version, they are seven or eight, sometimes sixteen. But, in their popular, non-Brahminical form, they expand upto two hundred. Such large lists are connected with the birth of Skanda-Kārtikeya, in the epic,[1] as well as the Purāṇas.[2] In the Mbh.[3] more than 18 Mātṛs are named as:

Vinatā, Pūtanā, Rakṣasī, Aditi (or Ravatī), Diti, surabhi, Saramā, Kadrū, Lohitāyani, and Āryā, and others. All but *Vinatā* and *Lohitāyani* afflict or devour children or pregnant women. Only three out of these are benevolent:

> *Pādapānāṁ mātā Karañjanilayā* (V. 22);
> *Lohitasyodadheḥkanyā dhātrī Skandasya sā smṛtā/*
> *Lohitāyanirityevaṁ kadambe sāhī pūjitā//* (V. 39); and
> *Puruṣeṣu yathā Rudrastathāryā pramadāsvapi/*
> *Āryā mātā Kumārasya pṛthakkāmārthamijyate//* (V. 40).

Sometimes Śakuni is also mentioned in the group. She is a hen-vulture and Pūtanā is a putrid female monster.[4] Pūtanā is also said to be the special goddess of the Mathura region.[5]

Mātṛs appear as ogresses and demoniac beings in these instances. These are known as *Bāla-Grahas.* They are malevolent towards children, either devouring or afflicting them with diseases. Many propitiatory rites are enjoined in order to appease them and ward off their evil influence. Skanda was their leader and his power increased when he married Devasenā. In *Suśruta Saṁhitā Uttarantara,*[6] Skanda sends his followers to *Śiva* who advises them to afflict only those children whose family does not honour gods, etc.

The worst or the most powerful of these Bāla-Grahas, is Revatī, who in the Purāṇas and in iconography is referred to as the wife of Balarāma.[7] She is of such high stature that, in the Mbh., she is referred to as equivalent to Aditi. Revatī and Ṣaṣṭī are two sisters of Skanda. Ṣaṣṭī is depicted in the Yaudheya (2nd-3rd cent. A.D.) coins with six heads, representing the six mothers whose son was Skanda.[8] In Vākpati's Gauḍavaho she is depicted as the attendant of the fierce mountain goddess Vindhyavāsinī. This is an instance of a popular malevolent goddess evolving into a benign goddess, by developing positive traits.

Revatī and Ṣaṣṭī are closely associated (in the *Kāśyapa Saṁhitā*) and both are identified with the Buddhist Hāritī. The cult of Ṣaṣṭī has been identified with that of Śrī-Lakṣmī.[9] Parallel to these mother goddesses who evolved into protectors of children, are the Cretan mother goddess, Roman Diana, and Teutonic Freyja[10].

Again, it has to be noted that the cult of the malefic beings was very popular in the first centuries A.D. of the Christian era, and they had to be Brahminised.

The *Aṅgavijjā,* a Jaina text[11] contains names of goddesses, who are said to be the wives and daughters of *Asuras,* Nāgas,

Gandharvas, Rākṣasaṣ Kinnaras, etc. Foreign influence, particularly Greek, is seen in the names of certain goddesses like Anāhitā, Airāṇī, Śālimālinī, etc.

In the Purāṇas and Sanskrit literature, these goddesses are said to be worshipped preferably by women. Their lists are said to contain Aryan and mleccha goddesses. Aryan, non-Aryan and folk elements played a part in the development of group goddesses' cult.

Origins of the Mātṛ cult cannot be historically proved. In the Indus Valley, we have a seal of seven figurines which have been identified by some scholars as the seven Mātṛs. The ṚgVeda has reference to the Sapta Svasāraḥ often identified with Sapta-Sindhavaḥ, the seven rivers. They could also have astral connections. Revatī, one of the prominent Mothers, is also a star. Further, they were connected with Apsaras. Both stars and Apsaras have malevolent connotations in Indian literature.

Examining the word 'Mātṛ' in the context of racial culture, we are brought to the culture of the Austric people. They had once spread all over North India. They were food-gatherers and used a common word for their digging stick, (its usage was earlier than the plough) and their cult icon, the phallus—Lakuṭa, laguḍa, and, liṅga. Their Mother-Goddess was called Mātṛkā (Polynesian *matariki*). This word has been used subsequently in India for the Divine Mothers.[12]

In spite of their early connections they are definitely referred to in literature only from the *Mahābhārata* onwards. The cult's formative years may have been the early centuries of the Christian era, and it must have grown in popularity over the centuries. This would have resulted in iconographic representations around the 6th century A.D.

The Mātṛs were never worshipped individually, and they always appeared in groups. This was their peculiar characteristic. The exceptions may have been Cāmuṇḍā and Vārāhī who were individually popular in the early Gupta period.

They are usually seven in number with Brāhmī leading them and Cāmuṇḍā bringing up the rear. Their names are: Brāhmī, Māheśvarī, Kaumārī, Vaiṣṇavī, Aindrī, Vārāhī, and Cāmuṇḍā. In iconography, Cāmuṇḍī is replaced by Nārasiṁhī, and it is contended that Nārasiṁhī is just another form of Cāmuṇḍī.[13] The point to be noted is they are the śakti or inherent power of the gods, and not their wives. For instance, Śacī is the wife of Indra, not Aindrī, Śrī-Lakṣmī is the wife of Viṣṇu, not Vaiṣṇavī. The one exception is Cāmuṇḍā, who is not the śakti of any god but of Durgā and is a goddess in her own right. The DM. gives an awkward derivation of her name,[14] as the killer of Caṇḍa and Muṇḍa. It may be inferred that the order and number of the Mātṛs were chosen from the non-Aryan groups of goddesses and became the Brāhminised local goddesses. Cāmuṇḍā must have been a powerful goddess with a popular cult, and therefore her name must have been unexplained.

The Aṣṭaka rites are domestic offerings to the dead. The Ekāṣṭaka rite was probably a new year rite performed to the goddess of the same name, as seen in the Atharva Veda.[15] Later on, funerary rites must have got assimilated with this rite. The Aṣṭakas also must have been Mātṛs to whom repeated offerings (svāhā) are made. The oblations of wine and flesh made at the cross roads point to the folk origins of the goddesses. The group characteristic also show "their low-graded, soil-born culture".[16] Goblins, ogres, and imps are thought of in the plural and this also points towards the ferocious or negative character of the Mātṛs. They are almost always connected with Rudra-Śiva, Agni, and Kumāra. They are goddesses without husbands and are analogous to the Dravidian village goddesses. They are standardised into seven types. These goddesses without consorts may have some relationship with Cybele[17]. No doubt the seven tongues of fire[18] represent the Sapta Mātrs: Kālī, Karālī, Manojavā, Sulohitā, Sudhūmravarṇā, Spulaṅginī, and Viśvarucī. There are also goddesses called Vidyās, eight in number according to Devī P.[19] and increased to ten in the Tantras.[20] They were known as Sāt-Bahinī or seven sisters in the Madhya Pradesh, which show the folk connections of the goddesses.

The literary sources for the goddesses cult would be the *Mahābhārata, Harivaṁśa,* the *Purāṇas,* namely *Vāmana, Varāha, Matsya,* and the DM section of the *Mārkaṇḍeya*, Bāṇa's *Caṇḍīśataka* and Gauḍavaho's *stuti* of *Vindhyavāsinī*. The epithets in the eulogies pertaining to the goddess are usually taken as a method of syncretizing autochthonous goddesses into the Big Tradition. Sometimes, though, the names describe the goddess only in an attempt to impress on her devotees the idea of her universality. Mbh. specifically gives seven names of *Mātrs : Kālī, Halimā, Rudrā,*

Bṛhalī, Āryā, Palālā and *Mitrā*. These are obscure names and must be belonging to the lowest layers of the folk-lore tradition.[21] In this age, the number of local goddesses were legion and this was an attempt to bring order out of chaos. Further, the Bhāgavata movement taught that all minor deities were but manifestations of the Great Deity. Similarly all local goddesses were made manifestations of the Great Goddess and this also resulted in unifying all minor cult deities.

Mātṛs had a distinct existence and characteristics, despite the growth of the cult of the Mother-Goddess. As mentioned earlier they are connected with Śiva, Agni, and Skanda. Their connection with Śiva is both in myth and ritual. Śiva produces twelve spirits who spread diseases amongst children and gives them to Skanda. Of these seven were female and five male.

Agni gets infatuated with the wives of the seven sages and Svāhā who is attracted to Agni assumes the form of each of the wives of the sages. Agni's seeds are deposited on the top of the Śvetagiri. This spot is protected by poisonous snakes, wild animals, Piśācas, and Rākṣasas. Skanda is born out of the tremendous energy of the seeds.[22] Skanda is so powerful that Indra and the gods ask the Mātṛs to vanquish him. This task proves impossible. The Mātṛs become supplicants and Skanda[23] asks them not to afflict children below sixteen years of age and they agree. In a further story, in the Śalya Par. of the epic, Skanda with the assistance of the Mātṛs defeats and destroys the demons Tāraka and Mahiṣa. The Mātṛs are essentially demonical. In the former episode, the Mātṛs are neither numbered nor named. In the latter there are 190 Mātṛs and they seem to be artificially thought up. In the earlier episodes, in the Mbh., the lists of the goddesses contain both good and evil deities. Their nomenclature could be an euphemism. In a further story, Indra hits Skanda with his vajra. The Mātṛs emerge out of his side along with Viśākha. They are seven in number, and are named.

In the Purāṇas, there are some accounts of the Mātṛs. The *Vāmana P.* account of the Mātṛs assisting Devī in killing Sumbha and Niśumbha is identical to that of the DM. The peculiarity of the *Vām P.* is that the Mātṛs appear from the limbs of the goddess[24]. After the killing of the demons, Śumbha and Niśumbha, the gods praise the Goddess and address her (62) by the names of the Mātṛs. In the DM, they help her kill *Raktabīja*.[25] In the *Varāha* and *Matsya*

Purāṇas the Mātṛs aid Śiva in killing *Andhaka*, similar to the *Raktabījavadha* in the DM. In the *Matsya P.*, the Mātṛs are created to drink the blood of Andhaka. After Andhaka's death, these *Mātṛs* become uncontrollable. Viṣṇu creates others under him and these Vaiṣṇavite Śaktis subdue the Śaivite ones. Many of the Vaiṣṇavite and Śaivite names overlap. After Viṣṇu leaves with his Śaktis, Śiva advises his śaktis to be benevolent and to bestow their grace .on their devotees. The Śiva-Andhaka fight is also said to be symbolic as the fight between Vidyā and Avidyā, each of the Mātṛs representing one abstract negative quality like Kāma, Krodha, *Madha*, *Lobha* and *Moha*. Since the Mātṛs are always represented in iconography as flanked by Vīrabhadra and Gaṇeśa, it may seem as an attempt to syncretise different mother goddess cults of the folk level with Śaivism. The fights involving the Mātṛs are also with Andhaka and Mahiṣa, both probably symbolically representing two tribes, Andhakas and Māhiṣmatīs, and may represent fight between rival sects.

From the Purāṇic accounts, it is seen that the Mātṛs were malefic: (1) they were sent to kill Skanda (2) they lap up the blood of Andhaka/Raktabīja; and (3) in the literary accounts of them which follow, they are seen as ugly and ferocious, and, their rites are performed in the night of the dark fortnight, on the crosroads. They were primarily fierce goddesses always appearing in groups. They were propitiated with ghastly rites. The lists of the mothers given in the *Purāṇas* are artificial and this is proved by the fact that there are imaginary names alongside names of well-known goddesses; and both benevolent and malevolent goddesses are grouped together. These could be divinized by villagers, of women who lost their children or died at childbirth and characterized as vengeful.

It is evident that there are a large number of autochthonous goddesses, Brahminised into amorphous groups of anonymous members, who were later made into the śaktis of male gods, and took their ornaments and weapons. Even after being Brahminised by settling their numbers and naming them, their essential evil nature and ferocity is never forgotten. Jarā was worshipped in homes in Rajagriha. Later she merged with Jātahariṇī. Just as all the Rākṣas, as horrible Grahas and Yakṣas were merged into the cult of Skanda, so also all terrible and destructive mother goddesses were assimilated into the cult of the wife of Skanda—

Ṣaṣṭī, Bhadrā or Devasenā.[26]

Literary References

A glance through the references to the Mātṛs in the Sanskrit literature would give an idea of the extent and popularity of the cult.

In the Bṛhat Saṁhitā, (58.56), it is mentioned that the icons of the Mātṛs should be made with the signs of the devatās whom they resemble in their names, like *Indra, Indrāṇī*, etc.

"Mātṛgaṇaḥ kartavyaḥ svanāmarūpakṛtacinnaḥ/"

In Bharata's *Nāṭyaśāstra* (III. 67), an offering is made to them: *"Namo(a)stu nāṭyamātṛbhyo Brāhmyādyābhyo namo namaḥ."*

In the *Cārudattam*, of Bhāsa (Act. I), the Vidūṣakas says, that he has brought flowers and undergarment for Cārudatta who has performed religious rites for Ṣaṣṭhī.

"Tat Ṣaṣṭhī kṛta devakāryasya tatrabhavatasCārudattasya kāraṇād gṛhītāni sumanaso(a)ntarīyavāsasca."

And (in Act III), Brahmāṇī gives a pearl necklace to *Vidūṣaka* as a formality of making a gift on Ṣaṣṭhī.

In Bāṇa's *Harṣacarita* (p.46), the king is shown by the Bhairavācārya a delapidated Mātṛ temple: *"Asya jīrṇaMātṛgrhas-yottareṇa bilvavātikā madhyaste"* (The śiṣya informs the Bhairavācārya, whose temple it was). There are further mentions of the Mātṛs in the same work. (5th *Ucchvāsa*, p. 21; 7th *Ucchvāsa*, p. 65).

In Bāṇa's *Kādambarī* (p. 145), Queen Vilāsavatī visits the Mātṛkā shrines of Māheśvarī, etc:

"Darśitapratyayāni sannidhāna Mātṛkābhavanāni jagāma." She propitiates the *Mātṛkas* to obtain a son, and speaks of the power and popularity of the goddesses.

In Śūdraka's *Mṛcchakaṭikam* (Act I), Cārudatta asks Vidūṣaka to offe r bali to the Mātṛs at the crossroads, in the evening twilight: *"... tvamapi catuṣpathe Mātṛbhyo balimupahāra"*. When the *Vidūṣaka* refuses to oblige, Cārudatta sets about to do so himself as it is an obligatory ritual for a gṛhastha (v. 16).

The casual way in which these references are seen integrated in these texts gives the impression that the cult was prevalent and popular in those periods.

Philosophy

The idea that the Mātṛs are śaktis of gods is definitely later than the metaphysical idea of a transcendental Feminine Principle because each god has a śakti. Though Tantrism is in evidence around the first century B.C., in literature, in *Bṛhatsaṁhitā* and iconography of the medieval temples, the *Tantric* support of the *Śākta* cult is only around the sixth century A.D. This is evidenced in the iconography of the period. But this is beyond the purview of this study.

The Varṇamālā or the alphabets are said to be correlated. The vibrations or the dhvanis of the alphabets are said to concretize as the Mātṛs.[27] It is understood that the Vedic metaphysics of the avyakta coalescing with the existing mother-goddesses cult must have flowered with Tantrism. This was ritualistically established in the post 7th century A.D. Tantric works, but the process was in the making over a long period. The correlation of the Varṇamālā, or the alphabets and the Mātṛs was seen as an example of a further correlation between the mundane and the sacred, or, the microcosm and the macrocosm. This leads to the esoterics of the *avyakta* (unmanifest) and the *vyakta* (manifest) philosophy of the *Upaniṣads*.[28]

Kālī

Kālī is the Terrible Mother. She is at the same time ambivalent as well as, not so. The term "Terrible Mother" is ambivalent. She is "Terrible" because she is the image of fierce negative qualities, and "Mother", because that is how her devotees approach her. The Great Goddess split into two images, and Kālī is the fierce half of her, personifying all negative qualities. Ambivalence is a common characteristic of South Asian Goddess cults[29] and has parallels in Indo-European religions. But Hindus prefer to have two goddesses to represent the two opposites. Her origin could be traced to a lone Nirṛti, though again the need to trace every popular (Purāṇic) god to a Vedic prototype is questionable.[30] Further back, it is traced to the IV civilization, and its nebulous ideologies, behind a lone artefact. As much as she answered to the needs of her devotees in the early periods, she is powerful and answers to those of the modern man. Her uniqueness is in the fact that, in spite of rationalising and belabouring metaphysical values to inexplicable mythical figures or incidents, she has grown steadily in strength, so much so that she has been a figurehead in modern politics. Unless gods are multivalent, they would not survive the changing values of any culture; further, the "motif" should be capable of varied interpretations—on sociological, as well as, psychological grounds, over and above the religious one. Kālī, the Mother, who anomalously has no children of her own in myths, has the strength and power to attract devotees through all ages down to Ramakrishna and Ramaprasad, in spite of her repelling fierceness. The following study makes an attempt to find an explanation for her popularity.

Origin the Goddesses

Tracing the origin of the goddess Kālī into IVC, it is surmised that the small figurines of the cult, may be her representations; or, she was represented not anthropomorphically but symbolically. IVC is seen as a society where the Great Goddess was worshipped along with an inferior spouse god. Particularly, the dancing nude girl is taken as the representative figurine of the priestess, who symbolised the Goddess. Because of this, there was no separate representation of the Goddess and many such examples may have been kept around the Great Bath, where ritualistic lustrations may have been involved in the goddess worship. But the dancing girl in her free and provocative attitude seems more a secular image than a cult figure. A connection between Kālī and the Zhob figurines could be seen.[31] Some scholars see a connection between the more benign Kulli goddess and Kālī or Caṇḍikā.[32]

Coming to the Vedic period where literary evidence can coroborate our premise, Nirṛti, the goddess of death and destruction seems the sure choice. One scholar[33] has mentioned Rātrī Devī, sister of Uṣas, as a prototype for Kālī. Both Uṣas and Rātrī were independent goddesses, untrammelled by a spouse god. But both these did not grow in stature and faded out quite early. Nirṛti dissipated her powers amongst Kālī, Chinnamastā, Cāmuṇḍā, Caṇḍī, etc., before fading out from the pantheon.[34] Further, Nirṛti is warded off by prayers, whereas Kālī is invoked in periods of war, etc., and revels in blood sacrifices. But, despite these few differences, it could be said that Kālī takes over from where Nirṛti left off. Pṛthivī, the great Mother Goddess, was paired more often than not with Dyaus. She had no independent stature.

Aditi and Diti developed into spouses of the Purāṇic Viṣṇu.

It is not that the idea of negative powers was not active in the Aryan mind and that the Aryan gods were purely luminous and belonged to the bright heavens. During the *Brāhmaṇa* period, certain gods were made guardians of the eight directions. Only East was ruled by *Indra* and other solar gods. The rest of the seven-eighths of the area of the directions are given over to dark gods: North-East-*Īśāna*, North-Rudra (a terrific god), and Kubera (a subdivinity) all these leaning towards the dark gods; West-Varuṇa, and the setting sun; S.W.-Nairṛta, South-Yama and the manes, S.E.-Agni, who is both malefic and benific. This is an important development in the religious thought.[35]

It is strongly felt that it is not right to trace every popular god to the Vedic pantheon. The tendency to trace Kālī to the Great Vedic Goddess is as puerile as to try and see Vedic antecedents for Skanda, Kṛṣṇa, or, Rāma[36] to an earlier Indra or Varuṇa. It is further argued that Kālī is a goddess of a great stature, and a goddess in her own right; she need not be subsumed under a Great Goddess, though it is more valid to state that she is a facet of the Goddess. Kālī has given far more to the Great Tradition by her entry into it, than she has received from it. If it is puerile to trace Kālī's resemblence to Vedic goddesses, it may be stated that a seed like Nirṛti, the Vedic goddess of decay, destruction and death is sufficient to take roots, envelope autochthonous symbols and luxuriate into the later fierce goddess Kālī. In the Tantras, her blackness is interpreted that all dichotomies resolve in her, like all colours cease to be differentiated in black.

Kālī is a goddess originally worshipped (propitiated would be a more appropriate word) by tribal and indigenous people of the hilly and peripheral areas like the Pulindas, Barbaras, the cowherd tribes, Ābhiras, etc. Mātaṅgī is the goddess of the Mātanga tribes, and Caṇḍālī of the Caṇḍāla tribes. These goddesses were associated with Śiva in a half-hearted way. These and other village goddesses were worshipped for their own powers, which they possessed, not due to any marital status. The cult of the village goddesses in Tamil Nadu, is closely related to Kālī worship, and the goddesses are malefic but addressed as Ammā or Āttāḷ. They are blood-thirsty and sacrifices are regularly offered to them. They have their shrines in the outskirts of villages. Māriammā, Māriāttāḷ (in Tamil Nadu), Polarammā, Gaṅgamma (in Andhra Pradesh) are goddesses of diseases who strike undevoted people with epidemics and are propitiated to ward off their evil effects. In North India, Sītalā is a similar goddess. There is evidence to note that Kālī and similar fierce goddesses were worshipped over a wide area of India.[37] She was absorbed slowly into the Great Tradition, whence her popularity grew gradually. But she retained her character of malevolency. She rejoiced in bloody sacrifices.

The name Kālī may have arisen from Greek thought, with a Sanskrit root which meant 'to rotate', 'to turn around'. This designation may have come to mean time as the destroyer. She could have been the consort of Kāla, Eternal Time and later on started to denote Death.[38] Her association with darkness and death seems to come much later. She could have been a regional deity of South India and the myths wherein she is shown as suffering defeat in a dance contest with Śiva may be to explain the defeat of her cult at the hands of the Brahmins. Though she was brought into the Śiva cult, by marriage in the DM, she retained much of her original fierceness.

Development

The AV mentions only the masculine Kāla (Time). But in the Śānkhāyana Āraṇyaka, the femine Kālī occurs but with ominous malefic connotations. A man approaching his death may see as a vision in dream, a yellow or black coloured woman with dishevelled hair or shaved head[39]. But in the KaṭhakaGS Kālī is a goddess, one among a list of deities, to be invoked at the time of the wedding ceremonies. The well-known verse in the Muṇḍaka Upaniṣad (1.2.4.) shows Kālī's affiliation to fire.

Kālī Karālī ca Manojavā ca
Sulohitā yā ca Sudhūmravarṇā/
Sphuliṅginī Viśvarucī ca devī
lelāyamānā iti saptajihvāḥ//

Manojavā the third name is one of the names of Yama and, this could be the reason why Devī was connected with Death in some Purāṇas.[40]

It is further felt[41] that Rudra was assimilated to Agni, and the Goddess, his spouse had to have a parallel development as seen in this verse. Moreover, the Goddess could be fierce due to developing these epithets, rather than to being worshipped by fierce tribals. So also is Durgā connected with Agni:

Tāmagnivarṇām tapasā jvalantīṁ Vairocanīṁ karmaphaleṣu juṣṭāṁ/

Durgāṁ Devīṁ Śaraṇamahaṁ prapadye sutarasi tarase namaḥ// (Taitt Ār. 10.1.2)

In the Kāṭhaka GS., Kālī and Bhadrakālī are mentioned as two goddesses worshipped in homes.[42]

Epic

In the Mbh., Kālī is mentioned in the Sabhā Parvan (II.2a) and in the Śalya Parvan (45.II.13). Kālikā is mentioned as two of the mothers associated with Kārtikeya. They are mentioned as wearing different kinds of clothing and speaking different languages. It may be an implication that they are goddesses belonging to the tribal fringes. In the Sauptika Parvan,[43] her terrible form is described, when she appears after the pāndavas are slaughtered. This is when Kālī entered the Great Tradition, but continued to be on its fringes.

Harivaṁśa

Viṣṇu goes to the nether world and asks the Great Goddess' help to annihilate Kaṁsa. He asks her to put her six embryos successively in Devakī's womb and he himself will be the seventh and eighth. At the same time as Kṛnisṇa's birth, in Śrāvaṇa. Kālī herself should be born to Yaśodā. Kālī thus becomes the sister of Kṛṣṇa. In the trinity Balarāma, Subhadrā, and Kṛṣṇa, in the Jagannath temple Puri, Subhadrā's origin has been traced to Durgā, and Ekānaṁśa.[44] As Ādyākālī in the nether world whom Viṣṇu propitiates she is the "elder one", and Kṛṣna's original mother.[45]

When Kaṁsa smashes and kills the baby girl, the terrifying form of the goddess comes out of the kośa of the dead infant similar to Aṁbikā's emergence out of Pārvatī's kośa in the DM.

In the Vaiṣṇava Purāṇas i.e., in the Viṣṇu and the Bhāgavata Purānas the role of Kālī is played down, whereas Durgā the luminiscent half is emphasized. This is seen as the influence of proper Smārta tradition which in the Pañcāyatana, included Durgā, not Kālī.[46]

Purāṇas

Devī Māhātmya (DM): This is the portion of the *Mārkaṇḍeya Purāṇa* slightly later than the main text. In this, the gods praise Pārvatī as she is going to take a dip in the Ganges. She asks to whom their praises are addressed. Out of her emerges a fair form and this form says it is herself they are praising. She is called Kauśikī because she emerged from the kośa of Pārvatī and the latter is left black in colour and gets name Kālikā. Kālī here can be seen as the dark residue after the emergence of the luminous one.

Devī splitting into Durgā or Kālī, or, into three goddesses, Mahākālī (Tāmasic), Mahālakṣmī (Rājasic), and Mahāsarasvatī (Sātvic) may be attempts to syncretize Aryan and un-Aryan goddesses, or, to mediate between them.

In Adh. 7.5., Śumbha's emissaries Caṇḍa and Muṇḍa meet Ambikā and tell her to accept Śumbha's hand in marriage. Looking at them Ambikā's face darkens in anger and from this anger Kālī emerges. She had a fierce face and held the following weapons in her hands - a noose, knife, and kaṭvāṅga; she wore a garland of human skulls, and was dressed in a tiger' skin. She was emaciated like a skeleton and looked frightening in her appearance. She had an enormous face, with eyes shrunken and red, tongue lolling and her roar filled the directions. She swallowed whole armies along with their weapons.

She killed and beheaded Caṇḍa and Muṇḍa and offered their heads to Durgā. Caṇḍikā, that is Ambikā names Kālī, Cāmuṇḍā, saying that because she killed Caṇḍa and Muṇḍa she gets this name. (26/27) This might be an effort, artificially syncretizing two powerful goddesses as the derivation of the name is not grammatically acceptable.[47]

Kālī again comes to help Durgā (8.53-54) to exterminate Raktabīja. She first swallows the asuras born of the blood drops of the demon (58-59), and then she drinks the demon's blood and Raktabīja falls dead. Blood is assimilated to semen. Thus when Kālī drinks the blood of the demon it is seen as the inversion of the act of procreation.[48] Kālī emanates from Durgā and is drawn back into her with all the other śaktis (10.4-5). Throughout, she is subservient to Durgā, comes to help her in a difficult situation and takes on to herself death and destruction, removing the stigma attached to such negative qualities from the Great Goddess. This is an example of the triumph of the Great Tradition over the Little Tradition. Kālī is the "embodied fury" of Durgā and helps Durgā out whenever the latter is faced with an enormous task.

Matsya Purāṇa

In the Matsya Purāṇa (chs. 146-60) Ekānaṁśā, the goddess of darkness goes to the room where Menā is giving birth to Pārvatī. She gives a portion of herself to the foetus, so that Pārvatī's form is complete. This goddess is born dark. Kālī in Kalañjara, Caṇḍikā in Makarandaka and Vindhyavāsinī in the Vindhyas are mentioned in this Purāṇa.[49]

Varāha Purāṇa : Raudrā Śakti of Śiva, his tāmasic Śakti, is known also as Kālarātri. She does penance on the Nīlā mountain. From her laughter, a number of goddesses who were deformed emerged and filled the world, and these helped the Goddess fight the demon Ruru. In this fight with Ruru (95.31). Devī kills the invincible asura and takes away his head and his leather shield. Therefore, she is known as Cāmuṇḍā. (32). The terrible goddess, who is the anmhilator, is called Kālarātrī. In a few verses (45-51), Śiva praises Devī by the epithets Kālarātrī, Mahākālī, Kālikā, Cāmuṇḍā, Kālī.

Vāmana Purāṇa

In Adh. 25 Kālī is born as the third daughter of Himavān and Menā. She is like a mass of collyrium and has eyes like a blue lotus. After Śiva and Pārvatī get married, Śiva playfully addresses Pārvatī as 'Kālī' (Adh. 28). Pārvatī feels insulted and goes away to do rigorous penance. Brahmā is pleased and grants her a golden complexion. Pārvatī leves her dark kośa behind, and this is called Kālī. Thus Kālī emerges from the negative nature of Pārvatī (23-24). Indra obtains Kālī as dakṣiṇā from Pārvatī, calling her Kauśikī, his sister, and installs her on the Vindhyas, and gives the lion as her vāhana. To connect an erstwhile most popular Vedic god to Kālī as her brother and involving him in establishing approved status to Kālī in her own natural habitat shows again the laboured attempt to push the Great Tradition over the Little Tradition. In this Purāṇa Durgā assuming many forms of the Mātṛs kills Caṇḍa and Muṇḍa herself[50] but is assisted considerably by Kālī. Durgā herself (V.56) is in her body half white and half black, i.e., the benign Durgā and the terrible Kālī, rides a donkey which animal is connected with Nirṛti.

Bhrukuṭīkuṭilād devyā lalāṭaphalakād drutaṁ/
Kālī karālavadanā niḥsṛtā yoginī śubhā// (29.56).

This Kauśikī has epithets Caṇḍikā, and Vindhyavāsinī in this Purāṇa. Durgā after beheading the two demons Caṇḍa and Muṇḍa, makes a fearsome ornament and offers this to Kālī, giving her a fresh name Caṇḍikā, and also a girdle of lion's skin. (78-79).

The episodes of the fights with Caṇḍa, Muṇḍa, Śumbha, Niśumbha and the Mahiṣavadha are earlier than those of the DM.[51]

Kālī's association with Śiva might have been due to the similarities in their origin and their characteristics. In this Purāṇa, in the marriage episode, the name merely means black in colour and she has none of the fierceness in character she acquires in the DM. But in the episode of the slaying of the demon, she is identical to the fierce goddess in the DM.

Devī Purāṇa

Devi Purāṇa which is an Upapurāṇa, but whose date is quite early c. 600 A.D., contains all the episodes between Devī and the demons that are in the Vāmana Purāṇa. Some new demons' names are also mentioned.

Viṣṇu Purāṇa

In this Purāṇa the Goddess' love of flesh and wine is referred to.[52]

Liṅga Purāṇa

Śiva requests Pārvatī to kill the Demon Dāruka. She merges in Śiva's person and comes out as Kālī, who exterminates Dāruka and his hosts, with assistance from her hosts of piśācas.[53]

Again she sets out to assist Śiva when he goes to annihilate the three cities. She is blood-thirsty, then becomes drunk with blood, and becomes unmanageably destructive. She is called the daughter of the Himālayas and is thus definitely identified with Pārvatī. She is born from Pārvatī's anger, i.e., negative emotions, and may be, is her alter ego.

In one more myth, Kālī is created out of the poison from Śiva's neck to kill the Demon Dāruka. After killing him, she goes berserk.

Śiva takes the form of an infant and suckles her anger out. She is calmed and both of them then dance.[54] In another variation,[55] Pārvatī creates out of herself a black maiden, to kill a demoness Dārukā. Śiva appeared as an infant at the cemetry. Kālī suckles him and he becomes angry, and she dances to calm him.

Between the two myths cited above, the gender of the demon is changed, creation of Kālī is changed and suckling angers Śiva and then Kālī dances to pacify him. In the former Śiva calms Kālī by reminding her of her role as the mother. In the latter her mother's role angers him and he is soothed by dance.

Dance is a metaphor for sexual intercourse. It is an auspicious occasion when a couple dance together. When danced alone, it upsets the world's equilibrium and is dangerous.[56]

In a Tamil version,[57] Kālī was created out of Pārvatī to kill the demons, and, after drinking their blood, she goes on a rampage. Śiva challenges her to a dance contest and he defeats her and clams her. Here again, Kālī is calmed not by an emphasis on her motherly aspect, but on her sexuality. In another South Indian myth,[58] after Śumbha and Niśumbha are killed, Kālī becomes uncontrollable, and she challenges Śiva to a dance contest and she is defeated and quelled by Śiva.

Kālī goes out of control and Śiva has to calm her and make her power positive and beneficent. Gods also go on a spree of killing, but they never go out of control. The corollary could be that good females and goddesses are controlled by their spouses, i.e., nature controlled by culture. It may be that gods (culture) are in control of the situation, whereas, the goddesses (nature/*Prakṛti*) have to be controlled by the god (culture). Male divinities kill with logical objectives. Goddesses do not. As a further corollary to this, the Spouse Goddesses, who are subservient to their husband gods are benevolent by nature, but the Mother Goddess can be, and is ambivalent.

In iconography, there are few depictions of Kālī as a quiescent audience to Siva's dance[59]. But in Tantric Art she is always shown standing on the inert form of Śiva. This form of Kālī with a quiescent form of Śiva under her feet, and of Mahiṣa trampled and beheaded by the Goddess is reversed in later regional variations of the myth. Mahiṣa is killed and a liṅga sprouts on his neck. Devī has his head sticking to her hand (like the parallel myth of Śiva with Brahma's head on his hand); she washes it and finds a liṅga inside it. Similarly, Satī who is dismembered in an earlier myth dances on her husband's corpse.[60] These would be examples of transformation of ideas in myths.

Skanda Purāṇa

Kālī emerges out of Umā, who became Gaurī. Kālī's skin was like a dark blue lotus, terrifying in looks, three-eyed, holding a bell in her hand. Brahmā blessed her. (The bell is later on associated with the untouchables, and Śiva had tied it to his leg as he wandered in the Pine Forest).[61] She is dressed in yellow and red garments, and fully adorned with ornaments. Kālī is told by Brahmā that she is wholly the Goddess Pārvatī, she being fashioned out of that goddess. By these words of Brahmā, she is not just a portion of Pārvatī. A lion born earlier out of Pārvatī's anger is given to Kālī as her vāhana, as well as the emblem of her flag. She is told to go to the Vindhyas to kill Śumbha and Niśumbha, the generals of Tāraka. The yakṣa, Pāñcāla is given to her as her attendant, followed by a hundred thousand yakṣas.

Devī Bhāgvata Purāṇa

In the two myths in this Purāṇa,[62] Śiva is frightened and subdued by the fierce form of Pārvatī. In the first, Śiva refuses permission to Pārvatī to attend the yajña of her father, Dakṣa. She assumes Kālī's form, and, frightens the whole world. Śiva cowers before her. She tells him, that this is her true from and she took on the saumya form of Satī because of the strength of his penance.

In the second one, Sītā takes the form of Kālī, and annihilates the thousand-headed Rāvaṇa. After killing him, Kālī gets drunk on his blood and goes on a frenzy of earth-shattering dance. Śiva requested by the alarmed gods lies at her feet. Kālī is brought to her senses and, ashamed, she quietens.

In both these myths, Kālī when out-of-control, is supreme. But when she is in the role of Satī, i.e., 'spousified', she is docile. Further, these myths show the transformation of the god's power to subserviate the goddess' power. When Śaktism ascended, the Goddess became supreme again. In some myths, even if she did not overtly kill or devour the demons, or, enemies of the gods, she seems to assist Viṣṇu when he kills Hiraṇyakaśipu, Madhu, and Kaiṭabha, and Śiva when he goes to destroy the Three Cities. Thus in myths where she is not seen in her malefic aspect she is shown as the subservient spouse of Śiva.

According to R.P. Chanda,[63] the cult of Caṇḍī was an early cult. As culture advanced, she was syncretized with Devī, who was herself a syncretic figure made up of the mountain goddesses of the Himalayas and the Vindyas, a goddess worshipped by the Ābhīra shepherds, a vegetation spirit conceived as a female spirit and a war-goddess.

Kālī being assimilated to Durgā is seen as syncretizing autochthonous goddesses; but on the metaphysical plane it could be seen as the elevation of the fierce side of life.[64] Durgā is seen as an agricultural goddess first, and Caṇḍī, Kālī, Cāmuṇḍā, Kauśikī, Kātyāyanī and Vidhyavāsinī are said to have been added on later, because of Śākta bias.[65] Caṇḍī is never connected with Śiva and she is always called the Viṣṇumāyā and worshipped as Nārāyaṇī.[66] Bhadrakālī is an auspicious and calm form of Kālī and she makes her appearance in the late Vedic texts like the Śāṁkhāyana and Hiraṇyakeśī *Gṛhya Sūtras*.[67] The elitist groups are said to have taken to the cult of the Mother Goddess reluctantly from the indigenous, and oppressed tribes[68]. This premise would be based on various assumptions:

(1) that the idea of a war-goddess is later than the agricultural goddess; we would see from Nuemann that the ideation of war-goddesses is inherent in the images of the Unconscious, or the Uroboros.

(2) that the war-goddesses were looked to as succour by the oppressed and the under-privileged. Again, fertility and not agricultural goddesses need to precede mother-goddesses. Culturally, fierce goddesses of the earth and death were seen to have wide diffusion.

(3) if temples, literature in the elitist language-Sanskrit, the *Purāṇas* are our only proofs, this could be afforded only by "elitist" "oppressor" groups.

(4) the antiquity of *Śākta Tantrism* is a controversial subject and beyond our purview.

This study of the development of the goddess from the Vedic to the Purāṇic period will not be complete without a brief mention of her occurrence in Sanskrit literature.

Kālidāsa's *Kumārasaṁbhava*[69] has a mention of Kālī, though she is not of great importance here. Subandhu's Vāsavadattā mentions goddess Kātyāyanī or Bhagavatī whose form and role are identical to that of Kālī. Bāṇa's Kādambarī (7th cent. A.D.) describes Caṇḍī worship by Śabaras. Bhavabhūti's Mālatī-Mādhava (late 7th and early 8th century A.D.) has human sacrifice in respect to the goddess Cāmuṇḍā. She is identified with Śiva here. Bṛhatsaṁhitā mentions Aparṇā. Kālī is also called by this name sometimes. She may have been the goddess of Nagna-Śabaras; the Buddhist goddess Pūrṇaśabarī is mentioned in the above work as worshipped by a tribe of the same name.

The Village Goddesses

The village goddesses are not goddesses of protection against diseases. They are fierce goddesses of diseases and they inflict people with illness. The devotee by repeated prostrations and thanksgiving begs her to desist from inflicting diseases on him. During Hinduisation of these goddesses, they were merged into Devī, and further Brahminised by marriage to Śiva.

Each village or tribe has a separate goddess, and even if many areas worship the same goddess, the people tend to treat the goddess as a particular deity of their locality, and do not attach universal significance to her. One opinion is that the Śakti cult originated from the Aryans' concept of the wives of the gods. It did not owe anything to the non-Aryan goddess worship, and the Dravidians were only worshippers of ancestral spirits and ghosts.[70]

These goddesses belong to separate villages, and they are often unheard of beyond their jurisdiction. They are aniconically represented by sticks or stones. In contrast to the "High Gods," whose precincts many villagers may not have entered, the village goddesses are worshipped with great intensity as they are involved in the local, existential problems. These goddesses are wild and out-of-step with natural order and are usually not benign. These may have become Brahminised into Mātṛs, or at least contributed much towards the formulation of the concept of Mātṛs. Though they are sometimes said to have gods of the Great Tradition as spouses , they are more "married" to the village and this relationship with the village is symbiotic.

The ambivalence in the independent and powerful goddesses

is that, as benificent deities, they look to the orderly cultivation of the fields and protect the village from inimical onslaughts. But they have to be dangerously powerful to face any threats from outside. They are propitiated by sacrifices of fowls and animals, but specially male buffaloes. These goddesses do not provide a traditional model for women to follow. Often a "husband" in the shape of an animal is killed to appease them and this may show that the goddesses do not care for marital status, but use it to revivify their strength and they either humiliate their spouses or dominate them.

Elmore[71] gives fifteen legends of goddesses of Purāṇic origins. The legend of Reṇukā[72] is most noteworthy. Since the myth is well-known, only the further deviation is stated here. The sword held by Paraśurāma flew and cut off Renukā's head and, returned and cut off his hand also. At his request Renūkā's head is restored. She is a princess and her father's kingdom is under threat from the Rākṣasas. She goes to help her father and fights valiantly against the Rākṣasa host. But from each drop of Rākṣasa blood that hits the earth, sixty thousand more appeared. As a remedy, she asks her brother to extend his tongue and drink up the blood before any touched the earth and by this device the war was won. The similarity of the Raktabīja episode in the DM. is striking. The Brahmins have tried to draw the village deities into the Great Tradition, by including these deities into their Purāṇic legends. Sometimes the folk population have taken the idea of a Brahmin legend and adopted it to their deities.

Pārvatī is said to have been born as Reṇukā. She brought forth hundred and one śaktis who became the village goddesses. Reṇukā persuades her husband about her immense śakti and assumes a fierce form, with a thousand hands, each carrying a spike with a body impaled on it, and, with goblins in attendance.

Another legend has it that the Brahmin-headed body became Reṇukā and the Śūdra-headed body became Mātaṅgī, goddess of the Madigas. A further variation states that Jamadagani refused to accept Reṇukā as she was resurrected, and bade her go to the Madigas and become their goddess. She is Ellammā.[73] The Brahminisation took place either by marriage to Śiva, like Mīnākṣī, or, a mother of an avatāra of Viṣṇu like Reṇukā.

The Turanians and the Babylonians believed in a feminine principle as a Supreme Power. This was there in the non-Aryan cults of the village goddesses. The Aryans had to assimilate this idea into their religion.[74]

These deities are seen as the forerunners of the *Sāṁkhyan Prakṛti* and the goddess cult.

In South India, with philosophic changes brought in from North Indian and Kashmir Śaivism, independent goddesses were brought into Brahminism as Manonmaṇī, Śakti of Sadāśiva. Those that were not so connected remained village deities and had the following names: Piḍārī, Ellaiyamman, Aṅgāḷamman, Māramma, Māriyamman, Śelliyammāḷ or Śellāyī, etc. The last two names particularly denote Durgā as the sister, Śelvi of Viṣṇu.[75]

The Ḍākinīs of Tibetan Buddhism are the exact counterparts of Indian Kālī and the Mātṛs. Originally demonesses, with the pacific influence of the Buddha, they are subserviated as assistants in Buddhist Tantrism.[76]

Appearance

Kālī is a fierce and fearful-looking goddess, though in the *Karpurādi stotra* (verse 1) she is described as young and beautiful, and, (verse 18) with gently smiling face and in some later portrayals she is depicted with a round and cherubic face and a well-filled form.[77]

Her hair is loose and dishevelled, her mouth is bloody, and with fangs, and from her open mouth the tongue lolls out gruesomely. She has shrunken pendulous breasts, and emaciated stomach. She is usually naked, holds a raised sword in one hand, and, a noose and a fresh cut head in the other two hands. She wears a girdle of severed hands, a garland of skulls; and a skeleton of babies as ear ornaments. She stands on a corpse as a vehicle. Her association and dwelling place also add to the gruesomeness of her character.[78] Her two haunts are the cremation ground and the battlefield. In the battlefield, she crushes the enemies with her kaṭvāṅga (the bone of a forearm topped by a skull), and, she crunches and eats the corpses, and drinks their blood. In the cremation ground, she is surrounded by snakes, jackals and ghosts. Her laughter is an eerie howl filling the quarters. Her temples may now be found in the areas of human habitation, but earlier they were built near forests or, cremation grounds, or, on crossroads. She is satisfied by sacrifices and bloody offerings.

Her tribal origins need not necessarily be deduced from her black colour, since colour may symbolise something else altogether. Śiva a parallel god with similar ancient origins white in complexion, and, Viṣṇu, an out and out Aryan god is depicted as dark.

Cāmuṇḍā

She is similar to Kālī in appearance. She has an emaciated body, shrunken belly, a garland of skulls and seated on a corpse. She bares her teeth, has shrunken eyes, with round protruding eye-balls; she has bald head, with flames issuing from it; she has four arms and she holds in her hands, a chopper, a śūla, and a skull. Though it may be said that she has inherited most of her appearance from the Vedic Nirṛti, the latter is more negative in her qualities because, she absorbed more from village goddesses.[79] In some late Purāṇa texts, she is described as Yamī, consort of Yama.[80] Kālī issued from Ambikā's forehead and is christened Cāmuṇḍā. The form of Caṇḍikā and name Cāmuṇḍā occur perhaps for the first time in the DM (7.6 and 27 resp.).

The ugra forms of the goddesses were always war-goddesses, and, they fought and exterminated demons and enemies of the gods. Their setting is different from the saumya form of goddesses, like Umā, Pārvatī and Gaurī. The main ugra forms of Devī are Kālī, and Bhadrakālī, though a few minor forms are also enumerated here. These goddesses are black in character and are invoked to win over enemies. Over and above the earlier description of Kālī, Devī Bhadrakālī wears bloodied red clothes, and smears red sandalwood over her body. She is surrounded by goddesses Ugra Caṇḍā, Kotrā Kaiṭabhī. Her tongue lolls out to one yojana. She has eight arms, holding śakti, mudgara, vajra, kheta and a shield.[81] A point to be noted is, in South India, Bhadrakālī is in fact Durgā as slayer of Śumbha and Niśumbha and usually worshipped in Piḍārī shrines.[82]

In the Skanda P. [83] and Devī Bh. P[84] she is described mainly as a war-goddess, having an army made up of non-Aryans. The Śiva P. says the goddess has hundred hands. She has eighteen hands according to the Bṛhaddharma P.[85] and according to Kālikā P., [86] she has sixteen hands. She carries in her right hands, a kheṭaka, a leather shield, a bow and a noose. and a noose. She shines with bright rows of teeth and three red eyes and stands by her lion, piercing a buffalo with her lance and placing her left foot on it.[87]

Tripura Bhairavī is comparatively mild in appearance, but she stands on a corpse.[88]

Śivadūti is the śakti of Kauśikī/Kātyāyanī/Cāmuṇḍā. She is fearsome in appearance, shouting like a hundred foxes. Since she sent Śiva as the messenger in the fight with the demon Śumbha, she was named thus[89]. Her uniqueness lies in the fact that she is the only Śakti of a goddess. As Cāmuṇḍa was sportively breaking with her arrows, the weapons sent by the demons, Kālī walked in front, pulverizing the fallen enemies with her kaṭvāṅga.[90]

Dikkarvāsinī is black, and wears black garments, and, tiger's skin. She wears a garland and girdle of snakes. She holds a cāmara, and, a sword in her right hands, and a knife and a pot in her left hands. Her left foot is on a corpse, and the right foot on the back of a lion.[91]

Carmamuṇḍā is a fearful looking goddess, fond of wine, meat, etc. She is black, seated on a corpse and is surrounded by dead bodies. She removes all troubles of devotees, and, is therefore remembered first on all auspicious occasions.[92]

Śāntādevī is mounted on a tiger, and is said to be Ekāṅamśā or Yoganidrā.[93]

Jyeṣṭhā, there is evidence to believe, was a folk deity of the autochthonous people. In the North, she, along with Gaṇeśa, may have been worshipped by the tribes in Central India. She has appellations like Hastimukhā, Kumbhī, and Vighnapārṣadā. Her elephant head may indicate her totemic origins like Gaṇeśa, as for example, amongst the Mātaṅga tribes. She is associated with tigers and lions which point to her wild habitat. Her chariot is said to be drawn by lions, which like Durgā would indicate that she was the goddess of forest regions. Her vāhana is a wild ass and she is the wife of Kāla.[94]

She seems an ambivalent goddess, whose worship was prevalent in the South. Her worship was popular as a parivāra devatā, receiving royal grants during the eighth to the tenth centuries A.D. She could have been the elder and more important of the goddesses of the original inhabitants of the area, giving her protection to agricultural wealth and progeny. When she was ousted from her status due to may be sectarian motives, she was bracketed with Alakṣmī, in the North, and, in the South, she was called Mūdevī, the elder goddess, but with bad connotation. Though a connection has been mooted with Nirṛti, Śītalā and Hāritī, Jyeṣthā is benevolent, has two children as seen in her icons. Her two children are Nandi on her right, and Agnimātā on her left.[95] Though a similarity is seen between the two goddesses, Jyeṣṭhā, and Nirṛti,[96] it stops with their vāhana, which is the donkey. She is of benign countenance, ample proportions, and is bejewelled. This image precludes any malignancy in her make-up. The Ajitāgama has fulsome praise for her and sets down ritual worship of the goddess for worldly prosperity. But the Purāṇas give her a malignant character. Jyeṣṭhā is said to be connected with the asterisk Jyeṣṭhā, and it is a known fact that stars have been ascribed malignant character. The queen of the Pandyan king Jatilavarman Parantaka had a Durgā shrine excavated at Tirupparankunram towards the end of the eighth century A.D. with a sculpture of Jyeṣṭhā also carved in high relief.[97]

Mātaṅgī stands on a lion; she has eighteen arms, and in one of them holds a bowl of wine. She is dressed in red silks. Tārā and Tripura Sundarī were goddesses who developed in the 9th to 12th centuriesA.D.[98]

Character

Kālī is ferocious and destructive. She is assimilated into the Great Tradition by myths, by being married to Śiva. In Tantras, her fierce aspect is not softened, but her devotee boldly faces upto her, conquers her and wins boons from her.

In the Vedas, her prototype could be Nirṛti. She is associated with tribals on the periphery of Aryan culture. She is the goddess of forests and hilly tracts. Her village counterparts have non-Brahminic priests and her propitiation is by bloody sacrifices. The diffusion of her cult attests to her wide popularity in time and area. She has her disciples in savants like Ramakrishna[158], and others. In recent times she was a symbol of suppressed Bengal in Bankim Chunder Chatterji's novels.

As a Great Mother she gives new life, but at the same time she needs to be sustained in her work with fresh and continuous sap of life, blood. Kālī's nature would suggest that our ideation of the divine has in it "the other" also. Underlying the orderly progress of the cosmos, is a taut, seething energy, which if untramelled, would annihilate the orderly existence, and return it to chaos. But this starts a beginning afresh, another cosmos.

There is a mistaken notion that subsidiary goddesses are benevolent whereas with the exception of Sarasvatī, whose worship is not of great popularity, all goddesses who are worshipped as main deities are fierce.[99] Even though Kālī is a war-goddess, her function is to protect gods and men from their enemies. Her very anger is a blessing to humanity, since it destroys their enemies.

Kālī breaks into the Great Tradition, in the Purāṇas, with a howl of laughter in the middle of a battle. None of her rough edges are softened. From the periphery of tribal origins, she became associated with Śiva through Durgā and Pārvatī. She is slowly accepted in the Great Tradition till in the Tantras, she is universalized. Tantric Vāmācāra rituals gave a superior position to Kālī. She is a bountiful, boon-giving, fear-dispelling goddess on the one hand and a forbidding and forbidden goddess on the other.

A vīra (a highest class of Tantric adept), by confronting her frightful form understands and conquers his own fears, and gains mastery over himself and her. The Tantric devotee goes beyond the Goddess's positive and negative aspects and reaches beyond the dualities of the world.[100]

The Judaic view of the Holy according to Rudolph Otto,[101] is that it is irresistably attractive and compelling on the one hand, and dangerous, frightening, and overwhelming on the other. Kālī fits this definition neatly. But Rudolf Otto[102] further suggests that the mysterium tremendum gets detached from other beneficent elements (specially in the development of Faust) and becomes mysterium horrendum. This is not fully borne out by the Indian Goddess, because to her devotees she is beneficent. Kālī is a goddess not distinct from Durgā, because she emerges from the frown of Durgā. Since Kālī emerges from the form of Pārvatī also, this would make her the same as Pārvatī. Kālī is distinct from these two goddesses inasmuch as she is their negative half. But she is not different in class.

To sum up then: Kālī is a destructive goddess, who destabilises cosmic order. When she labours to help the devas after annihilating the demons, she gets out of control and has to be restrained from destroying the world. She is the opposite of Pārvatī in her relationship to Śiva. She induces Śiva into a destructive frenzy of activity whereas Pārvatī soothes him.

Similar Goddesses beyond India

There is a similarity between Kālī and the thin-waisted Minoan goddesses.[103] Pattini in Ceylon is a counterpart of Kālī. She castrates her husband Palaṅga. She is ambivalent and this is a common feature of South Asian Goddess cults. But Indians are said not to prefer ambivalence in the same goddess and split the Great Goddess for the two functions and have posited maleficence in Kālī.[104]

There are two Sumerian seals from the ruins of the city of Lagash,[105] where a woman is seated on a prone male and in one of them another male has seized the female's arm and is threatening her with a staff. These seals are surmised as the heiros gamos, with the king substituted in the marriage with the priestess, and both of them put to death, later. This is assimilated to the Tantric figure of Kālī seated above the prone figure of Śiva. The analogy is further enlarged when it is seen that the god in the seal is Pfah, and his animal, like Nandi, is the bull and the goddess-consort has a lion vehicle like the goddess Pārvatī.[106]

Similar to Kālī's relationship to the dead is the finest example on the floor of an Egyptian sacrophagi, where Nut embraces the dead man.[107] She is dressed in black, and is bare-breasted which resembles Kālī. She is nocturnalistic and stands for the direction, West, killing and devouring. Further, a few examples are the Mexican Goddess Coatlicne-Aztec, the Grecian Gorgon, Ta-Urt and Hathor from Egypt who were popular from the 14th century B.C. to the 6th century B.C. The point to remember about these Mother Goddess figures[108] is that they signify the Great Mother. Since life and death are eternally bound with each other the epithet Great is justifiable.

Probable Reasons for the Kālī Motif

There could be two possible reasons for the rise and popularity of the Goddess Kālī: sociological, and psychological. A brief survey of the early Gupta period vis-a-vis the position of women is attempted, and the sociological set-up, of the women with the backdrop of the Brahminical rise in position and their efforts to stabilise their own pre-eminence is traced. Psychology has offered somewhat satisfying answers to the images thrown up from the unconscious and myths rising to explain the image. Jung who was the pioneer in this has been subsequently detracted, mainly by American psychologists. But, so long as there are no other satisfactory psychological explanations forthcoming, eminent scholars (Cassirer, and Lévi-Strauss), those in the historico-religious field (Eliade, O'Flaherty) and psychologists (Nuemann, Wulff) have all resorted to the Jungian explanation. An attempt has been made to find possible reason for the image.

Sociological Background

The position of women, of the higher classes, continued to deteriorate. In exchange for social security, her inheritence rights, and, rights over her husband's property were nullified. She was kept dependent on the males of her family, right through her life. Her education was stopped and marriage age was lowered to absurd limits. She was forced to treat her husband as her god and to self-immolate herself on her husband's funeral pyre.

This Brahmin attitude was due to his securing lineage rights and also his efforts to keep the family stock pure.

The lower class woman had equal, or, superior status to her husband. She worked in the fields and therefore, economically she was independent. The status of these classes of women is seen reflected in the goddesses they worshipped. Lakṣmī, who typifies the goddess who has power and status due to her marriage, is the example, which would reflect the status of the higher class women, and she is termed the Spouse goddess. Devī, i.e., Durgā or Kālī would reflect the status of the lower class women, independent, her position not dependant on any marital status. According to Śāktas, the more a śakti is distanced from the god, the more destructive she becomes.[109]

With the rise to power by the Brahmins, and the transition of statehood to the lands, Brahmins started acquiring lands as *dakṣiṇā*. They expanded their land-holdings further east and north. This resulted in their confrontation with tribal population, who were necessary for cultivation of the lands. The tribals were not given caste recognition, but their goddess cults along with Tantric rituals were assimilated by the Brahmins.

Worship of the Great Goddess or, Devī is said to be egalitarian. This is seen even in the IV goddess worship from the evidence that the majority of the population had enjoyed uniform prosperity and there was no great difference in the life-style dividing the elitist from the other classes. In the IV culture, there is a further surmise that there was a gender equality and role interchangeability between the sexes, and, independence in marital status, though no evidence is brought out to support the above view.[110] The IV goddess is thought to be the prototype of Mahādevī i.e., Devī, further exalted to a symbol of Monism. This is Kālī/ Durgā who is quasi-orthodox and free from marital control.

Sexual symbolism and worship for fecundity are implicit in Devī worship. This is also seen to be existing in the seal depiction of the goddess picturised as cult diagrams. This could have been the foundation for *Śāktism* and *Tantric* worship.

The Classical Age saw Brahminical ascendency, and, the rise of Mahādevī. The Spouse Goddess reflected the position of high caste women who had no choice but to play a subservient role in their marriage out of economic necessity. The presence or absence of orthodox marriage decided the class of the goddess. The Great Goddess, i.e., Kālī, Durgā, (also Rādhā), who were spousified Devīs, emerged in the same period.

Thus, the women of the elite class worshipped a transcendental metaphysical Goddess, while the lower castes by and large worshipped pragmatic goddesses. By the principle of reversion, women's status was so low in real life, that it was compensated by giving a dominant role for the goddess in the cult.

Belief in a goddess with a marked ambivalence is a part of the ideology surrounding the Goddess. Again, the goddess figure is a symbol and reflects the ideas, beliefs, and values associated with women. By studying a goddess, we may get an insight into the status occupied by women in that period and the dominant values attached to them. As a corollary, it may be possible to correlate the goddess images and the society which propitiates them and find out the reason for such worship.

Woman is Creation, Divinity, and Nature. Śakti underlies both creation and divinity, because it is power which distinguishes men from gods. Creation is accomplished by gods by their power. Nature is differentiated matter, whereas Puruṣa is differentiated (Spirit) code. Since nature is opposed to culture, according to Claude Lévi-Strauss, women are uncultured. If uncontrolled, they are dangerous. They are potentially dangerous. They have to be controlled by men. By submission they become "good" like the cow or the earth.

Woman=Power+Nature=Danger, is the equation which summarises the attitude of men towards women/goddesses.[111] Benevolent goddesses are those that are married, and thus transferred their power to their husbands.

There are two types of goddesses. One is free of male control, named here Devī. She is equal or superior to her male partner, and belongs to the Little Tradition. The other's position is due to her marital status, and, belongs to the Great Tradition, and here named the Spouse Goddess. In between these two, lies the goddess who is quasi orthodox, but, free from marital control. This is Durgā, or Kālī. She is termed Mahādevī. We are concerned with the last deity, but a better insight into her could be obtained if there is a grasp of the value and meaning of the two deities.

(1) Devī operates beyond the family circle and works for whole communities. The Spouse Goddess works only for the prosperity and welfare of the family, for a male progeny, etc.
(2) Both Goddesses have positive and negative qualities. Devī is ambivalent, her functions being creation and destruction, she performs these in the same form. The Spouse Goddess splits into two to show her malevolence; and her benevolence is also "insipid".
(3) Devī was primarily of tribal origin and continued to be worshipped so, till the Gupta period when she was married to Śiva, by the Brahmins.
(4) The Spouse Goddess cannot act without her marital status and heavy control by the god. Hindu men are said to approve of abstract fertility in their goddesses, but do not tolerate pragmatic sexuality. This ambivalence is reflected in the Spouse Goddess. Her bestowal of fertility to her devotees is approved, whereas her own latent sexuality is to be kept tightly under control by her spouse.

She may be absent altogether from rituals, eclipsed by her powerful husband. Devī, on the other hand, does not depend on marital status for her function and her stature is unaffected by her husband. In fact, she may leave her husband for long periods.

Mahādevī stands for monism and was spousified nominally in c. 400 A.D. She is Durgā, or Kālī, and in the villages called Mātā,

Ammā, or, Āttā. She is supreme in Tantrism, mysticism, and Śākta metaphysics. She re-emerged with Śāktism. Goddess Mīnākṣī of Madurai is an example of Mahādevī; she is married to Śiva with great eclat, yearly, and soon afterwards reverts to her superior single status. In the medieval period, spousification of a number of local goddesses took place. The regional goddesses provided the template for both Devī and Mahādevī.

The spousification may also be of three levels. There are village goddesses who had escaped Sanskritisation and who are worshipped by both high and low castes, and are identified by name with some Sanskrit deity. In the second category, there are goddesses who are superficially married to the god, e.g. Madurai Mīnākṣī. Mīnākṣī's mythic fight with Śiva may represent local cult's resistance against Sanskritisation. The third class shows an artificial manipulation where the two levels show like Ellamma, Reṇukā.

The Devī out-of-control is not the negative aspect of Mahādevī. Devī gets out-of-control because of lack of marital restriction. Mahādevī is negative because she stands for death and destruction, though both are called Kālī in these instances. Similarly, Pārvatī is beneficent because of her spouse status, whereas Durgā is beneficent by herself.

Kālī is uncontrolled power when she is called to annihilate the enemies, but if she continued her rampage, that is if she goes beyond her role, she is reminded of the mother/spouse part in her and she stands subdued and ashamed. This again is an instance of the ambivalent attitude towards the unspousified female power. High caste woman is potentially dangerous in her generatie functions for two reasons. The male loses his spiritual status (enjoined by ascetic restrictions on his sexuality), and social status (consequent to uncertainty of the paternity of the children). This is reflected in the sexual control of Kālī. When she outsteps the bounds of marital dignity, she has to be "punished" to expiate her sin (as Pārvatī) or be subordinated by Śiva (as Kālī).

The relationship between male and female deities of a pair may reflect the social values of a Hindu married couple. The husband has the authority and the wife the power and it is markedly delineated in public, though in private they are equal. The Spouse Goddess has no authority other than given by her consort. She is the power, śakti, of her husband. Kālī is a goddess out-of-control, and is all power, and has to be subdued. Lakṣmī's power is under the control of her husband's authority. It may have arisen out of the Sāṁkhyan philosophy, where the Male/Puruṣa has the authority and the Female/Prakṛti is the power.[112]

The two goddesses are different in their status and this can be gauged by the difference in the status of their devotees. Devī is worshipped by low caste women with comparative equality with men and who enjoy economic freedom. The devotees of the Spouse Goddess are high caste women who cannot interchange their roles with their husbands; they play specific roles related to their gender. The areas of popularity of Devī, that is, Bengal and South India are said to be areas where pre-Brahmin influence is extant.

But, it is going too far to say that high caste women worship only gods, while low class women show equal preference for gods and goddesses.[113] It is also not true that high class women do not participate in worships that concern the community, and that they confine themselves to domestic worship. Family is the concern of women irrespective of their status. Problems of communal concern like epidemics or climatic excess is bound to be equally the concern of women of both castes.

Marriage is the key factor which determines the symbolism of the goddess. Where orthodox marriage suppresses her into a spouse, she is equal or slightly superior to her spouse. She plays an active creative and destructive role, irrespective of her marital status.

In a late myth, when Rādhā places her foot on Kṛṣṇa, she is addressed as Caṇḍī, that is, the malefic goddess, or the goddess whose relationship with her spouse is not normal.

Historically, the killing of the demons Caṇḍa and Muṇḍa are seen as putting down un-Aryan resistance.

Sociologically, Kālī could warn us of a world devastated by a global war. If she stands for the material of life "out-of-place", it should induce us to strive towards peace in the world and learn our lesson through the goddess "controlled".

Psychological Reasons for Kālī's Image

If Kālī were not a major goddess with a wide diffusion over time and space, we could treat her as a goddess with terrible negative qualities, and as an aberration of a few tribes on the outer fringes of Hindu culture. But the very fact of her popularity in the mainstream of Hinduism upto today necessitates a deeper study into her image. Now the possible psychological reasons are taken up.

On the surface, Kālī is a menacing and cruel goddess, mystifying observers by her malefic nature. If her image is studied in depth, the truth that she embodies emerges and certain meaning evolves from the meaningless chaos. She stands for rebirth after death and for fresh life from pain and suffering. She confers no birth and life without pain. All deities in their destructive attitude are seen thus to give release to those who break natural laws, and go against established social structures. (Durgā, and Mahiṣa; Kṛṣṇa and Yamalārjuna, etc.)

Zimmer,[114] feels that devotees of Kālī do not understand her true essence because she is not a kind or merciful goddess. Devotees expecting these qualities from her, do not understand her, according to the above scholar. Propitiating her is seen as a sign of regression into infancy. If this were so, then how can one explain those who have attained peace and spiritual exaltation through her worship?

Too much Freudian meaning should not be read into Hindu myths, O'Flaherty states.[115] Though there could be sexual overtones in the myth of Mahiṣa or the beheading of the Tantric image of Chinnmastā, beheading could be just release or 'self castration' by the devotee to obtain release. Further down[116] in the same work, the author sees Freudian incest kept at bay in the devotees' seeing Kṛṣṇa as a baby or Kālī as mother. (The dictum of getting a young woman of a lower caste for a Tantric partner as also the devadāsī system are seen as further examples of avoiding incestuous relationships, because in such cases one cannot view the partner in the light of a mother).[117] It may seem strange to see in the motif of the Goddess, castration (beheading) and sex, that is her standing on an ithyphallic consort. Death and sex recur often together in myths, as for instance the Mahiṣī lying beside a dead horse, in the Aśvamedha sacrifice, Śiva dancing, carrying Satī's corpse, and Kālī standing on a couple, with a raised sword in one hand.

Freud

Freud had treated the father image of the deity and the reason for its arising in the human mind, elaborately. He has but given passing reference to the Goddess image before dismissing it.[118]

His two followers (Harald and Kristan Schjelderup) have seen it fit to correct this ommission. They see three stages in religious thought:

(1) The first is when self is thought of as God, when the psyche is undeveloped and in narcissistic stage;

(2) The second when the goddess is the deity, when the differentiation is not coloured by the ego's Oedipal complex in the consciousness, and,

(3) the third, when god is seen as the deity, when consciousness fully evolves, and the relationship of the ego to his father is coloured by Oedipal complex.[119] Thus, according to Freud, goddess—worship is a pre-Oedipal fixation.

Jung

The infant's first impressions of its mother as protective and nourishing on the one hand, and destructive and wanting to castrate it on the other, remain with it right through its later years, and the image of Kālī is one such image thrown up by the psyche.

There are again three qualities of the Great Mother.[120]

(1) Cherishing and nourishing goodness,

(2) Her orgiastic emotionality, and,

(3) Her stygian depths.

In the West, very early, this ambivalence in the (Greek) gods scandalised people and they tried to rationalise the myths and to read philosophical meanings into them. We, in India, have harmonized our relationship to the Great Mother by correctly accepting her ambivalence.

In the Goddess stage, there is a severe regression of wanting to go back into infancy and to return to the womb. Each person's individual psyche throws up its experience as dreams. The collective method of coming to terms with the various facets of the psyche's experience, turns into myths and fairy tales. According to Jung,[121] in our unconscious, there are archetypes which have no formal content. The archetypes are dynamic, impersonal forms. They are formed due to immeasurable psychic experiences, which are common to all humanity. Further, they are universally inherited factors. They throw up religious, that is, mythic forms, which lie beyond a person's experience.

To understand the Goddess figures, there are two elements encountered as the psyche transforms itself in the unconscious: they are the anima and the Mother archetype.

Anima is the unconscious femininity and also the female soul of the man. These throw up images of : (1) the Spouse Goddess, (2) the goal of the hero in myths, and fairy tales, and, (3) the guide way to the hero towards his goal.

The Mother Archetype is personified as the Great Mother, or, the Mother Goddess. The Mother Goddess has also two aspects: the positive, and the negative. The positive is Sophia or transcendent knowledge, positive instinct and impulse, container, nourisher of life. This springs from the outward mother-child relationships.[122] The negative aspect would be darkness, death, decay, destruction, the subterranean earth, and the negative destructive instincts and emotions. These arise from the inside and have no relation to objects in the physical world. The Terrible Mother is a symbol from the unconscious.

The images that the unconscious throws up are mainly feminine. It contains feminine "forces, tendencies, complexes, instincts and, archetypes, male and female gods, demons, spirits, animals and so on".[123] The image of the unconscious is given expression in esoteric teaching. This is the way of transmission of the contents of the unconscious into consciousness.[124]

The dark side of the Terrible Mother takes the form of monsters whether in India, Egypt, Mexico, Etrusia, Bali, or Rome, of the terrifying forms in myths and fairy-tales of all cultures all over the world, nay, even in our nightmares.

The womb of the earth becomes under the negative feminine characteristic the devourer, the maw of the underworld, as much as she puts forth, and nourishes as a positive feminine characteristic. She creates, and, pursues her creation with death, disease and destruction, and snares them back into herself. The symbol of the negative feminine characteristic is the goddess of war and hunt, who demands blood.

Further, the goddesses of war and hunt are the images of "man's experiences of life as a female exacting blood." "It is in India that the experience of the Terrible Mother has been given its most grandiose form as Kālī, 'dark, all-devouring time, the bone-wreathed Lady of the place of skulls'.[125] Moreover Kālī may be taken as the symbol of the primordial Mother figure representing the primordial mother principle, of life and death, death and resurrection. This image we have seen in the Kulli and Zhob goddesses and the Vedic Nirṛti; the last two are labelled as goddesses of Death.

The Kālī temples are famous for animal slaughter. The rituals attached to the goddess befit her personality. Kālī demands the life/blood of the creatures she herself has created. She has to be fed quickly on the life sap and since decapitating allows the blood to gush forth, sacrifice is performed. Kālī-Durgā are goddesses of war and hunt, because they are perpetually revived by the fecundating and revivifying blood; this is reinforced by the sight of the flow of death and rebirth on the earth around. This is constellated in the imagery of blood sacrifice to the goddess. This is why Kālī is represented with a raised sword in one hand. Continuing the symbolism, the mouth is the symbol of the female womb, the lips are the symbol of the feminine generative organ, and the tongue is that of the male. (Lf. Pls 27, 28) She is Jagadambā (the Mother of the universe), Jagaddhātrī (its preserver), and Annapūrṇā (the nourisher), all in one.[126] She is a gory goddess revelling in sacrificial dismemberment. She is phallic in her lolling tongue and raised sword. Thus she has in her, male and female which is the right image for the Uroboric Mother.[127] The mother goddess of the Aztecs was similar; she was also personified as the "white stone knife."

The phallic symbolism of the lolling tongue is a trait found in most representations of the Terrible Mother. That it is a seat of action and words is seen completely in the Loyalty Islands' nomenclature for the generative organ as "his word" and in New[128] Zealand and Oceanic Islands this association is overt.

The hands and heads used as ornaments by Kālī, symbolise sexual powers and are instruments in active sexuality in their own right. In Hindu myths, semen is stored in the head which further corroborates the castration by Kālī.[129]

The self-sacrifice to the goddess is seen as an unbidden wish to enter into the mother's womb. The act of sacrificing oneself is explained psychologically. In every human psyche, a certain quantum of libido is turned inward on the ego. This is termed primary narcissism by Freud. All infants have this tendency in the beginning. When there is an abnormal amount of this tendency, this persists through the ego's life and this is termed secondary narcissism.Hindus are said to belong to this latter class. This gives rise to idealism, a quest into ātman-Brahman relationship, yoga, love of the world, etc.; and the love for the aggressive mother Kālī is a small throw-up of such a tendency in a minority of aggressive people. This results in sacrifice, self-beheading by males, and satī by females. This narcissism is entirely contained in the unconscious, though a little bit of it shows up as a configuration in the conscious.

The Western ego, as opposed to this Eastern tendency, is said to be punitive. It is turned aggressively outward, representing sex and has a God who is aggressive and jealous. The narcissist has no compulsion about a male God and worships Goddesses freely. Their gods and goddesses are each individual's choice and are not mutually jealous.

Sacrificing the head to the Goddess then points to self-castration, in order to identify with the mother. Sacrifice or self-sacrifice is viewed by the Westerner as a corrective measure, or for a great purpose, and it is unwelcome. To the Hindu, sacrifice is justified in itself. Sacrifice and renunciation are among the two most emotive words in the religious vocabulary of the Hindu. Their worship of a war-goddess fits in not with their fighting qualities, but with their willingness to sacrifice themselves to her, and later on to her as their country personified.

In India, children are pampered and brought up with much leniency by their doting parents.[130] This is said to lead to a mother fixation, and another good reason for the popularity of mother-goddess worship.

Blood was assimilated to the seminal fluid, and therefore its fall would be potent. Loss of semen is equivalent to loss of power; loss of blood from the hero would decrease his power while increasing that of his enemies. Thus the decrease of magical potency due to sexual loss would parallel its increase in the opposing group. Therefore, Raktabīja's blood,[131] and Andhaka's blood[132] had to be prevented from falling on the earth. Since head was equivalent to the phallus, cutting off the head was tantamount to cutting off the storehouse of semen.

There is no Oedipal hatred as understood by the Western mind, behind the worship of Kālī. The Hindus usually deify and love the mother idea. Their narcissistic mentality makes them adore their goddesses. There is no aggression in the mind of the devotee to wards Kālī. She arouses two feelings in his mind. Neither is accompanied by any feeling of remorse or guilt, or for the expiation of sins. (1) She arouses "destructive fantasies" similar to the mother denying her breast to her child; and, (2) she arouses the feeling of the mother to whose womb the son castrating himself wishes to return.

Castration and decapitation are the same symbolically. To appease and quieten an avenging mother, the devotee has to submit totally and if necessary lose his manhood.[133]

Another way to appease her would be to become her infant and appeal to her maternal attitude from a position of total helplessness. This has been narrated in some Purāṇas where the gods become Devī's infants or Śiva puts on the role of her child.

Chinnamastikā, or, Chinnamastā is a reddish brown nude goddess, standing on a couple, with a raised head (her own) in one hand, and a sword raised in the other. The raised sword is phallic. The head again is a phallic symbol, and drinking the blood is revivifying, since it comes out of the head, again the creative fluid. This whole picture is a reflection of the devotee's desire for self-castration, and return to the mother's womb. This wish to return to the womb is seen even in the kumkum worn on the forehead.[134]

Zimmer,,[135] looks at the sword differently. Kālī's sword symbolises "physical extermination and spiritual decision; this sword cuts through error and ignorance, the veil of individual consciousness." And his justification for Kālī is that if the whole aspect of the Mother has to be depicted then her negative qualities have also got to be depicted.[136]

Many rituals associated with the goddess are aggressive. In the punitive ego (Western), this may be partly ascribed to aggression against oneself. In the Hindu narcissistic devotee, there is no guilt feeling in the devotee's mind and he desires it, and welcomes it, as a help to enter his mother. As a corollary to this theory, it may be stated that the worship could be aggressive in proportion to the degree of aggression in the devotee's ego. Those with very little aggression in them would worship the benign forms of the Mother.

Whitehead[137] has cited nine legends of goddesses, eight of which refer to castration and the last one to return to the womb.

This corroborates the theory of narcissistic attitude in propitiating Village Goddesses and it is similar to Kālī worship.

There have been misconceptions about mythic imagery and the psychology behind it. To quote one view: "... since mythology is born of fantasy, any life or civilization brought to form as a result of a literal mythic identification or inflation, as a concrete *imitatio dei* will necessarily bear the features of a nightmare, a dream-game too seriously played—in other words, madness; whereas, when the same mythological imagery is properly read as fantasy and allowed as nature—with irony and grace, not fierce daemonic compulsion—the psychological energies that were formerly in the capture of the compelling images take the images in capture, and can be developed with optional spontaneity for life's enrichment. Moreover....... such a transfer of accent may conduce, in time, to a life lived in noble consciousness, of its own nature".[138]

The psychological explanations of Jungians like Erich Nuemann may not satisfy non-Jungians. One may have to evaluate Kālī's importance in terms of Indian values in metaphysics. She may stand for Māyā, Duhkha, Prakṛti, and Kāla. Briefly these terms mean:

Māyā is the depiction of the world filled with negative aspects; one strives to look beyond Kālī and attain a true and unambiguous view of the world as it is.

(2) Duhkha is the inevitable realities of life like sickness, old age and death.
(3) Prakṛti is the seemingly relentless pulsating life;
(4) *Kāla* is Time which indiscriminately devours all things in its maw.

By confronting Kālī the devotee overcomes these entities she represents and gains ultimate freedom.[139]

Conclusion

There are two methods of viewing the mother-goddess-devotee relationship. Psychogenic, where psychology is used to evaluate, and sociogenic where social and economic values are used for adjudging. An evaluation of Kālī's image has been attempted under these two methods. Sociogenically, it was seen that rigid Brahminisation lowered the status of high class women further, but the status of the lower class remained much the same. Their status was reflected in the power and authority wielded by the Goddesses they worshipped. Kālī being 'spousified' became partially Brahminised, and was therefore popular with all classes of women. Under the psychogenic method, there could be two modes of relationships between the goddess and the devotee: that of a mother and her child and that of a marital partner. Kālī is able to fulfil both these modes well. The former is in the devotee's yearning to return to the mother's womb, and the latter in Śāktic mysticism.

There are many opinions on the metaphysical significance of this goddess. This could be due to her multivalency or her ability to adapt herself to any interpretation. On the concrete plane, Kālī stands for everything negative. But, on the metaphysical plane, she stands for the elevated idea of change as concomitant with time, mutability and ineluctible fate.[140]

Claude Lévi-Strauss says[141] that the sacrality of a thing is in its Being in its place. If so "Being Out-of-place", an abberration against order, is also sacred. Therefore Kālī leads us to *mokṣa* by giving us a vision of things out of place. Kālī's physical aspect is fierce. But intellectually she stands for Time, Cycle of birth and death and immutable Fate. She is seen as the ideal representative of the main Śākta theological terminologies of Māyā, Duhkha, Prakṛti, and Kāla. But it can be seen that the majority of Purāṇic goddesses can be made to fit the above ideologies. She stands for blood and death, which is unique to her. She may be our panacea for abnormal deaths and calamities, and may give us strength to face personal and communal catastrophies.

She is said to signify the unpredictable and uncomfortable weather with which the Indian peasant has had to struggle! "The life of the ordinary Bengal peasant must have been a hopeless and helpless one, and it is not difficult to understand his seeking refuge in a conception of the divine as destruction, in a deity unreliable, irresponsible almost, dancing a mad dance of death, and propitiated only by cruel rites and degrading practices".[142] This sentiment is echoed by Slater[143] when he compares the ambivalent Kālī to the unpredictable Indian weather bountiful or deadly, and quite sudden.

Kālī is a motner to her devotees. The devotee looks unflinchingly at the dark and forbidding aspect of the Terrible

Mother and in a flash of intuitive recognition calls her 'Mother' and this is the union of the soul with god.[144] Facing Kālī and coming to terms within oneself what she symbolises, one transcends her and with intuition is able to attain the next stage "Sophia", the transcendental Intelligence in spiritual progress.

When Kālī entered the Great Tradition, she ceased to be a tribal divinity. She represented Śākta metaphysical values. But she never lost her negative characteristics. She added these to the figure of the Great Goddess and made her complete. To the individual, she represented the negative elements in life, and the devotee by facing the truths she embodied, surmounted those. This is true of the village goddesses also who are only Kālī's versions. The vision of Kālī could also shake man out of his humdrum routine of life and jerk him into a new frenzied freedom which may exalt him.

Kālī is the projection from the inner core of Hinduism. She is dark, sensual and fearsome. Nirṛti who is her prototype could also have been the Vedic Indian's method of facing upto the negative aspects of life, by surrendering himself to her. Sāṁkya assigns to Prakṛti the three attributes sattva, rajas, and tamas (literally, goodness, passion and darkness). The Great Mother is thus well symbolised in her three major aspects of nourishing and protecting, orgiastic and Stygian, involved in death and destruction.[145] "Through the fierce and terrible he (the devotee) sees the sweet moonlight of grace that suddenly breaks forth, and Kālī is no more than a symbol to him—a symbol of divine punishment, of divine grace, and of divine motherhood".[146]

This brief survey concludes with an apt quotation about the lesson that the Hindu learns from the symbol of Kālī, to break out of his limitations, not become a creature of habits. She "directs man's vision beyond the limitations of an ego-centered, predictable, humdrum and deadening existence to an other world that is both terrifying and irresistably attractive in its transcendence."[147]

REFERENCES

1. Mbh. IX. 45. 1-28.
2. Matsya P. 179. 9 ff and Viṣn udharmottara P. I. 226. 7 ff; Tiwari, J.N. - *Goddess cults in Ancient India*, fns. 7 and 8.

3. Vana Parva 219.20-45.
4. Bhattacharji, S., *Op. cit.*, p. 167.
5. Kosambi, D.D., *Myth and Reality*, ch. 3, fn. 5
6. 37.12-22, Agrawala, V.S., *Ancient India Folk-Cults*, p. 77.
7. *Ibid.*, p. 5, fns. 30-32.
8. Agrawala, V.S., *Ibid.*, pp. 92-93.
9. Gonda, *Aspects of Early Viṣṇuism* pp. 218-9; Jaiswal, *Op. cit* pp. 99-100.
10. Sinha, B.C., *Hinduism and Symbol Worship*, pp. 130-31.
11. Tiwari, *Op. cit.*, p. 11.
12. Bhattacharyya, *History of Sākta Religion*, p. 18.
13. Santini, Asuranai Alitta Elu Śaktikaḷ, Tamil Article in *Amuda Surabhi*, Dec. '84.
14. DM. 7.27.
15. Agrawala, P.K., *Goddesses in Ancient India*, p. 116.
16. *Ibid.*
17. Dikshit, *The Mother Goddess.* p. 112.
18. Mund. Up. I. 2.4.
19. 39: 140, Sharma, P.K., *Śakti Cult in Ancient India*, p. 253, fn. 7.
20. *Ibid*, p. 236.
21. Agrawala, *V.S.-Ancient Indian Folk-Cults*, p. 80.
22. Mbh. II. Aranyaka Par., 219. 20-21.
23. *Ibid*, 22.
24. Adh. 30, 3-9.
25. Adh. 8.
26. Agrawala, V.S., *Ancient Indian Folk-Cults*, p. 87.
27. Aryan, K.C., The Little Goddesses (Matrikas), *Sunday Standard*, 10.8.80.
28. Aryan, K.C., *Ibid.*
29. cf. ch. II
30. Infra.
31. Neumann, Erich, *The Great Mother*, pp. 150-151.
32. Sinha, B.C., *Hinduism and Symbol Worship*, p. 121.
33. Sharma, P.K., *Śakti Cult in Ancient India*, p. 16.
34. Bhattacharji, *The Indian Theogony*, p. 85.
35. Bhattacharji, *Ibid.*, Intro. p. 7.
36. Kinsley, D.R., *The Sword and the flute*, p. 84.
37. Vide Sn. Matṛs.
38. Agrawala, P.K., *Op. cit.*, p. 120, fn. 780.
39. Coburn, T.B., DM, p. 110. fn. 74 quoting Macdonell, *Vedic Mythology*, p. 120.

40. Banerjea - *Paurāṇic and Tāntric Religion*, p. 117.
41. Bhandarkar, R.G. - *Vaiṣṇavism Śaivism and Minor Religious Systems*, p. 114.
42. Vide also Śāṇk. GS. 2. 14,14, Agrawala, P.K., *Ibid.*, p. 120, fn. 781; Hiraṇyakeśī GS. Banerjea, *Paurāṇic and Tāntric Religion*, p. 117; Kauṣītaka GS. 3.10.14; Vaikhānasa GS. named Kālakā, 3.7.18.
43. 8.65-68.
44. Mukherji Shyam Chand, The Cult of Ekānaṁśā, pp. 189-208, The IHQ, XXXX. 1, Mar. 1959.
45. Vaudeville, Charlotte, *Krishna, Gopala, Radha and the Great Goddess*, pp. 7-8.
46. Vaudeville, *Ibid.*, p. 8.
47. Bhattacharyya, IMG, p. 121.
48. O'Flaherty, *Sexual Metaphors and Animal Symbolism in Indian Mythology*, pp. 33-34.
49. 13.22 ff.
50. 29.23.
51. Sharma, P.K., *Śakti Cult in Ancient India*, p. 88.
52. V.2.84, Bhattacharyya, IMG, p. 121, fn. 253.
53. Kinsley, D.R., *Blood and Death Out of Place*, p. 146, fn. 6.
54. L.P.I. 106; O'Flaherty, *Sexual Metaphors and Animal Symbolism*, p. 140.
55. O'Flaherty, *Ibid.*, Quoting Kennedy citing this *Purāṇa*.
56. O'Flaherty, *Ibid.*, p. 143.
57. *Tiruvālaṅkāṭṭu Purāṇam* quoted in O'Flaherty, *Ibid.*, pp. 141-42.
58. Kinsley, *Blood and Death Out of Place*, p. 147.
59. Kinsley, D.R., *Ibid.*, p. 147, fn 10; quoting C. Sivaramamurti in Nataraja In Art, Thought and Literature, pp. 378-79 and 384, etc.
60. O'Flaherty, *The Shifting Balance of Power in the Marriage of Śiva and Pārvatī*, p. 86.
61. O'Flaherty, *Hindu Myths*, p. 259, fn. 28.
62. Kinsley, *The Sword and the Flute*, p. 106-108.
63. Indo-Aryan Races, p. 148, quoted in Srivastava, M.C.P., *Mother Goddess*, p. 117, fn. 1.
64. Bhattacharji, *Op. cit.* p. 174.
65. Bhattacharyya, *History of Śākta Religion*, p. 78.
66. Bhattacharyya, IMG, p. 59.
67. Banerjea, *Purāṇic and Tāntric Religion*, p. 117.
68. Bhattacharyya, IMG pp. 60-61.
69. 7.39.
70. Elmore, W.T., *Dravidian Gods in Modern Hinduism*, pp. 152-53.
71. *Ibid.*, p. 80-106.

72. *Ibid.*, p. 87-93.
73. Elmore, *Ibid.*, pp. 82, 83, 89, 92, 95, 99, 100.
74. Oppert, Gustave, *The Original Inhabitants of India*, Preface, p. viii.
75. Venkataraman, K.R., *Devī Kāmākshī in Kāñchi*, p. 63.
76. Zimmer, Heinrich, *The Art of Indian Asia*, p. 200.
77. Woodroffe, Sir John, Karpūrādi - Stotra pp. 283 and 326 in Hymns to the Goddess.
78. Devī Bh. P.V. 26.39-43; Varāha p. 26. 48-54.
79. Bhattacharji, *Op. cit.*, p. 90.
80. Banerjea, J.N., *Paurāṇic and Tāntric Religion*, p. 117.
81. Bhadrakālī may be just an euphemism of Kālī - Hopkins, E.W. EM, p. 226.
82. Nagasami, R., Ninnayum Pakaluven Tāye. Tamil Art. in *Kalaimagal* pp. 212-214.
83. 7.278.1-4; Sharma, P.K., *Op. cit.*, p. 261, fn. 6.
84. IX. 20. 40-45.
85. 1.18.16; Sharma, P.K., *Ibid.*, p. 262, fn. 2.
86. 60. 115-122; 62. 55-67; 63. 89-98, *Ibid.*, fn. 3.
87. Sharma, *Ibid.*, p. 262.
88. Kālikā P., 74. 90-94, *Ibid.*, p. 263, fn. 1.
89. DM. 8.28.
90. DM. 8.32.
91. Kālikā P. 83. 80. 34; 64-65; Sharma, *Op. cit.*, p. 264, fn. 1.
92. Skanda P. 7. Arbuda Kāṇḍa 23-34, *Ibid.*, p. 265, fn. 3.
93. Skanda P. Dharmāraṇya Mahātmya, 17.1-10; *Ibid.*, p. 265, fn.4.
94. Srivastava, M.C.P., *The Mother Goddess*, p. 175.
95. Tamil Article in *Kalaimagal* July 1988; R. Kalaikkovan, pp. 60-64.
96. cf. ch III Sn. Nirṛti.
97. *Swali, haridas* - Jyeṣthal, The Ambivalent Goddess, JASOB, Vol., 56-59. 1981-84 pp. 326-34.
98. Sharma, *Op. cit.*, p. 266.
99. Spratt, P., *Hindu Culture and Personality*, p. 223.
100. Zimmer, Heinrich, *Myths and Symbols in Indian Art*, p. 216.
101. Quoted in Kinsley, *The Sword and The Flute*, p. 152.
102. The Idea of Holy, p. 103. Quoted in Payne, E.A., *The Śāktas*, p. 111.
103. Gilbert Slater, *The Dravidian Elements in Indian Culture*, p. 77.
104. O'Flaherty, *The Shifting Balance of Power in the Marriage of Śiva and Pārvatī*, pp. 112-13.
105. Campell, Joseph, *The Masks of God, Oriental Mythology*, pp. 42-43.
106. Campbell, Joseph, *Ibid.*, p. 90.

107. Neumann, Erich, *The Great Mother*, p. 164.
108. Neumann, Erich, *Ibid.*, p. 153.
109. Boner, Alice, *Principles of Composition in Hindu Culture*, p. 228.
110. Gatwood, Lynn, *Devī and the Spouse Goddess*, p. 27. Further Ideas on Devī, Mahādevī, and the Spouse Goddess are taken from the same book.
111. Wadley Susan, *Women in the Hindu Tradition* p. 115.
112. O' Flaherty, *The Shifting Balance of Power in the Marriage of Śiva and Pārvatī* p. 117.
113. Gatwood, Lynn, *Devī and the Spouse Goddess*, p. 98.
114. Quoted in Kinsley, D.R., *The Sword and the Flute*, p. 132.
115. *The Shifting Balance of Power, in the Marriage of Śiva and Pārvatī* pp. 86-87.
116. *Ibid.*, p. 110.
117. *Ibid.*, p. 38.
118. Wulff, Prolegomenon to a Psychology of the Goddess; in *The Divine Consort* p. 286.
119. Wulff, David. M., *Ibid.*, p. 287.
120. Jung, *Archetypes and the Collective Unconscious*, Part II, p. 81.
121. cf. I ch. Sn. Psychological Assessment.
122. Wulff, *Op. cit.*, p. 293; also Neumann, *The Great Mother*, p. 148.
123. Neumann, *Ibid.*
124. Jung, *Archetypes and the Collective Unconscious*, Part I, p. 5.
125. Neumann, *Op. cit.*, pp. 149-50.
126. Zimmer, Heinrich, quoted in Erich Neumann, *Ibid.*, p. 152, fn. 5.
127. Uroboric would mean the original "psychic situation" which contains all opposites of gender, direction, and conscious and anticonscious elements, Neumann, *Ibid.*, pp. 212-13.
128. Neumann-*Ibid.*, p. 169.
129. Wulff, *Op. cit.*, p. 290; Also Spratt., *Hindu Culture and Personality*, p. 249.
130. Jeannine Auboyer, *Daily Life in Ancient India*, p. 166; Basham A.L., *The Wonder That Was India*, p. 162.
131. DM. 8.53-55.
132. Matsya P. 179.5-7.
133. Carstairs, quoted in O'Flaherty, *The Shifting Balance of Power in the Marriage of Śiva and Pārvatī*, p. 110.
134. Spratt., *Op. cit.*, p. 267.
135. Heinrich, *Myths and Symbols in Indian Art and Civilization*, p. 214.
136. *Ibid.*, p. 213.
137. H., *The Village Gods of South India*, quoted in Spratt, *Op. cit.*, p. 261.
138. Campbell Joseph, *The Masks of God*, Oriental Mythology, p. 96.
139. Kinsley, D.R., *The Sword And The Flute*, pp. 137-146.

140. Bhattacharji, *Op. cit.*, p. 174.
141. *The Savage Mind*, 1966, p. 10. quoted in Brubaker, Richard - Comments; *The Goddess and The Polarity of the Sacred*, p. 204, fn. 1.
142. Payne, E.A, *The Śāktas* pp. 86-87.
143. Gilbert, *The Dravidian Element in Indian Culture*, p. 92.
144. Sr. Nivedita, *Kali as Mother*, pp. 35-36, quoted in Spratt, *Op. cit.*, p. 242, fn. 34.
145. Jung, *Archetypes And The Collective Unconscious*, p. 81.
146. Sen, D.C. - *History of Bengali Language and Literature* p. 714; quoted in Payne, *Op. cit.*, p. 97.
147. Kinsley, D.R., *The Sword And The Flute*, p. 158.

CHAPTER V
DURGA—THE GREAT GODDESS

Durgā compounded with Kālī becomes the Great Goddess, and crystallises into Mahiṣāsuramardinī. As seen earlier, the goddess cult has a hoary past buried in antiquity. She is a goddess of war as well as of fertility of corn and vegetation. This ambivalence is also inherited from the ancient cult.

The Vedas have literary records of the antecedents of the Goddess. The Purāṇas elaborate it with different myths of the powess of the Goddess. If, in the Vedas, she developed to suit the traits of Rudra-Śiva, who himself had tribal or non-Aryan antecedents, in the Purāṇas her stature was enhanced by her adaptability to the changing needs of the period and to syncretise into herself millions of popular goddesses and ideas, and become The Goddess. Her tribal origins Brahminised, her myths concealing social and political upheavals, she rises as the symbol of supremacy of the goddess cult, obliterating by her popularity the earlier and similar exploits of Skanda, her son. The anomalous situation of the status of women in this period is subconsciously compensated by the build up of the Goddess.

The literature of the period is thrilled with the effulgence of this composite figure of lissom grace and a casually fierce valour. These moments are frozen by devoted artists in imperishable media, literary as well as visual, almost all over the country. This is not a minor aberration but is lovingly elaboated and reiterated by successive legends and ritualised in myths, giving hope to the troubled. She binds us with delusion in the here and now, but herself releases us into the beyond.

The following survey attempts to trace the Goddess' possible origin and development through Vedic, Purāṇic and (Sanskrit) literary works upto and around the eighth century A.D. and her delineation in iconography.

Origin

Almost all scholars are agreed with Marshall's verdict that the Goddess originated in the IVC, and her consort was Śiva-Yogi. Being patriarchal, the Vedic Aryans could have accepted Śiva-Paśupati (specially with their preoccupation with cattle wealth), and it must have taken longer for the Goddess to take root in the Vedic religion, and been a slower process to develop.

In the Harappan cemetery, discovered by Vats, pots used for partial burial are painted with bovine animals and peacocks. This could be the influence on the Durgā cult, specially when she is described as being surrounded by animals. She wears peacock feathers as an ornament on her head, and her connection with death is also surmised.[1]

There has been a suggestion[2] that Śiva or a form of him is the buffalo-demon. This cult goes back to the IV. The proto-Śiva has a headdress which is ridged at regular intervals like a buffalo's horns. Also in Maharashtra, the buffalo god called 'Mhasoba' is worshipped in a small shrine in proximity to the Devī shrine. Sometimes, this god is married to a local goddess who represents Durgā or Pārvatī. The frequent recurrence of the buffalo on IV seals also shows the probable popularity of this animal. The Tantric picture of the Goddess trampling on Śiva may be a development of Devī trampling on Mahiṣa. This is based on the folk traditionss, where Śiva is assimilated to the buffalo. The Purāṇas show no such connection. In ancient Indian myths, the buffalo figure may have symbolised darkness and death; or, the sacrifice of this animal to the Goddess may have given rise to the myth. From the historical point of view, it seems as though Śaktism is the result of indigenous beliefs acting on Aryan religion.

There should be a nucleus around which the cult has grown. Vedic gods Rudra and Agni have contributed towards the development of the Goddess, who under various names has attained the position of Mahādevī. Durgā has a more strong affiliation to Agni than to Śiva, whereas the goddess Umā grows slowly through her association with Śiva. It is to be noted that Durgā's connection to the Vedas is slender, and from these sources her glorious rise to heights as Mahādevī cannot be explained. But her contribution to the cult cannot be belittled. In the ṚgVeda, the word Durgā is used, but never in the feminine. The two Vedic Goddesses Rātrī and Vāk come nearest to contributing towards the ideology of the Goddess, though Vāk Devī could have developed into the Mahā Vidyās (emanations equivalent to the ten avatāras of Viṣṇu), and Rātrī Devī could have developed into Nidrā Devī.

In the early hymn to Rātrī Devī in the ṚgVeda.[3] Here, the goddess is not the dark night personified but the starlit, bright night, and the goddess sweeps away the darkness.[4] There are four sūktas in the Atharva Veda[5] to Rātrī Devī. Sūkta 47 is repeated in the Yajur Veda,[6] Yāska's Nirukta,[7] and in the Pariśiṣṭa sūktas of the ṚgVeda.[8]

In the apocryphal hymn, in the ṚgVeda, she is made into a Great Goddess. The epithets change to Bhadrā, Bhagavatī, Kṛṣṇā.[9]

Rātriṁ prapadye Jananīṁ sarvabhūtaniveśanīṁ/
Bhadrāṁ Bhagavatīṁ kṛṣṇāṁ viśvasya jagato niśām//,

Śivā,[10] and Durgā.[11] The name Durgā is noticeable here, which is seen to have been derived from the Atharva Vedic idea adya pārayati durgāṇi viśvahā[12] that she transports the devotee over all difficulties. In the Ath. V. hymn quoted above, she is called tamasvatī, ramyā. In a lightless, dark night movements for human beings and most creatures are difficult. This idea could have also given rise to her appellation Durgā. But this name gave into easy interpretation as a goddess who was difficult of access, or, as a goddess who helped her devotees across difficulties. This name does not occur prior to the Ṣūtra literature.

BṛhadDevatā, dated between 500-400 B.C. mentions Durgā, while enumerating the middle forms of Vāc;[13]

["She on becoming Durgā (and) uttering a stanza may own a (whole)hymn]. Her (other) names are *Yami, Indrāṇī Saramā, Romaśā, Urvasī;* she first becomes *Sinivalī* and *Rākā, Anumati, Kuhū"*. The square-bracketted portion is considered an interpolation, but a very early one.[14]

In the Sāmavidhāna Brāhmaṇa[15] a Rātri vṛata is prescribed for those who do not wish to be reborn. She is called Punarbhū (who appears repeatedly), Kanyā (virgin), Śikhaṇḍinī (crested), Pāśahastā, Yuvatī (youthful), Kumāriṇī (who has Kumāras). She is seen here as the virgin Mother, and with śikhaṇḍa, (like Rudra), and Pāśa (like Varuṇa).[16]

Just as Rudra is associated with hills and mountains in the *Śatarudrīya* the forms of his consort are also connected with the hilly regions. Umā in the *Kena Up.*[17] is not a consort of Śiva, but is Brahman herself, the Ultimate Godhead.

In the Taitt. Ār.,[18] various names like Kātyāyanī, Kanyākumārī, Durgī a variation of Durgā, is mentioned:

Kātyāyanāya vidmahe Kanyakumāri dhīmahi tanno Durgīḥ pracodayāt.

In the second verse,

Tāmagnivarṇāṁ tapasā jvalantīṁ vairocanim karmaphaleṣu juṣṭāṁ/
Durgām devīm śaraṇamaham prapadye sutarasi tarase namaḥ ....//

The germ of the later development of the Goddess is contained. This as well as the Rātri Sūkta (RV.IV.2) would be around the first century B.C. - 1st. century A.D. In a later text, Maitrāyaṇīya Saṁhitā of the Kṛṣṇa Yajurveda there is a Gāyatrī mantra of Girisutā Gaurī which mentions Gaṅgā, Girisutā, and Gaurī.

TadGaṅgaucyāya vidmahe Girisutāya dhīmahi/
Tanno Gaurī pracodayāt// II. 9.

The mountain-goddess aspect is taken together with the corn-goddess. This is slightly earlier than the 1st century A.D.Syncretization of goddesses seems to have started in this period.

The fire with whom the Great Goddess is assimilated is consuming, destructive, but also transformative. This association was important to the Egyptians in their rites to their dead, and also to the alchemists.[19] It is but natural that the Goddess associated with death and fertility, should be connected with Agni in the Hindu myths.

The mountain-goddess Umā-Haimavatī could not have suddenly come into prominence as the teacher of the gods, in the Kena Up. Prior to this period she must have been a popular deity. Ambikā[20] is described as the sister of Rudra in the Vāj. Saṁ. of the *Śukla Yajurveda*[21], "*Eṣa te Rudra bhāgaḥ saha svasrā Ambikayā,*" and in the *Taitt. Br.*[22] it is said, "*ityāha śarad vai asya Ambikā svasā tayā vai eṣa hinasti.*" Sāyaṇa in his commentary says that Durgā is like the autumn which kills people with diseases.[23] Sarasvatī is also connected with autumn and the rainy season.[24] In the Tait. Āṛ, Sarasvatī is called Varadā (X. 26), Mahādevī, and Sandhyāvidyā,[25] which epithets are subsequently given to Durgā. Thus a connection is seen between Sarasvatī and the Goddess.

Ambikā is Rudra's sister in the Yajur Veda.[26] In the Śūlagava sacrifice,[27] the wife of Bhava is mentioned.[28] Pāraskara GS.[29] mentions Rudrāṇī, Śarvāṇī and Bhavānī. As mentioned earlier, *Kena Up.* does not speak of her as Rudra's wife. The syncretisation of Rudra and Śiva was far quicker than that of the Goddess. Śiva emerged from the syncretisation of the Vedic Rudra and Agni. A similarity can be seen in the growth of his wife. She is seen as the syncretic figure of two streams one from Umā-Haimavatī, Ambikā, and Pārvatī belonging to Rudra, and the second from Kālī, Karālī, Sulohitā, Manojavā, Sphuliṅginī, and Viśvarūpā connected with Agni. Assimilated to Agni, she is the Devourer as well as the Expiator of sins. In her benign character she is the Mother of the hillsides.

It is thought that the Vedic goddesses Aditi, Uṣas, and Sarasvatī have developed into the Purāṇic Mahākalī, Mahālakṣmī and Mahāsarasvatī.[30] If we search for Vedic antecedents for the idea of feminine power or śakti, we may find it as the personification of the Will to Create. This of course has been enlarged to an eminent position in the Tantras.

Possible Development of Durgā from the Vedas

The Mother Goddess cult of the post-Vedic age must have been influenced by folk-cults and undergone a change. But it cannot be gainsaid that the Vedic goddesses like Aditi, Puraṁdhi, Sarasvatī and others had a certain influence on the Purāṇic goddesses like Durgā, Pārvatī, Umā, etc.[31]

When a deity has to be raised high above the level of the existing gods, she has to show extra prowess and power. If a goddess, then she has to show that she is superior to the gods' valour in their field of excellence, that is, war. The gods in the Vedic age were not much worried by the Asuras.[32] They were able to face their enemies after a generous draught of Soma. A similarity could be seen in the Purāṇas, when Devī quaffs wine, before killing Mahiṣa.[33] The hymns in the Mbh., as well as the DM. refer to the goddess as Durgā. This would indicate that her cult was well established at this time. One opinion against any connection of the Goddess to the Vedic goddesses should be mentioned. The Vedas or the epics do not know of the goddess

Durgā.[34] Judging by the hymn in the Virāṭa Parvan of the Mbh. she is stated to be related not to Śiva but to the Gopas,[35] that is the Ābhīras; further she is connected with the Vindhyas and not the Himālayas. The Mahiṣa killing episode is falsely attributed to her, because Skanda kills him in an earlier myth.[36]

Purāṇic myths or their figures could not have erupted out of nowhere, suddenly. They should have their seed in the Vedas.[37] We usually miss out their Vedic origin because we do not interpret Vedic gods themselves in their "multivalency". If we take Durgā's antecedents to Vedic Aditi, we should interpret the Goddess according to Yāska's rules. These would be :

(1) Ādhyātmika—the inner essence of the goddess,

(2) Ādhibhantika—her relationship to other bodies and elements,

(3) Ādhidaivika—her relationship to other gods, ie, mythology.

On the premise that Aditi is proto-Durgā, Aditi's inner essence is her all-encompassing motherhood. Durgā is also the Mother of all creations.[38] In the second classification Ādhibhautika, Aditi creates all gods. But with Durgā there is an exception. She is created by the tejas (luster) of all the gods. But she transcends all these gods in her powers and prowess. This may sound an anomaly. But myths have their own logic and they should not be forced to fit the logic of other disciplines. In the last qualification Ādhidaivika, Aditi is never supremely powerful. She is in the hymns always mentioned with her sons. But Durgā is transcendental. She is the ground of all beings as well as being the manifestation of the powers of the gods. Aditi is a creatrix, but is neither immanent, nor transcendent. Her Purāṇic model is both. This could also have been a cause of Aditi becoming a deus otiosus. She becomes Viṣṇu's wife in the Purāṇas, whereas Durgā, nominally spousified, grows enormously in stature, and has her Māhātmya recited by her devotees to this day. A god protecting or destroying exists in the Vedas themselves and this legacy is reiterated in the Purāṇic mythologies. The best example of such an ambivalence is the Goddess' fights with the Asuras, and especially their leader Mahiṣa. Further the Goddess tells Śumbha that she can only marry a person who can defeat her in battle. This is a typical characteristic of virgin war-goddesses the world over. The ambivalence is further seen in the characterisation of the Mothers, the Village Goddesses, Śaṣṭhī, Manasā, etc. The Śakti of the gods as picturised in the Purāṇas is an immensely powerful woman, which thought could naturally lead to the idea of the country as personified as a Mother.

Battle-myths are quite common in the early period all over the world. These are of three types. The myth may conceal opposition to the cult which finally overcomes the existing cult. It may remember the invading hordes subduing the original inhabitants. Thirdly, it may show the ambivalence of the gods, a brought-over memory from the Vedas, or, the alternating cycles of rest and activity of the gods. The Mahiṣāsuramardinī myth could be categorised both under the first and the third types.

We take Kālī and Mahiṣāsuramardinī as war-goddesses. War has been an occasional and inevitable occupation of civilizations of all stages, and war-deities have been popular in people's imagination. In the comparatively primitive stage of culture, a war deity qua war deity alone is popular. But as culture advances, the deity can remain popular only if she/he can take on beneficent attributes also. Kālī is an exception as she continues in her image of a goddess of destruction.

The *background* and *development* of the Goddess could be assessed by studying her various names. This would facilitate a better understanding either of the one Great Goddess and her multi-facets, or the characters of the multitudinous goddesses who coalesced into her.

Names

Since the Goddess is said to have an indigenous origin, which was Brahminised and brought into the Great Tradition later, the names which point to this background are taken up first.

Vindhyavāsinī

As the abode of the Goddess points to her origin. These ranges were the home of proto-Australoids. *Āryāstava* in the Mbh. calls her *'viśṛtā Vindhyavāsinī'* (6). She is said to be pleased with flesh, *māṁsaudanapriyā* (10). In the HV, (47.48), *Yoganidrā* is requested by Viṣṇu that, after helping him kill Kaṁsa, Indra will institute her in the Vindhyas, and she will be pleased by daily offerings of flesh, *'nityaṁ māṁsabalipriyā'* (41). In the apocryphal hymn of the Mbh., *Virāṭa Parvan. 'Vindhye caiva nagaśreṣṭhe tava sthānaṁ hi śāśvataṁ'* (18). Similar references are in the Matsya P.[39] and Vāmana P.[40] The literary references of this goddess will be taken up along with Durgā. In the apocryphal *Āryāstava* of the epic, she is said to be worshipped by forest-dwellers and tribals. *'Śabarair Barbarairścaiva Pulindaiśca supūjitā'* (10). Ethnically Śabaras are identified with the Kols, Kolis according to B.C. Mazumdar,[41] and Pulindas are the people west and north-west of India.[42] The word *Niṣāda* means *'ni'* to come down, and *'sad'* to settle.[43] Therefore, these along with the other tribes mentioned above may have been hill-tribes who came down to the plains and settled down. They were very devoted worshippers of the mother-goddess. These tribes were admitted into the Aryan society, when they changed their way of living, but they were kept on the outskirts of society as lower castes. But the Aryans absorbed their goddesses into the Brahminic religion. This may have been one way that Durgā and the other goddesses entered the Aryan fold. A similar case was when the god Kṛṣṇa was married to numerous powerful indigenous goddesses, thus bringing them into the Aryan religion. She is also referred elsewhere as Aparṇā, Nagna-Śabarī, and Parṇa-Śabarī. (This is said to be the *Vajrayāṇa* Goddess).[44] These names would indicate that, unlike Śiva who also had non-Aryan elements in his make-up, Aryanisation of the Goddess was much slower. Śābarotsava was till recently celebrated in Bengal, on the tenth day of the autumnal pūjā of Durgā. This substantiates the above opinion. Kālikā P. states categorically that this utsava should be performed according to the custom of the Śabaras.[45] Devī P. treats the exploits of Devī as Vindhyavāsinī. This Purāṇa gives a new list of demons killed by Devī. Vindhyavāsinī.'s manifestations, feats, and places dear to her are elaborated here. She kills the demons Ghora, Vajradaṇḍa, and Kāla.[46] Her fondness for flesh, her odd dress, and loud laughter all point to her origins from the tribal areas. Aryanisation of tribal goddesses helped to bridge the gap between the elite and folk elements.

Umā

The name Umā is non-Sanskritic in origin, related to words in Ma of Cappadocea, also the Chaldean mother-goddess, Babylonian Ummā, or Umā, Akkadian Ummi and the Dravidian Ammā.[47] The suffix Mā was thought to mean negation by the Brahmin priesthood, but it indicates the mother-goddess: Umā, Ruśamā, Rumā, Holimā, etc.[48] But another opinion is[49] that Umā is connected with the Himalayan region, and was later Aryanized. But Umā is always associated with the hilly regions in the epics[50] in her epithets.[51] In the Bhīṣma Parwan. of the Mbh., she is identified with Durgā. Umā's association with the hilly tracts has its parallels in Śiva's similar affiliations.

Durgā

The name Durgā occurs along with Kātyāyanī, Kanyākumarī and Vairocanī in the Taitt. Ār.[52] Sāyaṇa explains the name Durgī to be the same as Durgā. This name is explained in various ways in later religious literature. The name Durgā is said to be a lucus non,[53] because she is said to save people from difficulties, durga. In the Mbh.,[54] the derivation of the name is given. Another meaning would be that she is inaccessible, or that she lives in inaccessible places. In view of the antiquity of the word, the last meaning may be appropriate, since her abode as seen earlier seems to be on hills and in forests. In the Virāṭa Parvan when Durgā answers the King Yudhiṣṭhira, she speaks of the people living in atavī, durgā-kāntāra, sāgara, gahana-giri, which shows that she is the goddess of these people.

In the DM,[55] the derivation is given as *'Durgāsi durgabhavasāgaranaurasaṅgā,'* You help (us) cross the difficult ocean of *saṁsāra* by the boat of nonattachment. Another interpretation of this same is *'duṣprāpe Parabrahmatattve sāgare rāgādi rahite Durgā duṣprāpā naukā'*.[56] In the DM. itself, another fanciful explanation is given that she got this name because she killed the demon Durgama. This Durgama is seen as the demon of drought; for that matter even *Mahiṣa, Śumbha,* and *Niśumbha* are all seen as personifications of drought.[57] In the DM. (11.49), Devī says, *"tatraiva ca vadhiṣyāmi durgamākhyaṁ mahāsuram"*. In the *Skanda.* P.[58] Śiva asks Pārvatī to help kill the giant Durga. When she accomplishes this task, she is called Durgā.

In the DM.,[59] the Goddess promises that she will be born as Bhīmā Devī to kill the Asura Aruna. She will be renowned as Bhramarī. The Bhramaras are mentioned as the descendants of the Niṣādas, in the Padma P.[60] Bhramarāmbikā, is also the goddess of this tribe. There is a hymn about 'madhukaśa' in the *Ath. V.*[61]

We now take up the Brahminised names of the Goddess.

Kātyāyanī

Kātyas and Kuśikas were Brahmin families who adopted the Goddess as their tutelary deity. This shows the Goddess' slow rise to power, through Aryanisation, from small beginnings.[62] The Mbh.[63] *Bhīṣma Parvan* starts with Arjuna addressing the Goddess as Āryā (7). He calls her 'Kātyāyani mahābhāge (11), and 'Kauśikī pītavāsini' (15) showing the acceptance of the goddess by the Brahmins. This work is ascribed to the fourth century A.D.[64] In the Rām., the sage Kātyāyana is mentioned always in a list of venerable sages.[65] The name Kātyāyanī is given an origin in the Vāmana P. (Ch.19).

Taccaikatāṁ parvatakūtasannibhaṁ jagāma tejaḥ pravarāśrame mune/

Kātyāyanasyāpratimasya tena Maharṣiṇā tena upākṛtam ca// 7.

Tathārṣitejottamamuttamaṁ mahannāmnā pṛthivyāmabhavatprasiddham/

Kātyāyanityeva tadā babhau sā nāmnā ca tenaiva jagatprasiddhā// 13.

The appearance of the Devī from the lustres of the gods is given in the Devī Bhāg.[66] and Saptaśatī,[67] but the mention of Kātyāyana is not there.[68]

Skanda P.'s account of Kātyāyanī tallies with that of the DM.69 She is credited with the feat of killing Mahiṣā in this Purāṇa.[70] She is identified with Kṣemaṅkarī goddess of Saurashtra, called Camakkārī Durgā by folks; she was installed and worshipped by the King Kṣemaṅkara in his city. She is said to have mounted on a lion given to her by Gaurī, she went to the Vindhyas inhabited by Kirātas, etc. and she killed Mahiṣā. She was worshipped by the Kirātas. She is equipped with 12 arms having different weapons, given by the gods.[71] In the Matsya P.[72] she has ten arms.

Kumārī

The Goddess is often called a virgin and a brahmacāriṇī or Kumārī. *"Kaumāraṁ vratamāsthāya tridivaṁ pāvitaṁ tvayā"*.[73] "Having taken a vow of chastity, you have purified the three worlds." Kumārī, the Goddess in the southern most tip of India is mentioned in The Periplus of the Erythraean Sea, by an unknown author of circa 1st cent. A.D.:[74] "Beyond this[75] there is another place called Comari, at which are the Cape of Comari and harbour; hither come those men who wish to consecrate themselves for the rest of their lives, and bathe and dwell in celibacy; and women also do the same; for it is told that a goddess once dwelt here and bathed."

Sākambharī

In the DM., when the Goddess kills Caṇḍa, Muṇḍa, Śumbha, and Niśumbha, she says she will be born again in the Vindhyas assuming many names and kill many demons. These show not only the different names of the goddess but different goddesses syncretised into the Goddess. She says,

"Śākambharīti vikhyātiṁ tadā yāsyāmyahaṁ bhuvi/

Tatraiva ca vadhiṣyāmi Durgamākhyaṁ mahāsuram//. (11.49)

Durgā could be the logical extension of the Vedic Nirṛti, and Yamī. As such, she has underworld connections with the dead. Since death is drawn into the cycle of rebirth, Durgā is also the creatrix. This is particularly brought out in her Śākambharī aspect, connected to the vegetation cult. As life decays, dies, and is buried under the soil, it revivifies matter into life again, and sprouts new life. Hence Durgā calls herself Śākambharī in the DM. This idea of the Goddess as the fertilising power in vegetation is seen in the ghaṭasthāpana of the Durgā pūjā. Leaves of different plants placed in a ghaṭa full of water, assimilated to the womb, symbolises plants brought into contact with the female generative organ, for abundance. But, the name Śakambharī is seen as a historical name.[76] She is said to be the goddess of the Saka-Kushanas, under Kanishka, Huvishka and Vasudeva, whose composite rule lasted for 98 years. In the Śākambharī narrative, no enemy of the Goddess is mentioned. The memory of the Sakas must have been fresh in the minds of the people who had accepted the Devī of the Sakas. This idea is further confirmed by the name Śatākṣī of the Goddess, etymological derivation of which seems contrived.[77] Dhavalikar[78] finds the above argument far-fetched and prefers to believe that the Lajjā-Gaurī icons found on the Deccan plateau, are representations of Śākambharī, worshipped in the arid regions. The popularity of the Mahiṣāsuramardinī form of the goddess in the Kushana period is attested by the most numerous icons of this period. Durgā assimilated one by one each cult goddess, her traits, rituals and mythology, and the process was necessarily slow. Since these goddesses were of different traits, Durgā showed ambivalence in her make up as well as metaphysical superiority.

The three daughters of Menā, and Haimavān, as given in the Linga P. [79] are Aparṇā, Ekaparṇā and Ekapāṭalā. It is noticeable that all these names are connected with vegetation. Further Durgā is worshipped as embodiment in the leaves of nine plants, in the Navapatrikā ceremony in the Durgā pūjā festival. This is a clear example of plant theophany. The mystic relationship between humans beings and trees is seen all over the world, from May-Pole trees, Persepone and Demeter, Ceres, Attis and Adonis, to the Islamic and Hebraic importance given to the tree of Happiness.[80]

Durgama is taken as the personification of drought, and it is natural that a vegetation deity should vow to kill the Asura, "Being at once the goddess of fertility worshipped in a great variety of local vegetation cults, the Durgā was the author and giver of life to the fruits of the earth as the primordial essence, manifestation of cosmic vitality in perpetual process of regeneration, and at the same time a destructive force in the universe identified with Kālī and the 'grama devatā'.[81] Durgā's worship in the autumn is also connected with the harvesting festival. Rituals of Durgā show that she is a vegetation goddess, whereas her legends and iconography suggest a war deity. Her name suggests her association with inaccessible places. Her war-like characteristics are seen in Caṇḍī, Kālī, Cāmuṇḍā, and others. These qualities are not seen in Pārvatī and Umā. From this, it may be surmised that the Goddess Durgā is a syncretisation of two disparate streams. Kokhāmukhā is an epithet of Viṣṇu. Therefore, calling the Goddess Kokhāmukhā would connect her with the cult of Viṣṇu; it would not signify that she is wolf-faced.[82]

Durgā as Pārvatī becomes the wife of Śiva. This gave her an enormous potential. In the Aṣṭādhyāyī of pāṇinī, four names of Pārvatī are mentioned. These are—Bhavānī, Śarvāṇī, Rudrāṇī and Mṛḍānī.[83] Of these Śarvāṇī and Bhavānī were the local designations of one and the same goddess, whereas, Rudrāṇi and Mṛḍānī would be her local epithets.[84] The epic does not connect Durgā with a husband. She is mentioned as the sister of Viṣṇu. Her connection to Śiva is not always spelt out, except may be as the goddess of the mountainous regions.

The name Caṇḍikā, literally means the "violent" one. This seems to be derived from Caṇḍa. This is an epithet of both Śiva, and Skanda.[85]

The Purāṇic gods who are seen really as Vedic gods,[86] ask Devī's help to get their dominions back from their enemies. The Śākta cult's monotheistic influence is noticed here. Durgā is usually seen as a war-goddess, fighting for her devotees and actually participating in the war. She is Bhairavī, the terror-inspiring; Caṇḍī—the fierce; as Pārvatī she is the daughter of the Himalayas; Kumārī— the maiden; Umā—the mother-goddess of gracious appearance, connected with the mountains, Gaurī—either as the goddess whose colour is likened to the ripe corn, or, of the colour of the yellowish Gaur buffalo.

It is sometimes deduced that the Purāṇic Durgā's antecedents are through Ekānaṁśā to the Vedic Aditi.

Ekānaṁśā

According to the Matsya P., 87 Ekānaṁśā is the development of the Vedic Sinīvālī who was the goddess protecting childbirth and children. Brahmā requests Niśā Devī to give a share of her beauty of Pārvatī "Rūpāṁśena tu saṁyuktā tvamumāyāṁ bhaviṣyasi".[88] In the following ślokas, Brahmā praises the goddess (sl.s 76-83), in almost similar epithets as used in the DM, (Adh. 11). The connection to the Vedic goddess is seen in the prayer "Garbham dehi Sinīvālī" ṚV (X. 1842). Rātri Devī also gives a portion of herself to complete the form, tinging the foetus with her dark shade. Pārvatī's luminosity and Rātri Devī's darkness merged to give birth to Skanda, Agni's progeny.

In the epic, *Vana Parvan*,[89] she is *Kuhū*, daughter of Aṅgirasa. In Nīlakaṇṭha's commentary it is said

"Ekā cānaṁśeti Ekānaṁśā/
Bhagavatī ekā sati avibhaktā"//.

In the HV.[90] she is said to be born as a part of Brahma-Prajāpati, to protect Kṛṣṇa,[91] and that Ekānaṁśā should be worshipped on the ninth day of the śukla pakṣa fortnight with wine, animals and other sacrifices.

"Kṛtvānuyātraṁ bhūtaistvaṁsurāmāṁsabalipriyā/
Tithau navamyāṁ pūjāṁ tvaṁ prāpsyase sapaśukriyāṁ"//.

In another place in the epic,[92] it is clearly stated that *Kuhū* and

Ekānaṁśā are the same.

"Yaṁ dṛṣṭvā bhagavatīṁ janaḥ kuhukuhāyate/
Ekānaṁśeti yāmāhuḥ Kuhūmaṅgirasaha sutām"//.

Aditi is called Ekānāṁśa in the ṚgVeda.[93] A further nebulous connection between Durgā and Aditi is that Aditi is assimilated to the Sky sometimes; and, Durgā in the Mbh.[94] is called "Candrādityavivardhinī".[95]

Aditi, in the HV,[96] is born as Devakī, the mother-goddess Devagarbhā.[97] HV. identifies the goddess Yogamāyā as the goddess Ekānaṁśa, and states about offerings of wine and animals to the goddess. In the HV., Viṣṇu Parva, (Adh. 48), when Kaṁsa tries to strike her on a stone slab, she rises towards the heavens. She is Kanyā, endowed with good looks, adorned with the best of ornaments, and clothes (śl.. 30/31). She drinks wine and laughs loudly (śl. 33). She vows to drink warm blood tearing his body as he is being killed by his enemy (śl. 35).

She is the family deity of the Yādavas as she saved the life of Kṛṣṇa. her name is derived as Ekā and Anaṁśā (Bhagavatā Ekā satī avibhaktā). Another variant of her name is Ekānaṅgā, Ekā and Anaṅgā (one without a body). She is sometimes identified with Rukmiṇī, Subhadrā and Lakṣmī, wrongly so according to an opinion.[98] Her identification with Durgā and Ambikā is also considered promiscuous. In the Viṣṇu Parvan,[99] the goddess Nidrā plays an important part in the killing of Devakī's children by Kaṁsa. She puts six demons called collectively Saḍgarbhas into Devakī's womb successively. These were killed by Kaṁsa. The seventh foetus she transferred to Rohiṇī's womb. Then Nidrā and Viṣṇu simultaneously entered the wombs of Yaśodā and Devakī. Nidrā is variously called Yogamāyā, Ekānaṁśā and Ekānaṅgā. Viṣṇu goes down to Pātāla to request Nidrā to enter the womb of Yaśodā, and thus be the ninth of his family. In the dark fortnight, on the ninth day she would be born. But in the eighth month itself, they would exchange places. Indra will give her a permanent abode in the Vindhyas, and she would be known as Kauśikī (47/48). She would be worshipped on the ninth day of the fortnight, *"tithau navamyāṁ pūjāṁ ca prāpsyase sapaśukriyām"*. (51). In the Mbh., in the interpolated *stuti,*[100] she is called *"Gopendrasyānuje jyeṣṭhe Nandagopakulodbhave"*. Her malefic[101] and her beneficent[102] qualities are juxtaposed. She is accepted as the sister of Indra, and her abode as the Vindhyas. In the stutis stated above, her role as a sister of

Viṣṇu or Indra is emphasised. She is *Nārāyaṇī, Vāsudevasya bhaginī,* Kauśikī. In the Viṣṇu Parvan,[103] Balarāma and Kṛṣṇa after a war, return and offer their worship to Ekānaṁśā, established in the shrine by Vāsudeva, and looked after as his own daughter. "Putravat pālyamānā vai Vāsudevājñayā tadā" (śl.13). They show their indebtedness to her in killing Kaṁsa. "yatkṛte saganaṁ Kaṁsaṁ jaghāna Puruṣottamaḥ" (śl.12). Worshipped by the Vṛṣṇis she increased in her popularity.

Her origin is explained thus: *"Tāmekāmāhurutpannāmekānaṁśeti mānavāḥ"* (śl. 14).

She is described as Yogamāyā or as Yoganidrā of Viṣṇu in both Mbh., and the Bhāg P. In the Bhāg. P. (X. 2), she is called Yogamāyā, Viṣṇu's transcendent creative energy and also Bhadrā. Her sectarian (i.e., Śaivite or Viṣṇavite) affiliation may be doubtful. But iconographically she is placed between Kṛṣṇa and Balarāma as their sister. (śl. 6). Viṣṇu commands her to remove the seventh foetus from Devakī, and place this (Balarāma), in Rohiṇī. He states that he will be conceived simultaneously by Devakī and Yaśodā will bear Yogamāyā (śl. 8f). It is said elsewhere[104] that she is one day younger than Kṛṣṇa. In the Bhāgavata P. episode cited, Viṣṇu does not give the reasons but prophesies that she will be known as Durgā, Bhadrakālī, Vaiṣṇavī (śl.7), Cāṇḍikā, Kṛṣṇā, Kanyakā, Māyā, Nārāyaṇī, Iśānī, Śāradā, and Ambikā, (śl. 12), amongst other names. When Kaṁsa whose affection had been uprooted by self-interest, raises the infant to smash her against a stone slab,

"Sā taddhastāt samutpatya sadyo devyambaraṁ gatā/
Adṛśyatānujā Viṣṇoḥ Sāyudhāṣṭamahābhujā//
Iti Prabhāṣya taṁ Devī Māyā *Bhagavatī* .... (X. 4. 9ff).

She is called Yogamāyā in another place (III. 5. 47).

In the Skanda *P.* it is mentioned that Subhadrā should be propitiated with hymns from the Devī Sūkta.[105]

Many references make out that Subhadrā, and Durgā-Ekānaṁśā are one and the same goddess.[106] Bṛhatsaṁhitā states that Ekānaṁśā should be placed between Balarāma and Kṛṣṇa. When Subhadrā replaced Ekānaṁśā in the Skanda P., Durgā is removed from Viṣṇuite references. Ekānaṁśā is said to be originally a Viṣṇuite deity. She is said to be later associated with Yoganidrā and Yogamāyā, and was the sister of Kṛṣṇa. She was replaced by Subhadrā who had the same Viṣṇuite associations as Ekānaṁsā

Though some scholars have refuted the sister/consort relationship of the goddess Subhadrā to Kṛṣṇa[107], there seem to be clear indications that Subhadrā is treated as a consort of the god, specially from a painting in the bhoga maṇḍapa of the Jagannatha temple in Puri, where both these are depicted as standing on the same pedestal. In Tantras, the goddess is said to be both the sister and wife of Śiva.[108] There is a hypothesis linking the wooden post God Jagannātha worshipped in coastal Orissa and the wooden pillar goddess Stambheśvarī (i.e. Durgā) worshipped mainly in Western Orissa. This seems to have occurred due to religious and political link-ups[109]. One slight indication of the similar tribal origin of the goddess Subhadrā would be that, during the Ratha Yatra in Bhubhaneswar, tribals offer her worship. Further, the right side of the car of Subhadrā, is decorated with the icons of Caṇḍī, Cāmuṇḍā, Ugratārā, and others. She is said to have Buddhist Vajrayāṇa connections and is said to symbolise Śūnyatā of this branch.

The cult of Ekānaṁśā is said to be popular in the eastern districts of India. In the cave tample at Ellora, there is a stone relief of Ekānaṁśā which agrees with the iconographic details of the goddess as given in the *Viṣṇudharmottara;*[110]

Ekānaṁśāpi kartavyā Devī padmakarā tathā/
Kaṭisthavāmahastā sā madhyasthā balakṛṣṇayoḥ//

and, as in *Bṛhatsaṁhitā,*:[111]

Ekānaṁśā kāryā Devī BaladevaKṛṣṇayormadhya/
Kaṭisaṁsthitavāmakarā sarojamitareṇa codvahatī//

From these descriptions, it is seen that the goddess in this period was associated with Baladeva and Kṛṣṇa. As seen earlier, her role in the epic justifies such an association.

In the Kālikā P.[112] Yoganidrā is called Yogamāyā, Viṣṇumāyā, Mahāmāyā. She takes the form of Kālikā, dark in complexion, mounting a lion, with four hands, holding a sword and a blue lotus in two hands, and varadābhaya mudrās in her two other hands. She has a beautiful face, and red eyes. She is the power of Viṣṇu in the Devī Bhāg. P.[113] All Purāṇas which mention Yoganidrā connect her to the power of Viṣṇu, i.e., as his Śakti.

In the Matsya P.[114], Brahmā blesses Pārvatī with a golden complexion. The dark-hued goddess Rātr is separated from Pārvatī. She is three-eyed, dressed in golden coloured clothes, and holds a bell. She is asked to go to the Vindhyas, with Pañcāla, a

Yakṣa as an attendant; her vāhana is the lion and one hundred thousand Yakṣas follow her. She would be known as Ekānaṁśā and in the Vindhyas will do work for the devas. Then Kauśikī (Rātrī/Ekānaṁśā) went to the Vindhyas while Pārvatī joined Śiva.

The Goddess in the Epic

There are three stutis in the Mbh. on the Goddess. The first in the *Virāṭa Parvan.*;[115] the second in the *Bhīṣma Parvan.*;[116] and the third in HV.,[117] the Āryāstava. All these are considered late interpolations. The idea of the Goddess as expressed in these stutis, and the epithets used are similar to the eulogies in the DM. This leads to the dating of these epic stutis to the same period as the DM., i.e., fourth cent. A.D. circa.

In the *Virāṭa Parvan stuti,* as Yudhiṣṭhira goes towards Virātanagara, he praises the goddess Durgā in 26 verses. The relationship to *Viṣṇu* is immediately established, *"Yaśodāgarbhasaṁbhūtāṁ Nārāyaṇavarapriyāṁ"* and, *"Nandagopakule jātām"*(2), and *"Vāsudevasya bhaginīṁ"* (4). She is made the supreme goddess, *"tribhuvaneśvarīm"*(1). Though the verse 8 says *"Caturbhuje"*, she is visualised as aṣṭabhujā because, of the various weapons she carries (10-11) in her hands, and the varada and abhaya mudrās are considered to be implicit. Her connection to the South Indian goddess Kanyā Kumārī is established in the epithets *Kumārī Brahmacariṇī*(7), and *"Kaumāraṁ vratamāsthāya trididvam pāvitaṁ tvayā"*,(15). Her assimilations to other goddesses are further stated in the epithets *"Jayā"* and *"Vijayā"*(17), "Kālī" and "Mahākālī"(18). The Mahiṣāsuravadha is explicitly stated in *"trailokyarakṣaṇārthāya Mahiṣāsuranāśinī"*,(16). The Durgā *stotra* in the *Bhīṣma Parvan.*[118] is seen to be similar to the earlier one in that the conneection to Śiva is stressed in this, whereas her relationship to Viṣṇu is established in the *Virāta Parvan stuti.* Kṛṣṇa advises Arjuna to pray to the goddess, who is primarily a war-goddess, *Jayā, Vijayā*(11) and *Raṇapriyā* (16). In the fierce epithets "Kālī" "Kapālī", "Bhadrakālī", "Mahākālī", "Caṇḍī", Caṇḍe", and "Karālī", her connection to Śiva(11) may be seen. Attempts at syncretisation are seen in the epithets "Umā"(16), "Āryā", "Kātyāyanī"(11), etc. Later her relationship to Viṣṇu is also stated in *"Gopendrasyānuje Jyeṣṭhe Nandagopakulodbhave"*(14). Hopkins[119] interprets *Kokamukhā* as wolf-faced. But this is an epithet of Viṣṇu. Her loud laughter(18) and her residences on mountain(7), and forests(22), and epithets as Durgā(22), or allied names (15,22,16) all point to the character of the goddess already established by the time of this *stuti*. Just as in the earlier stuti she is called "Kṛṣṇā", here she is also called "Śvetā"(16). That her permanent residence is the Pātāla may point to her un-Aryan antecedents. She is "Kumārī", but also "Jananī" (8,30). Her Mahiṣavadha episode is mentioned only in that she is fond of the animal's blood(15). Lofty epithets are used more than in the last stuti. Her benign and fierce aspects are constantly juxtaposed. This may shgow that she was in the process of Aryanisation. Folk goddesses like Jambhani, and Mohini are mixed with Vedic deities like Śrī, Hrī, Māyā (29). The alternating of fierce and benign epithets are seen in the other eulogies of Mbh., DM., and *Lalitāṣahasranāma.*

The various names given to the Goddess may be seen as an attempt to syncretise different goddesses. But it could also be that the same Goddess has different names and forms to fulfil different purposes. When Viṣṇu goes to Pātāla to request Yoganidrā to assist him in killing Kaṁsa, she manifests herself as Durgā-Kātyāyanī, and is born as Kṛṣṇa's sister to Yaśodā and Nanda.[120] This shows an attempt to syncretise the Śiva and Viṣṇu cults. The composite figure of the Goddess which emerged had an amalgamation of different disparate groups of different levels. Her episodes are always to help her devotees out of their oppressive travails.

In the *Āryāstava,*[121] though her relationship to Viṣṇu is stated in *"Bhaginī Vāsudevasya"* (16), and *"Nandagopasutā"*(17), more epithets connect her to Śiva, *"Raudrī"*, *"Mātā Bhūtagaṇasya"*, *"Pārvatī"*(42). Though Aryan assimilation is seen (1) *"Āryā Kātyāyanī Devī Kauśikī Brahmacāriṇī"*, her habitat in inaccessible places is mentioned, *"parvatāgreṣu ghoreṣu nadīṣu ca guhāsu ca"* (7) and *"viśrutā Vindhyavāsinī"* (12). As mentioned earlier she is worshipped by tribal people. She is called Vālmīki's *Sarasvatī* and Vyāsa's *Smṛti* (29); very high praises are showered on her *"sarvabhūtānāṁ niṣṭhā"*, *"paramā gatiḥ"*(17), *"Brahmavādinyaḥ dīkṣā"*, *"parama śobhā"* (25, also 32,34,45). But her malefic character is also brought to our attention is such epithets *"yamasya bhaginī"* (4), *"mṛtyu,"* *"kalahapriyā"* (19,16), *"Alakṣmī"*(20). Her Earth-Mother quality is seen in the epithets *"karṣakānām ca Sīteti bhūtānāṁ Dharaṇīti ca"* (33). The folk element in her makeup is seen in *"Śakunī, Pūtanā, Sudāruṇā Revatī"* (39). Since in the previous chapter (i.e. 47), she is told by *Viṣṇu* that after helping him she would be installed on the Vindhyas by no less a deity than the Vedic god Indra, it may be surmised that she gained a foothold in the Aryan religion through Viṣṇu's assistance. She is also not called Durgā here. It might also be that a forced relationship is thought out with Viṣṇu, seeing the power she wielded amongst the masses. This connection later peters out and she is stable in her Śaivite affiliation. But the point to remember is that she was a Great Goddess in her own rights and her exploits are always to help out the gods who seek her out.

Her assistance here is in killing Kaṁsa, and no mention is made of *Mahiṣā*, though her fondness for flesh is mentiond. In the *Virāṭa parvan stuti*, and in other Viṣṇuite legends,[122] the Goddess is given Viṣṇu connection, and this is made out to be the cause of her future greatness. These texts call her the Mahāmāyā, or the Yoganidrā of Viṣṇu. These further may point to her Ābhīra or Gopa origins.[123] Others opine that though her Viṣṇuite connections are stated, her relationship to Śiva is more clear[124] Umā, Durgā, Ambikā, Gaurī are all melded into the Great Goddess only in the Gupta period. Moreover, Umā is the Brahminisation of the Village Goddesses like Ellammā, Kālammā, etc. She is Ammā of the indigenous cult, transformed.[125] In modern mythology Ellammā is elevated and made the mother of the three gods.[126]

There are three forms of the goddess-ugra, *saumya* and the sensuous. In these stutis from the epic, her sensuous form is not mentioned at all. There may be fear shown towards the Goddess. It is only in the Tantras that this form is developed fully and emphasised. That the goddess has become the deity of the elitists can be surmised from the stutis by kings and princes like Yudhiṣṭhira, Arjuna, Aśvathāman, Pradyumna, son of Kṛṣṇa,[127] and Aniruddha, grandson of Kṛṣṇa[128] and others. Yudhiṣṭira particularly begs for protection *"trāhi mām"*, because he is exiled, *"rājyāt paribhraṣṭaḥ."*[129]

The Goddess in the Purāṇas

The Purāṇas may be generally dated between 200 A.D. and 800 A.D. Though they were composed by Brahmins they had an appeal to a wider audience. The Supreme Reality was Puruṣa in the Vedas,[130] the Upaniṣads[131] and the epic.[132] With the advent of Śāktism it became feminine, and a Mother Goddess. In Śākta literature she ordered the three gods and their wives in their respective roles. She was Durgā, or Parāśaktī, Mahādevī, etc., in the DM, *Devī Bhāgavata, Devī,* and *Kālikā Purāṇas.*[133] She is usually addressed as the Supreme Being, the Mother underlying and pervading the universe. The epithets are sometimes the same for the Purāṇic gods and most generally for all goddesses.[134] The popularity of the Purāṇic deities arises to a certain extent from their amalgamating 'popular' deities with theriomorphic forms, and this allowed a rich mythology and symbolism. They are cosmic as well as terrestrial forms. The traits of the avatāras may be termed as the conscious development of a single trait of the deity through multiforms.[135] There are various names of goddesses in the eulogies of the Purāṇas. The idea of syncretisation apart, the epithets may have been brought in to give the complete picture of the qualities of the goddess, which the composer may have had in mind. Half the epithets in most of the eulogies are abstract ideas, or, compounds which look obviously contrived. The Vāyu P. gives different lists of goddesses and states that these are not different names of the goddess, but they indicate different goddesses altogether.[136] This *Purāṇa* mentions for the first time the white and black forms of Devī, that is, the benign and malignant forms, Gaurī and Kālī.[137]

In the Vāmana P., (Adh. 30) Kauśikī sees the demon Raktabīja multiplying from the droplets of blood; she addresses Caṇḍī as Keśinī, and requests her to drink the demon's blood (27). This Caṇḍī is same as Ambikā, and, Carmamuṇḍā (28). Ambikā is Durgā, who dragging the demon by his hair throws him into her mouth, rending his chest with her *śūla,* thus allowing the blood to flow into her mouth (29). Again Durgā as Kauśikī, resides on the Vindhyas after killing , Mahiṣa. Raktabīja is a friend of Mahiṣa on earth, and Caṇḍa and Muṇḍa are his generals, fleeing for their lives. Śumbha, Niśumbha and Namūci are three demons, sons of extraordinary valour of Kaśyapa and Danu. Śumbha and Niśumbha conquer the gods and come to earth and make friends with Raktabīja, Caṇḍa and Muṇḍa. Dhūmrākṣa goes as an emissary to a Durgā with a proposal of marriage and is destroyed by Devī with 'Huṁ'. Caṇḍa and Muṇḍa are killed by Durgā; and the others, in the following chapter. When Śumbha and Niśumbha are killed, the gods praise the Goddess with the epithets Mārī and Carmamuṇḍā - the carrier of dead bodies (62).

The Devī P. treats the exploits of Devī as Vindhyavāsinī. This

Purāṇa gives a new list of demons killed by Devī. Vindhyavāsinī's manifestations, feats, places dear to her, are all elaborated in this Purāṇa. She kills the demons Ghora, Vajradaṇḍa and Kāla.[138] In the Devī Bhāg P. Durgā is described as holding weapons in four or eighteen arms; dressed in excellent clothes and ornaments.[139] This is her saumya form. In this Purāṇa she is called[140]. Viṣṇumāyā and also Śaivī.[141] Madhu and Kaiṭabha episodes and Viṣṇu killing them are narrated in Book I (6-9) and in the fifth book are narrated the killing of Mahiṣa, Caṇḍa, Muṇḍa, Raktabīja, Śumbha and Niśumbh.

The three gods take fright when they confront Mahiṣa on the battlefield. They take to their hells and retire to their abodes. Brahmā had earlier given the boon to Mahiṣa that he can be killed only by a woman. Since there was no woman, not even Umā, or Śacī, mighty enough to meet the demon, they take *Viṣṇu's* advice, and with their collective tejas (splendouss) create a woman.

"... Devānāṁ tejapuñjasamudbhavā/
*Babhūvātivarā nārī ...//*43
*"Triguṇā sā Mahālakṣmīḥ sarvadevaśarīrajā/...//*44;
Aṣṭādaśabhujā devī sahasrabhujamaṇḍitā/
*Sambhūtā(a)suranāśāya tejorāśisamudbhavā//"*46.

There is an explanation as to the various forms sported by Devī:

"Yathā naṭo raṅgagato nānārūpo bhavatyasau/
*Ekarūpasvabhāvo(a)pi lokaranjanahetave//*58.
Tathaiṣā devakāryārthamarūpāpi svalīlayā/
*Karoti bahurūpāṇi nirguṇā saguṇāni ca//*59
Kāryakarmānusāreṇa nāmāni prabhavanti hi/"...60.

In Adh. 14 Devī spurns the marriage proposal sent by Mahiṣā through various messengers and kills a few war-leaders also. Finally Mahiṣa comes and proposes to her and is spurned and challenged by Devī to a fight. In Adh. 18, she drinks a fortifying draught of liquor, and cuts the head of the Asura with a sharp discus.

Similarly Śumbha gets infatuated with Devī. He and his brother also have a boon, this time from Śiva that they would be invincible, to all living creatures excepting women because they are by nature 'abalā'. The similar episodes to DM. are narrated in Adhs. 22-31.

The other popular forms of the goddess are as *Umā* or *Pārvatī*. These forms fulfil the roles as wife and mother, and are not involved in activities of war. The earlier Purāṇas like *Vāyu, Brahmāṇḍa* and *Matsya* and, the later ones like Kūrma, Śiva, Garuḍa and Brahma do not depict her as a demon-slaying goddess. The DM., *Vāmana* and other Devī or *Śākta*-oriented *Purāṇas* depict her so.[142] Whether a demon-slayer or a saviour, Durgā is equipped with eight, ten, or sixteen arms. Umā or Pārvatī is always depicted with two or four hands.

At the time of the compilation of the lists of the goddesses, the cults of these deities must have existed, though the goddesses may not have borne the same name as in the Purāṇas. Unless the cults were popular in that period their inclusion in the Purāṇas would be anomalous. The episodes in the myths may also have been composed to justify their inclusion in the Brahminic cult.[143] The groups of goddesses mentioned in the *stutis* in the Purāṇas, sometimes show foreign influence; e.g: Apata, Anādita, Airānī, Sālimālinī. These are called mleccha goddesses. They may have evolved from Pallas-Athene, Anāhaitā, Irene, and Seline respectively.[144] Sometimes the names sound purely imaginary like Sumahābhāgā and Mṛtyucchāyā[145] but elaborate details of their rites and the time and mode of worship are given. The many names and the myths point to a long and complicated history of the evolution of the Goddess cult. The popular village agricultural goddess Vaśinī was first ignored by the Aryans, but later was adopted by them and made into a wife of Śiva.[146] Vaiṣṇavism did not integrate into their cult tribal goddesses which Śaivism successfully accomplished.

Originally Durgā could have had an ugra aspect. She must have reflected the qualities of the tribal deities whom she syncretised into herself, having the same background. She could have absorbed the Sapta Mātṛs and reflected their fierce temperament. Her violent aspect is seen in the snake which is used as her kucabandha. She also uses the snake as a pāśa to bind the Mahiṣa before killing him.[147] (Snake is also the border dividing magic and religion). The serpent cult thus associated with her, her gruesome attendants and her own ugra form, all made her easily accessible to the Śiva cult. The Matsya P.[148] distinguishes between Pārvatī and Durgā, by apportioning to the latter hilly and forest regions as her habitat. But once Durgā was established as the Great Goddess, her saumya aspects were developed. It is easier to approach a mother for succour, and in her saumya aspect as Pārvatī, Gaurī, etc., she was the protective mother. After her marriage to Śiva she acquired a family also. Though, in the epic, she was connected with Viṣṇu in the DM. her affiliations are definitely with Śiva. The Ekānaṁśā episodes and the Nārāyaṇī stuti are seen as a late accretion to the Viṣṇu cult. In the Purāṇas she is a supremely powerful goddess, destroying the enemies of the gods easily. The episodes of the Śakti Pīṭhas enlarge the area of influence of the goddess enormously, spreading her cult all over the country. Though the cult did not seem to have an exclusive and organised sect,[149] the goddess cult seemed to have been widespread. This cult had definitely not sprung from either the Śiva or Viṣṇu cult but seems to have had indigenous roots going deep into the soil. She must have been a very great and popular goddess of the Vindhya regions that two hymns.[150] were devoted to her in the Mbh. The merging of Durgā and Vindhyavāsinī is also seen as a cultural coalescence. Durgā may be said to have reinstated the Vedic gods to their posts, if not to their original glory, as she keeps them subservient to her.

The Śākta oriented texts make Durgā as transcendental, or the Śakti of Brahman. The Tantric concept of the goddess is that she is fierce, and the rites connected with her are mostly vāmācāra. The Purāṇic concept of the goddes is ambivalent, but the rites recommended are Dakṣiṇācāra.[151] In the Mahānirvāṇa Tantra it is said that the goddess assumes various forms to assist her devotees and to rid the world of its afflictors, for its benefit.[152] In the Pāñcarātra texts like Lakṣmī Tantra, Durgā is named as the wife of Nārāyaṇa.[153]

The various goddesses who are all manifestations of Durgā may have been different deities with varied historical background, i.e., Bhīmā, Bhramarī, Śākambharī Kumārī and Ekānaṁśā.[154]

Mountains and forests are held to be sacred and the dwelling places of the gods. They are sacred because they were considered difficult of access and therefore assimilated to the heavens; the sacred tribal meetings were held there.[155] The primitives think of the cosmic god as likened to their totem animal-ancestor. The Mother-Goddess thus becomes the mother of the totem animal and, as the genetrix she becomes the protector of forests, and their denizens.[156]

The goddess cult alters the structure of religion. It softens the austere aspect of religion and infuses it with a sentiment of tenderness. It sometimes did contribute towards the improvement of the position of women in society.[157] There are three aspects to a deity, which have to be kept in mind, while studying a god or a goddess. Taking the goddess, there is the immanent form, which is Durgā; the pantheistic form when she is called Gaurī, Caṇḍī, Sarasvatī, Lakṣmī, etc.; then the transcendantal form when she is above all these manifestations and has the Virāt Svarūpa; she is praised in the Sahasranāma as being Sahasrākṣī, Sahasrabahū, etc.[158] In the Purāṇic Devī stutis all epithets which would describe other goddesses are used for Devī.[159]

The incarnations of goddess Durgā are different according to different legends. In the Skanda P.[160] Durgā is given eight forms, Aṣṭa Durgā, to match the eight forms of Śiva. Each of these forms signify a direction. In the Devī P.[161] she is Nava Durgā, to match the Nava Grahas. These are said to be her most important emanations. According to the Devī Kavaca,[162] these are: Śailaputrī, Brahmacāriṇī, Candraghaṇṭā, Kūṣmāṇḍā, Skandamātā, Kātyāyanī, Kālarātrī, Mahāgaurī, Siddhidā. In Skanda P.[163] her sixteen forms are explained as different incarnations in different Kalpas. Her sixteen, ṣoḍaśa forms are divided into sāttvika, rājasika, and tāmasika.

In worship, the Nava Durgā form is very popular. One icon is put in the centre, and the other eight are arranged around the centre one to face the eight directions. All of them are seated on lotuses, the middle figure has eighteen hands, and all the others have sixteen hands. Their names are differently given[164] as: Rudracaṇḍā, Pracaṇḍā, Caṇḍogrā, Caṇḍanāyikā, Caṇḍā, Caṇḍavatī, Caṇḍarūpā, Aticaṇḍikā, and Ugracaṇḍikā. The centre figure is that of a Mahiṣamardinī, the others seated in rathas, shaped like lotuses.[165] The Āgamas mention different names for the Nava Durgās: Nīlakaṇṭhī, Kṣemaṅkarī, Harasiddhī, Rudrāṁśā, Durgā, Vana Durgā, Agni Durgā, Jaya-Durgā, Ripumāri-Durgā.[166]

In the DM.,[167] the Devī assures the devas that in future whenever the world is troubled by unlawful oppression, she will incarnate herself to annihilate it.

"Ittham yadā yadā bādhā dānavotthā bhaviṣyatī"/54
"Tadā tadāvatīryāhaṁ kariṣyāmi saṁkṣayam"//55

Vibhūtivāda similar to the Bhag. G.[168] seems the only answer to explain the various emanations of the Goddess.

"Ahaṁ vibhūtyā bahubhiriha rūpairyadāsthitā/

Tatsaṁhṛtaṁ mayaikaiva tiṣṭhāmyājau sthiro bhava// (Adh. X, 8)

After Niśumbha was killed and Śumbha comes to fight, he taunts Devī that she depends an others to fight her wars, and Durgā replies with the above lines. She is immanent and transcendent in this world. She is the creator, preserver and destroyer of this world. She is immutable, but her mutation is this world. She is beyond the three Guṇas, but with the Guṇas she creates the world.

Taking up the different forms of the Goddess, on the north of Iḷāvarṣa, in a mountain where the river Kāmadughā originates, Goddess Mīnākṣī resides. She is dressed in blue clothes, has bluish black hair, a fearful contenance, and is wellornamented. She is worshipped by both *devas* and *asuras,* and fulfils wishes of her devotees.[169] The same Purāṇa (VII. 38) gives an exhaustive list of the different goddesses and their places of worship.[170] The goddess' name. Kāmākhyā must have arisen from the name Kāmā, which has malefic connotation in Austric language. This also shows that[171] most goddesses were ambivalent to start with. In the Viṣṇuite temples like Pandharpur and Dvaraka, the existence of an earlier and separate temple to the goddess Rukmiṇī is explained that she was peeved with Kṛṣṇa's dalliance with Rādhā and came to these places and lived alone, and Kṛṣṇa followed her later. This is a late explanation obviously by the Brahmins in an attempt to syncretise the goddess into their fold. Rukmiṇī is called Rukhumāi in Marathi. The 'ai' suffix shows she is a mother-goddess, possibly of great antiquity. Similarly the rustic god Khaṇḍobā and his wife Mhaḷsā are also installed separately.[172] These instances show the cults of two distinct deities belonging to different societies, brought together. The goddess belongs to a society of food-gatherers, whereas the god is of pastoral people. The couple reflect the conjoint society of a later period. Yet another instance of such a coalescence is of the mother-goddess of Maḷvalī[173] represented by aniconic stones, besmeared by red ochre paint and called "sati ai". A sati stone is a few meters away, showing the way the goddess derived her name. Further the goddess in Pandharpur is assimilated to Masānī a local goddess, and worshipped as such.[174]

Buddhist

Buddhist *Jātakas* mention goddesses only in the context of tree-spirits. In the *Mahājanaka Jātaka,*[175] there is only a reference to a vague character *Maṇimekalā,* daughter of the gods, appointed by the gods of the four quarters to protect devout sea-farers, so that they do not come to harm. A definite conception of mother-goddess occurs in the *Śirikāla Kanni Jātaka.*[176] Here two opposite types of goddesses are mentioned. One is the malevolent Kalakanni, daughter of Virūpākṣa, and the other is Siri, daughter of Dhataraṭṭa. The negative type is the personification of hypocrisy, wantonness, morosensess, envy, greed and treachery. Siri, the positive goddess resembles the Vedic Śrī. She is the goddess of wisdom, good-fortune, and luck. Just like the belief that Lakṣmī enters the house after Alakṣmī is driven out, so also the Buddhist Siri enters after Kalakanni is driven out.

South Indian

The South Indian burials of the Iron Age have a buffalo's head or a trident. The former is the symbol of Yama, later associated with Durgā and the trident is Durgā's weapon.[177] Thus there is the earliest evidence of the goddess, though associated with death, symbolically represented. Durgā, seen as the non-Aryan divinity, is traced through a connection between the Cretans, and the Dravidians.[178] Dravidian civilization could be connected to Crete via Mesopotamia. The proto Dravida, i.e., *Dramila-Dravida* could be connected to what the Lycian inscription calls one section of the Cretans, *Trmmili,* or, *Termilai.* This presumes the Mediterranian origins of the Dravidians. Certain Lycian words have a great similarity to words of Dravidian origin. One such example of striking similarity is seen in the Lycian *Trqqas,* a divinity, and the Indian Mother Goddess Durgā of non-Aryan but of Asiatic origin.[179] Umā as a goddess with a similar foreign origin has already been commented on . The Dravidians could have originated in Crete and passed through Asia Minor and the Mediterranean into Sumer and Elam. The Kols[180] culturally an inferior race have lent a lot of words to the Indian language, like liṅga, lāṅgala, lāṅgūla, etc.[181] So also did the Dravidians lend linguistic and religious ideas to the Aryan religion.[182]

In Tamil Nadu, Durgā was a popular goddess in the fourth, fifth centuries B.C. seen from the Tamil literature *Śilappadikāram.* In this period, it is learnt[183] that people of the forest regions, and the Maravars and Eyinars offered worship to the girl children in their families, dressing them up like Durgā and seating them on deer skins. She is called Koṟṟavai ruling over Pālai region in *Pattuppāṭṭu,*[184] *Kurunthokai*[185] and *Tirumurukāṟṟuppaḍai.*[186] She has a tribal or folk dress, ornamentation and appearance. She likes buffaloes sacrificed to her. Her weapon is a triśūla, trident. She is a fierce goddess whose displeasure is dreaded as it can be calamitous. Her influence over the forest regions is well attested in the regional literature of a very early period.[187] *Koṭṭavī*[188] was a popular goddess of South India. Originally she was supposed to have been a rākṣasī. Later on she was worshipped as Durgā or Umā. In Jaina literature Koṭṭakiriyā is the name given to Durgā, as she rides a buffalo. This must have been the result of syncretising a tribal goddess with Durgā. In the Bhāg. P. there is a mention of this goddess Koṭarā, mother of *Bāṇa,*[189] *"Tanmātā Koṭarā nāma nagnā muktaśiroruhā."* She must have been the South Indian goddess *Koṭṭavī.* There are literary evidences to support this.[190] In the Himalayan regions she was known by various mutations of this name, like Koṭṭakīriyā, Koṭṭavī, Kotarā, Kotavī, or Kotamāi. The goddess seems to have developed in three layers. Before the Christian era, she was known as *Koṭṭarī,* or *Koṭṭavī.* Under the Scythians, she was known as Nānī, or Nanaiā, around the beginning of the Christian era. And lastly in the Gupta period she was called Carcikā in the *Vāmana* P.[191] She was obviously a very popular goddess from the South upto the Himalayas. Pinnai is seen as the Tamil Durgā, though this is suppressed in Viṣṇuite records.[192] But this is refuted as it is dangerous to read too much into slender vernacular evidence.[193]

The worship of the goddess in Kanchipuram by the Śākta sects was of the Devī as Kālī, and later as the saumya from Rājarājeśvarī. Legends have it that the original fierce rites of worship in the temple were replaced by the pacific rites of Dakṣiṇācāra. This may be veiling the fact of one cult replacing another, just as this is symbolised by the legend of the fair Pārvatī emerging from the dark goddess. In Tamil, the word Kanni denotes Durgā, a maiden, and Kanchipuram is referred to as Kannikkāppu, a city protected by Kanni, a maiden. This further supports the view that the Kumārī of the deep South is another form of the goddess Durgā. That Kāmākṣī is a form of Durgā is proved by the Purāṇas Devī Bhāg.[194] and Matsya,[195] and inscriptions in Tamil Nadu, Andhra and Karnaṭaka.[196] Koḍi is Durgā between the ages of nine to twelve years, that is a maiden. Kāmāksī is not only Durgā, but she is also

Durgā or Kālī of some villages, in Tiruchi and Madurai districts. Since there are no iconographic details specially pertaining to this form of the goddess, most mūrtis over this area are called Kāmākṣī, or Durgā. Kāḷāmukha influence was on many Devī temples in the South. Śaṁkara is said to have changed the Kaula rituals into saumya form early in the eighth century A.D. He had installed Śrī Yantra in front of the goddesses, who were independent of the gods. Moreover, Golaki Lakṣādhyāyī Santānams which established Mutts, wielded great influence over the ruling powers. They brought in their influence of North Indian and Kashmri Śaivism. Prakāśa was Śiva's aspect of subjective illumination. Vimarśa was his objective experience of Himself. Sadāśiva tattva comprises both Sadāśiva and Manonmaṇī. If Sadāśiva is represented, his Śakti Manonmaṇī also has to be represented. This philosophy necessitated for the first time in the early eleventh century, during the Coḷa regime building of subshrines for Devī, either by transforming goddesses nearby independently under worship, as Manonmaṇī of the resident god, or building fresh subshrines for Devī in the building complex. It has to be noted that till now there were only shrines of parivāradevatās, not a separate subshrine for Devī.[197] The old Durgā temples which did not come under the Vedic or Āgamic modes of worship or where such modes were discontinued, the goddesses continued to be worshipped as Grāma Devatās, such as Pidārī, Ellaiyamman, etc.[198] In the North, the appeal of the worship of the female principle behind the god was so great that all the gods were provided with spouses and worship was established for the couples together. But this did not satisfy the masses. Therefore, the goddess had to be raised to the supreme status to be emotionally satisfying.

Superior Position of the Goddess

"In mythology, as in life, only the fittest survive. And mythological fitness is determined by the capacity to assimilate".[199] This dictum would give one of the reasons for the goddess' superiority. The deity should also have a vague outline for her character, which could grow and allow for syncretising other characteristics of other deites. Further, the atmosphere should be ripe for the emergence of such a figure, which has as a goddess strength and stature. When a deity has to be raised far above the level of the existing gods, she has to show extra power and capacity. If a goddess, then she has to show and maintain her superiority in their field of strength, that is war. Myths in the Mbh. were composed to show the certain superiority of the Goddess. In the Purāṇas, her elevated state is further exalted and substantiated with further myths. This rise to a high position would necessarily take time. It can be reasonably deducted that this period covered from 500 B.C. to around 400 A.D., that is, the period just after the non-Hindu cults, to the Gupta period. At around the late fourth century, or early fifth century A.D., the Great Goddess had crystallised into Mahiṣāsuramardinī. Durgā had to rise to power exactly like the Vedic gods earlier had, by feats of prowess and killing demons. Durgā's battles with Asuras can be commented on that she had to fight her way into orthodox Hinduism. Indra was the hero-god of the semi-nomadic pastoral tribes. He was a lusty drinker, cattle-raider, and a powerful leader. He could, with his personal charisma, collect the tribes and lead them to victory, against the non-Aryans. A similar situation could have arisen when India was constantly battered by foreign invasions. The faith in the Vedic gods was not sufficient to overcome the enemies and the people could have not only discarded them but belittled them in the episodes of the war-goddess. The milieu must have been just right for a fertility goddess who was also always victorious against powerfully evil enemies. In the myths concerning the Goddess, the gods are never shown as participating in the wars alongside the Goddess. But they are ever ready to eulogise her in extravagant terms in their lauds. They are mere by-standers, ever ready to applaud her when she surmounts a tricky encounter.

This supreme power invested in Devī, as she rose in her stature, may also have been helped by philosophy. Sāṁkhya had the two principles Prakṛtī who was an active participant while Puruṣa merely looked on. Advaita Vedānta postulated a neuter Brahman. Creation was possible through Māyā who was the eternal capacity (nityā śaktī) of the Paramātman. Lest it be misconstrued that this śaktī acted without the active effort of the Supreme Soul, they said Māyā was the Prakṛtī, and Māyin was Parameśvara. The other meanings of Māyā were insight (Prajñā), and Moha (delusion). This Wisdom and Stupefying Capacity along with Creative Energy, became Mahālakṣmī, who created all beings including the gods; Durgā, who fought and defeated asuras; Devī, who taught Śākta literature; and Yoganidrā, who sent all beings to sleep.[200]

Similar Goddesses Abroad

Durgā's character as a Goddess of war and fertility can be seen in many of the goddesses of Near East, Egypt, and Greece.

In Egypt, Anat[201] was known as the goddess of war. She had battled violently and victoriously with the enemies of Baal. She delighted in war and slaughter. She loved to wallow in bloodshed. She was also the goddess of love and fertility. *Anat* was also called the "Lady of the Mountain" since Baal also resided in the mountains. Asherah,[202] an ally of Baal was similar to Anat. She was also a goddess of love and fertility. These goddesses were perennially fruitful, but were virgins. They thus became the sister and consort of the leading god. This is a recurrent theme in the cult of the goddess. Another similarity is that these goddesses are called "Goddess of Many Names".

Similar to the Goddess' help to the devas, is an episode of Goddess Ishtar. In one of the three versions of the battle against the demon Kur, Ishtar, that is the Goddess Inanna vows to the gods who are powerless against the might and evil of the Demon, that she will exterminate him. After the victorious battle, she installs herself on the mountain Elish. As a result of this war, agricultural produce is abundant, granaries are full, and there was no more mourning on the earth.[203] The recitation of these myths at times of travail or natural disasters, restored peace and plenty. The mimetic rites or the recital of the cult legends had the effect of restoring fertility on parched lands, by propitiating and reinstating the agricultural deity who had disappeared; or, winning over a dragon whose ill-will caused hardships for gods and men, (by the storm-god or his equivalent). This fight between pairs of opposites was initiated at the start of the civilization in the Fertile Crescent and spread both east and west. But it changed in form, content, and its contenders to suit local needs. But the basic theme remained unchanged. Just as Durgā was equipped by the gods with various weapons in her fight with the demons, so also in the fight between Marduk and Tiamat, the gods assemble and equip Marduk with an array of invincible weapons, according to the *Enuma Elish,* the Babylonian creation myth. One of the main features of the creation myths is the opposition of good and evil in a primordial struggle of pairs of opposites. The pairs are gods and demons, light and darkness, etc. It was understood that the world was created out of this fight and order was reinsteated out of the primordial chaos. By repeating or acting out ritually this contest, man siding with the victorious contender, triumphed over not only natural calamities like famine or floods, but also his own sins or rebellion against the gods. Parallel to the growth of Durgā by assimilation is seen in Isis of Egypt who was Nature, universal Mother, primordial child of Time, Queen of the Dead, and of the immortals, manifestation of all gods and goddesses.[204] The goddess Ishtar also absorbed practically all Assyro-babylonian deities, and became so powerful that her name itself came to mean 'Goddess'.[205] Kybele, the Phrygian goddess, *Britomartis*, or, *Diktyannan* were also similar goddesses.

The cult of the resurrection of Osiris was very popular and was performed as a drama during the Ptolemaic (c. 1900 B.C.) period, but the cult predated this period by many centuries. It was an official cult of the Nile Valley, and was taken over by the Greeks. A similar situation arose with regard to Durgā as Śākambharī.[206] This has a hoary past through the Bhita seal to the IVC seal of the goddess connected with vegetation. Durgā is a virgin goddess, resides on mountains and is accompanied by a lion. These characteristics are found in the Minoan goddess of Crete and the Aegean.[207] She was the mistress of the wild beasts and was the mountain mother. She was accompanied by lions. She often held or was encircled by snakes. Sacred mountains are thought of as the centre of the earth. The fierce characteristics of Durgā is a common trait in all early goddesses. Just as Ardokhsho influenced Lakṣmī icons, the possibility cannot be ruled out that the goddess Nana may have influenced the goddess Durgā, or Umā-Pārvatī with her lion mount. Since Śiva appears both with Umā and Nana on Kushana coins, it may be deduced that the two goddesses may have held the same status in this period.[208] In the Middle East, the goddess Hatra was found to be the prototype of Durgā. She is attired like a soldier, wears a fierce mask, and holds a spear in her right hand. She is a warrior and a huntress, also accompanied by a lion . She is a domestic goddess as well as ruling over vegetation, mountains, earth, sea, and sky. With the Hellenist thrust over the Arab world she was taken over by the Greeks and became Athena.

Lion is a symbol of sovereignty in most ancient countries. Durgā has her lion mount to show her universal sovereignty and she became the leader amongst lesser cult goddesses.

The Romans pictured the goddess Venus as stepping out of the mussel-shell. Her antecedents are traced to the birth of Aphrodite in Homer and Hesiod. But this again goes further back to the goddess Anodyomene of an even earlier period.[209] This is an example of how the goddess changes names and contexts, but the basic character remains the same. The origins go back to the hoary past.

Hecate is also a goddess similar to the goddess Durgā. Sacrifices of animals and corpses of men who were executed were all thrown at the cross roads. The cross roads were dedicated to her.[210] What Lang,[211] says about the goddess Athene that she shows manly virtue when she is armed and warlike, and is womanly when she is protective could easily be said for Durgā.

Historical Background

Mother-right is associated with agricultural societies. It could, therefore, have been present in the IV culture. Aryans were predominantly pastoral. Therefore, no prominence was given to women. In the post-Vedic religion, there were always two strands of thoughts, the pre-Vedic and the Vedic. Where societies progress to agriculture without going through the intervening pastoral stage, mother-right is popular. Whereas in societies where pastoralism was the mode of life, before shifting to agriculture, patriarchy is the order of the society.[212] The religious outlook of the ṚgVeda is therefore patriarchal reflecting the pastoral society. Mother-right and mother-goddess worship is still popular in India, because we are still a predominantly agricultural country. Indian economy is stunted in its growth and this is said to be the result of strong tribal elements in the culture.[213] We are also economically dependent on the fertility of the land, which has resulted in a religion giving importance to the goddess worship.

The Kushanas were well-known devotees of Śiva. The native dynasties of Yaudheyas and the Nāga-Bhāraśivas who ruled after the Kushanas were also ardent devotees of Śiva and Kārtikeya. Mahākāla Śiva is famous at Ujjain.[214] A new inscription of the period of Chandragupta II mentions Bhairava worship.[215] This is dated to about 380 A.D. This would point to two facts. The fierce form of Śiva must have been in worship much earlier than this period, and the fierce form of the goddess must have also had a parallel development. Before metaphysical explanations of the Great Goddess came about in the DM., her affiliation to Śiva must have been established. Wema Kadphises was a Śiva Bhāgavata. Lākulīśa, founder of the Pāśupata sect was ascribed to the 2nd century A.D. Since there is seen an affinity between the two cults, Wema may have been a *Pāśupata* before the cult was formalised by Lākulīśa. Though the imperial Guptas had *Vaiṣṇavite* affinities and were *paramabhāgavatas,* there were many tribal chiefs like Yashodhaman of Western India, in the first half of the 6th century A.D., Bhimavarman, chieftain of Kosam, as seen from an inscription of 458-459 A.D., Parivrājaka Mahārājas, *fuedatories* of the Guptas in the Madhya Pradesh, almost all the Vakataka rulers, most of the Maitraka rulers of Vallabhi and probably the Maukhari kings of Kanauj, etc. who were ardent Śaivites.[216] This would indicate that the Vindhyavāsinī goddess developing from indigenous cults was named Durgā Mahiṣāsuramardinī, and was extant in Western India, as a popular goddess in the Kushana, and early Gupta era, mixing with the Śiva cult of this region. The relevant dynasties when the goddess cult developed and attained supremacy would be the Kushanas, the native rulers, and the Early Guptas. In the Gupta period the society is said to be sharply divided between the landed and the toiling masses. The latter due to being oppressed are said to have resorted to idealism in the Goddess as a saviour of the oppressed.[217] This is doubtful because in the DM. is the king and the *vaiśya* who ask the sage Mārkaṇḍ eya about the Devī's exploits. In the Gupta period the goddess was worshipped by herself as well as in a group as *Mātṛs.* In this period, Goddess worship had mainly two characteristics—sensuousness and fear of the Goddess.

Going to the pre-Maurya period to study the state of affairs in the country, K.A. Nilakanta Sastri[218] says that, after Alexander had left the country: "The great economic and political revolutions initiated by the establishment and the early breakup of Alexander's empire, the increase in trade due to the multiplication of armed camps in the wars of the 'successors' and the divisions of the empire, the accumulation of large fortunes by some and the coming up of a proletariat, the dispersion of the large gold treasures of Persia and the quickening transition from a rural to a money economy, and the rise of several large territorial states under absolute monarchs were the chief features of the new epoch. India was drawn more and more into this welter and Chandragupta and his teacher grew up in this atmosphere of rapid change and new formations." Epigraphy and contemporary Greek records show that Brahminism was still the religion of kings, nobles and rich Brahmin householders. The popular religious movements had as yet not caught people's fancy. The Brahmin priests were held in very great esteem and they were busy either advising the kings or performing elaborate *yajñas.* The Pāli canon mentions some of the Vedic sacrifices performed during this period: The *Śamyaprāsa, Nirargadam, Samāprabhāram* and *Śrauta* ceremonies, performing which the priestly class stood to gain great wealth. Alongside these, the *Somayāgas* like *Vājapeya, Aśvamedha* and *Puruṣamedha* are also mentioned which would indicate that the previous set of *yāgas* also would have involved large amounts of wealth.

Great quantities of wood and cattle for these sacrifices must have been wrested from villagers, which is mentioned in the *Brāhmaṇadhammikasutta.*[219] In the earlier periods Brahmins were intent on their own work in their own sphere of life. But they became greedy and used to "persuade" the Ikṣvāku kings to perform expensive *yāgas,* and expected huge presents *(dakṣiṇās)* in the form of women, cows, wealth, beds, clothes and horses. In the *Majjimanikāya,*[220] the suffering and loss of wealth in the shape of calaves (male and female) and wood, the villagers used to experience, is graphically described. They had to comply with the wishes of the priests who advised the king, out of fear of chastisement and punishment. Greek historians, beyond a solitary remark about the Buddha, do not mention anything further about Buddhism.[221]

Kauṭilya's work contains records of Brahminical mode of life. It confirms[222] the gift of Brahmadeya lands to *Ṛtvigs, Ācāryas, Purohitas* and *Śrotrīyas*[223]. Buddhism and Jainism instead of repressing Brāhminic culture seems to have given a fillip to it in religion and art.

The sociological background of this (Nanda-Maurya) period was only tribal and primitive. Agriculture, industry, and commerce were practised on a small scale. This picture is painted in the *Jātakas.*[224] In spite of some solitary references, in the Mbh., there were a lot of small states or kingdoms ruled by tribal chiefs or kings. Slowly the tribal outlook was widening into political outlook.

In the Mauryan period, there were three streams of goddess cult: one in the North-Western portion conceiving of a mother-goddess united with a father-god; one in the East which represented the goddess in diagrams; and one far South which worshipped the goddess as a virgin. In Kauṭilya's *Arthaśāstra*,[225] temples to goddesses Aparājitā and Śrī Madirā are mentioned. The first is definitely seen to be the goddess Durgā. The native dynasties must have helped in the formation of the Great Goddess. The Guptas who came later were Brāhminic and were tolerant. They must have seen the popularity of the Goddess cult and must have given the cult metaphysical meaning and stabilised its formation.

Social Milieu of the Period

Studying the religious trends amongst artisan, middle classes of Europe of the Middle Ages, Max Weber[226] finds that there is no uniform determination of religion by generalising the economic background of a class. But a class or a caste does formulate the particular type of religion to suit its own requirements which is peculiar to its economic background. The castes who have involvement, physical or economic in politics wielded by power or in wars, would not find a religion with ethical compensation as its tenets, palatable. The traders who would form the urban middle class can manipulate their earnings, and would not resort to magic. Normally, they would resort to an ethical religion. The lowest class of the population, that is the class of slaves and labourers, would not be the ground for any congregational religion or religious mission. It is this class which would resort to a magical religion; or in a magical supervention of grace. The peasant, entirely dependent on nature and its vagaries, would necessarily believe in a magical religion. The artisans and others of the lower middle class would believe in an ethically based religion, and the warrior class would prefer to believe in a soteriological religion which would assure them of heaven for leading a life of a hero, or dying like one.

The salvation religion may have its origin in the socially privileged class. The elitist class would "assign to religion the primary function of legitimising their own life-pattern and situation in the world".[227] But when this religion moves down to the lowest strata, spreads amongst the masses, its complexion changes. The lowest class are those castes "to whom intellectualism is both economically and socially inaccessible", and, "who are not particularly or professionally concerned with the cultivation of intellectualism".[228] Religion as it changes its character to suit the needs of the masses, creates a personal, divine or human-divine saviour. Cultic religion changes in two ways: it becomes magic-ridden, or, it changes to saviour religion, which again resorts to wizardry. The middle classes would not have recourse to a hero-oriented religion but to sentimental, *bhakti* cult and *avatāra* concepts in religion. For instance, in the case of the Goddess, she was married to Śiva and led a spousified life surrounded by family and children, reflecting on the family life, and importance given to it by this class. Thus, the soteriological cult is typical of the middle class with its saviour who is an *avatāra*. This has a very wide diffusion all over the world. Belief in a god who incarnates himself to allenviate human suffering and shower down his abundant grace on the suppressed people is further helped by soteriological myths, where the god fights the demons to release the oppressed victims. There are many forms of liberation depending on the situation, at hand. It could be the god of the Jews who liberated his people from the corrupting influence of a lesser god; it could be Jesus who liberated a people from hypocrisy and atrophied values; it could be Durgā or Kṛṣṇa leading the people out of varied types of suffering. "On the other hand, the notion of an impersonal and ethical cosmic order that transcends the deity and the ideal of an exemplary type of salvation are intellectualistic conceptions which are definitely alien to the masses and possible only for a laity that has been educated along rational and ethical lines."[229]

The Hindus believe in the continuation of the stratification of their caste system beyond death. This may be reason enough for their belief in a mother-goddess who delivered them from their troubles. On the other hand, the Jews thought their most down trodden were the chosen people of their wrathful god, to deliver them from their state of enslavement. Their god was thus a stern father figure, vengeful against his own children if they erred.

If a god were a deity of polity, it is but natural that he gains supremacy over other gods. When the political power expands his territory, those gods of the subjugated people also come under the wings of the god of the victor. There is no hard and fast rule about the suzerainty of such a god, and the territory over which he could hold sway. But if a god rises above all other gods, then he takes on their roles also. His functional capacity increases. But as mentioned earlier, there is no hard and fast rule about such a deity's area of popularity. The new responsibilities taken by the god would be according to the requirements of the new society, and his capacity increases. If such a god remains constant in the new responsibilities assigned to him, he retains his popularity, and superiority. Our goddess, amalgamated into herself all the indigenous deities, and remained supreme. Metaphysical justifications, and rituals of the cult followed as a natural corollary. Her capacity to alleviate any type of travail over any period of time ensured that she would never attain divine otiosus. A god's dominance of a pantheon would definitely substantiate the proposition that he is a universal or, transtribal deity. When there was an expansion of culture due to conquests, the alien gods were sometimes equated to their own existing gods and thus were universalised. This took place in China as well as in Greece.[230]

Position of Women

Manu had already laid down the freedom that should be given to a woman. In one verse,

"Bālayā vā yuvatyā vā vṛddhayā vāpi yoṣitā/
Na svātantryeṇa kartavyaṁ kincit kāryaṁ gṛheṣvapi// (V.147)
and
"Bālye piturvaśe tiṣṭhetpāṇigrāsya yauvane/
Putrāṇāṁ bhartari prete na bhajetstrī svatantratām//(V.148)
"Viśīlaḥ kāmavṛtto vā guṇairvā parivarjitaḥ/
Upacaryaḥ striyā sādhvyā satataṁ devavatpatiḥ//(V.154)
"Nāsti strīṇāṁ pṛthagyajño na vratam nāpyupoṣaṇam/
Patiṁ śuśruṣate yena tena svarge mahīyate"//(V. 155)

The wife or the daughter always held a secondary position in the family. But motherhood was held in very high esteem. This may also be due to the feeling of compensating the low status held by women. As it was, in the Ath. Veda there was a charm given to change the foetus of a girl into a boy. Ait. Br. treats the girl child as a source of trouble. Though Varāhamihira gave women a high status in his *Bṛhatsaṁhitā*, the epics, *Dharmaśāstras*, and the

Smṛtis, all degrade women.[231] Literary evidence may not usually reflect the social background of culture. Sītā, Sāvitrī and Draupadī are all idealised in literature, but, the position of women in real life seems to have been quite the opposite. In agricultural societies, where men do the major share of the work, it is natural that men have a prominent status in society, and women are subservient. Fear of sexuality, and fear of the loss of semen may also have contributed to the low status of women. To view the Indian society from the Western point of view and divide the sexes as nature and culture would be too simplistic and wrong.[232] It is also noticed that the underprivileged tend to give equality to women. This[233] would depend on whether they belong to the warrior caste. One thing to be noted is, that this equality is not dependent on the cult participation allowed to women.

Manu had allowed fathers to keep their daughters unmarried if a suitable or acceptable bridegroom was not available. But in the Gupta period, Yājñavalkya and Nārada condemn this in very strong terms. A father or brother would go to hell if he did not marry off the girl before her puberty. Since girls married before the age of twelve or thirteen, they had no say in the settlement of their marriage. There could be no Upanayana as there was no time available that could be set aside for studies. A few affluent families educated their girl children. Yājñavalkya categorically states that women should not recite the Vedas and they should not even hear it recited. Though Vātsyāyana in his *Kāmasūtra (I-Sādhāraṇa Adhikaraṇam, Vidyāsamuddeśaprakaraṇam)*, says that young girls (3.3) and princesses (3.12) should be taught *Kāmaśāstra* as well as be educated in the *Śāstras*. They should have knowledge of the sixty-four arts (3.6). He goes further, and says that a housewife should find out how much income there is in a year and accordingly budget her expenditure[234] *"Sāṁvatsarikamāyaṁ saṁkhyāya tadanurūpaṁ vyayaṁ kuryāt"*.[235] This would necessitate a certain fluency in the three 'Rs, There are literary evidences of this period of women hermits, poets, and students enrolling for studies along with boys. In the *Aṣṭādhyāyī* there are separate terms to be used for the teacher's wife *'Upāddhyāyānī'* or *'Upādhyāyī'* and for a woman who is herself a teacher *'Upādhyāyī'* or *'Upādhyāyā'*; similar terms used for the *Ācārya*, that is his wife should be referred to as *'Ācāryāṇī'* and who is herself one she should be called *'Ācāryā'*.[236] But it was generally laid down in this period that it is better for the wife if she worshipped her husband and if he is dead then to remain faithful to his memory.[237]

There was doubt whether the widow could inherit the share of her husband in the joint family. If at the time of his death he was still a member of the joint family, then his widow would only get a maintenance. But, if he had already separated, the wife got her husband's share. Daughters had no share in the father's property, if they had brothers. But her brother or her father was expected to spend about a quarter of the son's share at her wedding.[238] Nārada and Parāśara permit widow remarriage. There were occasional remarriages but, puritanical society frowned at this. Satī was also occasionally practised. The widow did not deform her looks, but neither did she decorate herself. All Smṛti writers emphasise that she lead an ascetic's life. Otherwise women could move about freely, but high class women veiled their faces when in public.

The Purāṇas emphasize the ideal marriage as a wife subservient to her husband and this is stressed in the Gupta period. The wife is said to enjoy social privileges by virtue of her marriage but she had no independent status. This state of affairs is emphasised by Lakṣmī and surprisingly contradicted by Durgā. Durgā and Lakṣmī were closely related and may have been worshipped together as two aspects of the pre-Aryan fertility goddess.[239] In the Purāṇas with Lakṣmī affiliated to Viṣṇu and Durgā to Śiva, there was a gap between the two goddesses which with time widened.

In the south Indian literature, women are said to possess a special power known as *'aṇaṅku'*, posited in their chest and womb.[240] Likened to fire, this power should be culturised by man, so that it is beneficial to him. This is achieved by marriage. Thus goddesses who cannot be controlled by their husbands tend to be dangerous and malevolent. The Sanskrit outlook on the feminine power could be analogous. It is called Prakṛti, Māyā, or, Śakti. The power is natural and being so, could be unpredictable and ambivalent. Like the power in nature, woman is productive, attractive, but, potentially dangerous, unless her power is harnessed. To understand women's relationship vis-a-vis men, the best available prototypes would be the goddesses, because there is a close relationship between the status of women and the goddesses as they are depicted. But the insight gained by studying the goddesses may not present an unbiased view, because they present the male view point. But viewing goddesses or women, one views onself, one's own self in relation to other selves in a particular socio-cultural background.

Psychological Origins

This is very similar to that of goddess Kālī, since all religious images and symbols have the same originating ground, except that Kālī is more malevolent than Durgā. Durgā is a war-goddess first and foremost.

Freud took the unconscious as the repressed or the forgotten contents of the mind.[241] Jung said there were two layers in our unconscious. The superficial layer is derived from personal experiences. Underneath this personal unconscious is the collective unconscious. This latter is common to all individuals and owes its existence to heredity. The archetype is contained in the unconscious. Its image is the Great Mother. Archetypes are not disseminated by language, cultural migration, etc., but it can arise anywhere at any time. Its form may be determined, but it gets its content when it rises in the conscious, and is filled with a latter's experience. The specific images of the archetype cannot be deduced from the archetype alone, but depend on other factors as well. The symbols of the Mother Archetype constellate in symbols which are wholly benign, like the benign symbols associated with fertility and fecundity, protective Mother Goddess, or, personal female relations; or, fully negative like the devouring demons, dragons, snakes, underworld, death, and darkness; or, again ambivalent, which contains both positive and negative characteristics. This is only a very rough list. The ambivalent symbol would be the Terrible Mother.[242]

The archetypes can never be got rid of, just like the body with its limbs cannot be got rid of, unless by suicide. Our mind connects the archetypes to our present existence, and, links our past to the present, and finds or tries to find a new interpretation of these symbols at every stage of differentiation of the consciousness. If the link-up does not take place then neurosis occurs in the psyche, which becomes rootless. Since the Mother Archetype belongs not exclusively to the individual, but to the whole race, it can be described as the pre-conscious mother aspect of the whole race.[243]

It should be noted that the real-life mother is not the cause and pre-condition for the existence of the mother 'motif'. And, the mother 'motif' is one of the, not the only, way of expressing the empirical 'mother' in psychology. Therefore, the mythological mother is not a carbon copy of the empirical mother, but the symbol is clearly discernible. The divine mother is a supra-human, her origin be-speaks of this; her form is also supra-normal and her multi-tudinous hands hold the weapons of the gods. She is accoutred in a strange way, and her *vāhana* is one which cannot be used as such by any human being. It is a lion/tiger. The Mother archetype symbol is mythologically irrational. Her physical make-up, her character, and her deeds are miraculous or monstrous.

The Western ego is said to be punitive, whereas the Eastern is narcissistic.[244] The war-deity in India is a goddess which suits the narcissistic make-up. Following such a deity, Indians are not thinking of success in the encounter, but they welcome it as an opportunity to sacrifice themselves to their mother goddess, Kālī, Durgā or to the country personified in the goddess.[245] The narcissist ego has not much aggression in him. What little there is, is directed outward in identifying oneself with the aggressive goddess. But the Mother Goddess has a benign character also. The fully narcissistic ego would identify oneself with the benign forms of the goddess. He approaches the goddess like a child unto its mother.

The philosophy of Sāṁkhya must have contributed greatly towards the evolution and subsequent exaltation of the goddess. Originally Sāṁkhya must have been oriented towards Prakṛti. Later on Brahminic and patriarchal ideas must have been imposed on it, its philosophy made to agree with Vedānta in a forced way.[246] Puruṣa is taken to mean soul, and, if so, there is a multiplicity of souls. Over and above the Sāṁkhya, Upaniṣadic philosophy also could have influenced the Goddess in attaining her greatness in the DM. She is in the DM. transcendent as well as immanent. She is behind all creation and is the cause for it. The philosophical concept that emerges from the study of the goddess in the DM. is monism. The Bhakti cult and the avatāra concept have also contributed their ideas to the concept of the Goddess. She is not only metaphysically transcendent beyond all dualities, above the trinities whom she has created, but, she listens to her devotees and comes to their aid and removes their afflictions. Thus she is equated to the Vedic or rather Upaniṣadic Brahman, the Prakṛti of Sāṁkhya.

Devī as Māyā is both delusion (moha) and knowledge (jñāna). This pair of opposites is necessary not only in themselves but they influence each other and impel the goddess either to quiescence or to fierce activity. There are two levels in the role of Devī as a deluder. She deludes the beings in the world into craving and bondage, and, she deludes the demons like Śumbha and Niśumbha into being attracted by her. She herself gives knowledge to the human beings so that they may break their bondage of saṁsāra, and be led back into a proper perspective. She kills and releases the deluded asuras from their bondage. The world is thus not abandoned by the humans beings nor annihilated by the asuras. She lets the earth proceed in its fertile cycle, and she herself leads the beings into liberation. Opposites, or, polarity,[247] is seen in the Yoganidrā Śakti[248] who has really created the demons Madhu and Kaiṭabha, and has made Viṣṇu sleep the while. Only when she leaves Viṣṇu, can the Śakti of Viṣṇu slay the demons. When the demons are killed the world returns to normalcy, but bound alternately by the Śaktis of bondage and liberation. Moreover, an aberration from the normal in the relationship between male and female, and, divine and human could be a powerful instrument for liberation. Male meekness and female power is by Hindu standards abnormal. This dynamic and dangerous power erupts into situations leading the world towards liberation. Following the path of Dharma, is seen as motivated by self-interest, and may therefore enmesh one further into bondage of the saṁsāra. Since it is Devī who enmeshes us into bondage it is she alone who can liberate us.

This study now takes up reference to the Goddess in Sanskrit literature, roughly belonging to the same period as Devī Māhātmya. The latter, our main text, is treated separately as deserving a more detailed scrutiny.

Literary Development of the Goddess

In Sanskrit literature Bhāsa is the earliest dramatist (circa 3rd cent. A.D.). In his Bālacarita,[249] he describes the Kaṁsa-Durgā episode. When Kaṁsa tries to strike the baby girl Kātyāyanī on a stone slab, she rises to the air and warns him,

"Śumbhaṁ Niśumbhaṁ Mahiṣaṁ ca hatvā kṛtvā surāṁstān hataśatrupakṣān/

Ahaṁ prasūtā Vasudevavaṁśe Kātyāyanī Kaṁsakulakṣayāya"//.

She tells her followers that to enjoy Bhagavān Viṣṇu's playful exploits as an infant they should be born amongst the Gopas in the dress of cowherds. Two things to be noted in this episode are, she does not talk of decimating Kaṁsa herself, but is going to be only the instrument in the annihilation of his family. This is in keeping with the idea of the Goddess being the Śakti of Viṣṇu as his Māyā, Vaiṣṇavī Śakti, or Yoganidrā. The second point is, after Kaṁsa's 'assault she does not rise towards heaven, but she disguises herself and with her followers goes to Nanda's village.

Bhāsa is said to be coeval with *Śilappadikāram* of South India.[250] He is also said to belong to the South, to around 3rd cent. A.D. It is further averred that the above episode may not have any Purāṇic background but may be based on folk-tales.

The act of offering one's head to the Goddess Kumārī is mentioned in *Śilappadikāram*[251] and *Maṇimekali*[252]. Medieval literature is full of the act of sacrificing one's head. This is deemed an act of worship. In other references, instead of severing his own head, the devotee inflicts the injury on somebody else. In folk-tales and medieval romance such references are numerous. *Kathāsaritsāgara* is full of this. Most usually these acts are towards the Goddess only. Buddhist literature gives little importance to goddesses in the early period. The *Niddeśa* passage does not mention goddesses.[253] If the epic and the Purāṇas are somewhat coeval with the post-Kushana and the Gupta periods, the stutis to Devī said to be later interpolations, could be of this period.

Bāṇa around the period of DM. or slightly later, treats the goddess and her cult oftener in *Kādambarī*. He mentions a Caṇḍikā kānana in the Harṣacarita,[254] as he narrates his travel to see the king. At the entrance to the forest, the images of the goddess Caṇḍikā were seen carved on trees, and marks of the worship offered by the travellers could be discerned. The grass growing around on the soil burnt by the forest fires was of asparagus, which was also called śatavarī or Nārāyaṇī.

In *Kādambarī*,[255] Queen Vilāsavatī goes to the Caṇḍikā shrine and offers worship to obtain an issue. She observes various vratas, and the temple is described as being dark, because of the guggulu offered by the devotees was burning night and day, and was covering the shrine with its thick pall of smoke. In the subsequent section of the story,[256] Candrāpīḍa, on his trip to Ujjain, sees on his way, a lonely, deserted forest;[257] He sees the red flag from afar. The temple[258] and its precincts are described, as being decorated with red flowers. The Goddess is described as having a bali pītha in front of her icon.[259] She is dressed in red clothes and is worshipped by Śabara women, with red flowers. Her forehead is decorated with a golden band, and she wears a red sindūr tilaka. She wears pomegranate flowers in her ears, which reflecting on her cheeks, gives them a reddish glow. This is enhanced by the red betel juice on her lips, tawny eyebrows and red eyes. She is beautiful to look at with her body graceful like a creeper. She is called the lover of Mahākāla. The pious old Dravidian who looks after the shrine and offers worship to the goddess is described in the following words: *"Jaraddraviḍadhārmikenādhiṣṭitāṁ Caṇḍikāmapaśyat"*,[260] and in the following pages his description continues.[261]

In Harṣa's *Nāgānandanāṭakam* (the same period as Bāṇa), in the first Act, Princess Malayavatī goes to Malaya parvata to propitiate the goddess Bhagavatī Gaurī. In the final Act,[262] the goddess is derided by the princess that her lover is dead. Goddess Gaurī appears and gives life to Jīmūtavāhana.

In Bhavabhūti's *Mālatīmādhava*[263] references are numerous about the gory rites associated with the goddess cult. Kapāla Kuṇḍalā enters the temple situated near a cremation ground. She speaks about her Guru and says that Aghoraghaṇṭa has gone to the city to try and fetch a comely maiden to sacrifice to the goddess. Meanwhile Mādhava comes to sell flesh to the inhabitants (goblins and spirits) of the cremation ground.[264] The *Kāpālikas*[265] praise the goddess Cāmuṇḍā, and mention the *Niśumbhavadha* episode (though the commentator says this word stands for a type of a weapon).

In Vākpati's *Gauḍavaho,* the goddess is referred as the Great Goddess, Mahādevī. She is Vindhyavāsinī, killer of Mahiṣa,[266] resting in the Himalayas . The goddess herself is addressed as *Śabarī* and there is also a reference to Koli women, may be of non-Aryan tribal origin offering worship.[267] A Śabara man dressed in turmeric leaves[268] offers pūjā to the goddess. Epithets such as *Mādhavī* and *Nārāyaṇī* suggest her relationship to Viṣṇu. But, even though the episode of Kaṁsa trying to kill her and her slipping away heavenwards is also mentioned, her affiation to Śiva comes out clearer by her epithets such as Śaṁkarī, and Bhairavī, as also her residence in the Himalayas. The fierce aspect of the goddess is dealt with, along with mention of harsher rites. In this fierce aspect the Goddess is closer to Bāṇa's *Kādambarī*, and the rituals in Bhavabhūti's *Mālatīmādhava*.

In *Daṇḍin's Daśakumāracaritam* the Goddess Vindhyavāsinī blesses[269] her devotee Suhmadeśa's king Tuṅgadhanva with two children, a boy and a girl. The daughter was to be told to propitiate the goddess by pleasing her with *Kandukanṛtya* every month on the Kṛttikā-star day, from her seventh year to the time she would marry, so that she may obtain a good husband. In a later chapter,[270] mention is made of Kāpālikas in the cremation ground, and propitation of Goddess Vindhyavāsinī.

Subandhu's *Vāsavadattā* mentions the episode of the killing of the demon Niśumbha.[271] In the *Mṛcchakaṭika*, she is mentioned as *Sahyavāsinī.*[272]

These literary evidences show that the goddess' Vaiṣṇavite relationships were mentioned in the earlier works. Though these mentions continued in the later works, the Śaivite affiliation comes out clearer. Irrespective of the age of the work, bar a few exceptions, the fiercer aspect of the goddess seems to be more popular with the people of the respective periods. Otherwise, literature would not bring out these traits in the cult. The association with the mountains, or forest regions, the existence of bali or sacrifice in her temples, all point to her un-Aryan origins, and Sanskritisation is one successful method of assimilating the cult into the Big Tradition. There is an opinion that literature may not portray actual life, religious or secular.[273] By and large, literature may give us a rough idea of the society and its mores. For example, *Bṛhatsaṁhitā*[274] lays down the rules of worshipping different deities. But this need not be taken as an exhaustive list, because it does not mention Skanda-Kārtikeya or Gaṇapati whose cults were popular at this period.

Devī Māhātmya (DM)

The DM. forms part of the Mārk. P.[275] This Purāṇa is amongst the early Purāṇas, according to most scholars[276] that is 3rd to 5th centuries A.D. In the Mārk. P. the DM is a late interpolation. But the cantos 1-44 of the Purāṇa are later still. The DM glorifies the sanguinary aspect of the Goddess worship. "Some hymns breathe deep religious feeling, express enthusiastic adoration, and evince fervent spiritual meditation. On the other hand, the descriptions of the battles abound with wild and repulsive incidents and revel in gross and amazing fancies. The *Devi-mahatmya* is a compound of the most opposite characters. The religious out-pourings are at times pure and elevated: the material descriptions are absurd and debased."[277] This is one early view of the work which has held the attention of devout Hindus over the millenia. From the Śaivite affiliation of the Goddess, it has been inferred that the probable place of the myth's origin could be Mandhata. This is supported by the internal evidence of the residence of the birds which figure in the earlier cantos of the Purāṇa. Though it is held that in the DM itself Viṣṇu connection of the Goddess is more prominent than her Śiva affiliation,[278] the Viṣṇu accretions are thought to be later.[279] The Goddess is not called Umā, nor is she Mahādevī, because she is the wife of Mahādeva Śiva. She is the Great Goddess in her own right.

It has been generally agreed that the dating of the DM. is between the late fifth or early sixth centuries A.D. There is agreement also that the DM. treating the divine as feminine is unique, but it shows as Hinduism did of this period, non-Aryan influence on the Aryan religion. There is seen influence of Sāṁkhya philosophy in the formulation of the goddess idea, but *Sāṁkhya* cannot be pinpointed as either Aryan or non-Aryan.[280]

The questions that arise in our minds on taking up the DM. are: Is this a Purāṇa; by itself; or is it just part of the big Mārk. P.? What is its connection to the Vedic thoughts and, if the goddess cult has a stronger base in the indigenous population, how did it rise to be accepted by the Big Tradition?

Taking the last question first, it is seen that local cults are made acceptable to the Brahmin culture through a process of "Sanskritisation".[281] "Sanskritisation" has many connotations at different levels. Religiously, it is the process of local cults gaining importance and being accepted by the Big Tradition. In literature, the language becomes literally Sanskritised.

Culturally, the inter-caste movement is more fluid than hitherto thought of. A group may give up meat and drinks in their diet and feel spiritually pure enough to move up the caste scale. But this entails the Big-Tradition to come down and impose its norms on the local cults, and if they are popular or deep-rooted, they are syncretised. Thus, it is as much moving up as coming down in Sanskritisation. Writing in Sanskrit lends the piece dignity and respectability, and elevates it in status. This could be said of the other forms of Sanskritisation also, since Sanskrit is a language of respectability and culture. This process culturally makes the rites and rituals of the caste part of that people's living. This could be put in another way. This process is parochialism percolating down or the local cults moving up.

In Western thought, knowledge is discovered. In Indian thought, it is recovered.[282] Since knowledge exists for all times, the DM has to have a connection to Vedic thought. Absolute truth of the beginning of time (i.e., sacred time), was lost, but not irrevocably. It is still made available through such religious texts like the DM. Śṛuti once states what is the Truth. Smṛti keeps on explaining this Truth in various ways and at different levels, to enable humans beings to understand. It Vedas are to be recited and heard only by the twice-born. The Smṛtis are meant for the "others". Therefore, the importance of the Purāṇas, to particularly allow those others to hear and understand the eternal and immutable truths embedded in the Vedas, attractively clothed in myths and legends. A short study of the origin and contents of Purāṇas is taken up, to enable us to understand the DM. better.

Purāṇas

Itihāsa-Purāṇa is the ancient Indian historical tradition. It was composed by *Sūtas* (bards) and *Māgadhas* (panegyrists). Vedic literature also contained historical facts imbedded in them. These were *nārāśaṁsīs, gāthās, dāna-stutis,* and *ākhyānas.*[283] These were preserved partially because they were incorporated into the texts of the yajñas. The *ākhyānas* were recited at rituals and contained the mores of the community, and these were changed to social custom, containing some elements of history in them. The Purāṇic literature can be traced back to the ṚgVedic period, and this was as sacred to the Aryans as the Vedas themselves. They delt with five subjects:[284] (i) *Sarga*-creation, (ii) *Pratisarga*-recreation, i.e., periodic annihilation and renewal of the worlds including the geography of the earth and the atmosphere, as well as the distribution of the different races on the surface of the earth; (iii) *Vaṁśa*—genealogy of the gods and sages; (iv) *Manvantara*—cosmic cycles or the Manu periods of time, i.e., those great periods, each of which is reigned over by a Manu, or, primal ancestor of the human race; and, (v) *Vaṁśānucarita* - the history of the royal dynasties.

There were two stages in the development of Purāṇas. In the first stage, it was only one Purāṇa, the *Brahmāṇḍa* P. This single Purāṇa is said to have been composed by Brahmā himself constituting one hundred crores of ślokas. In the second stage, this has evolved into the eighteen *Mahāpurāṇas*. It is said that Vyāsa learnt this from Brahmā and gave them to the mortals.[285] If Vyāsa is the arranger of the Purāṇic material, then this would presuppose that the Purāṇic material was already existing and Vyāsa merely rearranged it. The second tradition says that Vyāsa taught the Purānic material to Lomaharṣaṇa, who dispersed it further into six versions. Since Lomaharṣaṇa was a Sūta, that is a non-Brahmins, the authorship of these works vacillates between Brahmins and Sūtas.[286]

The Purāṇas could have grown around the Purāṇa mentioned in the ṚgVeda, and the following Smṛti material, exactly like the Sanskrit religious literature grew around the ṚgVedic nucleus. In the ṚgVeda, 'Purāṇa' is an adjective meaning an old story. The later usages of the word might have grown from and around such an old format.

There are seen four stages in the development of the Purāṇas.[287] First is the word as mentioned in the Atharva Veda, second the Dharma Sūtas, and in the third stage the Purāṇas had Pañcalakṣaṇa. In the fourth and last stage, the Purāṇas no more had the Pañcalakṣaṇa format, and also they must have been composed after the Sūta/Māgadha tradition had ceased.

Central to the *Itihāsa-Purāṇa* tradition was the genealogical data, *vaṁsānucarita*. They were in Prakrit originally, and the Brahmins changed them into Sanskrit, introducing into them Brahminic fables, philosophy and rituals. This *Itihāsa-Purāṇa* tradition was contained in the epics also, before they were edited and incorporated into the Purāṇas. The Purāṇic lists of kings were not meant to give historical and chronological exactitude. They were authentic to a certain extent in lineage forms and in geography. The composers looked to the past for a framework and fitted the contemporary events into it. Since these were finalised around the Gupta period, there was a considerable historical change in North India, the *vaṁśānucarita* section became a book of origins, used by those wanting political legitimacy.[288] The royal dynastic lists from the earliest period upto the Andhras and the Guptas have been corroborated with epigraphical and numismatic evidences.[289] Purāṇas have also contributed to the emergence of the modern science of comparative mythology, in the West. Studies in Aryan mythologies have revealed common origin to (or parallels in) Greek and Roman on the one hand and Purāṇic legends on the other.

When the Purāṇas were transmitted orally, the texts underwent radical changes. These could not be called interpolations but additions and amplifications. This was arrested to a certain degree when they were committed to writing. The variations in the myths of the Purāṇas were due to local traditions. Vedic texts were confined strictly to particular families, and there were no mutations. The Purāṇas were popular and were accessible to all castes. In the Purāṇic text there could sometimes be a lacuna, when the meaning is obscure. But one of the manuscripts of local versions would give a meaning which would correct and complete a text.

There were also *Upapurāṇas,* and *Aupapurāṇas,* whose numbers were fixed by tradition to eighteen. The *Purāṇas* were classified according to their contents. *Mārkaṇḍeya Purāṇa* is bracketted with *Liṅga* and *Vāmana Purāṇas* as a sectarian Purāṇa.[290] They were also divided similar to the four Mahāyugas.[291]

Purāṇas are the real encyclopaedia of Hindu religion. From ancient religious and secular stories and cosmological stories of the Brāhmaṇas, which formed the kernel, the Purāṇas elaborated them into a vast and complex literature treating every aspect of religion. They had always kept abreast of current events and kept incorporating them into the Purāṇas. That is why the Purāṇas were recited by a wide number of people, and were more popular than the epics. The material of the *Purāṇas* has therefore increased vastly over the years, but they should not be considered spurious.[292] There is an opinion that a text may be considered spurious if it did not support the sectarian view contained in that particular Purāṇa. This may not be a proper criterion, because truth is reiterated in different ways and from different angles. This is a living tradition and a continuous process. This precludes existence of any spurious passages. In the West, written tradition is respected better than oral traditions, whereas, in India, the oral tradition has an aura of sanctity about it. A better term than oral tradition would be 'revealed truth received through hearing'.[293] The epics and the Purāṇas, though classified as Smṛti, contain religious material in agreement with the Vedas, and this evaluation is done by Brahmins who are well-versed in the Vedic lore. Purāṇas are *upabṛhmaṇa,* elaboration of the Vedic truth. There could be no critical edition of the Purāṇas, and there could be no interpolation or later additions.

The epics and the Purāṇas had an oral tradition till they were transcribed. The difference between oral and written traditions is that sacrality changes to historicity, immediately as the work is put down on paper; and it lays itself open to a critical study. But, Purāṇas are a continuous and fluctuating tradition and it is wrong to apply Western rules of critical appraisal. The authenticity of a Purāṇa and its author, Vyāsa is purely according to one's inner faith, *śraddhā,* in the work which is outside critical enquiry.

If we examine a myth from the structuralist's or the phenomenologist's point of view, it takes into account the relevance of the text in the religious beliefs of the people, but it ignores the history which necessitated the myth, since such a study is 'ahistorical. This may suit us as historicity has not been our strong point. But religious feelings must not be overlooked while examining the meaning behind the texts. The Hindu accepts that *upabṛhmaṇa* does take place in a text. Therefore each text has two view points: its importance to an individual which differs from person to person; and the study of its history which would be the study of the sum of all the individual's view points. This latter is the historical view point which is the accumulation of the individual faith of men. The historical accretions to the text are called *upabrahmaṇa.* To just study the meaning behind a text, and the significance of each accretion without paying proper emphasis to the history which necessitated each such accretion is inadequate. From the historian (of religion)'s point of view, one should stand above the contemporary influence of meanings and emphases and appreciate the wholeness of each individual's experience of the text. But even this has its lapses that, if we study each facet that goes to make up a *Purāṇa,* they overlap at a certain stage and are not water-tight independent compartments. Myth should be studied from the individual's view-point as well as from the "cumulative tradition".[294] The study of the cumulative tradition allows us to study the myth from the objective and historic stand; while the individual's view-point gives a subjective illumination to the understanding. Any religious text is originally an expression of an individual's faith, but later on it becomes part of the Hindu tradition. One opinion is that the historic value of the Purāṇas would be limited, because they were redacted by the Brahmins, and changed from the composers who were the custodians of the tradition.[295] But another opinion is that India does not lack the sense of historicity, though her understanding of history is different.[296] It is not a string of mundane events, but a true understanding of the purpose of human existence as revealed in the Purāṇa. For this, we have to understand the basic concept of the Paurāṇika which underlay and illuminated the narrative. Such concepts were Sanskritisation and Purāṇisation, i.e., any idea could be made into a Purāṇa, the only criterion being that it should be old. To the Indians, historicism was understandable only with reference to the Vedic system and the changes were judged against the rearrangement of ideas with reference to the Vedas which were immutable and primordial.

Sometimes, a local version of a myth is more important as encased in the *Sthala Purāṇa,* than the Brahminised version. But Sanskrit tradition would look down on the local myth and try to ignore it. The existing *Purāṇic* version of a myth may convey no meaning at all, till a local tradition would give a minor detail which would shed light on an obscure point and make it meaningful.[297]

Coming to the text proper, the DM. is examined against the Vedic backdrop from which it has developed, and, its history, i.e., its relationship to the anterior stutis of the Mbh. and the HV. are considered. (It would even answer to historical and symbolical divisions.)

It would seem that the DM. had an earlier independent status as sacred literature before it was appended to the *Mārk. P.* Its intrinsic importance is not derived from its inclusion in the *Mārk. P.* There have been sixteen editions of the text and it has been translated into many European languages, including Greek and Latin. The French translation is as early as 1788 A.D.[298] DM's intrinsic importance is that it is a culmination of the literary, i.e., Vedic, and archaeological evidence. It has suggestions of a germ of ideas which later evolve into Tantrism and Śākta literature.

Thus DM. is generative for later Śākta literature and integrative for earlier literature. In the DM. the non-Aryan origin of Devī is played down, as opposed to the hymns in the Mbh. and the HV. (Since the latter have been treated already, only some salient features are touched here.) The DM. gives emphasis to both the benign and terrific aspects of the Goddess. Though the *stutis* in the DM. are similar to those in the HV. they are grander in conception and contain more elaborate and abstract ideas. They seem the logical conclusion of the epic lauds. As for the emphasis on the ambivalance of the Goddess, the best example would be the *śloka* in the *stuti*, popularly called the *Śakrādi stuti.*[299]

"Kenopamā bhavatu te(a)sya parākramasya rūpaṁ ca śatrubhayakāryatihārikutra/
Citte kṛpā samaraniṣṭhuratā ca dṛṣṭā tvayyeva Devī varade bhuvanatraye(a) pi//"

What can be compared to your this valour? Where this beauty which creates fear in the enemies? Boon-giver! In all the three worlds only in you can be seen together compassion and harshness in battle at the same time.

As a watershed for future developments, the DM. is seen as similar to the *Devī Bhāg. P.*, and the *Brahmavaivarta P.* It is also the jumping board for future Tantric works.

The Function of the DM

The whole of the DM. is important as a ritual. Devī herself assures her devotees[300] by their just hearing the *Māhātmya* read,[301] or reading it themselves,[302] she would relieve them of all their travails.

*"Smaran mamaitaccaritaṁ naro mucyeta saṅkaṭāt/*29...
*Dūrādeva palāyante smaratascaritaṁ mama//"*30

Therefore, whoever composed the DM. must have foreseen its cultic importance, and woven into it ritually significant matter. It is natural for the religious Hindu to weave the important events of his life with the rituals of the text. Myth and ritual have the same objective, that of gratifying desires. This the DM. fulfills admirably. Even if the DM is a later accretion to the Mārk. P., it does not lose its sacrality, because of its recent origin, exactly like the late khilas of the Vedas, some of the late Purāṇas and Upaniṣads. The DM. is treated similar to a Vedic mantra, with a

Ṛṣi, chandas, and devatā, for each of the three episodes. Proper pronunciation necessary, just as in the Vedic mantras. The analysis of the DM. is to recognise its functional importance in the religious context. But analysing a text is of subsidiary importance, because once its parts have been synthesized, its history begins. There is a distinction between the content and function of the text. DM.'s content is Smṛti, and its function is Śruti.

The DM. is both Śruti, and Smṛti. When recited, its form or contents is not important. It is as good as the Vedas, where the reciter need not know its meaning. But its contents would classify it as a Smṛti. It is a frozen moment, of unusual importance, which has been made eternal and immutable. Its position as part of the Purāṇa makes it sacred like the Vedas. But by itself it is sacred, in its function as a Smṛti. The Vedic antecedents could be the 'will to create' personified as a feminine power, or, Śakti. This has been enlarged in the DM. and from here she has been made the pre-eminent deity of the Tantras. This does not gainsay the aboriginal contribution in her make-up as much as it is in Rudra-Śiva.[303] The polytheistic nature of the godhead as thought of in the Vedas is further elaborated here. The DM. is seen[304] as developing directly from the *Vāgambhṛni Sūkta*.[305]

The difference between oral and written traditions is as between *Śruti* and *Smṛti*. If we adjudge the DM. as an oral epic, to be recited, the problem that arises is that it is more than just that. The martial activity of the Goddess predominates the DM, but this is balanced by the stutis. These stutis are so beautiful by themselves that they impose their presence over the narrative portions also. The narratives help in our understanding Devī in her hymns. Similar hymns in the Mbh. and the HV. assisted in the emergence and development of the Goddess. Oral reciters make changes in the format and without any conscious effort. This is to make it relevant to that particular period. But, tradition is preserved even though it is constantly re-created. This leads to variations in different editions of the same myth.

Some of the Epithets of the Goddess in the DM

The true function of an epithet is to distinguish a particular person or object, from other such similar entities. Therefore, the epithets are chosen with great care to bring out a particular picture the composer would have in mind. They also reveal the historic background. There is power in the epithets which gets transferred to the reciter, and he holds it over the god. In this, it is similar to the Vedic sūktas. The importance of an epithet would increase if it were used often. Many of the epithets have Vedic antecedents, or, epic ones. The DM. makes the Sanskrit tradition contemporary, and the Goddess worship traditional. The new figure of the Goddess is made traditional by using epithets which have Vedic roots.

Durgā in the DM:

There are four mentions of this name in the text.

(i) *"Durgāsi durgabhavasāgaranaurasaṅgā/"*4.11.

You are Durgā, a ship, personification of non-attachment, in the difficult ocean of saṃsāra world.

(ii) *"Durge smṛtā harasi bhītimaśeṣajantoḥ svasthaiḥ smṛtā matimatīva śubhāṁ dadāsi/"*4.17

If remembered by creatures you remove all their fears

(iii) *"Durgāyai durgapārāyai ..."*5.12

As Durgā you help (people) over difficulties.

(iv) *"Bhayebhyastrāhi no Devī Durge Devī namostu te"*11.24

Protect us from fear, O Durgā! Devi! we bow to you.

If we look over these references it would be seen that the goddess is a protector of her devotees from worldly calamities, but herself is at the same time hard to approach. There is mention of the word durgā in the ṚV., but not in the feminine. It is used as a neuter and masculine only.[306] The Taitt. Ār.,[307] and other references have been gone over already. Durgā's cult must have been well-established by the early centuries of the Christian era, as attested by iconography.

Caṇḍikā

This has absolutely no reference in the Vedas or the epic. This is a most popular (by its frequency in occurrence) epithet in the DM. Only in contemporary, or slightly later literature do we find references. In Bāṇa's Caṇḍīśataka, Caṇḍī is not solely malefic, but is beneficent also. She has marked Śiva affiliations in this work. This occurs for the first time in our text.

Ambikā

At the root of the form of the Goddess is an attempt at homogeneity of heterogenous forms. Though Ambikā emanates from the kośa of Pārvatī (5.85/6), Pārvatī herself has almost no references in the text. It is in Ambikā all the fighting hosts merge (10.6). Though she may seem a subsidiary of Pārvatī, she is the more powerful goddess. The roots of this epithet have already been traced to the YV.

Mahāmāyā

The meaning of this would be either "one who possesses great delusive power", or, "one who is delusion", "existing in, or of māyā", mithyādarśanam.[308] Māyā has associations with asuras in the ṚV. Mahāmāyā should therefore have asuric connections. In 1.78, she is called Mahāsurī. Her popularity may be due to a certain extent to her asuric or non-Aryan connections. Māya, here might mean prakṛti and also illusion. She is transcendent, but when she has some purpose to fulfil, she takes on forms.

Nityā

In the ṚV., this word has three connotations: (i) one's own-*svīya, sahaja;* (ii) dear-*priya;* and (iii) constant and permanent-*dhruva.* It came to mean, over a period of time, the essence of a thing, which is immutable, and eternal. In the DM., Nityā is applied to the goddess, and we may take it that she is not only eternal, but this "eternality" is her inner essence.

Śivadūtī

There are three noticeable points about this epithet. Firstly, she could subordinate Śiva. Secondly, it could mean two opposite things, auspicious and a wolf. Thirdly it is a goddess who puts forth a Śakti. The purpose of this epithet may have been to make auspicious what is really fierce.

Gaurī

In the ṚV. this word means literally a female buffalo, or figuratively milk.[309] This word is correlated to Pārvatī, and both have few mentions in the text. She was earlier thought of as the wife of Varuṇa and so represented in iconography.[310] Her Śiva connections are firm. Her mention in our text may be to show up the contrast held within the Goddess. Gaurī is said to have emanated from Pārvatī, beautiful and fair, leaving the latter dark, whence she gets the name Kālikā.

Kṛtyā

This strange epithet occurs once.[311] Kṛtyā is an evil spirit born out of the third eye of Śiva. Brahma P.,[312]and Skanda P.[313] mention her as the "womb of fire", and the "tongue of death. She is said to be riding a monkey. In the Padma P.,[314] she is described as a terrible goddess, with all attributes complementing this picture.[315] Kṛtya may appear in a male form also, and appears usually to afflict particular persons.[316] This epithet in the *Nārāyaṇī stuti* emphasises the malevolent origin of the Goddess, and her associations with Śiva, and Agni.

Prakṛti

In the DM., this word means the material earth, though the Goddess identifying herself with it, raises it to divine heights. In the Mbh., the Saptarṣis are called Prakṛtis.[317] This word is from the Sāṁkhya philosophy where it is made up of three guṇas, and evolves into the material world. The Śvet. Up.[318] says:

"Māyāṁ tu prakṛtiṁ viddhi māyinam tu maheśvaram", and makes the Sāṁkhyan world theistic. In the Bh. G.[319] Prakṛti is the lower nature of God. In the DM. this word is used to denote the material world in various degrees of relationship to the divine.

Yoganidrā

She is the creator of this world and its destroyer. In the first episode, she shows her grace by leaving Viṣṇu after which only he is able to wake up and slay the demons. This is implicit in the episode. Putting this differently, it is only due to the Goddess that the world exists and human beings have life and consciousness. This epithet has levels of meaning.

Viṣṇumāyā

She is the power of Viṣṇu. But, she is praised as Pārvatī, wife of Śiva, when the gods go to the Himalayas to praise the Goddess.

"iti kṛtvā matiṁ devā Himavantaṁ nageśvaram/
*Jagmustatra tato Devīṁ Viṣṇumāyāṁ pratuṣṭuvuḥ//*5.7.
*Namo Devyai Mahādevyai Śivāyai satataṁ namaḥ"*5.8.

Another opposing trait in her is, she gives knowledge, but deludes by clouding our discrimination.

Parameśvarī

This would mean that the goddess is beyond any comparison. Śakti in the DM. means not what the Goddess has, but, is. Śakti does not denote the word as understood in the Tantric context.[320] In the Tantras, Śakti is connected to Śiva, and to Yoga. In the DM. her connection to Śiva is slight. She is the ultimate principle and creatrix of the world. Durgā is formed by the tejas of all the gods. Their Śaktis form a separate group as Mātṛs. Svāhā has connections with Agni and the epithet shows Durgā's similar connection. As for the epithet Nārāyaṇī, in the Durgāstava by Yudhiṣṭhira,[321] she is called wife of Nārāyaṇa : *"Bhāsi yathā Padmā Nārāyaṇaparigraḥ"* You shine like the wife of Nārāyaṇa.

The Śakti aspect of the goddess is as important a fact as her syncretised figure. This power is not only mental, moral, etc, but is biological, physiological, as well as physical. We are just the media for the expression of this power. We are not separate from it which is identical with God.[322]

Kātyāyanī

In the DM. she has Śiva connotation. Her earlier epic connections have been already dealt with. The goddess is not designated with overtly Śivaite relationships. This is similar to the epithets Aindrī, and Māheśvarī. These show a relationship to the respective gods on a slightly more profound plane than a mere physical one. It can also be seen that the Goddess is suprême by herself and not due to any help from a god.

The Myths

The importance of the myths in the *DM.* is that these three different episodes are brought together for the first time in our text; and, though there have been earlier episodes of the gods fighting the demons, this is the first time the Goddess has been requested to slay the enemies herself, and she is the sole instrument in their annihilation. As mentioned earlier, this is also an instrument to make the Goddess cult traditional by the language, and Sanskrit made contemporaneous. There are three myths, or *caritas.* The first is the *Madhu-Kaiṭabha vadha*; the second, is the *Mahiṣa vadha,* and the third is the *Śumbha-Niśumbha* and other attendant demons' *vadha.* These three episodes are treated in earlier religious literature in great detail. But in the *DM.*, their lengths are in inverse proportion to those in the above. In the *Madhu-Kaiṭabha* episode, the Goddess is transcendent, but this gets scant treatment in one chapter. But in the epic and the Purāṇas this is treated in great detail. The Goddess appears in the world in the Mahiṣa episode. Her encounter with Mahiṣa is treated in four chapters, whereas this gets scant treatment in the Purāṇas. The Śumbha-Niśumbha episode gets an elaborate treatment in the DM. whereas it is almost unknown earlier.

The first episode, *Prathama Carita,* is set in the *pralaya* period when the worlds were covered by water. This episode is mentioned in the Mbh.[323] The HV[324] says that the world was created from the fat; medas, and marrow, vaśā of these demons and hence derived the name Medinī. In the Matsya P. Madhu and Kaiṭabha ask Viṣṇu to kill them on dry earth, urvi. Viṣṇu chooses the pun in the word and interpreting it as thighs, kills them there. This is a patently cosmogonic myth, the god creating order out of chaos, and the world out of the waters. Because of this aspect of this myth, it is mentioned in the epic, as well as in many Purāṇas.[325] The relevance of this myth in the DM. as the opening myth is that this battle is on a cosmic scale, and it results in the re-creation of the earth. It is but appropriate that the Goddess makes her debut in this episode. She is cosmic in scale, and she is connected with creation. She is called the Great Deluder here, because she deludes the demons into thinking they can outwit the Divine. This is patently a Viṣṇuite myth. Some scholars have gone to the extent of saying that the exaltation of Durgā as a goddess is entirely due to the help she renders Viṣṇu as Yoganidrā, in the Kaṁsa episode as well as here. Here the power of the Goddess is shown in a curious way. Only when she leaves Viṣṇu can he combat the demons. By her grace or power, Viṣṇu is able to kill the enemies.

The second episode, the Madhyama Carita, deals with the Mahiṣa vadha. Battle-myths both in the Vedas and the Purāṇas are common. They contain a change in religious ideas, or some political event. Myths of Śiva's fight with Arjuna and Śīsupāla reflect probably the struggles Śaivism had to face against stiff opposition. The myths of Rāma and Agastya camouflage the Aryan expansion of territories. The Goddess' fights with demons in her role as the protectress is seen as the continuation of the ambivalence seen in the Vedic deities, for instance in cycles of the gods' rest and activity.[326] The Goddess being desired by Mahiṣa, or Śumbha, Niśumbha is a common motif of a virgin war-goddess. The culmination of the goddess made beneficent as a wife is, as Satī.[327] Just as the Madhu-Kaiṭabha episode is connected with Viṣṇu, the Mahiṣa episode is connected with Skanda in the Mbh. But the parentage of Skanda is in a flux in the epic, and finally,[328] Brahmā tells him that Śiva and Pārvatī are his parents. Since this is the first time a god is created, though there are innumerable instances of the emanations of a god, the confusion could be justified. Since Skanda is born for the express purpose of killing Mahiṣa, even Śiva desists from killing him, remembering his son's role. Mbh. is consistent in ascribing this role to Skanda. It may be surmised that, just as Skanda was attaining fixed myths by variations of his background, so also the Mahiṣa episode may have gone through earlier variations, before being fixed to the Goddess. Iconography supports the popularity of the Goddess' claim to Mahiṣavadha, and there is not a single icon pertaining to Skanda's similar involvement. Padma P. says[329] Mahiṣa was killed on the Mandaragiri by Vaiṣṇavī in the Svāyambhuva Manvantara. He was destroyed by Nanda in the Vaivasvata Manvantara on the Vindhyas. In the Vāmana P. the treatment of Mahiṣavadha is not given much importance, and Skanda killing Mahiṣa is further elaborated. In this Purāṇa in the Mahiṣa episode,[330] Devī leaves her lion mount, and rides on the back of Mahiṣa (46). She presses him with her soft feet (47), though he jumps about to unseat her. He loses his strength, though resembling a mountain (48), Devī cuts off his head with the śūla.

*"Sā cāpi padbhyāṁ mṛdukomalābhyāṁ/ mamarda taṁ klinnamivājinaṁ hi//*47

*Sa mṛdyamāno dharaṇīdharābho/Devyā balī hīnabalo babhūva"*48.

She is related to Pārvatī in this P. and subservient to Śiva, whereas Pārvatī or Śiva get very little importance in the DM. The strange conclusion of the Mahiṣa episode is at the end when the Goddess sits at the feet of Śiva and is hymned by the gods. She then promises to help them out in future and she enters back into the gods: "Evamuktvā praviveśa Durgā" (52). This may support the view that this Purāṇa is later than the DM. But there are similar considerations to put its date earlier than the DM. In Hindu myths, integration of earlier accounts of the myth is quite common, as mentioned earlier, and are considered equally sacred. Mbh. is unequivocal about Skanda killing the Mahiṣa demon. DM. is equally so about Devī's role in the same episode. But, Vāmana P. seems aware of both the versions and is in the transition stage when both are presented. This Purāṇa seems to treat the goddess not as a Supreme Goddess, and though she promises she will be born again to help the devas in their difficulties, her emanations are not mentioned.

Different Interpretations of the Myth

In the Padma P.,[331] the Asura is mentioned as the personification of ignorance and the Goddess is Jñāna Śakti, wisdom. The Purāṇic fight of Daśabhuja Durgā with Mahiṣa is assimilated to the Vedic Indra-Vṛtra fight.[332] Indra is the sun, and Durgā is the autumnal sun. Vṛtra and Mahiṣa stand for the dark clouds holding back the waters. The sun strikes them with his rays, i.e., the ten arms of the Goddess, and releases the rains.

The conflict between Devī and Mahiṣa is seen on a universal scale.[333] Devī is said to preside over Mahat or Virāj, i.e., the universal plane. She faces the universal enemy in the Mahiṣa. The words 'mahat' and 'mahiṣa' are said to come from the same root 'mah' to magnify, to become great. The devas are said to be order, Yajña, and the asuras the opposite, disorder and a-Yajña. This is the polarity symbolised in the conflict between Devī and the asuras. The motif of the devāsura conflict is implicit in worldly existence. The harmony between the devas and asuras is necessary for order. Again this struggle could be seen as between forces of light, goodness, and truth against darkness, evil and arrogance. This is a cosmic struggle. Devī is the cosmic power. The asuras pose a danger if they transgress the area allotted to them, and cause disruption to the daivic order. If this happens then the devas have to find strength and support from the cosmic power to subdue the evil and confine it. The asuras are Tāmasic and the devas are Rājasic. Therefore, the asuras start a battle, and the devas have to reunite with the transcendent reality to enable them to subdue and defeat the asuras. The asuric tendencies are eternal and everpresent.[334] These fights are seen as fought within each individual between true powers and arrogated ones.[335]

This victory over the Mahiṣa by Devī is seen as the victory gained by the Mother-Goddess principle. This has been the theory universally acclaimed. But,[336] it is seen as victory of the mother-goddess against the aggressive, self-centered and chaotic male force. She restores order from chaos, and channelises the unbridled manly fury. This is almost the only opinion which tends to view the male power as tending to get out-of-control, and the female curbing and channelising it by her beneficent powers.[337] This devāsura struggle is similar to that between the Olympians and the Titans. The universe is conceived to be supported and controlled by various gods. When this orderly government is dislocated by an asura, through his pride and ambition, a struggle ensues. The asura usually accumulates psychic energy sufficient to become a reservoir of power, and poses a threat to the gods. He would usually ask a boon of invulnerability, or immortality, which the higher gods, like Viṣṇu, Śiva, etc., have to concede, otherwise their world would get disrupted. The asura in this episode assumes the form of a huge buffalo, commensurate with his immense arrogance. The Mother-Goddess becomes the integrated power, collected from the particularised, and one-sided abilities of the devas. She is not exerted by the fight at all. This is the resurgence of the pre-Aryan mother-goddess, who had waited gracefully in the side-lights, for nearly a millenia, before taking the centre-stage in all her full glory. "She simply stands here again: spotless womanly charm, the life-force incarnate; the same irresistible, unattainable one as ever; unwearied and betraying no sign of having suffered even a moment of anxiety and incertitude before emerging in her own true character again, triumphant."[338]

In the *Mahiṣavadha*,[339] the emphasis is on Devī, pressing the asura down, with her foot, and then killing him with the śūla. Quakenbos[340] states that "... the emphasis seems to be laid on the efficacy of Caṇḍī's kick as the final coup de grace that ended the struggle". This thought is a unifying idea in Bāṇa's *Caṇḍīśataka* also where the glory of the foot of the goddess is praised rather than the Goddess herself.[341]

The third episode, Uttama Carita, is in the main the

confrontation of the Goddess with Śumbha and Niśumbha. The supporters and generals of Śumbha-Niśumbha are also annihilated in the process. The fights with others culminate duly in the ninth and tenth chapters where the main villains are killed. Just as the devas praised Devī,[342] after Mahiṣa was killed, so do they sing her praises after she finishes off all the enemies of the devas in a beautiful panegyric (11), called the Nārāyaṇī Stuti. Of the thirteen chapters that make up the DM. Adhs. 11,12, and 13 are considered to be later additions, because they seem loosely strung as compositions.[343] But this may not be the correct view. As mentioned earlier the devas praise her (11) after she killed the demons exactly as they do affter Mahiṣa's death. In the twelfth chapter, Devī herself foretells about her future emanations and their glory, and in the thirteenth chapter, there is a logical round up of the theme, as it was started in the first chapter by the king and the Vaiśya.

The Vāmana P. (29) records the Śumbha-Niśumbha episode as follows. Their ancestry is traced as the sons of Danu and Kaśyapa (1-2).[344] Because Indra craftily kills their third brother Namuci (4-10) with foam, they start harassing and vanquishing the gods, and taking away their wealth (11-14). They descend to the earth after over-running devaloka, and there meet Raktabīja, a friend of Mahiṣa (15-17); also Caṇḍa and Muṇḍa, the ministers of Mahiṣa (22-23), and jointly they decide to kill the Goddess. Raktabīja wants to marry the Goddess (26) but is prevented by Caṇḍa, who says that she is fit only for Śumbha. (27)

The Goddess in the episode of killing Caṇḍa, Muṇḍa is called Śuṣkarevatī and Caṇḍamārī (82). She is the personification of fearsome death. As for calling her by the star's name, the bad connotations of asterisks has been noted earlier. Her dress after this battle is tribal. She is ornamented with snakes, Garuḍa's feathers (not with peacock's as in the epic), and a girdle of small bells made of lion's skin (78/9). She also quaffs wine and blood (80), and sports a crest of the skulls of the two demons (83).

In the DM., the goddess Caṇḍikā is not connected with the mountains and the emphasis is on her character as a war-goddess. Further the Himalayas are rarely mentioned.

The Stutis

The stutis are taken up now. There are four hymns in the DM. They are the Brahmā stuti, Śakrādi stuti, Yā Devī stuti, and the

Nārāyaṇī stuti. Brahmā is threatened by the two demons Madhu and Kaiṭabha, while Viṣṇu is sleeping. He lauds Devī, in the form of Yoganidrā, and requests her to delude the demons and also that Viṣṇu should wake up and the thought of killing the demons must strike him. The Goddess herself gives delusion to creatures and they lose their discrimination. The way to get out of this is to pray to the Goddess who is personified as Mohamāyā.

In the Śakrādi Stuti,[345] the devas praise the Goddess after she kills Mahiṣa. They are filled with awe and wonder at her power and the ease with which she destroyed Mahiṣa. They realise her ambivalence as also their own puny and helpless state. She is transcendent and immanent. The asuras killed by her are all now led into heaven. Her tender hands which wielded powerful weapons against the enemies, should be used by her now to protect her devotees from all directions. The phalaśruti contained in the laud itself is that she should protect whoever recites this and she should come to protect the devas whenever they are troubled again.

In the third hymn,[346] the gods reach Himalayas to hymn the Devī, requesting her to keep her promise of coming to their aid, as they are now troubled by Śumbha and Niśumbha. She is called Viṣṇumāyā, and the anomaly of her residence and her relationship to Śiva contained in the laud itself has been mentioned. Her immanence is emphasised in this laud. All abstract qualities of excellence found in living creatures, not humans alone are the personification of the Goddess herself, and there is no other origin beyond her. But she is also *'bhrānti'*—delusion, *'nidrā'* sleep, *'kṣudhā'* —hunger, *'tṛṣṇā'*—Thirst. And the significance of the *'namastasyai'* repeated thrice is bowing down to her with the body, word and mind. *"Namastasyai iti padatryeṇa kāyikavācikamānasikanamas kāratrayaṁ pradarśitam"*.[347] This stuti is said to be supported by numismatic proof of the Chandragupta II Vikramaditya period.

The last stuti is the *Nārāyaṇī stuti.*[348] Here the subsidiary goddesses or Mātṛs, are praised as her innumerable forms. Her fierce aspect is also brought to our attention. Her weapons used to kill the enemies are praised and Devī requested to use them for their protection. Her ambivalence is touched on in verse 29.

"Rogānaśeṣānapahaṁsi tuṣṭā ruṣṭā tu kāmān sakalānabhīṣṭān/

Tvāmāśritānāṁ na vipannarāṇāṁ tvāmaśritā hyāśrayatāṁ prayānti//"

If you are pleased you remove all diseases. If angered you remove all our desires. There is no danger to those who have come to you for refuge, for they themselves become a refuge for others.[349]

Searching for the roots for these *Stutis*, one could reach down to the two *Vedic Sūktas*, the *Rātri Sūkta* and the *Vāgāmbhṛṇī Sūkta*. These are considered so much related to the Goddess' exploits that they are recited prior to and after the main text in rituals.

In the first verse of the *Rātri Sūkta*, the beauties[350] or, the glories,[351] are mentioned *(śriyaḥ)* In the last (8) verse the goddess is requested to accept this offering of verses offered to her as if to a conqueror.[352] This is seen as a prophesy of Durgā's future victorious encounters. But, another reading is "as the eulogy of one about to conquer".[353] This reading would assimilate it to the lauds by Yudhisṭhira, and others before the wars. In the *Śrī Sūkta* and the *Pariśiṣṭa Rātrī Khila* of the RgVeda,[354] the goddesses are assimilated to the god Agni, as a mark of auspiciousness, and beauty. The *stavas* in the epic has been noted earlier.

The three *caritas* of the DM. present three names of the Goddess: Yoganidrā in the first episode has not caught people's fancy. She is more popular as Kauśikī / Kālikā of the third episode. But, she is most popular as Mahiṣāsuramardinī of the middle episode. Some icons of this form are dated earlier than the DM. Since icons represent crystallisation of ideas, the Mahiṣāsuramardinī aspect of the Goddess might be even earlier. From among the many forms of the Goddess, Mahiṣāsuramardinī aspect of Durgā became the finally popular form.

The whole of the DM. is seen as a symbol for our spiritual progress.[355] The Brahmin Ṛṣi Sumedhas stands for Jñāna as Medhas means this. The Kṣatriya king Suratha is the soul bound by the physical body.[356] The Vaiśya Samādhi is the personification of one-pointed concentration of the citta. This is an important instrument in Yoga. This condition of the Yoga and the Jivātmā are embroiled in Duhkha .and Moha of saṁsāra. When these two appeal to the Ṛṣi and ask him the reason for their delusion, the Ṛṣi points out that it is Devī herself who is the cause of their plight and she is also the instrument of their release. In the Devī Sūkta, Devī declares that whomsoever pleases her she will make him a Ṛṣi, and Sumedhas.

*"Yaṁ kāmaye taṁ tamugraṁ kṛṇomi taṁ brahmāṇam taṁ ṛṣiṁ taṁ sumedham//"*5

Whom I like, I make him exalted, Brahmā, Ṛṣi or the best.[357]

Conclusions

In the DM. the non-Aryan goddess is presented in Sanskrit and her full account is given. Sanskrit was not only a language giving culture and respectability, it was also a language of piety, giving tradition an eternality. The process of Sanskritisation makes a social, cultural or religious norm appreciate in status. DM. was a part of a Purāṇa. Purāṇa was an accepted elaboration of the Vedas, or their revision, and its aim was to make the eternal truth embodied in the Vedas understandable in the contemporary society. The content of the DM. as a text is important by itself in integrating past history, and to serve as a footboard for future Śākta religion. In function, it is liturgical and helps the ritual of the cult. This latter shows a similarity to the *Vedic* tradition. Western theories of oral composition show a set of formulae repeated whenever a situation or, metre arrangement requires it. But this would lead us away from the hymns which are more important than the narrative episodes. Epithets are important in Indian religious literature, to judge the historicity of an episode or a characteristic of the Goddess. The Vedic antecedents are traced and similar myths of an earlier period have also been mentioned.

The composer of the DM. does not know that Śakti is feminine and its possessor is masculine. The Goddess though formed of the śaktis of the gods herself puts forth śaktis in the narrative. The ultimate reality is feminine in the DM. She is transcendent, as well as immanent. She can be realised internally. Since she is immanent she can always be requested to help the devotee in times of danger, which can be anything from crossing a jungle, to annihilating the enemies. Because she is transcendent none of these are contradictory. DM. has a retrospective Śruti aspect as well as a prospective Smṛti aspect. To integrate many goddesses into one, many myths are needed to be integrated. Many of the epithets and ideas can be traced to the Vedas. As for Skanda's involvement in the Mahiṣa episode it can only be surmised that Skanda and Agni played an important part in the formulation of the Goddess.

The IV culture and other folk deities would have formed the substratum of the goddess cult. There is certain connection seen in the Vedas. The popularity during the Kushanas and the native dynasties gave the cult concrete expression in icons, and the Śiva cult gave it a fillip. Guptas gave it a philosophy and Brahminised the rituals for its cult. It emerged in the form of the Great Goddess, Mahādevī, and her exploits were regularised in her *Māhātmya.*

Bāṇa's Caṇḍīśatakam

In more than sixty of the verses, it is Caṇḍī's kick on Mahiṣa which is panegyrised. This glorification is said to have its origin in the personal marital life of Bāṇa.[358] In the DM. in her fight with Mahiṣa, the emphasis is on Caṇḍī's foot which presses Mahiṣa's neck, and which lays him low. After this she hits him with her trident,[359] and finally cuts his head off with a big sword.[360] This same emphasis of the foot is given in the *Caṇḍīśatakam.* The unity of thought which runs through the work is the foot of Durgā, and praises are given more to the foot of the Goddess than to the Goddess herself.

The whole poem picturises the fight between Devī and Mahiṣa, which is dealt with more elaborately in the DM. In the *Kathāsaritsāgara*[361] is mentioned:

"Namastubhyaṁ Mahādevī pādau yāvakāṅkitau/
Mṛditāsuralagnāsrapaṅkāviva namāmi ahaṁ//".

....

Paritrātāstvayā lokā Mahiṣāsurasūdani/"

Though the poem is called Caṇḍīśatakam, there are only five stanzas which have the epithets Caṇḍī, or, Caṇḍikā. The various other epithets that are used are: as daughter of the Himalayas; as wife of Śiva and the benign and malefic aspects of the Goddess.

Caṇḍī is said to have killed Mahiṣa with her left foot.[362] Left side is considered evil. Death is also evil. It sends the good to the heavens and the evil to hell. (It may also be mentioned, that women were considered evil and therefore the goddesses were consigned to the left side of the gods.) The arrow which was sent by Pārvatī killed Mahiṣa and entered Pātāla.[363] There is covert eroticism in certain verses. Śiva says,[364] "I cannot call you Mahiṣī, now that Mahiṣa is dead."

"Drān nīte dīrghanidrāṁ dviṣati na Mahiṣī 'ty ucyase prāyaśo' 'dya"

(p.2) and, Mahiṣa compares himself to Śiva (76), and also in verse 20:

"Śūlenīśo yaśobhāg bhavati parilaghuḥ syād vadārhe 'pi daṇḍaḥ" *(p. 2) Mahiṣa* is hit by the arrow. But if he were killed by the trident it would be lying beside him and he would be famous as *Īśa.*

Verse 74 says:

"Saṁdhyāsevāparāddhaṁ bhavaṁ iva purato vāmapadāmbujena/ Kṣiptaṁ daityaṁ ..... //" (lines 3 and 4)

"She kicked him with her left foot, the Daitya who was changed into a buffalo, as though it was Bhava who was similarly spurned by her earlier for committing a fault in his *saṁdhyā pūjā."* Again in verse 77,

"Bhadre krīḍābhimardī tava savidhaṁ ahaṁ kāmataḥ prāpta Īśo." (line 3)

I have come just like Śiva wanting to hug you in amorous sports. Such approaches are made in verses 75 and 85. Pārvatī is described as having a forest of arms.[365] Even when she is fiercely fighting the Mahiṣa, the beauty of her limbs and body are described.

"Pārvatyā Mahiṣāsuravyatikare vyāyāmaramyaṁ vapuḥ" (verse 72, line 3) The Mahiṣa is also compared to the Vindhyas or Kailasa where Pārvatī and Śiva live. The Goddess is always portrayed as a bashful wife,[366] embarrassed[367] by praises of her valour and taking refuge in her husband's embrace. Śiva subserviates himself in love, by kissing her foot which had killed Mahiṣa. He admires her physique while she is killing Mahiṣa.[368] We are constantly reminded of her role as the mother of Skanda, daughter of Himavān and Mena, and as the wife of Śiva. As the proper Hindu wife she kills Mahiṣa as he derides Śiva.[369]

In verse 37, punning is used in the word Paśupati, and Śiva and Mahiṣa are juxtaposed. (75 also).

In one verse, the Goddess herself derides the gods, including Śiva:

"Aibhī tvaṁ niṣṭhureyaṁ bibhṛhi mṛduṁ imām īśvareti āttahāsā Gaurī ....". (Verse 29, lines 3 and 4)

Oh! Īsvara! the elephant skin you are wearing is rough, please take this soft skin of Mahiṣa. Her maid Vijayā also taunts the gods that they abandoned their weapons in fear.

The picture that we got of the goddess in DM. as a supreme deity not leaning on any gods, coqutry unknown to her, eroticism completely deleted, is changed into a spousified goddess, constantly reminding us that she is a dutiful wife and mother first, and then only as a secondary role she is a war-goddess. Bāṇa might have intended this piece as a literary work and changed the character of the Goddess subtly to suit his period.

Asura

To complete the analysis of the goddess Mahiṣāsuramardinī, a study of the demon Mahiṣa is necessary. This in turn entails an analysis of the clan asura to which Mahiṣa belonged, shades of the meaning of the word asura, its historical development from the ṚV. through the Brāhmaṇas and the Purāṇas, the cultural and religious contribution of the asuras to Hinduism, to the extent that it would help in our better understanding of the demon. Attention is also paid to the sociological necessity which gave rise to the concept of demons, the polarity of opposites, and the concept of good and evil which gives rise to deities good and evil.

Consubstantiality of gods and demons

In the earliest literature there is no distinction between gods and demons. They have the same father Prajāpati. They are consubstantial before the beginning of creation. But after creation they are deadlocked in battle. In the main, both demons and gods are the same, but functionally they are different. There could even be a potential deva in the asura, or, the deva could by his nature be an asura. The designations of deva or asura could be applied to the same person, deity or power.[370] The asura may be only a transformed deva. Thus though they are the same before creation, afterwards they are always at war.

In Vedic mythology, gods and demons could change their places fluidly. The bridge between the two could be crossed again and again. The antithesis between the devas and the asuras is almost unknown in the Vedas, but is perfected in the Brāhmaṇas. This antithesis divides these two people exactly like the demonisation of the devas divides the Avesta from the ṚgVeda.[371] The eternal fight between the gods and the demons seems to have as its cause hegemony "rājyahetoḥ", of the world.[372] The word asura is frequently used to denote a god, and the word deva could have been used to designate the demons and the others. "*Devajana*" denotes demons of any kind like serpents and demons.

Meaning of the word Asura

The word asura is thought to mean "living".[373] This must have been originally an epithet of certain powers of Nature, particularly the sky. Since devas also derive their name from similar origin, there does not seem much difference between them. Again the word is thought as originally to have meant only "possessor of occult power" in a neutral sense, belonging to both good and evil things. In the long run it must have taken on a bad connotation in India.[374]

The word asura was first used in the Vedic religion as one possessing the highest occult power. Asu is thought of as originally being a supernatural fluid, like the primitive "mana", and "ra" was the possessive termination.[375] This occult power could be used for good as well as bad purposes. The magic miracle possessed by Varuṇa was the orderly progression of the cosmos, which he binds with his ṛta. The occult power asu is equivalent to the Huron Indian's Orenda.

Asura is said to be derived from the root "as" to be. Thus asuras would be the existence of life itself. The Brāhmaṇas and the Purāṇas derive the word from asu - breath. Those who disliked their dwelling or were driven away from it, or those in whom the breath or living energy is strongly knit are *asuras*. It could also have been derived from 'as' to frighten away. The name is seen definitely to be Indo-Iranian in origin.[376] In the god *Ashura (Asura)* two gods are seen to coalesce. They are the Sumero-Babylonian god of fertility Osiris and Ra, the Egyptian Sun god.[377] *Amarakośa* calls a demon a pūrva-deva, one who was a god earlier.[378]

Tracing the Role of the Asura in the Vedas

The Vedic gods did not portray evil as such. Varuṇa was firm in his justice. Nirṛti represented the manes and therefore death and decay. But both dropped out of the pantheon. In the Purāṇic religion evil had to be explained. It could not be part of god. Therefore metaphysical explanations were sought for. The ṚgVeda states the conflict in a straightforward way. The Brāhmaṇas embroider it with ritual language. ṚV. records a continuous victory, whereas the Brāhmaṇas have a prolonged struggle and gain victory by guile. Indra and Viṣṇu were thought to be historic figures and they helped in the war against the asuras and used guile to attain victory. The pañcajanas mentioned in the ṚV. were the Asuras, Gandharvas, Rākṣasas Yakṣas, and Piśācas.[379] These were all seen as historical tribes whom the Aryans had to subdue or rout to gain comfortable access as they proceeded inwards. Real events could have been described in the ṚV., and mythicised in the Brāhmaṇas and further elaborated. There are innumerable mentions of the devāsura conflicts in the ṚV.[380] and Ait. Br.[381] mentions that the devas and asuras were children of Prajāpati. In the beginning, the demons were stronger and better than the gods who were evil like the younger brothers.[382] The gods took away the Soma and thus became more powerful than the demons.[383] Varuṇa, Soma and Agni belong to the asura group, but they leave and join the devas.[384] At first Varuṇa was the lord of the asuras, lost his position and later regained it.[385]

In the early books of the ṚV., that is, books II-VII, there is no hostility between the devas and the asuras. Only in the tenth book, which belongs to the period of the Brāhmaṇas, is the hostility well delineated. In the second book, the Aryans are on the eastern banks of the Sarasvatī, far from the asuras, who are in the Western regions. Therefore, there is no enmity between them.[386] In ṚV., III 55.1-22, the refrain is *"mahad devānāmasuratvamekaṁ"*, asura here meaning great and unequalled (is the might of the gods). In ṚV III 38.4, the asura does not only possess "asu", but is capable of transferring it to others. In the Vedas there is no unambiguous personification of evil. There is no major demon standing for evil. But there are a few terms used to show evil as an opposition to the gods, such as "hostility", "violence", "resistance". The terms which are used to show opposition to the above mentioned ones are *"dhāman"*, *"ṛta"*, and, *"indriya"*, *"tejas"*, and *"vaja"*.[387] Sometimes there is ambivalence in the figures of the Vedic myths. Pipru and Namuci have their benevolent side. Rudra has an integral part of him which is benign. The two parts together made the later figure of Śiva. Rudra and Śiva had nothing in common. Terms like *ari, manyu, māyā, yakṣa* have two sets of meanings and, in a particular context, their meaning would depend on whether they are used with *devas* or *asuras.* The Maruts and the Rudras have given rise to a host of demons who interfere with the human affairs. In the ṚV., there is a containment of the evil forces, whereas in the Ath. V. there are many invocatory verses addressed directly to the demoniac forces. In the Brāhmaṇas, the ancient colourful rivalry described in the ṚV. metamorphoses into monotonous accounts of the devāsura conflicts. The groups of demons are not wholly good or evil. The members of a group may stand out as individuals. They may be considered evil or good according to which group they are affiliated to, at any particular period.[388] But, this opinion that there are two different divine groups named devas or asuras, or, that the words deva and asura denoted the same being depending on whether he was good or evil, are found not tenable.[389] The word asura is used for gods like Agni, MitrāVaruṇau, Rudra, etc. Further both devas and asuras are used in the same verse, and if interchanged, they would indicate the same beings, i.e., the words had the same connotations. As for example:

"Tamu ṣṭuhi yaḥ sviṣuḥ sudhanvā
Yo viśvasya kṣayati bheṣajasya
Yakṣvā mahe saumanasāya Rudraṁ
Namobhir devam asuraṁ duvasya"

"Praise him who has good arrows and a good bow, who rules over all medicine. Sacrifice for great well-being to Rudra; favour the god, the asura with prostrations".[390] Though there are instances of various beings called deva and elsewhere asura, this is the first instance of a god being called both at the same time. It has been mooted[391] that the rivalry between Indra and the asuras must have been confused with the enmity of the Aryans and the Assyrians, the asuras being erroneously assimilated to the latter. But there is no evidence to prove that the Aryans and the Assyrians met anywhere.[392] The word asura seems to mean leader, thus there being an asura of gods, one of humans, of wise ones, and of the heavens. This last epithet is usually associated with Śiva. The ṚV. treats of gods, and therefore the asuras have to be taken as gods. Further, asura is always mentioned in the singular. This would refute the theory that the asuras were a group of people. The impression gained from the study of the word in its derivatives and compounds is that an asura is chosen and made the leader by the consent and support of those who followed him. He was not an asura by birth or by nature. This was true for the gods and it would follow that this was true for humans also. Thus an asura after being elected by his followers maintained his position by their support. His insight or planning ability (kratu) must have been above the ordinary. Other than the family books, which are the earliest of the ṚV., the word asura is used for humans, and has evil connotations. In the plural, as applied to humans, the word means demonaic qualities, and the description comes closer to the later meaning of the word as enemies of gods. In the ṚV., the feminine principle is always designated as asurā. This is seen as the people inheriting their Aryan ancestry through the father - right, and the mother - right through the non-Aryan or the asuras.[393] It is seen that the word asura gets a bad connotation only in the later books, where the meaning changes to "a demon" or "antigod". But this usage is closer to human dāsas and dasyus, rather than inhuman rākṣasas.

In the AV, Śaunaka recension,[394] in the singular, the word has a good connotation. In the plural; the word meant lord, but later it came to be used as enemies of gods. In many instances it is not clear whether the enemies of Indra are humans or mythical beings. The word dasyu or dāsa could be interchanged for the word asura, and there would be no change in the meaning, thus showing that they could be human enemies. In the ṚV X. 123 the Gandharva is eulogised as the solar god. In the ṚV X. 177, Asura is mentioned as the source of all creative energy. Connecting these two, the asuras are seen as solar the gods.[395] In the Brāhmaṇas, the shift in the meaning of the word asura has already taken place. It does not occur in the singular. In the plural it had come to mean demonic beings in opposition to the gods. Taking up the ṚV hymn X. 124, it is seen not as a war between an individual deva and an asura but between two groups.[396] Agni, Sōma and Varuṇa are benign Asura Lords. Indra seen in this verse was not attempting to bribe the asuras, but as offering rewards for services already rendered. This is a late hymn, judging by its grammar.[397] Innumerable scholars have given contradicting opinions. It is best not to put too much weight on the relationship between Varuna and Indra.

Thus, the earliest usage in the ṚV. of the word is as a lord who led vīras, and who had kratu, planning ability or insight. In the later books, though the singular had good connotation, the plural had come to mean human beings. Perhaps the word meant a leader of men, but since, in the ṚV., the subject was the gods and not men, it came to mean the enemies of gods. AV. also had plural usage of the word but it had a bad connotation. In the

Brāhmaṇas, Indra fighting asuras could mean human enemies. There was never much history in the ṚV, it is felt, and it is much less so where asuras are concerned. The human enemies of the Aryans became mytologised into supernatural enemies.

In the Later Literature

In the Matsya P. (24. 23-24) in the Purūravas-Ūrvaśī episode, Purūravas is mentioned as a winner over the demons and being a helpmate of Indra, in his battles against the demons. This could be traced to the ṚV,[398] where he is mentioned as a great hero.[399]

The rivalry between gods and demons is seen as one of phratry rivalry. Both had to join together in the ritual of *Amṛtamanthana*. Even in the Mbh., the later generations of kings were harassed by *asuras* and the kings were praised for finally defeating the *asuras*. This shows that the conflict between the devas and asuras did not end with the ṚV. but continued. In the Tait. Saṁ.,[400] it is mentioned that the devas were defeated, which in the Purāṇas, they do frequently in the beginning, and later, with the help of a god or a goddess, they manage to defeat their rivals. The Ait. Br.[401] describes how the devas were prevented from entering the svargaloka by the rākṣasas and asuras. In the Mbh., a few gods more freely amongst ṛṣis and asuras. They obviously have no uneasiness in moving amongst their counterparts. Śrī Lakṣmī left the asuras because they had become arrogant, and were filled with desire and anger.[402] In the Mārk. P.,[403] it is said that, when the demons eat the evil nature of men, the latter become virtuous. This gives an ethical justification for the demons. Further, it is believed that people doing evil karma are either born as demons or are born to evil mortals.[404] The gods and the demons are not seen as eternally opposed, because Patañjali does not mention this twosome in the examples he cites for enemies opposed eternally.[405] It is also said that the god Prajāpati created the demons first, and was not pleased, and this was the reason for the dull gold colour of the sacrificial fire. He was pleased with his creation of the devas and therefore the sacrificial fire was bright.[406] There is an artificial etymological explanation for deriving their nomenclature. They were Asuras, that is, they refused to drink the immortal drink, surā, which the devas did. This could also mean that the Aryans and the asuras were originally of the same clan. But the asuras came earlier from Persia, and the Aryans hated them amongst other things for this their cultural difference.

Asuras were so powerful and valorous in battle they could be defeated only by guile or trickery. They are seen as obstacles to men who are on the path of self-realisation. Those that are helpful to man towards this quest are the devas. The dividing line between the devas and asuras could be quite fluid and not at all rigid. Some asuras could move up and become devas and similarly some devas could slide down and become asuras. The asuras were some of the earlier gods of the Vedic religion. These antigods were not destroyed for their sins, but for their powers which may pose a threat to the gods. There were good Brahmin asuras like Bali and Prahlāda. A few of them after their defeat turned to Śiva as his devotees. When they were good and pious, Lakṣmī dwelt amongst them, and when they stopped performing sacrifices due to their pride and arrogance, Lakṣmi left them and joined the devas.[407] Some of the asuras who were great and whose strength and wisdom were untarnished became attached to Viṣṇu's incarnation myths, or such similar myths.

The Taitt. Br. mentions that Prajāpati created them from his breath. Śat. Br. says that they emerged from Prajāpati's digestive breath. The Taitt. Ār. mentions that the god created gods, men, manes, gandharvas and apsaras from water and the asuras, rākṣasas and piśācas were created from the drops which were spilled. They were very powerful in battle. They possessed magical powers by which they could change their forms. But this quality the gods also possessed.

The Brahmins of the Purāṇic age called themselves gods of the earth. They wrote most of the Purāṇas. Therefore, they warn their patrons to be bountiful towards them. Then they would raise their patrons to their own level. Those who do not listen to this admonition, or, are unable to comply because of their birth are cast aside or even thrown into the nether world. The Bhakti cult elevated the good demons and men to the heavens. The ambivalence of the Vedic gods must have deterred the mythologists of the Purāṇas, because, there are no wholly evil figures in those myths. There are good demons and also some are devotees of gods. In most of the Purāṇas, the pious ascetic, that is, the good man is seen as a serious threat to the devas and has to be distracted from his austerities. The pious demon, because he swerves from his svadharma of demoniac quality, has to be punished by being sent to the nether world in spite of being good.

Character of the Asuras, as seen from their Culture, Religion and History

Culture

The asuras knew pottery made by wheel, whereas the Aryans made it by hand. There fore, the aryan's suspicious prejudice against the more modern method could have resulted in the injunction against using wheel-made pottery for certain rituals like the purodāsa offerings. The herbs (or the knowledge of them) belonged to the asuras,[408] but appropriated by the devas later. The seasons[409] were refused by the Aryans a share in the sacrifice and therefore they joined the asuras. The asuras prospered after this. It might mean that the *asuras* had knowledge of the seasons for agricultural purposes. Yājñavalkya calls their type of marriage, where dowry is paid to the girl's relatives and to the girl, *Asuro draviṇādānāt*. Manu strictly forbids such a marriage.[410] According to some law books, asura form of marriage is allowed only amongst Śudras and Vaiśyas.[411] About their burial rites, Aryans buried their dead directly placing them on the earth, whereas the asuras buried them in a stone basin "camū", on a mound.[412] The burials were either in round graves,[413] or in graves jutting above the earth.[414] They have a barbarian speech.[415] It could be that these were a people of different language, religion and culture. But, since these passages are late, it could be that the asuras were made to look as outlandish and bizarre as possible. Many of the agricultural terms are not of Sanskrit origin, but borrowed from Mundari, etc.[416] The Aryans became agriculturists, and sinre their language did not contain terms relating to this, they could have borrowed them from the asuras who were very good at cultivation. Asuras could have been primitive iron smiths settled in Central India. They could have been wealthy as iron miners and smelters. Their land, power and wealth were taken away from them by the Aryans through guile. The hand of Viṣṇu, the solar hero is seen in this, in the myth of *Trivikrama*. The asuras performed different sacrifices or observed different customs in the sacrifices. This is the main point of the feud with the devas. When a custom was rejected because it was unsuitable it was called an āsura custom.[417]

Religion

The religion of the asuras could be older than that of the devas. The later could have altered it to suit their needs. The asuras had ukthya and the devas had agniṣṭoma. Both had twelve recitations, but the ukthya had three more.[418] Most of the asuras and allied groups were followers of the Śiva or Viṣṇu cult. They may have been strongly opposed to the establishment of the Vedic religion. The sage Kapila is said to have studied the ancient and almost forgotten wisdom of the asuras, and taught it to the Aryans. Dānavas are said to be more god-like than the other groups of asuras. Asuras, are said to be opposed to the caste system, Brahmin power, and the seers[419] Āsuri was a well-known teacher of the Vedas.[420] The asuras did not know the midday savana, but knew only the morning and evening savanas.[421] The mode of piling up the smaśānas is also different from the eastern asuras and the Aryans.

History

The Aryans, hearing of the richness of the Saptasindhu, came to India and after many defeats at the hands of the asuras, conquered them with wile, assisted by Viṣṇu. The asuras were settled in the Harappan region. They were flushed out by fire in the settlement. Those who helped the Aryans in their cause were deified. Those who resisted and were defeated stood for evil which had been overcome. The Aryans took over certain of the religious ideas from their enemies.

As represented in the ṚV., the asuras were slowly driven out or defeated by guile by the invaders. Their home was in the North. The events of this conflict were mythicised and the asuras branded as demons and evil beings. The attempts by the beseiged asuras trying to reach the North-West by the tributaries of the Indus were blocked by the Aryans. These movements are seen from the Buddhist, Jain, epic and Purāṇa evidence. They went up to Magadha in the east and Ceylon in the South. Their last strong hold in Ceylon was vanquished by Rāma.[422]

Varṇa was seen as the basis of differentiation between the Aryans and the Dāsas, and speech was a distinction between the Aryans and the asuras.

The devāsura conflict is seen in the Dāśarājña battle[423] as between the Aryans and the asuras. The asuras were lead by Viśvāmitra and lost. They went to the Madhya Desa, in the Brāhmaṇa period, and were finally driven upto Magadha. The Turvasa and Vṛchivants brought in by Indra, from across the seas in the above battle may mean from across the Indus. These people are surmised to be the Jhukar people.[424] The Kuru-Pāñcāla and the asura Pūrus[425] merged in the Kurukṣetra field. The AV. authorship depends either on the Bhṛgus or Angiras. Bhṛgu is of the asura camp. The asuras metamorphose into Brahmins in the AV. In the area of the Ganges-Jamuna doab, the AV. saw the gradual absorption of the Atharvan asura into the Aryan body-politic. Thus the asura Pūru-Bhṛgu clans get absorbed in the Pāñcāla group who again merged as the Kuru-Pañcālas. The epics popularised the Aryanisation of the asura clans and the Purāṇas elaborated and strengthened the idea. In the ṚV. the asuras lost the areas of the Indus river upto the Sarasvatī. In the Yajur, Sāma and Atharva Vedas they are driven neastwards. Some of them merged with the Aryans in the Ganges-Jamuna doab, with the rest going eastwards towards Magadha. The vanquished asuras in the South merged with the Dāsas.

Magadha is seen as the last settlement of the asuras who had crossed continents and every vicissitude of geography and culture and still managed to influence the conquerors with their own culture. From the Noṛth-Western part of India, the asuras were pushed into the Ganga-Jamuna valley. They are seen thus as being absorbed into the invading population or forced to settle in the forest areas, clearing them and creating fresh lands for cultivation.[426] The asuras must have been matrilocal people. The marriage between Pāṇḍu and Mādrī was considered an asuric type of marriage, where the bridegroom had to pay the bride and her people a certain amount of money. Asuras became an essential part of Vedic India.

In the myths, Andhakāsura came to power after Hiraṇyākṣa and Hiraṇykaśipu were killed. Andhaka and Mahiṣa may have been two tribal kings, who were defeated by the Aryans. The tribes could be Andhakas and Māhiṣmatis.[427] The Andhakas were a branch of the Yādava tribe living near Mathura, but moved later to Kathiawar. The Sātvatas regained their region near Mathura, after their enemy, Śatrughna, brother of Rāma died. The asura king Bhīma had two sons Andhaka and Vṛṣṇi. The Andhakas continued to rule over Mathura, while the Vṛṣṇis moved to Dwaraka. Ugrasena of the Andhaka family was the ruler of Mathura at the period of the Mahābhārata war. The ancestors of the Yādavas were the ṚgVedic Yadu clan, who were defeated in the Dāśarājña war and moved from the Sarasvatī region to the Yamuna near Mathura.[428]

One *asura* is called bull-asura in the ṚV,[429] Vṛṣṇa.[430] The bull could be the clan name which occurs so frequently in the early literature: Vṛṣṇi, Vṛṣabha, Ṛṣabha, etc. In this connection, the Harappan seals depicting the bull may be noted.

The asuras include amongst them dynasties of Magadha and Kalinga. In some Purāṇas the nandas are called Śūdra-prāyāstv adhārmikāḥ.[431] The epithets Śūdra-like and irreligious suit the Mauryas well because several of the kings had a predilection towards Buddhism. The DM. labels the Mauryas as asuras.[432] People beguiled by the Buddha are called Suradviṣ.[433]

The contrast between state and non-state is brought out from the contrast of the administrations of Lanka, and Ayodhyā/Kosala. Presuming that the former was under the asuras and the two latter were under the Aryans, the former had no trained army; there seemed a lot of gems and precious metals in the king's treasury, but there were no taxation or revenue.[434] Though the asuras' wealth is said to come from their knowledge of iron mining and smelting, there is no evidence to support the view that the Aryans with their knowledge of copper learnt iron smelting from the asuras settled in Bihar as iron smiths. The non-Aryan terms for agricultural implements would point to the fact that there was a settled agricultural community before the Aryan invasion. These could be the asuras. The Pūru community knew agricultural pastures well, on the banks of Sarasvatī; S'B[435] speaks of the asuras knowing the seasons well, for agricultural activities. These agriculturists subordinated to the pastoralists because either the lands may have been worth the risks of cultivating in a settled way, or, they may have come to a symbiotic relationship with the pastoralists. The latter could have afforded them protection in return for fodder for their cattle.

Influence

The asura influence is seen in their tracing their descent in the female line, the king succeeding in the matrilineal line, and in the brother/sister marriage and the niyoga form of marriage mentioned in the ṚV.[436] The Vedic Aryans learnt to respect women from the asuras, it is surmised.[437] But as seen earlier, the position of women was quite high amongst the Vedic Aryans in the early period, and it started deteriorating later. The matriarchal asuras had merged into the Aryan culture, diffusing their ideas widely into the latter's religion and society. They could even have had a mother-goddess worship which changed the Aryan religion to a very great extent. The asuras' superiority was marked in agriculture, pottery, marriage, and burial rituals. They were given the subtle compliment of wielding magical power. They are treated with ambiguity right through the ṚV, though they are said to have common origins and powers with the Aryans. The asura culture whether from the IV or not, has influenced the Aryan religion and culture to no mean extent.

Māyā: The Special Power of the Asuras

Like the meaning of the word asura, developed into negative connotations in the Brāhmaṇas, so did Māyā, their special power. In the ṚV the word Māyā is used to denote special ability, the ability to project oneself externally. Asuras had special prowess in this regard. It is not correct to say that the word got a bad connotation only after the people who possessed it became classified as demons, nor is it right that, Māyā, which meant special magic power, was at a period when a special class of people, the asuras, possessed it. In the Ath. V., the combination of asura and Māyā is not taken to be antagonistic to the welfare of men, in which the devas were actively interested.[438] Asuramāyā meant "the power to achieve wonderful deeds inherent to lordship."[439] But as the asuras were believed to be associated more and more with the powers of darkness, the above word got new connotation in the Brāhmaṇas. Māyā is also the tremendous power of Varuṇa, which is the cause of the regularity of the universe.[440] Earlier Māyā meant wisdom, extraordinary and supernatural power. But, later, it came to mean illusion, unreality, deception, fraud, sorcery, witchcraft, magic. Varuṇa loses his asura māyā, when Prajāpati rose to power in the pantheon. This power is shared by the gods and demons, in two different forms. The devas practised white magic, beneficial to the gods and men. The asuras practised witchcraft or blackmagic. Thus, creative power became illusory power.

There is an interpretation that, because Māyā was associated with evil beings, the asuras became evil after they obtained this power.[441] If the asuras were the indigenous people the attribution of the power of Māyā with bad connotation could be the conquerors' distrust and prejudice of the enemies' culture and religion. Thus Māyā could become witchcraft.

When viewed as a goddess of the asuras, she could most probably be a fertility goddess. She had wombs on all her limbs. She was also called Dīrghajihvī.[442] She is said to lick away Soma from the sacrifices. Indra was unable to exterminate her, and finally he used Ṣumitra, a handsome young man and killed her by guile. Her role in the Vedic period and the DM has been mentioned earlier. She was Maiya, the goddess of rain and fertility of the Gangetic valley. In Prākṛt, her names were mā, māiyā, and māyī.[443] Thus Māiya of the third century B.C. could well be Māyā the mother-goddess.

Opposition of Good versus Evil

The recurring theme in the myths is that the devas and asuras are eternally locked in battle. The devas usually win and the asuras are sent down to the nether world or to the heavens. If the former, then, this is not permanent. They appear again and the battle restarts. The gods, demons and men are said to be fighting for power which is limited. Therefore, the gods feel threatened by ascetic men, who would not give them sacrifices, and by good demons who refuse to treat the gods as their superiors. Further, the demons themselves are a source of threat to men. Since men would turn to the gods for protection, the gods are assured of sacrifices. Thus it is in the gods'own interests to leave the demons without annihilating them. It is seen that the gods are fully capable of killing the demons but choose not to do so.[444] The divine powers are divided into beneficent and maleficent according to their function, that is, whether they are helpful to men or harmful. If the former, they are gods and, if the latter, they are demons. At first, there was no differentiation between the gods and the demons. Later, if the demons were not wicked, they ceased to follow their svadharma. They became morally neutral enemies and later they became fully evil. Mahiṣa is a composite figure of good and evil, opposites or polarities. He is Śiva, consort of the Goddess in folk-tales, and enemy of the gods and the Goddess in

Purāṇic myths. If he were not partly good, he would not have been given mokṣa by Durgā, after killing him. The Goddess became transcendental, above polarities, annihilating both good and evil, transmuting the evil into good and releasing Mahiṣa into the Beyond. Mahiṣa is worshipped at the side of the Goddess according to *Vaikṛti Rahasya.*[445] *"Pūjayenmahiṣaṁ yena prāptaṁ sāyujyamīśayā/"*

Two Polarities: Cosmic and Human

There are two polarities : cosmic and human. 'Cosmic' can be many types like the seasons, agricultural cycles, light and darkness, etc. The human polarity is mainly male and female, sacred and profane, etc. In the early stages of religion these polarities were considered necessary parts of the whole. It cannot be pinpointed with surety when the negative elements were thought of as evil. The idea of evil arises slowly and with some difficulty in the development of religious thought.[446] Evil spirits were incipient personification of evil. When the evil got to be the focus of attention, these developed into demons. This was true also for the gods. They were the personification of power, helpful to humans. And, sometimes, they were deified for their functional superiority, as for example, Isis of Egypt who, originally, was the literal deified throne.[447] Opposites are necessary for the cosmos. It impels activity and creativity.[448] The devil in the Catholic religion is autonomous, free and eternal. His metaphysical qualities are so much in common with those of God, that he is eternally in opposition to God.[449]

In the primitive mind, there is not much distinction between good and bad. But, by and by, he needs to go into the cause of such a difference. He associates brightness with light, etc., as being behind godness, and darkness, gloom, etc., as causing evil. Good and evil have always been the contending forces. This has given rise to an elaborate system of demonology in all ancient religions, as for example in Babylonia, and Assyria. This necessitated pacificatory and expiatory rites of great complexity.[450] The examples illustrating the above opposition are innumerable. In Egypt,[451] it is Osiris versus Set. In Babylonia, Merodach, the Sun, fights against Tiaiwath, who is Chaos. In Greece, it is Zeus opposed by Typhon, the deity of gloom. In the Nordic countries, it is Loki the vindictive god opposing Odin, the Sun-spirit. This idea is also prevalent amongst the Algonquin Indians of North America, ancient Peruvians, Tupi Guarani of Brazil, Australian aborigines, and many more. In the primitive mind, evil cannot succeed, but good is not all-powerful; it is slightly more powerful than evil by virtue of its possessing a magic trick or two.

Seth, the Egyptian god, was perfectly at peace with his brother Osiris and nephew Horus. When a feud developed between them, Seth became a demon, the personification of evil. In a Sumerian myth, the goddess Inanna slayed the dragon Kur, who had grown invincible, with her copper sword. Afterwards, she stationed herself on the mountain Elish. This myth is placed around the third millenium B.C. There are Anatolian, Hittite, Hurrian, and Babylonian versions of the above myth, mainly portraying gods personifying beneficent powers and demons personifying evil powers, opposed to each other, and the demons being defeated in the end. This myth is said to have its cradle in the Western Mediterranian, from whence it had spread both to the east and to the west.[452]

The ancient mythical combat between good and evil is the creation of the cosmos from chaos. The opposing pairs were usually good versus evil, light against darkness, life against death. Man while enacting these myths sided with the beneficent powers. He hoped not only to fight the powers of evil around him, but tried to overcome his perennial struggle against his evil nature, pitting against the gods. There were also the resurrection of the vegetation after a blight or after winter. All these myths were enacted at particular times, like New Year or spring and autumnal harvest festivals. The malice of the dragon or demon resulted in a blight over the land. When the demon was vanquished, peace and plenty were restored on earth.

The periodic ritual enactment of the myth was necessitated by the belief that the universe might slip back into chaos from a nebulous order. There was hope that, from a restoration of order at the end of time, periodical renewal need not be necessary. The combat was said to have taken place in ancient times. By ritually recalling or recounting or enacting it, the potency is transferred to the present time and it is hoped the transcendental powers would restore order to the earth, and bring back peace or fertility as the context warranted. Differences in myths took place to suit the particular climate and environment of a place. But the basic theme of opposition between good and evil never changed.

All opposing dualities are seen only as outward oppositions. It may be deduced that good and evil exist or come to play only under the sun, in existence, but merge in the Supreme Being without any opposing identity.[453] As seen so far, these opposing dualities are not unique to the Hindu religious ethos alone, including its communication in ritualistic format, but quite common in extra-Indian traditions. But, what is unique to each country is its own traditions which colour the concepts transmitted through its religious myths.

Later Types of Asuras

In later Vedic times, there were two classes of demons, asuras, who were opposed to the devas, and rākṣasas who were of a lower order. They were flesh-eating enemies of humans. But gods, manes, and humans join hands in fighting asuras, rākṣasas, and piśācas. Though the rākṣasas were distinct earlier, in the later literature, asuras were connected with them. The words Dāsa, and Dasyu are dropped in the later hymns of the Vedas, when asura starts being used in the bad connotation. It is felt that the human enemies of the Aryans became mythologised into these types of demons. Thus rākṣasa was always used in the pejorative, and could be black magicians, and sorcerers. Similarly Dāsa and Dasyu could have been related to the rākṣasas. They may be human, historical beings.[454] There are plenty of evidence that the asuras were historical people, as seen earlier. Similarly Piśāci-Prākṛt is a language used by Guṇāditya in his Bṛhat Kathā. The political and cultural milieu of the rākṣasas are well delineated in the Rāmāyaṇa. . Rākṣasas were stated to be the sons of Pulastya, the fourth son of Brahmā; they were thus the brothers of yakṣas. The function of these could be inferred as to either cause injury or to protect. The first meaning could be the older, and when they took over to protecting forts, the second meaning could have been ascribed.[455] It is averred that the asuras and rākṣasas were from the figment of Aryan imagination, but that the Dravidians elaborated the idea, and considerably enlarged it from the folktales.[456] The Nāgas who fought on the side of the asuras, are mentioned as kings. Piśācas were tribes, and asuras were the euhemerised native races. The asuras were sometimes picturised to be as generous as the gods. Devas, manuṣyas and Pitaras were opposed to asuras, rākṣasas and piśācas, respectively. The difference between the Brahminic and other demons is the former are supernatural beings while the others are spirits of dead people, and the latter could possess people.[457] Manu [458] says, the gods, the Dānavas, the Gandharvas and the Rākṣasas give enjoyment only if they are tormented by punishment.

Economic situations or political events definitely have a hand in shaping mythological figures, be they gods or demons. But, because of the distance in time, we are not able to gauge properly the reason behind the rise of a particular god or demon. The powers of good and evil deified at first are only relatively superior to men. But they lead their glamourous existence due to imbibing some magical potion or food. The primitive believes in supernatural powers, be they gods or demons, when he finds he is not able to control the powers of nature.[459]

Lastly, *Śakti*, is said to incarnate herself on this earth to vanquish demons who are no other than ill-natured and powerful politicians.[460]

Comparison with Ahura

Ahura in the *Yasts* is a ruling prince leading a group of fighting men. *Ahura* is said to possess *xratu* which is the same as *kratu* possessed by an asura. In the *Avesta, ahura* is very much like the *asura* of the *ṚV*. He is a powerful and respected lord and leader. The connection with *xšaorya* is explicit in the *Avesta,* whereas it can only be deduced from *ṚV* 7. 21.7. where kṣatram is associated with āsuryam. But the Ahura is mentioned as a hereditary power, whereas, Asura is selected by a group.[461]

Mahiṣa: The Buffalo Demon

The use of the buffalo in depicting certain ideas in religion has been popular since Palaeolithic times. In the Dordogne caves, a man is portrayed as being killed by a bison, which in turn is killed by a rhinoceros. Both these animals were sacred in the IV religion. The connection of rituals of buffaloes with fertility cults had been popular in the Palaeolithic period.[462] In India, as in Africa, the wild buffalo was feared as a dangerous animal. In the IV, there are many seals and amulets, portraying this animal as a cult object. Fear could have been the cause for its deification and this could be the cause for its connection with Yama, the god of death, it is thought.[463] The animal seals in question could be the representation of some attribute of the divinity, the divinity itself, or, they were worshipped just as buffaloes.[464] Second only to the unicorn, the buffalo appears next in frequency on the *IV* seals. The germ of the story of the *Mahiṣa* episode may be connected, though in an indirect way, to a few seals from the IV. In the first one, a woman, surmised to be the tree-spirit is transformed partially into a buffalo. In the next one, she is seen retaining her horns but is transformed further into a tiger.[465] The buffalo being speared is seen in another seal no. 279.[466]

In the ṚV. X. 123.4., the Gandharvas and the buffalo are connected in the same way as the solar god asura and the bull.[467] ṚV. I. 141.3 states about making Agni by a twirling motion. Mātariśvan does so on the ground from the buffalo's image.[468]

In the HV,[469] Pradyumna advised by Indra, via Nārada praises Devī Kātyāyanī to overcome Śambara. In line 371, he says "Triśūlinīm namasyāmi Mahiṣāsuraghātinīm". In the Mbh.,[470] Skanda severed Mahiṣa's head, after the latter demoralised the deva army. Crooke[471] states that this Mahiṣa is the Mahiṣoba of Berar, and like Bhainsāsura occupies waterways and has to be propitiated. This severed head of Mahiṣa is said to have barred the entry to the Northern Kuru country. This was opened by the god, to enable the devas to visit the plains from Kailāsa. According to Manu[472] sons born of a Kṣatriya father and a Vaiśya or Śūdra mother were called Mahiṣya, Ugra. An inscription of Kulottunga's time A.D. 1118 at Uyyakkondan Tirumalai, lays down the same sentiment, on the strength of various earlier Smṛti writers.[473] Buffaloes were domesticated during this period, since their wild state is not mentioned.

In the AV,[474] Varuṇa is identified with Yama. In the Maitrāyaṇī Saṁ.[475] it is stated that buffaloes should be sacrificed to Varuṇa. It should be noted that, in the later Vedic literature, the buffalo became Yama's mount. Kāṭhaka Gṛhya Sūtra,[476] and Mānava Gṛhya Sūtra[477] mention Mahiṣikā along with other goddesses like Hrī, Śrī, etc.

In the Purāṇas

Devī incarnates herself for the express purpose of annihilating Mahiṣa, in the DM. Mahiṣa hurls insults at Devī. Mild eroticism can be read into his death by decapitation at the hands of Devī. A parallel is seen between the insulting language of Mahiṣa and Nindā stuti, a way of worship in the Bhakti cult. These insults really cover praise.

In the Mārk. Purāṇa,[478] saint Supārśva was disturbed by the heat of the austerities of Diti. He cursed her that her son would be a buffalo. Brahmā, towards whom Diti was praying mitigated the curse, that only his head would be that of a buffalo. Thus was born Mahiṣāsura.

In the *Varāha Purāṇa,*[479] Māhiṣmatī, in the guise of a female buffalo, disturbed the sage Ambara. He cursed her that she will retain that form. Relenting after her entreaties, he mitigated the curse and said she will regain her human form after giving birth to a buffalo-son. In a round-about way, Sindhudvīpa is the father of Mahiṣa and also of Māhiṣmatī.

In the Vāmaṇa P.,[480] Mahiṣa is the son of Rambha, and a she-buffalo, Śyāmā in the entourage of the Yakṣa Mālavaṭa. He is described as "śubhraṁ Mahiṣaṁ kāmarūpiṇam". The Devī Bhāgavata. Purāṇa,[481] is similar to this. In the Bhāg. P.,[482] Mahiṣa fought in the ranks of the asuras against the devas. He confronted Marīchi, (and other sons of Brahmā), after the nectar was distributed to the devas alone, by guile. Goddess Bhadrakāli fought Śumbha-Niśumbha in the same war.[483] In this same Purāṇa, the birth of Mahiṣa is treated.[484] Anuhrāda, the second son of Hiraṇyakaśipu and Kayādhu, by his wife Sūrmyā, had two sons, Bāṣkala, and Mahiṣa.

In Literature

In Bhāsa's Bālacarita,[485] Kātyāyanī foretells how she will kill Śumbha, Niśumbha, and Mahiṣa. In Bāṇa's Kādambarī, Candrapīḍa travelling through a forest, on his way to Ujjain, sees the sun setting from near a Caṇḍī temple where buffaloes had been offered as bali. The sun looked as though he was coming down to save his son Yama in the guise of a buffalo from being cut up.

"suta mahiṣa rakṣaṇāvatīrṇadinakarāvatarita śaśineva virājita

śikharam..."[486]

In the Caṇḍīśatakam, Mahiṣa is juxtaposed with Śiva. Or, he is described as making erotic gestures towards the Goddess, as mentioned earlier.[487] His epithets always point to his enemity towards the devas, and connections with the daityas, dānavas or asuras. He is also called Mahiṣavapuḥ, or, disguised in the body of a buffalo. For the Tantric equating of Śiva to Mahiṣa, DM[488] has been mentioned earlier.

Horns

There are various interpretations about the significance of the horns. They are the masculine aspect and symbolise the hot element of passion.[489] They are phallic symbols. It also symbolises the sun's rays in both its creative and destructive aspects. It also stood for strength and power.[490] It symbolised the raging fury of bulls.[491] The horns symbolised divinity and this idea since Neolithic times has had an uninterrupted history.[492] In the IV religion, they are thought to have magico-religious significance. The victims of sacrifice were also depicted as having horns as these were signs of consecration.[493] The horns are very popular amongst the tribals, in their religion. The Gonds of Mandla erect theriomorphic horned menhir figures exactly like the ones worn by the seated god of IV. The Maria of Bastar wear bison horns. The Gonds of Bastar have wood-carvings of dancers with buffalo horns. Horns were depicted by themselves as portraying an animal or as a magic symbol. All the West Asian countries used the horn as a symbol of magic power, and "breaking the horn" meant destroying power. But, in these areas, the bull was more popular than the buffalo[494] in the third millenium B.C.

Sacrifice of Buffaloes

Ehrenfels[495] has studied exhaustively[496] over eighty tribes and found a connection between matriarchy and buffalo sacrifice. Such a sacrifice and an offering of blood would belong to primitive agricultural tribes like the *Parayan* and *Pulayan* in India. The beast to be sacrificed is not divinised, or, demonised, but for the qualities it stands for. In common rituals, the god, the sacrificer, and the beast to be sacrificed are all confused to be the same. Animals were sacrificed to particular deities either because of a magical identity of nature, between the god and the animal, or, that the beast was sacred to a hostile tribe or clan.[497] The most numerous examples of the buffalo with the rituals of death are in the *Adichanallur* burials.[498] It is a strange fact that there are no oxen found here. These burials could belong to the period before the ox was introduced, and after the successful domestication of the buffalo. Dravidians in pre-Vedic time must have used the buffalo to plough the fields, and associated the animal with agricultural fertility.[499]

In the Mbh,[500] Devī is called "Mahiṣāsṛkpriye", fond of the blood of Mahiṣa. Paśubali is condoned or even advised as pleasing to the Goddess, if offered on the navami tithi, especially during the Navarātra festival.[501] But, both Devī Bhāg P.[502] and Kālikā P.,[503] specify that Brahmins should not indulge in this. They consider this not an act of cruelty to the animals, but they are believed to attain heaven. Bali is offered only to the ugra form of the Goddess, and not to the saumya form. Though many animals are mentioned as fit to be sacrificed to the Goddess, buffaloes are most commonly mentioned. In Tantric rituals, buffaloes are advised as suitable offerings, for worship done in the cremation ground,[504] and spirituous liquor is advocated as a compulsory accompaniment for blood offerings. Flesh offerings are hesitantly advised in the Purāṇas, but condoned in the Tantras. The Purāṇas call this Tāmasic worship. The goddess cult might have overcome a rival group, and assimilated the animal sacrifice. Or, the goddess may have been worshipped by tribal people, who had this custom.

There are diverse myths about Mahiṣa. The evil in Mahiṣa is of different kinds, and many myths are thought necessary to represent these.[505] The animals considered as sacred usually have some characteristics more powerful than normal, like strength, speed, courage or virility. This may be seen as their Mana.[506]

References from Folk Traditions

In the North, the buffalo was thought of as a dark demon of the waters. As Bainśāsura, he was thought of as the personified god of corn, and, during the harvest season, was propitiated. He was essentially a malignant demon. If he could be taken in a group, along with the bull, ox and the wild bison, his cult was very popular in the Sind, Punjab and Baluchistan, during the Chalcolithic period.[507]

In the South : Andhra

A buffalo which had been dedicated to the Goddess by the Mādigas in the Bellary district is killed and taken round the temple of the goddess Ūrammā, literally goddess of that place. His head is covered with omentum. The fat from the stomach is put in a lamp to burn on top of his head. The right foreleg is severed and kept cross-wise in his mouth. In the Cuddappah district, a similar custom of sacrifice took place and was performed by the Mādigas and Mālas. The goddesses here are Peddammā and Chinnammā.[508]

The buffalo sacrifice is performed in a similar fashion all over South India, in Tamil Nadu, Andhra Pradesh, Karnataka and South Maharashtra.

In brief, a potter makes a clay image of the goddess, and installs it, on rice poured on the floor. Ram, sheep and buffalo are killed and blood allowed to pour over the rice. The buffalo's head is severed and placed in front of the goddess. Fat from the animal's entrails is smeared over its forehead and face. Some boiled rice is put on the forehead, earthenware lamp installed on it and kept lit right through the festival. The buffalo is called Devara-Potu, devoted to the goddess. The people do obeisance to the beast before killing it. If there is an epidemic, a buffalo is dedicated to the Ūrammā. When the epidemic subsides, a newly prepared image of the goddess is installed and the special pūjā done usually on a Tuesday, (favourite day for the Goddess Durgā), and the buffalo called Ganda-Kona that is husband-buffalo is sacrificed. Ganda-Kona is, according to tradition, the outcaste husband of the goddess, who pretended to be a Brahmin, and married the Brahmin girl now worshipped as Ūrammā. A new buffalo is always dedicated to the goddess, immediately after the festival, so that the goddess is not left a window. The ritual is an exact replica of the one described earlier.

In Karnataka, the legend is that a sweeper of the Holaya caste married a Brahmin girl Dayamava, daughter of Mataṅgi, and had children by her. Discovering his true identity, the girl killed all her children, and chasing her husband who ran and hid inside a buffalo, killed him also. In the Dayamava festival a holy buffalo pattadakona is sacrificed. This is supposed to be Dayamava's Mahar husband. The severed head of the buffalo is taken to Mataṅgi's hut. A fresh buffalo is always kept dedicated to the

Goddess.[509]

In the city of Mysore there are seven Maris who are sisters, who are worshipped. A Caṇḍāla put on a Brahmin's guise and returned after learning all the Śāstras from Benaras. He married a Brahmin girl and had children. Later, the girl discovered his low-caste and cursed him and herself, that she would be born a Māri and worshipped only by low-caste people, and he would be the buffalo fit to be sacrificed to her. Their children would be born as chicken and sheep. This is said to be the reason that in Māri festivals, chicken, sheep, and a buffalo are sacrificed. The buffalo's foreleg is always put crosswise in his mouth.

In Tamil Nadu, the village goddesses were named Māriamman and Yellammā. Though there is a distinction that to the former was sacrificed goats, to the latter only buffaloes were sacrificed. But generally, though these goddesses are thought to show preference for male animals or birds, the buffalo was the preferred animal. In Tiruchy district the goddess is called "Ujinihonkālī", that is the Kālī of Ujjain.[510]

In Maharashtra, though *Saṣṭhi* (or *Sathi* or *Satavi*) has been identified with Durgā, in popular belief, she is unmarried. Thought a mother, the goddess tolerates no spouse. Mhasobā is the demon Mahiṣa killed by Durgā. But he is worshipped as a god, and sometimes near her temple. In Pune, a living Mhasobā cult thrives at the foot of the Parvati hill temple. The many indigenous goddesses had no spouse. Jogubai's husband is Mhaṭobā in Kothrud and Vakad. Mhaṭobā is really Mhasobā, that is Mahiṣāsura. Jogubāi is Yogeśvarī, that is Durgā. This is not an isolated case. Mhasobā became Maskobā and is married to Jogubāi at Vir. The Vir god belongs to the pastorals of the area. Jogubāi's shrine shows a stone-relief of Durgā as Mahiṣāsuramardinī. The various gods Maskobā, Bhairav, Khaṇḍobā, Vetāl, Mhāṭobā are all equated to Śiva. The anomaly of the goddess killing Mhasobā in icons is not given much thought by the villagers. The goddesses called "ai" or mother are all primitive autochthonous goddesses. The gods all belong to a later period of highland pastoral origins.[511]

Similar to the buffalo sacrifice was the rite called Taurobolum. This was a ceremony performed in Rome by a priest on the Vatican Hill in the sanctuary of the Magna Mater. He ceremoniously speared a bull and splashed himself with its blood. Earlier, this symbolised ritual rejuvenation enacted on behalf of the king. Later on, this became a baptism of all people irrespective of their status.[512] The buffalo sacrifice could also have a similar rejuvenation concept behind it. Though many metaphysical explanations have been brought forth to justify the sacrifice, that the buffalo represents evil, darkness, etc., emotional catharsis is reached only when the devotees smear themselves with the animal's blood, and join in the communal participation of the worship. Further, a totemic connection is seen, in the sacrifice when the whole community share the meat.[513]

Symbolism

The demon is not a symbol of a specific person. He represents the human concept of such a person. Though he is born out of an individual ego's imagination, he is a superhuman figure. Mythic images are thus not important for what they are, as for what their form represents. Mahiṣa would thus symbolise unbridled human passion in an animal form, blind power with his instincts overwhelming his reason and will.

The animal demon thus is highly representative of our negative instincts. Man is the only being who can control his instincts by his will. But, this may injure his inner personality. It becomes a dangerous situation when his lower, negative emotions may get out of hand. Just as uninhibited emotions were dangerous for the primitive, suppressed emotions are dangerous for the civilized man.[514] Just as it was necessary for the primitive to control his instincts and subserviate them to his will, so is it necessary for the civilized being to heal the animal in himself, come to terms with it and control it. This need is universal. The popularity of animal themes in religious art and mythology, and its wide diffusion all over the world, would be the outcome of man's effort at trying to subjugate his baser instincts. Needless to say there are good symbols of animals, like the Egyptian Hathor, Viṣṇu's Boar avatār, as well as bad representations like Mahiṣa and his allies.

Conclusion

Thus, it is seen from the above study that the asuras and devas were consubstantial in the beginning. The bad connotation to the word came in the later literature. They were historical people with a distinct culture and religion, which played a substantial part in shaping the Aryan religion. Lastly, asura and Dāsa or Dasyu came to have a similar meaning, referring to human enemies. Mahiṣa was a demon with deep roots in the folk culture of India. In many areas, he is confused with Śiva (which Bāṇa deliberately attempts) and the relationship between the Goddess and Mahiṣa, inimical though it be, seems to have sexual overtones, (though this is non-existent in the DM) ending with the beheading. Metaphysical and euphemistic explanations have been attempted later by the Brahmins to come to terms with this myth. The folk element is prominent in buffalo sacrifice during the Goddess worship and the participation in the rituals has a cathartic effect on the devotees. The image of Mahiṣa helps us overcome our baser instincts through our will power, with the Mother Goddess symbolising the victory over our "nature"

The Vāhana of the Goddess : Lion/Tiger

The association of animals with deities is of great antiquity in the religions of the world. It could either have come into later Hinduism from the IV culture or from the Vedas themselves. It is generally accepted that the animals would have been worshipped for themselves. Many hundreds of years later, symbolism could have been attributed to them. Thus the original reason for their worship is now obscure. An animal could present certain traits which would express more strongly the might of the divinity.[515]

In the IVC, there are a large number of seals with animals depicted on them. It cannot be deduced whether these were worshipped for themselves, or, as the representation of the essence, or attributes of a deity. It may be incorrect to state that the people of that period associated the buffalo with Yama, god of death. Similarly the tiger is associated with a cult figure who could be proto-Durgā. It cannot be gainsaid that the animals represented some aspect of a deity. Neither can it be ruled out that these were the "doubles" of the deities. Thus Skanda-Kārtikeya with his peacock and Durgā with her lion mount may have some pre-Aryan origins. In Indian myths, the tiger is ridden only by a woman. The tiger is a symbol of great power. It may have personified the magical power of the goddess on the seals. When the goddess was Brahminised, it is thought, she abandoned the tiger and took the lion.[516] Tracing this further back, the Egyptians and the

Sumerians had only lions depicted on their seals and in the myths. Since there are only tigers on the Indus seals, and, no depiction of lions, it is felt that the change could have occurred as the idea travelled eastwards into India, to suit the ethos.[517] Both animals are seen to represent an aspect of the Goddess. The tiger represents her as imbued with magic and mystery; the lion stands for her protective and benign aspect. It should be noted that the tiger is never portrayed in the IV seals as aggressive. He seems always benign and protective. The tiger is symbolic of the virile heroic male. This composite tiger and human figure on the IV seal could also be the origin for the Huligamma (tiger-mother) goddess of the present-day South India.[518] The association of the animal as a vāhana to the Goddess could be traced to this syncretized figures on the IV seal. This connection of the Goddess, as the tree-spirit with animals is very popular in the Hindu and Buddhist iconography of the 2nd to 1st centuries B.C. These are the Yakṣis, as tree-spirits, standing on animals.[519]

The terrible nature of the goddess could take two forms in representations. Either she could be represented as a wild beast like lion or tiger, or, she could be shown as being accompanied by them. This is supported in the folk traditions of North India,[520] where the mother-goddess in her cruel aspect takes the shape of a tiger, as for example the Gonds of Berar worship her as Vāghai Devī. Amongst the Bhils, though it is a male god, Vāghaika Kuṁwar (Tiger Prince). At first, the goddess is represented as the beast itself. Later on, she ceases to "be" the beast, and rides on it. Still later, she takes a human form and becomes the protective Mother of Beasts. Her domination of the animal world is our subconscious projection, and her role is to rule over our "nature", as against Śākambharī, the "culture" goddess. As a Goddess of Wild Beasts, she is close to the untrammelled nature of man, or, to put it bluntly the beast in him.[521]

In Taitt. Saṁ.,[522] there is a mention of a relationship between an animal and god. This was such a close relationship that they were considered "yolk-fellows" or "companions". In Taitt. Br.[523] also, there is seen such a connection, that an animal which had a close affinity with one particular deity, later on became his vāhana. Further, such animals as those with very close association with particular deities, both in the Vedic and later religion, were considered as the theriomorphic representation of an aspect of that particular god's essence or nature. This is seen as the Haṁsa associated with vāc and purity which are symbolised in *Sarasvatī*, the power of lion/tiger associated with Durgā, (cf Pl.18,) and the owl or such other portents of evil with Nirṛti. The particular way in which the deity is portrayed in association with the animal, as a vāhana is important to the role of the deity in a particular context. (cf. Phs. 9-13 & 14). If there is a change in the attributes of the vāhana of a deity, then there has been a change in the character, function, and qualities of the god. In this context, (cf. phs 9-13 814) it should be noted that the Vedic gods sported chariots, and only the Purāṇic deities had vāhanas.

Durgā in the role of Agni-Durgā rides a lion and has a terrifying look; as Ambikā she is seated on the animal in a pose of granting boons; as Vindhyavāsinī the lion should be portrayed as standing near-by; as Bhadrakālī, she rides a chariot drawn by four lions; and, when killing Mahiṣa the lion assists her.[524] The Vedic gods are seen as the prototypes of this concept of association of a deity with an animal or a chariot. Hindu gods are particularly anthropomorphic and play a similar role to the king in cosmic and terrestrial planes. Their anthropomorphous character is more pronounced in the Vedas than in later Hinduism. Thus the concept of vāhanas of deities could be traced to the Vedic religion as seen in the close association between a deity and an animal. The animal could either be a draught animal or the theriomorphic representation of the god's personality or his inner essence. Though these concepts are seen to spring from the Vedas, the latter had not yet crystallised the idea of vāhanas.

This was well represented in art and iconography in Hinduism, along with the division of the deities into three classes: Sāttvika-in meditation pose; Rājasika—the deities well ornamented and attired, holding weapons, with varada mudrā, sitting on a vāhana; and Tāmasika—where a deity is armed with weapons, sitting on a vāhana, and fighting the enemies of gods. Thus, the vehicle is not only the representation of the god's power but denotes the god's sphere of influence and his realm. The animal could be depicted not only as a mount, but as being close to the standing or seated form of the god, or depicted on the base of the throne of the seated figure. These representations are used as a means during meditation. The vāhanas mediate between the devotee and the deity, helping him to cross over his baser nature and pull himself across to the deity's level[525] Lion is seen as the power of the sun. Tradition in Orissa associates the lion with strength, signifying *dharma* and prowess; the tiger is the symbol of mokṣa. The lion or the tiger is seen as the fury of Devī, externalised.[526] Devī herself was the externalisation of the wrath of the gods.[527] Curses are also personified as demons or other monsters. The vāhana of Devī is seen to have its origins in the mediterranian countries. Though the attitudes, mudrās and weapons may be shared by many deities, in iconography, vāhanas are never shared.[528] Thus vāhanas are of a great help in identifying the deities. The Vāhana depictions could be a meeting point of Sanskritic and folk art traditions, and as such may symbolise truths at both these levels.

There are three stages in the post-Vedic concept of the association of an animal with a deity, as vāhana. Firstly, the animal may represent an important aspect of the god. Second, in iconography, the concept has a set format. Thirdly, the deity rides on the vāhana.

In the Purāṇas, the goddesses Vindhyavāsinī, Kauśikī, Gopajā, Bhadrakālī, Dikkaravāsinī and Mātaṅgī all have the lion as their vāhana. Śāntā Devī alone has the tiger as her vāhana.[529] The icons of the Goddess of the Kushana-Gupta period have been identified with the help of the lion mount. There are coins of this period showing the Goddess Durgā-Ambikā riding a lion. Even if these are identified as Lakṣmī Siṁhavāhinī, Lakṣmī's association with lion could only be due to the influence of the goddess Durgā. In the early centuries of the Christian era, there was mutual borrowing between the two cults of the deities.[530]

The lion associated with the Goddess in terracotta plaques has been assigned to the Kushana period of mid 1st century B.C. to mid 1st century A.D. Jyeṣṭhā is depicted as riding in a chariot drawn by lions, and followed by tigers. The goddess' association with lions and tigers show her origins as the goddess of the wild beasts, and forest regions. She could have been popular originally with forest-dwellers, and could have provided protection against wild beasts. Unlike the male gods in myths, the goddess shows no antagonism towards beasts.

On the seals and intaglios of the Neolithic Cnossus, Potnia Theron, the Mistress of Wild Beasts is portrayed with a lion preceding her. This idea survived in Greek mythology and religion. These goddesses are always associated with mountains and high places.[531] This comes up later in the 2nd millenium B.C. in Anatolia, in the Hittite and Indo-European culture. This pantheon is headed by Teshub, the storm god with a sacred bull, and his wife Hebat, with a panther. In around 5700 B.C.., the goddess is shown in association with leopard as her sacred animal.[532]

Thus, we see that the concept of vāhanas has a connection with the Indus Valley Culture, as well as with the Vedic religion. It has its origins in the mediterranian cult of the goddess from the fifth millenia B.C. The idea of an animal associated with a deity is not unique to the Hindu religion, but is a stage in our evolution of religious ideas.

Iconographic and Numismatic References

Starting from the Kulli and Zhob culture, in the Aurignacian period, there were two types of goddesses portrayed. They were portrayed either as earthy goddesses with exaggerated reproductive. organs, or, they looked etherial with these same organs glossed over. Both the concrete and abstract portrayals are symbols of fertility. The Kulli goddesses of about 2" height fall into neither class. She may be classified as "Earth Mother", because of certain features. She has a narrow forehead, broad shoulders; her splayed bottom seems to merge into the earth. She is well ornamented. The Zhob goddess of about the same height is a goddess of death, and destruction. The negative aspect of life is personified as feminine. The round holes as eyes, the beak nose, and a cavity for mouth are features which inspire horror in the viewer.

The representations of the Indus Valley Culture have been dealt with earlier.[533] From the available artefacts, it may be surmised that the art had reached its climax just as the civilization had attained its apogee and decadence had set in. The people must have been highly urbanised, industrial, and feudal in their social and economic structures, sophisticated and living in luxury. They must have had a highly developed appreciation of art forms, and the artisans must have had a long tradition of artistry behind them and experience to match it. But one opinion is that the number of artefacts which are more art forms than cult objects in IVC, show no particular artistic attainment.[534] Many opinions are unanimous in labelling the statue of a girl as the Dancing Girl. But this may not be the pose of a girl in the middle of a dance.[535] Her provocative stance may be due to her status or need. Her features are also proto-Australoid and she may have belonged to the lower strata of the society of Harappa. Thus, she may also not be the ideal standard of beauty. The tree-goddess of IVC is transmuted into the dryads of Buddhist art.[536] Later she grows to eminence and is given a supreme stature metaphysically. The architecture of the sanctum of temples itself bespeaks of a fertility connection, as their shape resembles the yoni. This is true of the sanctum of many West Asian religious places also. Particularly in Mesopotamia, there are many temples built to resemble the Goddess' fertility symbol, and by analogy, worshipping the bearing and nourishing aspect of the Goddess.

The stone discs from Bhir Mount (Taxila), Hathial, Kosam, and Rajghat show female figurines interspersed with creeper-like designs. These are definitely fertility cult figures. The carved stone-rings have been found also from Rupar, Mathura, Sankisa, Śrāvastī, Kauśāmbi, Patna and Vaiśāli. Excluding the last, from where the artefacts have been dated to 150 B.C. - 100 B.C., all of them belong to the Maurya-Sunga period. They are about 1½"-3½" in diametre, with or without central perforation. Some of the ring-stones have female figure in stiff postures, and the resemblance of these figures to those in Lauriya-Nandangarh and Piprawah is striking.[537] These are seen as a connecting link between the Indus Valley ring-stones and the later Tantric yantras. Marshall's identification of the ring-stones of IV as objects of the Goddess cult may be appropriate but that they anticipate Tantrism may be doubtful. In a ring-stone found from Taxila, there are two bands of decorations on one side round the central hole. On one band there are a row of alligators and on the second band are nude goddesses whose forms extend into the hole. The association of godhas with the mother-goddess has been represented right through the years though they are not too numerous. In medieval images of Caṇḍī, and Kalaketu of Bengal the godha is always carved on the pedestal. The association of the animal is also evident on the Umā-Maheśvara icons of South India. On the Chandragupta cave façade of Udayagiri, M.P., the

Goddess Mahiṣāsuramardinī is shown stretching a *godha* between her two hands.[538] This is one more important point to infer that the cult of the mother-goddess has roots in the Indus Valley in India. In the Maurya-Sunga period, the alligator disappears, and nude, or semi-nude goddesses appear. The Basarh disc has couples in erotic postures depicted on it. These are similar to the Yakṣiṇī figures on the Sānci Stūpa. These Yakṣiṇīs were very popular during the Maurya and post-Maurya period.[539]

Śrī Lakṣmī

There is a winged goddess from Basarh, (cf Pl.11,) which could be the earliest representation of Goddess Lakṣmī. This figure is nude, well-ornamented, standing on a lotus, and having lotus buds at her sides. Her wings may be an adaptation from the Mesopotamian deities, where they are always portrayed with this appendage. In an inscription from Khoh (MP), the goddess Piṣṭapurī is mentioned. She is believed to be a form of Lakṣmī. There are innumerable depictions of the goddess on coins covering a wide range of dynasties. A coin of the king Sujeṣṭha identified with the Śunga king Sujeṣṭha or Jyeṣṭhamitra shows the goddess standing on a lotus and holding a lotus in her right hand. Two elephants stand on either side of her, and pour water from a vessel held in their trunks. They stand on lotus leaves. Variations of this theme occur on coins of the kings Vāyudeva, Viśākhadeva, and Śivadatta, the kings of Ayodhya, as also of the kings of Ujjain. These belong to the first century B.C. The elephants on the Gaja-Lakṣmi motif point to her Nāga (that is elephants or cobra) antecedents. She may be a fertility symbol of Nāga origin. Her original association with asuras and her leaving them on their degradation could also point to her non-Aryan origins. She is on the coins of Gomitra, Brahmamitra, Ghoṣadatta, and Dṛḍhamitra, depicted as standing with a lotus in her hand. She appears to be famous with the Śaka rulers also. She replaced the Greek goddess Pallas on the coins of Mahākṣatrapa Rañjuvulla, Aziles (28-40 A.D.), and Śoḍāsa (15 A.D.),[540] whose coins depict her on both sides. Foreign rulers identified her with one of their deities, and this increased her popularity. The abhiṣeka motif of the goddess was very famous in almost all reigns from 3rd centruy B.C., on coins from Kausambi and Ayodhya. In the centuries just before and after the Christian Era, she was worshipped in her own right.

Maues (20 B.C.-22 A.D.), and Azes I (5B.C.-30A.D.) may have had a Hellenised version of her. Kausambi was a trade and commerce centre with powerful merchant guilds. It was no surprise that the goddess was very popular in such places. On the coins of the Ayodhya kings she is shown mostly as seated. Lakṣmī without the elephants but with lotuses is seen on the Azes II, and Hagāmaṣa coins of the second to first centuries B.C.[541] These are thought to be Roman goddesses or, variants of Lakṣmī.[542] In an Indo-Scythian coin of about the first century A.D., made of gold, there is depicted a Pukhalāvatīdevatā, who is identified as Lakṣmī, or, Ambā (Pārvatī). The latter is more probable as there is a bull device on the obverse side of this coin.[543] The Śaka rulers also adopted the Abhiṣeka motif of the goddess as their insignia. Gupta sealings in Bhita, Basarh, etc. have already been mentioned. Some of the feudatory kings of the Guptas also had the device on their copper plate grants. There is no Śrī-Lakṣmī on Kushana coins, but she reappears in the Gupta period. On Kumara Gupta I coins, Lakṣmī is associated with lion. Many icons of this goddess have lion as a mark, though Viṣṇu-dharmottara[544] specifically allots the lion as a vāhana to Durgā. Lakṣmī's images decorate the lintels of the Viṣṇu temples of Badami and Aihole. But she deteriorated into a parivāra devatā in the temple of Brahmā as Viśvakarma. The goddess standing or seated on a lotus was common in the Mathura kings' reign. Some of these goddesses have also been identified as Durgā. A Gajalakṣmī motif appears on the door lintel of Anantagumphā, an Orissan cave. Brahminised versions of the Jaina goddess Śri Devī, or Padma Śrī was a favourite numismatic device.[545] On the tribal coins she is depicted always as standing, rarely seated, washed by two elephants.

Lakṣmī's connection with Viṣṇu was only in the third to fourth centuries A.D. in the Kushana-Gupta period. There are many inscriptions justifying this opinion. She appears for the first time with Viṣṇu emblems on Gupta coins. The lotus, an emblem of Lakṣmī, was added to Viṣṇu.[546] On a Bhita seal, she is shown holding a conch in one hand. Mihirakula's Gwalior inscription refers to Śrī's association with Viṣṇu, that the Sun temple will stand as long as Śrī adorns Viṣṇu's chest. The Junagadh rock inscription of the Gupta age refers to Lakṣmī's abode on Viṣṇu. Another inscription of the last quarter of the fifth century A.D., the Kadamba record, as also the Saranath inscription of Prakaṭāditya, and the Aphsad inscription of Adityasena, all mention the mutual connection of Śrī and Viṣṇu.[547] The lotus was provided as a seat for deities, most commonly, and it was not unique to the goddess Lakṣmī alone. The benign beauty of the seated goddess of the Coḷa period can be seen at the Brihaeśvara Temple (cf. plate 15). Many of the goddesses with associations with the flower may even be forms of the Great Goddess. In Bali, the goddess is connected with rice and thus vegetation fertility. Most cultivators with surplus food became traders and Śrī became the goddess of the Vaiśyas. There is Brahma Śrī, connected with Brahmins, and Rājya Śrī of the Kṣatriyas. Since the Śūdras were not expected to possess any wealth, they were not allowed to worship Śrī. The wide representation of the goddess on Gupta coins might also have been due to the Pāñcarātra influence on Vaiṣṇavism.

Lakṣmī on the coins was for the same reason very popular. Her associations with Kubera connected her with wealth, and the coins of Chandragupta II, and Kumargupta depict her. She is also seen on the seals of the guild of merchants and bankers.[548]

Sarasvatī

Sarasvatī is not as numerously represented as Lakṣmī. There is an icon of the goddess belonging to the third century B.C. She sits on a swan, and has a noose in one hand. The Sunga period is considered an important water-shed in the representation of the goddess figures. Sarasvatī's icon is found on the railings of the Barhut Stūpa belonging to this period. She must have been very popular in this period, and she was adopted into Jainism and Buddhism also. On a Gupta style gold coin of the period 6th to 7th centuries A.D., most probably this goddess is represented with a swan at her feet. She had a variety of vāhanas; and over and above the haṁsa, there was a ram, and in the South, the peacock. There is a unique representation of Sarasvatī, lustrated by elephants seated on a lotus in Uttaramerur, of the Pallava period. There are abundant examples of this goddess on the Samudragupta-lyricist type of coins. On these, there is a figure of a goddess variously identified as Lakṣmī or Sarasvatī. On the Kumargupta I coins also the goddess is shown as a slayer of a tiger. Another depiction of the goddess in a tribhaṅga pose is on a coin of Samācāradeva (c. 550-573 A.D.). From the caves of Ujjain, there is a four-armed goddess inferred to be Sarasvatī, holding a book and a vīṇā. At Mahivara in the basement of an old temple, there is an icon of this goddess with an inscription Sarddha, which may either be Śāradā, or Śraddhā. She is four-armed, seated on a haṁsa, holding a vīṇā, and a book in her hands. Pāla period has a beautiful two-armed icon of the goddess.

In the medieval period, there are numerous representations of the goddess. One such is found in Gadag. There is a six-armed depiction of the goddess in the Western Chalukyan style belonging to the tenth century A.D. There are also her representations of the Coḷa (cf. Pḷ 16), and the Nāyaka periods, the famous one is her icon in the Madurai temple on a peacock.[549] There is an opinion that the Yakṣas and Yakṣīs depicted iconographically in the two centuries prior to the Christian Era, could have provided the model on which the gods' images were conceived, refined and executed. A headless statue of the goddess Sarasvatī has been discovered while excavating a Jaina Stupa near Mathura. It belongs to the first half of the second century A.D.[550] Sarasvatī was represented on coins on a small scale. Durgā was more popular in the South and North-West regions and, Lakṣmī was the most popular goddess on the coins in these periods.

The Mātṛs

During the Kushana period, numerous images of the goddesses have been found and catalogued.[551] During this period it seems as though their number was not fixed. They were represented in groups of even twos and threes, and these were very numerous. A group of four Mothers (Nos. 59 and 63)[552] are depicted possessing no distinguishing marks. Obviously, the numbers as well as the format of the icons were in a flux. Seven Mātṛs are depicted with water pots in their left hand, and Abhaya mudrā shown by their raised right hand (Nos. F 38 and 39). An Āyudhapuruṣa is seen standing by their side. There are again no distinguishing features. There are two Āyudhapuruṣas flanking the Mātṛs (G 57 and 126) in two groups. There are numerous depictions without this feature. They are seen in some icons holding a child in their laps. Sometimes, a vase like the ones in the Vasudhāra statuettes are also depicted. The infants in the goddesses' laps show their connection with Hāritī. The above features as also the vase show the Mātṛs allied to fertility and childbirth. One depiction (No. 2331) shows a relief of seven mothers each with a child in her hands, showing Abhaya mudrā. They are seen with animal faces, seeming to represent their vāhanas. But this surmise may be wrong and this feature may have been in consonance with their fierce nature. There is one very proper representation (No. 552) of the Mātṛs where they are flanked by Śiva and Gaṇeśa. Each of them is shown with her appropriate vehicle. The convention of depiction of the Mātṛs during the Kushana period was only with Āyudhapuruṣas. Later these were replaced by Śiva and Vināyaka.

In the Buddhist period, Hāritī was worshipped and depicted in paintings and icons from Magadha to Central Asia, and from Afghanistan to Ajaṇta.[553] In the Gupta period, each Mātṛ was distinguished by a distinct vāhana and āyudha, as described in the DM., but accompanied by Īśāna also.[554] The very early depiction of Mātṛs of this period is seen in the Udayagiri cave of the early Gupta period. All the Mātṛs have an identical look which shows that their iconography had become fixed. There are plenty of Mātṛs icons belonging to this period. During the late Gupta and early medieval periods, their depiction was popular as the seals from Nalanda attest. These depict the Mātṛs individually and not in groups. By the medieval period, the number and the format of the icons were fixed.

Seen symbolically, Ātma Vidyā as represented by either Devī or Śiva combats with darkness and ignorance represented by the demons Mahiṣa and others, or, Andhaka (in the case of Śiva). In this fight, the good power takes the assistance of the various powers of the gods as represented by the Mātṛs.

There may have been only three Mātṛs in early representations, as seen in the Imadpur metal images. From this, their numbers rose to seven, eight, and finally to sixteen. This cult rose to its zenith around eighth to tenth centuries A.D., but this gave way to the propitiation of Cāmuṇḍā among the ruling classes. During the Chalukya, Solanki and Vaghela dynasties, they were arranged in the periphery of the temples, in niches, along with various other deities. In a few South Indian temples the Mātṛs were added later to satisfy the ritualistic needs of the period.[555]

The divine mothers were sometimes called *Dākinis* and *Ghoṣiṇīs.* There are a few extant temples to these goddesses in Bheraghat, near Jabalpur, in Khajuraho, and in Hirapur, near Bhubaneswar in Orissa, belonging to the medieval period. Usually, these shrines are round in structure, emphasising the word "*maṇḍalakramavidaḥ*".[556] In Bhubaneswar, they gained great importance during the Kesari dynasty. Their icons were represented with babies in their hands, the exception being only Cāmuṇḍā. The accompanying Vīrabhadra and Gaṇeśa are also omitted. There are many more temples cited in Orissa for Mātṛs. Early Kadamba and Chalukyan dynasties accepted the Mātṛs as their tutelary deities. The temple of Aeśvara in the North-West of the town Sinnar (near Nasik, Maharashtra) has the Seven Mātṛs on the doorway to the temple. The Chalukyans were specially devoted to the Mātṛs. The temple belongs to circa 1025 A.D.[557]

The worship of Saptamātṛs by themselves in separate shrines existed in the Coḷa period till as late as Kulottunga II (1070-1120 A.D.) (cf Pl. 18). At Daṇḍīśvaram which may be a corruption of Taṇḍīśvaram, there is an independent temple to the Mātṛs, of the period of Sundara Coḷa (956-973 A.D.).[558] With regard to the shape of the Buddhist stupas, it is felt that its roots could be embedded in the hoary past of the South Indian worship of the Mātṛs in the villages.[559] There were seven clay mounds representing the Mātṛs worshipped in the villages. Even though there could be folk origins to the stupas, it seems far-fetched to see this connection to the South.

Varāhamihira states in his *Bṛhatsaṁhitā*, on the installation of images in temples that "...... *Mātṛṇāmapi maṇḍalakramavidaḥ*",[560] Utpala[561] commenting on this says, "*Mātṛṇām svakalpavihitavidhānena*", that is, the Mātṛs should be installed according to their individual tenets. Utpala gives their names as Brāhmī, Vaiṣṇavī, Raudrī (Māheśvarī), Kaumārī, Aindrī, Yamī, Vāruṇī, and Kauberī. There are also others like Nārasiṁhī, Vārāhī, and Vaināyakī. Though the Mātṛs were individuąlly popular as folk-goddesses they were installed and worshipped in a group. Some of the lesser known Mātṛs were : Deḍḍarī, Lampaṭā, Ṭhānī, Ṭakārī, Ṛiḍhālī, Ṣaṇḍinī, Audārā, Khemakhī, and a host of others, which have no iconographic representations.[562] Obviously, these were folk-goddesses. The wide diffusion of the cult is attested by a number of temples all over the country. Near Shadol at Antarā there are many images of śaktis, with labels on their pedestals. This script puts a date of tenth century A.D., to these icons. Many new names are inscribed, such as Tāraṇī, Sabhavā, Thabhā,

Tāmakā, Damakā, Itaralā, etc. There are little known ones in such places as Goa and the Simla Hills too.[563]

Yāmala Mantra Śāstra and *Śilpa Saṁgraha* deal in detail with the iconographic particulars of the Mātṛs. They are usually carved on a slab of stone and are flanked by Gaṇeśa and Vīrabhadra. In the South, the cult was very popular during the Pallava and Coḷa regimes.[564]

The Mātṛ cult was so popular that Jainism adopted it and we find their iconography in the Khandagiri caves (Bhubhaneswar, Orissa.[565]

In the worship of Mātṛkas, fear played a major part. But the Mothers were also made benign as seen from their iconography, as they hold infants in their arms. As seen earlier, in the Indus Valley icons, the mother-goddess with a child in her arms is an indigenous element, and this concept is prevalent in many parts of the world. As stated, sometimes, there are only three figures embossed on a rectangular piece of stone, and they are usually Brāhmī, Kaumārī, and Vaiṣṇavī.

In the DM, the śaktis are said to come out of the gods, Brahmā, Śiva, Kārtikeya, Viṣṇu and Indra. Brāhmī always leads them, though by this period Brahmā had ceased to be a popular god. These Śaktis are said to bear the respective forms, ornaments and mounts of the gods.

"Yasya devasya yadrūpaṁ yathā bhūṣaṇavāhanam/
Tadvadeva hi tatśaktirasurān yoddhumāyayau//" (8.14)

The first reference in vv. 14-20 contain descriptions of Brahmāṇī, Māheśvarī, Kaumārī, Vaiṣṇavī, Vārāhī, Nārasiṁhī and Aindrī. In verse 22, Caṇḍikā issues from the goddess' body and is called Śivadūtī. The panel in cave 14, Ellora faithfully represents the seven mātṛs, the set closed by Gaṇeśa; and Cāmuṇdā, as Durgā's śakti is outside this st. (cf. Pl. 17). Common iconographic lists would roughly match this : Brahmāṇī, Māheśvarī, Kaumārī, Vaiṣṇavī, Indrāṇī and Cāmuṇḍī, though there are other variations.[566]

It is seen that the cult of the Mātṛs rose from folk background, and they tried to absorb as many folk and tribal deities that were popular, as possible. Near Pune, the Māval region derives its name from the mother-goddess Māvaḷā-devī. They are identified with the seven apsaras, satī āsarā, worshipped always in a group near water. In the present day, blood sacrifices are not offered. These aniconic stones are coated with red oxide.[567]

Cāmuṇḍā

The depictions of Cāmuṇḍā in the early icons of the Mātṛs, in the Mathura region, of the Kushana period, is distinctive and she can be easily identified due to her emaciated looks and her pretāsana (cf Pl. 19). It is the same with regard to the Nalanda seals where there are her depictions, of the Gupta or early medieval periods. Numerous icons of an emaciated Cāmuṇḍā flanked by Gaṇeśa, and an Ūrdhvaliṅga Bhairava adorn the back and side walls of the main sanctum of Vaital Deul in Bhubaneswar of the eighth century A.D., as also the Vārāhī temple of Chaurasi belonging to the tenth century A.D.

On the hill of Mandhata, near the Omkāreśvara temple, lies a huge, 18″ tall figure of Cāmuṇḍā, with emaciated belly and a scorpion carved on her body akin to Vṛścikodarī. She is ornamented with a necklace of snakes and holds a garland of skulls in her hand. In her other hands, she holds a sword and mace.[568] This is said to belong to the same period as the Omkāreśvar temple, that is circa tenth century A.D. At Kolar in Karnataka, an inscription in the temple of Kolaramma (1072 A.D.) states that the main deity of the temple is Cāmuṇḍeśvarī. There are other deities and Saptamātṛs in other shrines in the vicinity.[569] These depictions of this goddess follow the iconic instructions given in the Suprabhedāgama, the manual on iconography. Here Jyesṭhā or Alakṣmī is described as having a crow ensign (which bird is an emblem of the nether-world spirits), seated on an ass, two-armed, with long nose and sagging lips, with long and pendulous breasts and belly, holding a lotus in one hand. Cāmuṇḍā is also to be fashioned similarly, but seated on a dead body, adorned with a chain of skulls, and flames issuing from a bald head.[570] In Jajpur in Orissa, considered a Tantric spot, colossal sculptures of *Cāmuṇḍā*, *Indrāṇī*, and *Vārāhī* were found, belonging to the early ninth century A.D. at the latest.[571]

Kālī

In South Indian traditions, Kālī is said to be calmed by Śiva in a dance contest. There are very few icons or references showing an encalmed Kālī. In iconography, Kālī is always shown as the more powerful of the pair. She is usually shown as dancing on the prone form of Śiva, who may even be a corpse. There are a few South Indian bronzes of the fifteenth to nineteenth centuries, A.D., showing Kālī in an attitude of devotion towards Śiva. In the cola period both the benign (cf. Pḷ 3-20,21,22,23) and fierce (cf. Pḷ 24 and 25) forms were well represented in bronze and stone media. Plate 27 shows vividhy the weapons and attributes of the goodess, symbolism of which have been earlier deal with (cf. IV Cḥ Sṇ Psychological Reasons). In maithuna pairing also, Kālī is shown as the more powerful partner.[572] A goddess Koṭṭamahika, is mentioned in a grant of the king Dhruvasena II, in the seventh century A.D. This could be the Tamil Koṟṟavai. The shrine of Jyeṣṭhā devī occupied the North-West corner of the temple prākāra during the reign of the early Coḷa kings. The adverse preaching by the Tamil poet saints discouraged and finally stopped the worship of the Mātṛs as well as Jyeṣṭhā devī. When the latter's worship stopped her image was removed, and in her place Lakṣmī's image was installed.

Geographically, the earliest record of the Seven Mothers belongs to the Chalukyan period. The well-known inscription is from the Gangdhar temple (in Malwa), of Viśvavarman of the years 423-24 A.D. The Mātṛs were popularly worshipped and were the titular deities of the Chalukyas and the Kadambas. As one would assume from the inscription it is not true that the temple itself was fierce, but the rites associated with the Mātṛs were fearsome.[573]

Lajjā Gaurī

Bubo or Lajjā Gaurī type of fertility goddess was very popular from the fourth century A.D. onwards as attested by archaeological finds. The Baubo figurine from IV which comes through the ages (including the Bhitta seal) is connected to the Purāṇic Śākambharī. Stella Kramrisch has called this Aditi Uttānapāda. This type of fertility-connected goddess is called Lajjā-Gaurī in Maharashtra and Gujarat. This goddess could be related to the Tantric yoni worship and viewed as the seat of the slumbering Kuṇḍalini śakti. The original triangular figures with sophistication may have transformed into Tantric Yantras. Since the goddess is related to rains, her icons are widespread in Rajasthan and Gujarat, in the step wells. in Ter, Mahurdzari, and Nevasa, in Maharashtra her icons have been excavated belonging to the early centuries of the Christian Era.[574] Recently,[575] in Curdi village near Goa, an eight-foot long image of the Goddess in laterite, probably belonging to the period of the Chalukyas of Badami has been discovered. She has a child pressing against her breast. The local people call her "Kalawant", a variation of the Goddess Durgā. The wide diffusion of these icons and her continued popularity shows the folk-element in the cult, and the later attempts to bring her into the Great Tradition through similarities seen in the Purāṇic Goddess.

The goddess' name Lajjā-Gaurī is derived from the old Kannada word Lañji, or Lañjikā meaning a harlot. Pārvatī was caught in an amourous pose with Śiva, by a devotee. She blushed and ran away, and hence the name.[576] Some Sthalapurāṇas connect this figure with Reṇukā, which show the folk-element in her. But, this source belongs to the late medieval period, whereas the icons belong to the 2nd cent. B.C.-6th cent. A.D. These were called Baubo figurines by H.D. Sankalia inferring that the cult was due to Roman influence by a goddess of the same name. Dhavalikar,[577] sees this goddess connecting the proto-historic Venus figurines of Europe, as well as the goddess Palghat, of the Warlis of Thana Dt., Bombay. He concludes that this is the Goddess Śākambharī of the DM.[578]

Tato(a) hamakhilaṁ lokamātmadehasamudbhavaiḥ/
Bhariṣyāmi surāḥ śākairāvṛṣteh prāṇadhārakaiḥ// 48
Śākambharīti vikhyatiṁ tadā yāsyāmyahaṁ bhuvi/
Tatraiva ca vadhiṣyāmi Durgamākhyaṁ mahāsuram// 49

Kesargutta is on a hillock hundred metres high, forty kilometres north-east of Hyderabad. In the three brick structures here, one has a peculiar carving of a goddess in relief on a 9 cms. square slate stone. The goddess is of the Baubo type, squatting on her haunches, hands resting on her knees, and extended palms supporting a lion's face and a liṅga. Her head is a huge lotus. Such figures are also found in Kunidene, Guntur District, belonging to the fourth century A.D. But here the lion has a human body. In the Chalukyan temples at Alampur, Bhavanasi, Sangamesvaram, Yellala and Pratakota, the deity is kept in the North-West koṣṭha, in replacement of Durgā.[579] A very early specimen is found in the Kāmākṣī temple in Kanchipuram, and is still under worship to obtain progeny. This icon could be the original goddess in this ancient seat of Śakti worship. There are larger versions of Lajjā Gaurī which are found from the Satavahana levels in Nevasa, Ter, Maharzari Kondapur, Yelleswaram, etc. These figures emphasise the generative organ as does the Nagarjunakonda limestone Yoni of huge size, in the shape of a huge ghaṭa, with leafy foliage entwined between the legs. The lotus head of these goddesses is supported by Viṣṇudharmottara (cf. Pl. 29-35).[580] It is a symbol of Saubhāgyam or auspiciousness. The Baubo figures have been found in the Deccan in terra-cotta, in the Kushana period. They were made out of stone in the Kushana-Gupta periods. They are surmised to have come to India through Roman contacts. But India being an agricultural country, worship of the fertility goddesses is as hoary as the Indus Valley Civilization.

Lauriya golden tablet of a goddess and such similar ones from Piprahva from a Buddhist stūpa, and a terracotta figurine from Bhitta (cf. Pl. 29) are all obviously cult objects. These could not have resulted from any systematic art movements. Passages in the ṚgVeda and the Gṛhyasūtras support the view that objects of deities should be fashioned out of clay and metal.[581]

Various names of goddesses are mentioned in inscriptions. In Rajasthan, there are names of goddesses Āraṇyavāsinī and Dadhimatī, of the period around seventh century A.D. In Orissa, Stambheśvarī Devī is mentioned in inscriptions of the sixth century A.D. In the Phabasa cave inscriptions of the 7th.-8th. centuries A.D. Kiraṇeśvarī is mentioned.[582]

Śiva was a popular deity in the Gandhara regions. Ambikā as his spouse could also have been popular here. Bhīmā Devī as the spouse of Śiva had a shrine in Gandhara. This view is supported by the coins from Ujjain.[583] The goddess cult could have started its conception in Madhya Pradesh, it is surmised, on evidence from inscriptions and coins.[584]

There are seen to be three major types of mother goddess icons in the first centuries of the Christian Era. A goddess as a Nourishing Mother is the figure from Mathura of the Sunga period. Her one hand holds a lotus near her chest and with her other hand she holds her breast. The Baubo figure with her reproductive organs exaggerated, or, who is a personification of these organs, is also well represented in this period. The third type is the Ishtar type with chest exposed, but with no touch of vulgarity, and with her divinity emphasised.[585]

Thus, there were a number of goddesses representing local cults in India of this period i.e., a few centuries before and after the Christian Era. Foreign influence also could have played a part in the formation of some of the deities. The popularity of some goddesses over others could have been due to their fertility symbolism which is possible in an agriculture oriented country like India.

Terra-Cottas

In the terra-cotta figurines, many styles overlap. Thus a particular style cannot be pin-pointed with certainty. But there is a continuity from the Mauryan, through the Sunga and Kushana periods upto the Gupta period. Mostly, they were mother-goddess figurines. In the Sunga period itself, iconography of the goddesses was getting fixed. Thus, particular goddesses could be identified by their attributes. They also started resembling stone icons.

There are a number of terra-cotta figures of the post IV and pre-Mauryan female figurines. They are nude or, semi-nude. These are very similar to the IV figurines (cf. Pl. 4). In Navada toli (Maheshwar) a bas-relief of a goddess figure is found, dated to one thousand B.C. On a potsherd, earlier to this period is found painted a group of female dancers in a circle holding hands. All these are fetishes of the fertility goddess cult. That this is a step in the evolution of the religious thought is borne out by the similarity between the Lauriya-Nandangarh golden plaque of the goddess and a Syrian golden plaque of the goddess Astarte belonging to the thirteenth century B.C. In the Maurya and post-Maurya periods, terra-cotta figurines were better developed.[586] Aditi had no special facial features. There have been a number of terra-cotta figurines identified as Aditi/Pṛthivī, showing the boundless aspect of the goddess, but with no specific features.[587] There are a large numbr of semi-nude figurines in the same medium, in the Buddhist and Jaina sacred places belonging to the Kushana period. All these cult figures are syncretised into the Great Goddess as seen in the Devī Māhātmya. In the Maurya and Sunga period the representations of the goddess contained only a single goddess figure, some resembling the gold leaf figure of Lauriya-

Nandangarh and Piprawah. These figures have been dated to 300 B.C. Gupta shrines were adorned with large terra-cotta plaques which contained complex compositions. In a terra-cotta panel of Viṣṇu Anantaśāyin from Bhitargaon (UP), Viṣṇu is seen as though emerging from sleep, Brahmā is looking terrified, and the demons Madhu, and Kaiṭabha, standing close to the tail of Ananta, seem to challenge Brahmā either to accept them as their overlord, or to fight them.[588] This could be an ideal representation of the Madhu-Kaiṭabha episode of DM., which as seen earlier is a creation myth. In the Sunga and Kushana periods and more so in the Gupta period, there are representations in this medium of different and definite types of goddesses, as for example : Śri Lakṣmī, Vasudhārā, Pārvatī, Durgā Mahiṣāsuramardinī, Cāmuṇḍā, Hāritī, (what could be) *Koṭṭavī*, many-headed *Ṣaṣṭhī*, *Carcikā* in a cat form, and *Nāginīs* and Yakṣīs.[589]

Two similar terra-cotta plaques from Nagar, near Uniyara in the Tonk Dt. near Jaipur in Rajasthan have been dated to the middle of the first century B.C., to early first century A.D. These are now preserved in the Amber Museum. This might be the earliest representation of the Goddess as *Mahiṣāsuramardinī*. The Goddess is four-armed. The lower left hand is placed on the back of the buffalo, and the upper right hand holds a trident. The left leg is placed on the recumbent lion. Bhita and Ahicchatra artists may have copied this motif in their images. Early representations of the demon depicted him as a buffalo. The lion is a later addition to the motif, and so this plaque had been assigned a much later period.[590] This was very popular in the later Kushana, and more particularly in the Gupta periods, as seen in the finds in Ahicchatra, Bhitta, Rajghat, in U.P., and the Udayagiri caves, the Śiva temple in Bhumara and Karavan, all in Madhya Pradesh. But it could be that the inspiration for this composition (with the lion) could be of folk origin, even earlier than the Devī Māhātmya. Just as there are a number of variations in the account of the killing of Mahiṣa, there could be different compositions in iconography portraying this myth. The Kushana figurines of Mahiṣāsuramardinī do not have inscriptions. Therefore it is hard to say whether in this period itself Durgā had become the Great Goddess or not. Be that as it may, this goddess certainly could have provided the germ for the later elaborations in the Devī Māhātmya.

A terra-cotta plaque has been discovered in Sambhar, made of white clay belonging to the first century A.D. with the same theme.[591] There are innumerable depictions of the Mahiṣāsuramardinī theme in Kushana art, and sculptures. Therefore, it could be assumed that the genesis of the text of Devī Māhātmya could have come to fruition during this period. Nana could have had a great influence in the formation of the Goddess, just as Ardokhsho influenced the icons of Śrī-Lakṣmī. This could be the reason for the formation of the Goddess' cult in the Kushana period and also that of the dynasties immediately following it. Since the Kushanas were great Śiva bhaktas, the goddess cult could have developed alongside that of Śiva. Thus, the lion mount could have been borrowed from Nana, or for that matter from Śiva himself, who in the Mbh. is mentioned as riding a chariot drawn by thousand lions.[592] Nana and Ardokhsho were prestigious goddesses worshipped by the ruling family. The local goddess cult could have gained in stature through an adoption by the Kushanas. After the fall of this dynasty, when the local monarchs grew in power, the cult must have had a further fillip. Affiliation to Śiva and a parallel growth of the goddess cult could have hastened her development along Brahminical lines.

Durgā Mahiṣāsuramardinī : Numismatics

Coins and seals provide good samples for fixing and verifying goddesses. But the continuing tradition in numismatics, or, the suitability or otherwise of a particular goddess for coins would be an impediment in fixing or corroborating evidence. In the Gupta period the characteristics of the Goddess are fully developed iconographically. She is shown as standing on a lotus or sitting on a throne on Gupta coins. There is seen an influence from Nana-Ardokhsho coins. On Chandragupta I's coins the goddess is shown seated on a high throne. On Chandragupta II's coins the circular mat at the feet of the Goddess is replaced by a lotus.

In the Devī Māhātmya, in the Nārāyaṇī stuti, Devī is called both Trayambakā-Gaurī,[593] consort of Śiva, and Nārāyaṇī-Lakṣmī,[594] wife of Viṣṇu. The gold coins of Chandragupta I-Kumaradevi type belonging to either Chandragupta I, or Samudragupta period, show on the obverse side the lion-slaying Goddess. Though the device could have been influenced by the

Nana-Ardokhsho coins, the theme of the Nārāyaṇī stuti could also have contributed towards its evolution. The Goddess is shown seated on a lion and holding a lotus in her hand.[595] The influence of the goddess Oesha of the Gandhara region, as well as the goddess Ishtar are seen in its formation.[596] These coins are seen not due so much to the influence of foreign goddesses as due to the Lakṣmī-Siṁhavāhinī idea, which is depicted on the Khajuraho temple. This has been described by Hemādri also. But since these coins are of a very early period, this is not possible. Lakṣmī's association with the lion is late. Durgā riding a lion or killing the buffalo demon appear on the seals of Nalanda, of the later Gupta and early medieval period. Near Chhattisgarh in M.P., a stone icon of Mahiṣāsuramardinī has been found.[598] Her lion mount is seen tearing the hind portion of Mahiṣa as he lies trampled under the feet of Durgā. This belongs to circa 400 A.D.

There is another icon of Cāmuṇḍā quaffing blood, surrounded by goblins. She is emaciated with pendulous breasts. Nalanda was Buddhist, but the Hindu religious tolerance is seen on the seals where Hindu and Buddhist deities are pictured side by side. Thus, Śrīmad-Deveśvarī is a four-armed goddess on a lotus seat placed on a lion. The obverse side of this seal has emblems of Buddhism. Another seal is of a goddess similar to the above, on a buffalo. Both these could be Durgā. An eight-armed goddess holding a trident and other weapons, also seems to be the goddess Durgā. Some goddesses are pictured as riding on alligators or iguanas All these attest to the popularity of the Goddess Durgā. Her fierce counterpart Cāmuṇḍā and the Mātṛs were also well represented on the seals and were very popular during the Gupta period.

Inscriptions

There are many inscriptions of this period. The earliest one is dated 491 A.D. near Udaipur, from Choti Sadri. Here the Goddess is mentioned as Mahiṣāsuramardinī and having a lion as a vāhana. Her anger is seen in her knitted eyebrows, but she is a devoted mother to her children. The inscription further says that a king Gauri built a palatial shrine for her. Many more inscriptions of the 6th-7th centuries A.D. are from Rajasthan, Orissa, U.P., and Bihar. Maukhari king Anantavarman (6th century A.D.) has two inscriptions for the goddess bearing his name. The second inscription mentions Mahiṣāsuramardinī, and the installation of

Kātyāyanī, in a cave temple and a grant of a village to the Goddess. An inscription of the year 625 A.D. in Sirohi (erstwhile state) in Rajasthan, states of the dedication of a temple to Durgā by a goṣṭī. There is a temple to Śākambharī in Sakrai, again near Jaipur in Rajasthan. An inscription here states that a group of bankers built a maṇḍapa to this temple. An inscription of Cāmuṇḍā from Jaipur, Orissa belongs to the 7th century A.D. It opens with an invocation to Durgā, accompanied by her lion, and her son Kārtikeya. An inscription to the goddess Bhavānī from Banaras, of the early 8th century A.D., describes the goddess wearing a garland of skulls.[599] The Nagarjuni Hill cave inscription of Anantavarman states that the Goddess placed her foot with its tinkling anklet on the head of the demon. There is also a mention of the icon of Devī Kātyāyanī in a cave in the Vindhya mountains.[600]

Iconography

Only in the Mauryan Age, we have a large number of artefacts made of stone. But Durgā images of the Kushana, Gupta, and early medieval period have been discovered in and around Mathura. There are about thirty-three statuettes catalogued.[601] The Goddess is identified by her lion mount. The heights of these vary between 5½"-1½". Some icons show her as a Vaiṣṇavī Śakti, holding a conch in front of her chest with both her hands (Nos. D 51, 1105, 2103). Some show Pārvatī doing tapas, (No. 1100) and between pañcāgni (No. 1044).

There are some Mahiṣāsuramardinī icons of the Kushana period.[602] The heights vary between 5½" to 3". One icon (No. 875) is six armed, and supports a bowl on her head with two of her hands. In the other two hands she holds the animal. These are mostly in red sand-stone. There are other similar ones (Nos. 889, 993). In one the Goddess is ten-armed (No. 541). Her lion attacks Mahiṣa. His head is broken and a divinity is seen emerging from the skull and ascending. The upper corners of the icon are decorated with a couple of Mātṛ. This belongs to the medieval period. In the early medieval periods, two icons (Nos. 842, 1087) show her holding the demon by his hair. Another icon of the same period shows the lion in the background as a docile vāhana (No. 2317). Another one (D 12) shows Durgā slaying the demon. Two hands hold a basket over her head. The left hand holds the tail of the demon, and with another hand she is piercing him with a trident. This is very poorly executed. In one (D 32), her right foot is on the lion and the left foot is on the prostrate Mahiṣa. A figure of a warrior seen between the two animals may be the same demon in a human form. This is also rudely carved and belongs to the late Mughal period.

There is a stone relief of the Goddess killing the demon in a miniature size found at Bhitta. Two reasons put forward that this might be a very early representation of the theme are that the Goddess is two-armed, and that the demon is in the shape of a buffalo. This Gupta period piece is surmised to be earlier than the DM.[603] But the number of hands alone does not date the sculpture, though the hands were multiplied in later representations. One of the earliest figures of the Goddess carved on the facade of the Varāha cave shrine of Udayagiri (near Bhilsa, M.P.) is twelve-armed. This is of the period very early fifth century A.D. In one of her hands she is holding an iguana.[604] The iguana has associations with Devī icons in her role as Pārvatī, in later periods. Mahiṣāsuramardinī's image has also been found in Bhumara also in M.P. A fine figure in bronze of this Goddess bearing an inscription as Lakshaṇā has been discovered in Chamba a hill state in North India. In this, Devī is four-armed, holding the tail of the demon in one hand and driving the trident with the other. Her foot presses the neck of the buffalo. This belongs to the eighth century A.D.[605] As seen earlier, a partial representation of this is found in the Bhitta seal. In the Gupta and the early medieval periods, the icons follow closely the DM. description. But in the early medieval icons, the demon as a buffalo is changed into a human figure with horns and Devī rides the lion.

On a quick survey over the period covered by the Kushana and the Gupta dynasties, with their interregnum also showing slight variations of the *Mahiṣavadha* scheme we could arrive at a certain broad generalisation. In the Kushana period. Devī encircles the demon,[606] depicted as a buffalo, with her left arm, her right arm pressing his spine. This mode of killing the Mahiṣa would be the literal picturisation of the word Mahiṣāsuramardinī, mardana meaning destroying and crushing. There is no lion in the early icons. In the later ones the Vāhana appears but Devī's foot is not placed on the lion, but is beside it on the ground.

In the period between these two dynasties, Devī presses the demon on his spine, does not encircle him with her left arm, but is pulling his tongue (Nagar tablet). In the Udayagiri Cave No. 6, which is of a slightly later period, she is applying the trident on Mahiṣā. In a still later depiction in the front courtyard of the same cave, the lion serves as the footstool for Devī, which pattern stabilises in the Gupta period.

In a couple of examples of the Gupta period, where the hind leg or the tail of the demon is held by Devī, and he is swung aloft, before being flung down in a mortal throw, a similarity is seen in the artist's conception of the theme to DM. 10.20ff.[607] It does not seem plausible that an artist should borrow from the same Māhātmya, another episode's[608] idea, to depict the Mahiṣavadha scheme. It could be that the depiction grew from each previous simplistic idea, and the elaboration resulting from the artist's intuition.

The Mahiṣāsuramardinī theme was very popular in India especially in the Eastern parts. A very rare figure depicting this has been found in Porsha (Dinajpur Dist., North Bengal) of the medieval age. There is one central figure of an eighteen-armed Devī, surrounded by eight other Mahiṣāsuramardinī images, each having sixteen arms. This is a representation of the Nava Durgā concept, as mentioned earlier.[609]

The central hall in the Buddhist cave at Lonad (Thane Dist.) contains three loose images of Mahiṣāsuramardinī. This cave must have been abandoned by the Buddhists due to a defect in the back wall of the cave, and the deity later installed is called Khaṇḍeśvarī. This icon belongs to the Vakataka period, fifth century A.D. This village goddess is a representation of Mahiṣāsuramardinī. The upper right hand holds a sword (Khaḍga) which in medieval Marathi is called Khaṇḍa, and the Goddess may have derived the local name from this.[610] There is a fragmented image of the Goddess belonging to 550-570 A.D. in the Hire Mahakutesvara temple at Mahakuta. The temple belongs to the period of the Chalukyas of Badami, and is in the style of Early Karṇāṭa, in the 6th century A.D. Another temple in Badami has a Mahiṣāsuramardinī icon of the period circa 745 A.D. the composition of which resembles the Mahabalipuram icon strongly.[611] There is another very early image of this form of Devī in a mould from Peshawar. Though the details are not clear the upper part of the body of the Goddess and the animal is clearly seen. A figure from Bengal shows Devī as thirtytwo armed slaying demons, not particularly Mahiṣa. There are also numerous representations of Devī accompanied by the lion, or riding on it, but without the combat with Mahiṣa in Bihar. These belong to the medieval period.[612]

Maukhari chief Anantavarman (fifth or sixth century A.D.) established *Devī* and Śiva in a cave shrine, and in another installed the image of *Devī* as Mahiṣāsuramardinī. The Gurjara-Pratiharas (8th-11th centuries A.D.) of Kanauj were also devotees of Mahiṣāsuramardinī.[613] There are a group of temples in Alampur of the early Chalukyan period, that is from 550-753 A.D. The principal shrine in this group is the Bālabrahma temple belonging to the early 8th century A.D. Here there are one icon of Durgā standing on a lion[614] and three of Mahiṣāsuramardinī type. The first icon of Mahiṣāsuramardinī is four-armed with a Śaṅkha and Cakra in her upper hands. She thrusts the triśūla with her lower right hand into the body of the buffalo and pulls the demon's tongue out with her lower left hand. She is well-ornamented. There is a lion carved at the bottom (Left. cf. Pl. 36).[615] The second icon[616] is a standing figure with eight hands holding weapons. The lower right hand thrusts the triśūla into the back of a half-human form, emerging from the mouth of the animal. The lower left hand rests on the head of the human (cf. Pl. 37). This emphasises the killing and release from bondage simultaneously by Devī. The third icon[617] is similarly standing on Mahiṣa. She is eight-armed, holding various weapons. The lower right hand thrusts a triśula into the body of the animal, while the lower left pulls at the tail she is well-ornamented (cf. Pl 38).[618] There is one of a similar type where Devī is thrusting the triśūla with one of her left hand, and pressing Mahiṣa's head with another left hand, while the right foot presses the demou's back. (cf. Pl. 39). Devī pulling the tongue of Mahiṣa has a wide diffusion in the post-Gupta period and is found even in modern depictions in Goan villages, the earliest representation being 1874 A.D.[619] The representations of Mahiṣāsuramardinī are most numerous in Gujarat and Orissa. In Bhubaneswar, she is under popular worship in modern period. A four-armed icon of the Pala period is still under worship in Dinajpur. At Midnapur, a ten-armed Goddess has been discovered.[620] A stone relief from Singaseri (Java) belonging to the period of Brahmin influence in that island, i.e., 950-1500 A.D., depicts the killing of the demon exactly as put forth in the DM. The Goddess is standing on the prone form of Mahiṣa, and is in the act of dealing the mortal blow to him. The demon is emerging in the form of a dwarf from the buffalo.[621]

Durgā's affiliation to Viṣṇu via Ekānaṁśā, could have been later, after her cult started gaining a loose form. When the idea of the power of the deity as his śakti and of his powerlessness without it gained credence, the further elaboration of the cult in the DM of portraying the gods as totally powerless may have taken place. Each single god is a power of one particularised energy. All of these externalise into one single Goddess. The wrath of the gods personified into the Goddess, just as in Śiva's case his anger is portrayed as the Kīrtimukha. The symbolism of the formation of the Goddess is seen as the Universal Life Energy absorbing back into its womb all the numerous tiny energies, as the Goddess goes to meet the enemy. In a manuscript illustration of the modern period, about 1800 A.D., the gods are shown giving their weapons, vessels and ornaments to her, thus giving up their valour and manliness.[622] In Pallava sculptures, Durgā is shown with the Vaiṣṇavite emblems of conch and discus. After the seventh century A.D.when Durgā was affiliated to the Śaivite sect, she still retained her conch and discus in iconography.

Though Kushana art picturised the lion's participation in Devī's encounter with Mahiṣa, even if only as a vāhana, Gupta sculptures did not portray the mount. The DM mythology must have been well-known all over Central and North India, but the sculptures in these areas do not show the lion mount.

Gupta Art

The Gupta art shows an intrinsic aesthetic sense. It cuts down on ornamentation, and makes the statue simple in line. Only Mauryans left behind art forms huge in size. They are deemed the first to use stone as a medium, since so far, we have no proof of earlier stone artefacts. The Gupta stone images are not massive representations. The emphasis is on elegance.

The result is not the effectiveness of a craftsman solely trying to show his excellence in art, but it is the experience in knowing the intrinsic essence of the thought portrayed, which his skill highlights with artistry. The beauty seems to come from inside and it seems to exemplify as it were the possible motto of the artists of that period, that virtue is an inherent part of beauty. Beauty was not pursued for satisfying the senses alone, but for guiding the mind towards higher ideals. This was made easier by the artefacts of beauty, which seemed to lead them towards their goal. Thus, the art was necessarily religious. The inspiration must have come from higher aesthetic plane. But religion did not stand in the way of aesthetic enjoyment. Hindu India had always had a religious foundation for all their fine arts. In the Gupta period this was no less so. The simplicity of style gives an impression of an easy manner of execution. This conceals great ideas. The outer form and the inner ideal are blended in perfect proportion. It could even be said that Gupta art was Indian art at its best. Because of its popularity, it was transplanted into countries abroad, from the Central Asiatic deserts to the islands in the east. Mahabalipuram and Ellora panels of this theme show a changed attitude in Devī's fight with the demon. Before taking up these two panels which are artistically perfect, a few other samples are viewed.

A panel from Aihole 6th or 7th cent. A.D.,[623] (cf. Pl. 40) shows an eight-armed goddess piercing the neck of the demon with the triśūla, while the lion looks on. Devī does not show any strain or effort in this confrontation. On the other hand, she looks languorously graceful and seems in serene repose as if this was something that had to be got through as a daily chore. The writhing Mahiṣa at her feet, looks imploringly up at her as though requesting her to give him release quickly. Though the lion looks fierce and as though he is advancing towards the foe, he is as yet not involved in the fight. All the eight arms of the Goddess are held aloft showing the various weapons held in them, but her serenity underlines her supremacy that though she holds the weapons, she has no need to wield them.

The other panel is from Haripur, (Mayurbhanj, Orissa)[624] a few centuries later than the Aihole panel. Here the composition is similar to the Aihole one, though a human figure is seen emerging partially from the felled buffalo. Devī's stance shows mental determination, though physically it is an effortless event. Her face looks harsh. Though the demon is not very clear, and is partly mutilated, it can be surmised from the fallen figure in a writhing pose, that the end has come and the demon realises his helplessness. The Pallava and Chalukya sculptors emphasize the effortless grace of the Goddess, whereas the Orissa sculptor underlines the calm but determined action of Devī.

In a very early sculpture of the goddess Durgā, in a Mahabalipuram panel, she stands benignly under an umbrella. She is four-armed, her back hands carrying a conch and a discus; she is surrounded by *gaṇas* and there are two seated human figures, one of whom is in the process of cutting off his own head. This Tantric attitude is surprising in such an early sculpture. In the Early Coḷa period also, Durgā is depicted in a benign posture, (cf Pl. 41) though standing on Mahiṣa's head, her many arms hold different weapons, but usually the back left hand holds a conch, and sometimes she has an abhaya mudrā in her front right hand. In the South, there are many depictions of Devī annihilating Śumbha and Niśumbha, but named Pidāri, or Bhadrakālī. Around the 8th cent. A.D., she is in the centre, surrounded by the Sapta Mātṛs in temples built by Śuvaran Māran, Varaguṇa Pāṇḍian, and others.[625] In the Southern depictions Durgā as Mahiṣāsuramardinī or, Vindhyavāsinī is always depicted with a kucabanda. In later iconography Nappinnai was given this vesture to distinguish her from other gopis.[626] The skull sometimes pictured in iconography, as held in Devī's hand is said to symbolise the universe. According to Rahasyāgama. Prapañcāmbuja hastā ca Kapālinyucyate parā.[627] Vijayālaya Coḷa thought that his victories in establishing the Coḷa kingdom were due to the divine grace of the goddess Niśumbhasūdani. Under the Coḷas Lākulīśa sect had good influence over the temples. In Coḷīśvaram, during Rajendra I's reign, the temple was under this sect's control. There is a Durgā idol installed in the Somesvara temple in Kunigal (Tumkur Dist.), a Ganga sculpture dated to circa 800 A.D. Here the Kālāmukha (Kaula) form of worship was changed into a saumya form by installing a Śrī Cakra in front of the deity. Mahiṣāsuramardinī sculptures in the South of notable importance excluding the Mahabalipuram one are one in the Kailasanatha temple built by Rajasimta in Kanchipuram, and one more in the vicinity of this temple. Pārvatī occurs only in the Ardhanārī form. It is to be noted that in the Pallava period the most popular depiction of the Goddess was as Mahiṣāsuramardinī. In a panel in the Kailasanatha

Temple, (fourth from the NW corner of Vimava, North Side) Devī, fully accrutred is standing gracefully poised, with one foot as the lion mount, ready to anntlulate any enemy (cf. Pl. 42). In the Mahiṣamardinī Cave in Mahabalipuram, the Madhu-Kaiṭabha episode with the sleeping Viṣṇu is depicted, but the Goddess is not depicted. But her involvement as Madhu-Kaiṭabha Praśamanī is suggested in the grouping of the characters.

The Pallava sculpture of Mahiṣāsuramardinī at Mahabalipuram is a seventh century master-piece. The Goddess' figure is svelte and taut, and she has not dealt the mortal blow yet. The demon is seen standing in a stunned and confused manner, preliminary to loosing his judgement and agility in self-preservation. His huge hulk as juxtaposed against the small, gracefully poised figure of the Goddess, can be seen as a personification of Tāmasic qualities. He stands with his arrogance shaken, with disbelief that he could be laid low by a mere woman. He had thought of this sex with such contempt that he did not consider it necessary to ask for immortality against any female enemy. (cf frontis piece)

Mahiṣa transforms himself into many animal forms, before finally emerging as a human being. These are seen as symbols of a particular characteristic or power he externalises one by one, and by steps his energies are wiped out. The ultimate in externalisation of the inner vision would be the Universe, a reflection of our Māyā, Illusion. The asura who is the lord of Māyā does not lack this illusory power and thus in quick succession he takes many forms. When Māyā is removed god-realisation sets in and there is no duality. The bison shedding his animal nature becomes Śiva and attains beatitude. The Goddess is unconcerned with the onerous task ahead of her. This is seen in the easy way she carries her weapons as she rides the lion. The demon is going to fall in a moment. The contrast in the massive form and stance of Mahiṣa and the slim figure of the Goddess is also symbolic of their respective spiritual status. Pallava work always depicts momentous periods in myths with restraint and lightness. They depict not the final climax when tensions may dissolve but a fleeting second earlier, when tension is taut and the excitement of the final denoument is building to a crescen do. A symbolic analysis of this sculpture has been attempted.

In Ellora, in the Rāmeśvaram shrine on the east wall, the same moment of annihilation of the demon is sculpted in massive proportions (cf Plate 43). [628] The demon is in the form of a buffalo, Devī holding his face in lower left hand and lifting the sword in the lower right hand to deal the mortal blow. There is resolution on her face, but she is slow in her motion, as though showing she is beyond Time. Mahiṣa is seen as the materialisation of self-centered forces. Devī is in repose even in this taut moment of annihilation, of the arrogant power which took onto itself the suzerainty of the universe, throwing it into disorder. Devī here shows not the tautness of battle but the serene assurance of carrying out whatever has already been fated. The calmness underlines her maternal characteristic that patiently undertakes the destruction of evil, to protect her children, who cry out to her in bewildered agony.

A century later, (circa 750-850 A.D.) the panel in Kailāsanātha temple[629] depicts the same dramatic moment of climax. The adversaries are actually fighting in the final clash, though the buffalo is moving forwards and has not been dealt the mortal blow. The deposed gods are hovering above the scene, anxious for the outcome of the battle, or rather since the outcome of the encounter is already predestined, they show anxiety to get their positions back. The lion is fierely moving forward, to attack the demon in its own right. Three arrows simultaneously discharged from Devī's bow are about to hit the demon, who is disturbed and distraught and heaving the mace in a massive effort to hit his adversary. Tension of the battle is shown by the fierceness of her own attendants and the lion's belligerent movement forward, and by the anxiety shown by the waiting devas. It is not shown by the principal actors themselves. In an Eastern Ganga (8th cent. A.D.) panel in the Someśvara temple, Mukhalingam, the buffalo is transformed into half-human, the mortal blow is to follow. There is grace and valour in Devī's stones (cf.pl. 44). This panel is unique because there is a narrative depiction at the bottom describing the event.

In Vaital Deul, Bhubaneshwar, (circa 1000 A.D.), the final moment of annihilation is again depicted. Unlike the Rāmeśvaram cave panel, here[630] there is grace and vigour seen in the Goddess as she moves against the Tāmasic, massive asura, fallen at her feet. He is also troubled by the lion, and his tail is held by Devī in one of her hands. Her right foot presses the demon down and the triśūla is sent in its final thrust. There is resignation of his fate and acceptance of mokṣa at her hands, and he seems not to fight but support Devī in delivering him from the Tāmasic coils enmeshing him to earthiness. All her hands are holding weapons aloft, for the final onslaught, but Devī is calm, as much as to show compassion in delivering him. The brutal strength overpowered by the vital force of Devī is depicted in such later sculptures. Where restraint and suggestiveness was the Pallava motto, liberal depiction of the power struggle was the hallmark of later iconography. The decadence of the theme is seen in the Belur sculphere of the 12th century A.D., where the emphasis shifts from the fight, to rich ornamentation. Mahiṣa is quiescent in the lower corner (cf. Pl. 45).

The Rashtrakutas had as their emblem on their flag "*śyena*", because the Goddess Vindhyavāsinī was said to have taken the form of a falcon and saved the kingdom. She became known as Rāṣṭra Śyena.[631] There is a Mahiṣāsuramardinī icon in the Gondesvara temple at Sinnar (near Nasik, Maharashtra). She stands on her left foot, and her right foot rests on a buffalo. Her arms are mutilated, but the weapons are partially seen. A lion in a fierce mein is looking on in the right corner. There is an icon of Cāmuṇḍā, emaciated, with pendulous breasts, also mutilated. These are in niches on the eastern doorway.

The temple of Aesvara, to the North-West of the town of Sinnar and in many temples in Maharashtra (Jhodgā, Ambernath, Chandor to name only a few) in the wall niches, there are small figures of Mahiṣāsuramardinī and sometimes figures of Kālī used as decorations. In Berar, in the outskirts of the town in Basri Takli, there are bands of mother goddess figures on the outer walls of the shrine. These temples would belong roughly to 1176 A.D. or thereabouts. Fiftysix miles north of Ahmednagar, in the village of Kokamthạn, in a subshrine of a temple there is an aniconic image of Jagadmbā Devī, washed with ochre. (Henry Cousens lists many more in his well-catalogued "Medieval Temples of Dekhan"). A copper icon now in the British Museum, of Mahiṣāsuramardinī, seated with the lion at her feet is unique in this that she is lustrated by two elephants. This was from Kashmir.

Conclusion

This rough survey would give an idea of the vast diffusion of the Mahiṣāsuramardinī icons in time and space. This attests to the popularity the Great Goddess enjoyed bridging many dynasties of rulers. The foreign kings came under the spell of her cult and built many temples to freeze their devotion to her in eternity. The icons show a slow evolution in the concept of the confrontation between the adversaries, and this necessitated slight variations in its depiction. The artistry which started with the Kushanas, who are a watershed in Devī iconography since there are none discovered earlier than these, burgeoned in the Gupta Age. The dynasties, either contemporaneous with them or slightly after them, did not let the idea fade, but took the theme up and presented it with great devotion and artistry. Thus no icon of Mahiṣāsuramardinī can be judged to be of a poor representation. The local cults earlier than the DM. must have helped in the formation of the literature and iconography. The interpretations were in varied media from terra-cotta to metals. Even today, folk art of Orissa, Gujarat, Maharashtra, etc., depict the theme on cloth.

It would be appropriate to conclude this survey on iconography with a brief study of the two important concepts underlying iconography: Symbolism which expresses philosophy in icons, and the principles of composition which governs the sculptures.

Aesthetics In Art

In language, the beginning is phonetic when the words and the object coincide, and when fully developed the difference is vast. Similarly, in the beginning of the expression of art, the aim is magical, not aesthetic. Therefore in the beginning of the evolution of the spiritual process, art makes images which have an immediate validity and truth. So also in a mythical dance; the player does not represent a god, but he *is* the god. This is also the truth of a mythical play which is the seed for all future dramatic art. It has no aesthetics as its norm, but the magical presence of the 'here' and 'now'. When we understand the magical potency in the mythical ideas, we can appreciate the resultant power in a name or an image. Thus, myth clings to the magical efficacy of the forms, language to signification, and then comes art, when it is only the representation of the inherent essence of a thing and ceases to be an image of its form. Thus, we find a gradation when the spirit creates forms, but understands and rises above them.

Coomaraswamy,[633] takes the two opposing terms 'parokṣa', and pratyakṣa' while explaining the stages towards understanding Indian art forms. Parokṣa, is indirect, and is the only means of depicting the devas, that is through symbolic referrents. On the human level, pratyakṣa is direct and is possible because we can depict what is obvious. Religious literature is a symbolic means to understand the divine. This and also the visual art forms are all the parokṣa method. If an individual is able to experience oneness with the Supreme through spiritual realization then he has a pratyakṣa experience of God. Icons act in a similar manner to language, and are the means to help us understand the Supreme. Thus iconography is a symbolic expression to make known to us what is unknown, but what we know as existing. The multivalency in the symbolism of an iconography can also be understood when we realise that parokṣa and pratyakṣa are two different levels of cognition. But this difference need not be unsurmountable but can be reduced as we progress through the various levels starting from the grossest and the earthiest.

Symbolism and the Principles of Composition In Iconography

An analysis of the composition of the forms in the famous panel of Mahiṣāsuramardinī at Mahabalipuram is attempted now, along with the symbolism underlying it.

In Hindu theology, Divine Truth is called *Īkṣaṇa* or *Darśana*, from the root 'to see', and one who perceives this truth is called a Seer or a Ṛṣi. Thus, a sculpture helps in the primary action of 'perceiving' truth, when at one glance we perceive, understand and assimilate the Truth.

The principles of composition of sculpture are considered so important, that only the illiterate are said to be satisfied with its aesthetic beauty, but, the true student of art is satisfied only on studying those principles underlying the art form. These principles are the basic laws which govern any visible representation of art. They are more necessary for a tradition bound art, where the symmetry of cosmic forms and metaphysical ideas together formulate a sculpture. Though these principles are only abstract theories, they are vital for any expression of art. Symbolism in art and principles of composition are two equally important legs on which any theory of art should stand. Some rules must have been laid down even in the distant period of our sculpture, because similar themes are found treated in a similar manner in the same period and diffused over a wide area.

The lines which break up a sculpture, beyond serving a functional act, might also have a symbolic value. For the Indian artist, line, form and space are not used arbitrarily, but, according to its primary significance. Every tiny or curve line has a special significance. Life-force animates matter and either by expansion or contraction it creates forms. These outer shapes lead us towards its inner conception. Different movements of the life-force create different forms in sculpture. Thus every line and space in a sculpture is a depiction of a facet of the life-force and is a direct example of God. The various fundamental Geometric forms have, inherent in them, symbolism of divine or transcendental concept.[634] Forms and lines have their individual function, character, and mode of expression. This is independent of their place in a sculpture. They show their primary significance in our subconscious. Their role in an art form is of secondary importance. We form symbolic concepts by imbibing ideas through literature or ideology. But form symbolism is of primary significance and therefore more potent. Such images which synthesize in themselves measure, proportion, form, line, movement, and space-direction are ultimate in visual beauty, and imbue us with the spark of the divine.

The sculptures were not merely using proportions to show harmony in composition, but had a certain symbolic expression as well. They have implicit in them a symbolic representation of metaphysical facts. They thus are representations of intuition and high standards of artistic evolution, but with roots deep in metaphysics. The uniform excellence and artistic mastery show that there were rules in this discipline which were followed seriously. The individual genius in each sculpture overlays archetypal symbols, which get concretised. Similar to theology, religious art expresses truth at different levels, according to the spiritual level of the beholder. Man's creativity transforms the impressions gained from his surroundings and with the symbols arising from his unconscious; he translates these into sculptures. Religious art is able to express itself in sculptural form, because these arise more from intuition than from intellect, and icons are primarily forms of intuitive symbolism. Sculpture is a gross representation, and farther away from the spiritual ideas it conveys than the word. Man thus lost in the aesthetic enjoyment of appreciating gross images, might lose the symbolic significance altogether. Thus, though language and sculpture have similar symbolism at work it is easily apparent, while reading, than when seeing gross representations. Though nāma and rūpa describe the same divinity, their mode of operation as much as their media are immensely different. Literature, that is, sound operates in Time, whereas architecture or form operates in Space. Visual representation is expressed at once whereas audio expression can be assimilated by stages. Sculpture suppresses the Time factor, preventing changes and preserving the timeless essence of things. Later, dhyāna ślokas translated Nāma into Rūpa, and helped the sculptor to understand the deity. These are not literally translated into icons, but he infuses them with life not at variance with the truth they symbolise through his intuition. True symbolism abounds in nature and man transforms it. Modern man who has lost touch with our great traditions appreciates art for aesthetics, not for its metaphysical symbolism. We have to rediscover the symbolism by retracing our steps to the religious texts. Since religious images are born out of intuition and not discursive thinking, these could be understood only by a person in total harmony with the surroundings and the cosmic law; the image is also delineated according to the relationship between the sculptor and the divinity.

These sculptures are not an end in themselves, but are only the means. Through intuition these material forms undergo a subtle change, discarding their phenomenal form and get charged with the transcendent meaning. Sacred images are primarily not to give us aesthetic satisfaction, but they serve to concentrate our will onto a spiritual focus. These images born out of spiritual intuition lead men back through meditation into the truths hidden in them. They serve as doors between the material and the spiritual worlds.

Analysing the sculptural compositions on the panels of cave temples, a similarity is seen between them and the Tantric Yantras and Maṇḍalas. The difference lies in this that the space between the intersecting lines of the triangles is filled with sculpted figures instead of geometric ones. The whole composition devolves inside a circle, sometimes as in the Mahabalipuram panel, two circles, the area inside them is triangulated with diameters and parallel chords. All lines relate to the central point of the panel, centre of the middle circle, directly or indirectly. They thus simulate the concentric layout of the Yantras, and assist the devotee in meditation.

Principles of Composition[635]

A panel of sculpture is divided into three levels of: lowest, physical (Bhūḥ); the atmosphere (Bhūvaḥ) denoting the psychic plane; and the heavenly plane (Suvaḥ). A circle symbolises compactness and a line, speed and direction. Since all lines have an inherent symbolism, they possess a fundamental character according to their direction and incline. When all these space-directions of lines and curves are brought together, they may complement each other or compete with each other, but never lose their innate character. These patterns give us a greater understanding of the sculpture, emotionally. Analysis of the sculpture along geometric lines does in no way detract from its value, but on the other hand strengthens its validity. It does not obstruct our understanding of the artist's perception. Principles of composition only help in the physical formation of the sculpture. The sculptures are not as is usually thought to help the illiterate understand scriptures. They appeal to the sensitivity of the highest order and assist in bridging the world or Māyā to the world of the Transcendental Reality. Its essence is understood only when the viewer is completely attuned to it.

It may be argued that every sculpture may not be the outcome of intuition, specially when royalty commanded sculptors to complete a complex within a specified time, as when commemorating some event. This would be true only for the minor ornamental embellishments, and not for the sculptures of some import. Further, whatever the branch of fine arts, the basic rules are imbibed and become part of the artist's ethos. Intuition overlays these with its imagery. Without grammar, art would not be harmonious, nor would it evoke in us a sublime response.

The excellence in the panel we consider below is in its happy balance of intuition and rules of the art. It satisfies both the devotee and the discerning critic.

The dynamic movements of the sculpture reveal the inner meaning of the composition. The forms cease to be mere embodiments and become representations of powers, actions or tendencies. The network of vertical and horizontal lines dividing the sculpture is the space-division of the sculpture. The chords running parallel to the oblique diameters divide the circle further, and this is called the time-division. The lines here denote movement and are kinetic. All these lines fix their own size and position and fix the forms in relation to each other.

The panel on first casual inspection looks as though the forms were loosely put together. But there is an underlying unity in the pairs of opposing figures balancing each other. On the top of the panel there are two opposing warriors. The umbrellas of Devī and *Mahiṣa* complement each other by their angle of inclination. There are the two warriors of the two camps, facing opposite (outside) directions on the topmost corners of the frame. Devī's sword and *asura's* club also slant in complementary angles.

Conclusion

The whole picture is of Durgā brandishing weapons and attributes in her extended hands, and advancing forwards, and Mahiṣa retreating slowly, but in a last attempt at defiance is turning his face towards Devī. In this configuration, contrasting Devī's rigid vertical posture with Mahiṣa's learing stance one would expect the later's victory. But the triumph of Devī symbolises the victory of divine power over brute strength.

There is tension between the main actors as they face each other. The shields of the soldiers on top are clashing, and a plumb line from this point divides the panel into the two opposing groups. The tensions are different. That of the Asura is heavy, tāmasic and earth-bound. That of Devī seems effortless with divine grace filling her form, and symbolised in the arms spreading out like the glorious rays of the sun. Mahiṣa's energy is coming from the nether regions and will be brought to nought very soon; whereas, Devī's form does not touch the ground at all, and she seems to descend on him in one fell swoop. Though the umbrella over Devī and the stance of the demon are parallel, while the former shows forward movement, the latter shows confused retreat. The parallel lines of the fleeing and falling warriors also hint at the end. The small rounded forms seem filled with divine joy, and are seen to advance in the wake of Devī's buoyant energy.

The alternating and antagonistic principles involved in this tableaux show the pulsating cosmic process where they are necessary for each other in the eternal circle of creation and destruction. The left and right portions of the panel symbolise negative and positive elements. The tension between them activates them into a constant flux of the renewing circle. Thus, the two opposing parts may have remained disjointed but are connected by the centre area between them symbolising *Brahmāṇḍa*, the Cosmic Engineering which encompasses Creation.

REFERENCES

1. Vats, M.J., *Excavation at Harappa*, ABORI, XXI, pp. 287-92.
2. Kosambi, D.D., *Myth and Reality*, pp. 2-3,90-91,122
3. X. 127. 1-8.
4. Sū. 2 and 3.
5. XIX, 47-50.
6. VS. 34.32.
7. 9.29.
8. Appended after ṚV.X. 127.
9. Stanza 3.
10. Stanza 4.
11. Stanza 5., etc.
12. AV, XIX. 50.2.
13. 2.77 - Coburn, T.B. - DM, p. 117.
14. Macdonell, A.A., *The Bṛhad - Devatā*, quoted in Ibid.
15. 3. 8. 2. ff
16. ŚB. 6.7.3.8; Kāṭhaka Saṁ. 24.5; Agrawala, P.K., *Goddess Cult in Ancient India*, pp. 108-10.
17. III. 25
18. 10.1.
19. Neumann, E., *The Great Mother*, p. 219.
20. cf. Ch.III Sn. Ambikā.

21. III.57.
22. 1.6, 10, 4-5.
23. Banerjea J.N., *Paurāṇic and Tāntric Religion*, p. 114, fn.6.
24. Agrawala, P.K., *Op. cit.*, p. 91, fns. 277-78.
25. X.30, Weber quoted in ERE, ed. Hastings, p. 117.
26. Taitt. 1.8.6.
27. Hiraṇyakesin GS. 11.3.8.
28. Sircar, D.C., *The Śākta Pīṭhas*, pp.101-02.
29. Pāraskara GS (III.8.).
30. Sharma, P.K., *Śakti Cult in Ancient India*, p. 277.
31. Das, S.K., *Śakti or Divine Power*, p. 41.
32. Quoting W. Norman Brown in O'Flaherty, *The Origin of Evil in Hindu Mythology*, p. 83-84.
33. DM. 3.34, *pānamuttamaṁ papau.*
34. Mazumdar, B.C., *Durgā, Her Origin and History*, JRAS, Art. XIII, 1906, pp. 355-8.
35. cf. also Hopkins, *Epic Mythology*, p. 225.
36. Mbh. Āraṇyaka Par.
37. Werner, Karel-Men, Gods and Powers in the Vedic Outlook; pp. 14-23, JRAS, 1982, No.1.
38. *Mātṛrupeṇa Saṁsthitā*, DM. V., 71-73.
39. Ch. CLV, 170.
40. Ch. 26, 26-8.
41. *Ibid.*
42. Payne, E.A., *The Śāktas*, p. 68.
43. Bhattacharyya, IMG, p. 68.
44. Banerjea, J.N., DHI, p. 492.
45. Sharma, *Śakti Cult in Ancient India*, p. 201.
46. *Ibid.*, p. 122.
47. Bhattacharyya, IMG, p. 62.
48. Kosambi, D.D., *Origin of Brahmin Gotras*, p. 71, JBBRAS, 26.1. 1950.
49. Chattopadhyaya, S., *The Evolution of Theistic Sects in Ancient India*, p. 52.
50. Rām. 3, 16, 43; Mbh. S 1, 172, 28; 1. 187.4.
51. Hopkins, E.W. - EM, p. 225
52. 3-X. 1.7.
53. Hopkins, EM, p. 224.
54. IV. 8.21 - *Durgāttārayase Durge tattvaṁ Durgā smṛtā, janaiḥ/*
55. 4.11.
56. Sarayu Prasad Sarma's *Saptaśati Sarvasvam*, quoted in DM. ed. "Aṇṇā",

p. 123, fn. 11.

57. Chanda, R.P., *Indian Archaeology: A review*, p. 69; quoted in Bhattacharyya, IMG, p. 61.
58. 6.11.83 - Srivastava, M.C.P., *Op. cit.*, p. 110, f. 6.
59. II. 52-53.
60. II.27.42-43, Bhattacharyya, IMG, p. 68.
61. IX.1.
62. Bhandarkar, R.G. - Vaiṣṇavism, Śaivism and Minor Religious Systems, p. 144.
63. VI.23; ensuing numbering in the brackets denote the line number.
64. Sharma, P.K., Śakti Cult in Ancient India, p. 31.
65. 1.7.5; 1.69.4; 2.67.3.
66. V. 8.
67. 2-4
68. Rai, Ganga Sagar, A Note on Kātyāyanī, pp. 102-3, Purāṇa, XIX.1.1977.
69. Skanda P, 6.116. 12-13; Sharma, *Ibid.*, p. 254, fn. 1.
70. 6.115. 21-22; *Ibid.* p. 253, fn. 6.
71. Skanda p., 6.114.8.
72. 259. 55-69; *Ibid.*, p. 254.
73. Mbh. 4.8.15.
74. Paragraph 58, p. 46, tr by Schoff, W.H.
75. i.e. Parlia which is Modern Travancore, cf. note 58. p. 234, *Ibid.*
76. Agrawal V.S., The Glorification of the Great Goddess, p. 218.
77. *Ibid.*, p. 219.
78. M.K., *Śākambharī: The Headless Goddess*, ABORI, LXVIII, 1987, pp. 281-93.
79. I. 70.331; 82.14-15; and 101.6; Gangadharan, M., Had Aparṇā (Pārvatī) Any other Sisters?; Purāṇa XVIII, 2, July 1976. pp. 153-161.
80. Eliade, *Patterns in Comparative Religion*, p. 280.
81. James, E.O., *The Cult of the Mother Goddess*, p. 242.
82. Hopkins, E.W., EM., p. 225.
83. IV. 1.49.
84. Srivastava, M.C.P., *Mother Goddess*, p. 65; quoting Agrawala, V.S. in India as Known to Pāṇinī, pp. 357-358, University of Lucknow, 1953.
85. Hopkins E.W., E.M., p. 225, Mbh. 6.23.5.
86. Bhattacharyya, IMG., pp. 60-61.
87. Chs. 146-60.
88. *Matsya*, p. 154-75.
89. 213. 118; Mukherji, The Cult of Ekanamsa, IHQ, XXXV, Mar 1959, pp. 189-208; this reference could not be located in the editions available.

90. Ch. 160.
91. *Ibid.*, this reference also could not be located.
92. Mbh. III. 208. 8.
93. Vaudeville, Charlotte, *Op. cit.*, p. 6.
94. Bhīṣma Par. 23.
95. Dikshit, *The Mother Goddess*, p. 101.
96. Ch. 45.
97. Vaudeville, Charlotte, Krishna Gopala, Radha and the Great Goddess, p. 8.
98. Critical notes to the above chapter, p. 794.
99. HV, Vol. 1, 47.
100. VI. 23.14.
101. Kālī, Kapālī,I. 10; Caṇḍī, p. 9.
102. Umā, Śveta, l.17; Brahmavidyā, l.21; Vedamātā, l.24.
103. 96. śls 11-16.
104. Vaudeville, - *Op.cit.*, p. 6.
105. Mukherji, S.C. - *The Cult of Ekānamśā*, IHQ. XXXV.1. Mar 1959, p.p. 108-208.
106. *Ibid.*, p. 193
107. Misra, K.C., The Cult of Jagannatha quoted in Vaudeville - *Op. rit* p. 9, fn. 21.
108. *Ibid.*
109. Joint article by Eschmann, A; Kulke H; and Tripathy G.C. eds. The Cult of Jagannath and the Regional Tradition of Orissa, Book Review by Sitakant Mahapatra in *The Time of India*, 23-9-1979.
110. Critical Notes on 48th ch. in HV. p. 794.
111. 57, 37.
112. Hazra, R.C., *Studies in the Upapuranas*, Vol. II, p. 198, in P.K. Sharma, *Op.cit.*, p. 123, fn. 2.
113. III. 2., 25-40.
114. CLVII. sl;. 3-19.
115. IV. 8.
116. VI. 23.
117. 47.53.
118. VI. 23; in the following account, numbers in brackets denote the line in the Stuti.
119. EM; P. 225.
120. Vaudeville, C. *Op.cit.* p. 6.
121. HV, after 47.52; the numbering in the brackets denote the line in Stuti.
122. Viṣṇu Par., chs. 47-48; Viṣṇu P. V. 1ff, Tiwari, J.N., *Op.cit.*, p. 67, fn. 52;

Bhāg. P.X. 1ff.

123. Srivastava, M.G., *Mother Goddess*, p. 114.

124. Payne, E.A. - *The Śāktas*, pp. 38-39

125. Hopkins, EM., pp. 226-27.

126. *Ibid.*

127. HV. Vi. Par. 108. 5-14.

128. *Ibid.*, 120. 4-47.

129. Virāta Par.

130. RV. X. 92.

131. Katha. Up.

132. Bhag. G. VIII. 22.

133. Gupta, A., *Eulogy of Parāśaktī by God*, With Notes, pp. 1-7; *Purāṇa* XIX. 1, p. 7.

134. Gupta, A.S., *Eulogy of Devī by Maheśvara, Purāṇa XV*. 1, p.3.

135. Soifer, Deborah. A., *Towards an Understanding of Viṣṇu's Avatāras, Purāna* XVIII. 2, p. 132.

136. Tiwari, J.N., *Goddess Cult in Ancient India*, p. 15.

137. Vāyu P. 9.82-84; Sharma - *Op. cit.*, pp. 69-70.

138. *Ibid.*, p. 122.

139. III. 26. 18-19.

140. IX. 38.55.

141. IX. 50. 54.

142. Bhattacharyya, *History of Śākta Religion*, p. 75.

143. Tiwari, *Op.cit.*, p. 17.

144. *Ibid.*, p. 12.

145. *Ibid.*, p. 13.

146. Banerji, Sastri, *Asura Institutions*, p. 517; JBORS. XII Part II.

147. *The Classical Age: History and Culture of the Indian People* ,Vol. III p. 446.

148. 154.561, Tiwari, *Op.cit.*, p. 70.

149. *Ibid.*, p. 68.

150. Mazumdar, R.C., *Op. cit*, p. 358.

151. Sharma, *Op. cit.*, p. 277.

152. 4.15-16; Sharma, *Ibid.*, p. 169. fn. 8.

153. Hudṣon, Dennis, Pinnai, Krishna's Cowherd Wife; in *The Divine Consort*, p. 260

154. Tiwari, *Op. cit.*, pp. 71-72.

155. Held, G.J., *The Mahabharata, An Ethnological Study*, p. 218.

156. Briffault, R., *The Mothers*, Vol. 3, p. 51.

157. Farnell, L.R., *The Attributs of God*, p. 50.

158. Gupta, A.S., *Glorification of the Goddess Rātri, With Notes, Purāṇa*, XVIII. 1. 1978, p. 6.
159. Gupta, A.S., *Eulogy of Devī by Maheśvara*, With Notes, *Purāṇa*, XV.1. 1973, pp. 1-5.
160. II. 2.4. 42-47; Sharma, *Op. cit.*, p. 233, fn. 5.
161. 50. 22; *Ibid.*, p. 232, fn. 1.
162. V. 2-5, *Ibid.*, pp. 6-8.
163. 4.272. 3-73; Ibid., p. 229, fn. 11.
164. Rao, Gopinatha, EHI, Vol. I, Part II, pp. 356 ff.
165. Skandayāmala, quoted in above.
166. Srivastava, M.C.p., *Op. cit.*, p. 110.
167. 11.54-55.
168. X. 41-42.
169. *Devī Bhāg*. p. VII. 6. 18.21.
170. cf. also *Ibid.*, VII. 30.
171. Sircar, D.C., *The sakta Pithas*, p. 15.
172. Kosambi, D,D., *Myth and Reality*, p. 86.
173. *Ibid.*, p. 87.
174. Vaudeville, C., *Op. cit.*, p. 9, fn. 27.
175. Cowell, E.B., The Jatakas, pp. 19-37, No. 539; quoted in Srivastava, *Op. cit.*, p. 66, fn. 3.
176. *Op. cit*, p. 165-68; quoted in Srivastava, *Ibid.*, p. 66, fn.7.
177. cf. ch. II, Adichanallur burials.
178. Chatterji, S.K., *Dravidian Origins* and the Begginings of *Indian Civilization*; The *Modern Revieew*, Vol. XXXV, pp. 665-79.
179. *Ibid.*, p. 678.
180. *Ibid.*, p. 679.
181. Przyluski, J., *Pre-Aryan and Pre-Dravidian in India*, p. 11.
182. *Ibid.*
183. Nagasami, R., *Ninnayum Pukaḻuven Tāye*, pp. 212-14.
184. vv 257-58.
185. 218, 1-2.
186. PP. 258-59.
187. Srivastava, *Op.cit.*, p. 82.
188. Agrawala, V.S., *Ancient Indian Folk-Cults*, p. 159.
189. X. 63. 20.
190. Agrawala, V.S., *Ibid.*
191. *Ibid.*
192. Hudson, Dennis, *Pinnai Krishna's Cowherd Wife*, p. 258.

193. Yocum, G.E., *Comments : The Divine Consort in South India*, p. 278.
194. VII.30.
195. XIII, Venkataraman, K.R., *Devī Kāmākshī in Kāñcī*, p. 13.
196. *Ibid.*
197. Venkataraman, *Ibid.*, pp. 16-23.
198. Vide ch. IV. Sn. Village Goddesses.
199. Bhattacharji, S., *The Indian Theogony*, p. 203.
200. The classical Age-Gen. ed. Majumdar, R.C., Vol. III, pp. 444-45.
201. James, *Myth and Ritual in the Ancient Near East*, p. 123.
202. *Ibid.*, p. 125.
203. *Ibid.*, p. 191.
204. Bhattacharji, S., *Op.cit*, p. 175.
205. *Ibid.*, p. 175, fn.1.
206. DM. 11.49.
207. Bhattacharji, - *Op. cit*, p. 165.
208. Tiwari - *Op. cit*, p. 91.
209. Jung, C.G. and Kerenyi, C., *Introduction to a Science of Mythology*, pp. 143-44.
210. Jung, C.G., *Psychology of The Unconscious*, p. 224.
211. Andrew, *Myth, Ritual and Religion*, Vol. II, p. 249.
212. Bhattacharyya, *History of Indian Erotic Religion*, p. 16.
213. *Ibid.*, p. 8.
214. Meghadūtam, I. 34; Raghuvaṁśa, VI. 34.
215. Diskalkar, D.B., *A New Inscription of Chandragupta II of G.S. 61 Found in Mathura*, pp. 166-70, ABORI XVIII.
216. Tiwari, J.N., *Op. cit.*, p. 90; Banerjea, J.N., *Paurāṇic and Tāntric Religion*, p. 101.
217. Bhattacharyya, *History of Śākta Religion*, p. 84.
218. *Age of the Mauryas and the Nandas*, p. 197.
219. *The Sutta-nipāta, Sastri*, K.A.N., *Op. cit.*, pp. 289-90.
220. *Ibid.*, p. 290.
221. *Ibid.*, p. 324.
222. *Ibid.*, p. 325.
223. II. I; III. 10.
224. *Ibid.*, p. 349-50.
225. Srivastava, M.C.P., *Op.cit.*, p. 74.
226. *The Sociology of Religion*, p. 96.
227. Max Weber, - *Ibid.*, p.. 107.
228. *Ibid.*, p. 102.

229. *Ibid.*, p. 103.
230. Max Weber, *Ibid.*, p. 23.
231. Refs. taken from Srivastava , *Op. cit.*, p. 9.
232. Jacobson Doranne and Wadley, Susan, *Women in India*, p. 9.
233. Weber, Max, *Op. cit.*, p. 104.
234. 4.1.32.
235. In Bharyā(a)dhikārika Adhikaraṇaṁ.
236. 4.1.49.
237. Majumdar, R.C., gen. ed., *The Classical Age*, Vol. III, p. 570.
238. *Ibid.*
239. cf. ch. III. Sn. Lakṣmī.
240. Yocum, Glenn. E., *Comments : The Divine Consort in south India*, p. 280
241. Jung, C.G., *Archetype and the Collective Unconscious*, p. 3.
242. cf. under Kālī.
243. Jung, *Op. cit.*, p. 161.
244. cf. Sn. Kālī.
245. Spratt, P, *Hindu Culture and Personality*, p. 82.
246. Bhattacharyya, IMG, p. 268.
247. cf. Brubaker, Richard, L., Comments, *The Goddess and the Polarity of the Sacred*, p. 205.
248. Prathama Carita, DM.
249. Act 2.20.
250. Hudson, Dennis, *Pinnai, Krishna's Cowherd Wife*, p. 256.
251. tr. V.R.R. Dikshitar, pp. 212-13.
252. 7.100-102; a mention is made of the Kāralar sect giving narabali after worshipping Durgā.
253. Banerjea, *Paurānic and Tāntric Religion*, p. 11.
254. Ucchvāsa 2, p. 26.
255. pp. 143-146, *Pūrvabhāga*.
256. pp. 455-65.
257. p. 453.
258. p. 456.
259. pp. 457-58.
260. p. 463.
261. pp. 461-63.
262. Act V.
263. Act V.
264. p. 103.

265. p. 109. 22.
266. vv. 285-86, 290.
267. v. 319.
268. vv. 338 and 305.
269. 6th. *Ucchvāsa*, p. 166.
270. 8th *Ucchvāsa*, pp. 272 and 278.
271. Tiwari, J.N., *Op. cit.*, pp. 77-78, fn. 127.
272. Act X, *Ibid.*, p. 77,
273. Renou, Louis, *Religions of Ancient India*, p. 52.
274. 59.19 ; Banerjea, J.N., *Paurāṇic and Tāntric Religion*, p. 120.
275. Chs. 82-92.
276. Kane, P.V. HDS. V. ii, 854-55; Bhattacharrya, The IMG, p. 120; Pargiter, F.E., *Markandey Puran*, Intro. p. xx; Tiwari, J.N., *Goddess Cults in Ancient India*, pp. 74-75; Mazumdar, R.C. - gen. ed., *The Classical Age*. p. 298; O'Flaherty, W.D., *Asceticism and Eroticism in the Mythology of Siva*, p. 14.
277. Pargiter, F.E., *Markandey Puran*, Intro. pp. vi-vii.
278. Coburn - DM, p. 98.
279. *The Classical Age*, Vol. III, p. 447.
280. For ideas of the non-Aryan influence a few western scholars would be Payne, Zimmer, Marshall, Piggot, Basham; and amongst the Indian Scholars are, Bhattacharyya, N.N, Sircar, D.C., Benerjea, J.N., Bhandakar etc.; D.P. Chattopadhyaya and recently Kingsley, and many others have seen the Sāṁkhyan influence in the Goddess formulation.
281. Srinivasan M.N., *Religion and Society among the Coorgs of South India*, quoted in Coburn, T.B.-DM., p. 10; for an exhaustive treatment of this idea, and also of the questions raised in the previous para., vide this author's Prolegomenon to his DM.
282. J.A.B. Buitenin, in Coburn, *Ibid.*, p. 15, fn. 43.
283. Thapar, R., *From Lineage to State*, p. 30.
284. Hazra, R.C., *The Upapurāṇas*, ABORI. XXX, Art. 6, p. 54, fn. 4.
285. Gupta, A.S., *Purāṇas and their Referencing*, *Purāṇa*, VII. 2, p. 324.
286. Thapar, R., *Op. cit.*, p. 136.
287. Gupta, A.S., *Purāṇas and their Referencing*, p. 324; also *Varāha Purāṇa*, Intro, pp. 3-4.
288. Gupta, A.S.-A Problem of Paurāṇic Text Reconstruction, Purāṇa, Vol. XII.2, p.p. 304-21.
289. Gupta, A.S.-Paurāṇic Heritage pp. 39-55, Purāṇa XVIII. 1.
290. Kane, P.V., *Op. cit.*, p. 842.
291. Gupta, A.S., *Purāṇas and their Referencing*, p. 348.
292. Gupta, A.S., Constitution of the Vāmana Purāṇa Text, p. 146.

293. Biardeau, Madeleine, *Some More Considerations About Textual Criticism*, p. 117; *Purāṇa* X.2.
294. Smith, W.C., *The Meaning and End of Religion*, Quoted in Coburn,-DM. p. 43, fn. 175.
295. Thapar, R., *Op. cit*, p. 137.
296. Coburn, T.B., *Op. cit.*, p. 47.
297. Biardeau, Madeleine, *The Story of Arjuna Kārtavīrya without Reconstruction*, p. 303; *Purāṇa* XII.2.
298. Coburn, *Op. cit.*, p. 52.
299. DM. IV. 22.
300. XII.2.
301. 4, 10, 12, 15, 16, 22, 24.
302. 7, 9, 10, 15, 16.
303. Bhandarkar, R.G., *Vaiṣṇavism, Śaivism and Minor Religious Systems*, p. 144.
304. Desai, Nileshwari, *Ancient Indian Society, Religion and Mythology as Depicted in the Markaṇḍeya Purāṇa*, p. 160.
305. ṚV. X. 125.
306. Coburn, T.B., DM, p. 116.
307. 10.1.
308. Gonda, *Change and Continuity in Indian Religion*, p. 171.
309. Coburn, DM, p. 154.
310. Banerjea, DHI, p. 526.
311. DM. 5.13.
312. 110. 125 ff.
313. VI. 168. 38.
314. Uttarkāṇḍa, 18.84-87.
315. Dange, S.A., Encyclopaedia of Puranic Beliefs and Practices, p. 951.
316. Vettam Mani—Puranic Encyclopaedia, p. 432.
317. Coburn, T.B.-DM. p. 184.
318. 4.10.
319. VII.5.
320. Desai, Nileshvari, *Ancient Indian Society*, p. 160.
321. Mbh., 4.8.9.
322. Coburn, T.B. - DM. p. 57.
323. 3. 193. 16.
324. Appendix I. 41. 1431-1434.
325. Coburn, *Op. cit.*, p. 215, fn. 11.
326. Renou, Louis, *Religions of Ancient India*, p. 62.
327. Only in later period was a myth found necessary to explain the various

sacred places of the Devī Cult, and the Sati myth fulfilled the purpose. In ancient times there was no anomaly in one man having different graves, and Tsui Goab, god of the Hottentots had more graves than Osiris of Egypt; Lang, Andrew *Custom and Myth*, pp. 205-06.

328. 3.220.8-10.

329. Srivastava, *Op. cit.*, p. 110.

330. Adh. 21.

331. Srivastava - *Op. cit.*, p. 110.

332. Choudhari, N.N., Mother Goddess Durga, pp. 32-38; *The Poona Orientalist*, XV. 1-4.

333. Agrawala, V.S., *The Glorification of the Great Goddess*, p. 5.

334. *Ibid.*, pp. xii and 8.

335. Coburn - DM. p. 58.

336. Zimmer Heinrich, *The Art of Indian Asia*, I. 95.

337. *Ibid.*, p. 100.

338. Zimmer, M., *Ibid.*, p. 101.

339. DM. 3. 40.

340. *The Sanskrit Poems of Mayūra*, p. 251.

341. cf. Infra.

342. 4; no. in brackets denote chapter numbering.

343. Agrawala, V.S., *The Glorification of the Great Goddess*, p. xiii, Intro.

344. Nos. in brackets denote śloka numbering.

345. DM. 4.

346. DM. 5.

347. DM - Aṇṇā, p. 143, fn. 16.

348. DM. 11.

349. A different meaning is given for the last part of the verse by Coburn, *Op. cit*, p. 301; For those who resorted to you have truly entered a refuge.

350. tr. by Wilson, H.H., VI, p. 223.

351. Coburn, *Ibid.*, p. 257.

352. *Ibid.*, p. 258.

353. Wilson, H.H., *Op. cit.*

354. 2.6 and 4.2 resp.

355. Raghavan, V. Śrī Devī Māhātmya, Tamil tr., Intro. p. iv.

356. *Atamāṇaṁ rathinaṁ viddhi sarīraṁ rathameva ca.*

357. *Devīsūktānī Upanisadasca, tr. Aṇṇā,* p. 20.

358. Quackenbos, G.P., *The Sanskrit Poems of Mayūra*, p. 247.

359. 3.40.

360. 3.42.

361. 7.37.44-46, Quackenbos, G.P., *Op. cit.*, p. 251, fn. p. 2.
362. Verses 42, 47, 74, 82, 89, 93, 94 and 101.
363. 18.
364. 14.
365. in vv. 39 and 64.
366. 26,47.
367. 14.21.
368. 30.
369. 91, etc.
370. Angel and Titan, *An Essay in Vedic Ontology, JAOS*, p. 374.
371. Hillebrandt, Alfred, *Vedic Mythology*, Vol. I, p.11.
372. Held, G.J., *The Mahābhārata*, p. 169.
373. Lang, Andrew, *Myth, Ritual and Religion*, p. 131.
374. Held, G.J., *Op. cit*, p. 169, quoting Oldenberg.
375. Dandekar, R.N., *Asura Varuna*, ABORI, XXI, p. 179.
376. Danielou, Alain, *Hindu Polytheism*, p. 140.
377. Shendge, *Op. cit.*, p. 195.
378. Amarakośa 1.1.7.
379. cf. ch. II, Sn. Harappan Civilization.
380. ŚB.I.5. 3. 2; 7. 2. 22; II.2. 2. 8; VI.6. 2. 11.
381. II. 36; Shendge - *Op. cit.*, p. 66.
382. O'Flaherty, The Origin of Evil in Hindu Mythology, p. 66.
383. Kātha Saṁ. 27.9 citing ṚV. 3.31.6.
384. ṚV. IV. 42.
385. *Ibid.*
386. Hillebrandt, A., *Op. cit.*, p. 269.
387. Renou, Louis - *Op. cit.*, pp. 19-20.
388. Hopkins, EM., p. 38.
389. Hale, W.E., Asura in Early Vedic Religion, p. 43.
390. ṚV. 5.42.11; verse and meaning from Hale, W.E. - *Ibid.*, pp. 42-43.
391. Dandekar, R.N., *Op. cit.*, p. 189.
392. Hale, W.E., *Op. cit.*, p. 14.
393. Coomaraswamy, A.K., Angel And Titan *An Essay In Vedic Ontology*, JAOS, p. 393.
394. Hale, *Op. cit.*, p. 102; *also the* Paippalādīya recension, *Ibid.*, p. 119.
395. Shendge, *Op.cit.*, p. 103.
396. Brown, Norman, *Proselyting the Asuras*, JAOS, pp. 100-103.
397. Hale, *Op. cit.*, p. 88.

398. X.95.7 and X.95.11.
399. Kantawala, Purūravas - *Op. cit*, ABORI, LVII, p. 52.
400. 2.3.7.
401. V.1; Shendge, *Op. cit.*, p. 67.
402. Mbh. 3.92. 6-10.
403. 47. 42-61; O'Flaherty, *Op. cit.*, p. 78, fn. 100.
404. *Ibid.*, fn. 98; quoting Dubois, *Hindu Manners, Customs, and Ceremonies*, p. 516.
405. *Ibid.*, p. 62.
406. Bhattacharji, *Op. cit.*, p. 324.
407. Mbh. 3.92. 6-10.
408. ŚB. VI. 6.3.2.
409. ŚB. I. 6. 1. 2-4.
410. Manusmṛti, III. 27-34.
411. Hillebrandt, A., *Vedic Mythology*, II, p. 271, fn. 109.
412. ŚB. XIII. 8. 1.1 ff.
413. ŚB. XIII. 8.1.5.
414. ŚB. XIII. 8.2.1.
415. ŚB. III. 2.1.24.
416. Shendge, *Op. cit.*, p. 137.
417. Hillebrandt, A., *Op. cit*, p. 267.
418. Bhattacharji, *Op. cit.*, pp. 93-94.
419. Hopkins, EM, pp. 47-48.
420. ŚB. II. 1.4.27; 3.1.9; 4.1.2 etc.
421. Hillebrandt, *Op. cit*, p. 271.
422. Banerjee, Sastri, A, *Asura Expansion In India*, JBORS, XII. ii, pp. 243-285.
423. ṚV. VII. 8.4.
424. Gordon, D.H., *The Pre-Historic Background of Indian Culture*, p. 95.
425. ṚV VIII. 8.4.
426. Thapar, *From Lineage to State*, p. 28.
427. Srivastava, M.C.P., *Mother Goddess*, p. 138
428. *Mathura-Govardhana Region: An Archaeological Assessment in Historical Perspective*, pp. 103-13; Indological Studies.
429. III. 38.4
430. Thapar, *From Lineage To State*, p. 44, fn. 21.
431. Nilakanta Sastri, K.A., *Age of the Nandas and Mauryas*, p. 141, fn. 1, quoting Pargiter, *Dynasties of the Kali Age*, p. 25.
432. DM. 8.6.
433. I. 3. 24 - Bhāg. p.

434. Thapar, *Op. cit.*, p. 134.
435. 1.6.1. 2-4
436. Banerji - Sastri, Asura Institutions, p. 534.
437. *Ibid.*, p. 537.
438. Gonda, J., *Change And Continuity in Indian Relgion*, p. 168.
439. AV. 3.9.4., *Ibid.*
440. Dandekar, R.N., *Asura Varuna*, p. 81, ABORI, XXI.
441. Hale, *Op. cit.*, p. 32.
442. Ait. Br. 2.22.
443. Agrawala, V.S., *Ancient Indian Folk-Cults*, pp. 150-53; fn. 803.
444. O'Flaherty, *The Origin of Evil in Hindu Mythology*, p. 80 ff.
445. DM. 30.
446. Eliade, M., *The Quest*, pp. 173-74.
447. Frankfort, H. and H.A., *Before Philosophy*, p. 26.
448. Eliade, *The Two in One*, p. 80.
449. Jung, C.G., *Psychology and Religion: West and East*, p. 59.
450. James, *Sacrifice and Sacrament*, p. 106.
451. This and the following examples are taken from Spence, Lewis. The *Outlines of Mythology*, p. 64.
452. James, *Myth and Ritual*, pp. 180, 191.
453. Coomaraswamy A.K., *Angle and Titan: A.. Essay in Vedic Ontology*, JAOS, p. 410, fn. 42.
454. Hale, *Op. cit*, pp. 140, 141.145
455. Hopkins, EM, p. 36.
456. Oppert, gustav, *The Original Inhabitants of India*, p. 526.
457. Elmore, W.T., *Dravidian Gods in Modern Hindusim*, p. 47, fn.1.
458. 7.23.
459. Malinowski, B., *Magic, Science and Religion*, p. 3.
460. Sharma, P.K., *Śakti Cult in Ancient India*, p. 228.
461. The whole information of Ahura is from Hale, W.E., *Op. cit.*, p. 189.
462. James, *The Cult of the Mother Goddess*, pp. 15, 17, 18; Jaffe, Aniela-*Symbolism In The visual Arts*; in Jung, C., Man and his Symbols, p. 261.
463. Mackay, Ernest, *Early Indus Civilization*, p. 64.
464. Gonda, J., *Change and Continuity in Indian Religion*, p. 87.
465. Jayakar, Pupul, *The Earthern Drum*, p. 53.
466. Pl. LXXXVIII, Mackay, Earnest, *Further Excavations of Mohenjo-Daro, quoted in Shendge*, M., *Op. cit*, p. 204.
467. Shendge, M., *Ibid.*, p. 123, This may not be the correct interpretation as the Mahiṣa is the Ṛsi Vena.

468. Coomarswamy, A.K., *Angel and Titan*, p. 376; here also Mahiṣa means mighty, not buffalo.
469. Appendix I, No. 30.
470. 3.229-231.
471. The Popular Religion and Folk-lore of Northern India, Vol. 1, p. 45; quoted in Quackenbos, *Op. cit.*, p. 248.
472. Sharma, R.N., *Ancient India according to Manu*, p. 93.
473. Balasubrahmanyam, S.R., *Early Chola Temples*, p. 153, fn. 1.
474. XVIII. 3.66; in Bhaṭtacharji, *Ibid.*, p.40.
475. III. 14.10.
476. 17.1; Srivastava, M.C.P. - Mothr Goddess, p. 64.
477. II. 3, *Ibid.*
478. Source untraceable, in Quackenbos, *Op. cit*, p. 256.
479. Adh. 94.
480. 18.60.
481. 5.2.28-31.
482. VIII. 10.32.
483. VIII. 10.31.
484. VI. 18.16
485. Act 2.20.
486. p. 455 ed. Parab.
487. cf. Sn. Caṇḍī Śatakam.
488. Vaikṛti Rahasya. 30.
489. Jacobi, Joland - *Complex /Archetype/Symbol*, p. 145.
490. *Ibid.*, p. 150.
491. Eliade, *From Primitives to Zen*, p. 279.
492. Eliade, *History of Religious Ideas*, p. 57.
493. James, *The Cult of the Mother-Goddess*, pp. 33, 128.
494. Eliade, *Patterns in Comparative Religion*, p. 89.
495. O.R., *Mother Right in India*, p. 130.
496. cf. caste register Index.
497. Lang, Andrew, *Myth Ritual and Religion*, Vol. II. p. 234.
498. cf. Supra, Sn. South Indian.
499. Slater, David, *Dravidian Element in Indian Culture*, pp. 75, 108.
500. VI, 23 line 15.
501. DM. 12. 10; *Devī Bhāg* p. 3.29. 20; *Devī* p. 22. 13-15, and *Kālikāp*. 71. 191-93, the last two references from Sharma, P.K., *Sakti Cult in Ancient India*, p. 202, fn. 2.
502. 3.26.32.

503. 71.49-51, *Ibid.*, fn. 5.
504. Yogini T. 2.9.158, *Ibid.*, p. 203, fn. 5.
505. Sinha, B.C., *Hinduism and Symbol Worship*, p. 145.
506. Marshall, Sir John, ed., *Mohenjo-daro and the Indus Civilization*, p. 74.
507. *Ibid.*, p. 72.
508. Thurston, E, *Ethnographic Notes on South India*, p. 460.
509. Jayakar, p., *The Earthern Drum*, pp. 26-28.
510. Whitehead, *The Village Gods of South India*, pp. 56, 62, 72, 80-84 and 117.
511. Kosambi, D.D., *Myth and Reality* pp. 88, 90, 91, 122 and 132.
512. James, *The Concept of Deity*, p. 49
513. Held, G.J., *The Mahābhārata*, p. 192.
514. Jaffe, Aniela, *Symbolism in Visual Art*, p. 264.
515. Farnell, *The Attributes of God*, p. 23.
516. Jayakar, Pupul, *The Earthern Drum*, p. 58.
517. Mackay, Ernest, *Early Indus Civilization*, p. 67.
518. Allchin, *The birth of Indian Civilization*, p. 67.
519. Marshall, *Op. cit.* p. 64.
520. Marshall, *Ibid.*, p. 20; quoting Crookes, *Religion and Folklore of Northern India*.
521. Nuemann, E., *The Great Mother* , pp. 183, 276, 277.
522. 7,5,19,1.
523. 3,7,4,8; Gonda, J., *Change and Continuity in Indian Religion*, p. 82.
524. Gonda, J., *Ibid.*, p. 71, fn. 2.
525. Smith Daniel, H., *Vāhanas in the Cultic Art of South Indian Temples* pp. 12-29.
526. Zimmer, H., *Myths and Symbols in Indian art and Civilization*, p. 189.
527. DM. 2.10-12; Vāmana p. 19.5-8, etc.
528. Zimmer, H., *The Art of Indian Asia*, pp. 43, 45.
529. cf. Sharma, *Sakti Cult in Ancient India*, pp. 245-266.
530. Tiwari, J.N., *Goddess Cults in Ancient India*, pp. 45, 47.
531. Eliade, M., *History of Religious Ideas*, p. 131.
532. *Ibid.*, pp. 139-40.
533. cf. ch. II, Sn. Kulli and Zhob, p. 108.
534. Gordon, D.H., *The Pre-Historic Background of Indian Culture*, p. 69.
535. Guha, J.P., *Seals and Statuettes of Kulli, Zhob, Mohenjodaro and Harappa*, p.5.
536. Campbell, J., *The Masks of God: Oriental Mythology*, p. 291.
537. Tiwari, J.N., *Mother Goddess*, p. 58.
538. Banerjea, J.N. - DHI, pp. 171, 172, Harle, quoted in Mitterwallner-*The*

Kuṣāṇa Type of the Goddess Mahiṣāsuramardinī as Compared to the Gupta and Mediaeval Types, p. 198, is of the opinion that the object held aloft is a garland of flowers.

539. Srivastava, M.C.P., *Ibid.*, p. 72.
540. Jaiswal, *Op.cit.*, pp. 63, 90-95.
541. Tiwari - *Op. cit.*, p. 45.
542. Bhattacharyya, *History of Śākta Religion*, p. 48.
543. Banerjea, J.N., *Paurāṇic and Tāntric Religion*, p. 77.
544. III. 94.38; Jaiswal S., *Op. cit.* p. 107.
545. Bhattacharyya, *History of Sākta Religion*, pp. 48-50.
546. Jaiswal, S., *Op. cit*, p. 65.
547. *Ibid.*, pp. 65, 102, 105.
548. Srivastava, M.C.P., *Op.cit.*, p. 123.
549. *Ibid.*, p.p., 73, 75, 128 and 133-35.
550. Bhattacharyya, *History of sākta Religion*, pp. 46, 51.
551. Agrawala, V.S., *A Catalogue of the Brahmanical Images in Mathura Art.*
552. The number indicates the catalogue numbering.
553. Agrawala, V.S., *Ancient Indian Folk-Cults*, p. 83.
554. Agrawala, V.S., *The Glorification of the Great Goddess*, Intro., pp. viii - ix.
555. Venkataraman, K.R., *Devī Kāmākshī in Kañchī*, p. 16, fn. 6.
556. Banerjea, J.N., *Paurāṇic and Tāntric Religion*, p. 129.
557. Cousens, Henry, *Medieval Temples of the Dakhan*, p. 41.
558. Balasubrahmanyam, S.R., *Early Chola Temples*, pp. 146-47.
559. Campbell, J., *Oriental Mythology*, p. 291.
560. 59.19; Banerjea, J. N., DHI, p. 505.
561. *Ibid.*, p. 482.
562. Banerjea, J.N., *Ibid.*, p. 35.
563. Aryan, K.C., The little Goddesses (Matrikas) reviewed by Kapila Vatsyayan, "Tantric Thought", Art, *Sunday Standard*, 10.8.80.
564. Santini - Asuranai Aḷitha Elau Śaktikal, Tamil article in *Amuda Surabhi*, Dec. '84.
565. Bhattacharyya, *History of Śākta Religion*, p. 66.
566. Banerjea, J.N., DHI, p. 503.
567. Kosambi, D.D., *Myth and Reality*, p. 61.
568. Gorya, B.S., Mystic Monuments of Mandhata, Art. in *The Times of India*, 23.1.1988.
569. Balasubrahmanyam, S.R., *Op. cit*, p. 147.
570. Bhattacharji, S., *Op. cit*, p. 90.
571. Kuraishi, M.H., List of Ancient Monuments Protected Under Act VII of 1904, in the Province of Bihar and Orissa, ASI Vol. LI, pp. 226-27

572. Kinsley, D.R., *Blood and Death out of Place,* p. 147.
573. Banerjea, J.N., *Paurāṇic and Tāntric Religion,* p. 127.
574. Materials taken from Pavetri Kumari Shivaram, *Lajjā Gaurī Sculptures with Special Reference to Gujarat,* MA. dissertation of the MS University Baroda, April 1987, pp. 15,16, 21, 24, 31.
575. *Indian Express* 23.7. 1988.
576. Dhere, R.C., *Lajjā Gauri,* pp. 19-38.
577. M.K., *The Headless Goddess,* ABORI, LXVIII, 1987, pp. 281-93.
578. Adh. 11.
579. Sharma, I.K., *Brahmanical Brick Temples and Cult Objects from Keesaragiri,* p. 236, Art. 43, in Kusumāñjali.
580. 3,82,8; *Ibid.,* p. 237.
581. Sastri, K.A.N., *Age of the Nandas and Mauryas,* p. 343.
582. Tiwari, J.,N., *Op. cit.,* pp. 42-43.
583. Banerjea, J.N. - DHI, p. 135.
584. Srivastava, *Mother Goddess,* p. 81.
585. *Ibid.,* p. 75.
586. *Ibid.,* pp. 68-70
587. Upadhya, B.S., *Women in ṚgVeda,* pp. 6-7.
588. Joshi, M.C., *Tantric Symbolism in Brahmanical Iconography,* p. 66.
589. Tiwari, J.N., *Op. cit,* pp. 48, 50-51.
590. *Ibid.,* p. 88.
591. Bhattacharyya, *History of Śākta Religion,* p. 50.
592. Mbh III .221. 1-2.
593. 11.10.
594. 11.5.
595. Banerjea, J.N., *Paurāṇic and Tāntric Religion* p. 59.
596. Srivastava, *Op. cit,* p. 82.
597. Banerjea, J.N - DHI, pp. 185 ff.
598. *The Times of India,* 21-4-88.
599. Tiwari, J.N., *Op. cit,* pp. 76-77.
600. Banerjea, J.N., DHI, p. 228.
601. Agrawala, V.S., *Catalogue of the Brahminical Images in Mathura Art,* pp. 51-56.
602. *Ibid.,* pp. 57-58.
603. Srivastava, *Op. cit.* p. 112.
604. This has been refuted as mentioned earlier.
605. Majumdar, R.C., *The Classical Age,* p. 448.
606. Agrawala, V.S., *Terracotta Figurines of Ahichchhatra District Bareilly,* U.P.

p. 133, calls this pose as holding the demon with affection.

607. Mitterwallner, *The Kuṣāṇa Type of the Goddess Mahiṣāsuramaradinī as Compared to the Gupta and Mediaeval Types*, pp. 209-10.
608. Devī, fight with Śumbha.
609. Banerjea, J.N., *Paurāṇic and Tāntric Religion*, p. 126.
610. Deshpande, M.N. and Jamkhedkar A.P. The Buddhist Cave At Lonada Art, 31 in Kusumāñjali pp. 163-67.
611. Meister, M.W. and Dhaky, M.N. ed. *Encyclopaedia of Indian Temple Architecture*, Vol I, Part 2; Illustration Plate 27.
612. Banerjea, J.N. - DHI, pp. 500-501.
613. Sircar, D.C., *The Sākta Pīthas*, p. 100 ff.
614. No. 47.
615. No. 48.
616. No. 49.
617. No. 50.
618. Rao, Rama, M, *Early Cālukyan Temples of Andhra Desa*, pp. 15, 27-28.
619. Mitterwallner, *Op. cit.*, p. 206.
620. Srivastava, *Op. cit.*, p. 112.
621. Quackenbos, G.P., *The Sanskrit Poems of Mayūra*, p. 249.
622. Zimmer, H., *Myths and Symbols in Indian Art and Civilization*, pp. 190-91.
623. Plate XLII, No. 8; Banerjea; DHI.
624. Plate XLII, No. 2; Banerjea, J.N., DHI.
625. Nagasami, R., *Ninnayum Pukaluven Tāye*, Tamil Article, pp. 212-14.
626. Venkataraman, K. R, *Devī Kāmākshī in Kañchī*, p. 9, fn. 3.
627. *Ibid.*, p. 15.
628. Zimmer, H., *Art of Indian Asia*, Pl,. 234. Vol. 2
629. *Ibid.*, Pl. 210, Vol. 2.
630. *Ibid.*, Pl. 326, Vol 2.
631. Ganguli, O.C., Text and Descriptive Notes, The Art of Rashtrakutas, p. 3.
632. Cousens, H., *Medieval Temples of the Dakhan*, Pl. L.
633. A.K., *The Transformation of nature in Art*, p.p. 122-33.
634. Boner, Alice, The Symbolic Aspect of Form, JISOA, XV, II, pp. 42-50.
635. For an exhaustive study of this Subject cf. Boner, Alice, - Principles of Composition In Hindu Sculpture. The terminologies and the concept are followed from Boner's book, p. 230 ff.

CONCLUSION

This study started with symbolism in myths and ends with symbolism in iconography. Iconography is after all concretization of myth. Covering various emanations and representations of the Goddess and her cult, to sharpen our perception of the Devī myth, we have traversed a full circle and reached the beginning, the circle itself symbolising the Uroboric Mother principle. She encompasses in herself both positive and negative aspects of life and nature. These are represented by various symbols even in the Palaeolithic period. The question is not whether a particular icon of her was 20,000 or 50,000 B.C., but, the emphasis is on the uniformity in the symbolic thought of man even before he thought discursively. This symbolism embedded in a concept is our Goddess, containing in herself creation and destruction, ignorance and knowledge, moha and mokṣa.

To answer some questions that would arise regarding our subject a quick resume would not be out of place :

The cult of the mother-goddess was popular and important in the Palaeolithic era as seen from its artefacts diffused over a very wide area. Psychology has an answer for the ambivalence in the motif of the goddess as shown in its representations. The motif of the Great Round as the Mother Principle thrown up from the archetypes of our unconscious contains in it both the negative and positive aspects of the goddess concept. The Kulli and Zhob goddesses are seen as representing the polarities of life and death. The Goddess as the deity of the forests/vegetation, and protector of the beasts is depicted on the seals of the Indus Valley Culture. The Vedas do depict the ambivalence of the goddess by the two goddesses Aditi and Nirṛti. During the period of the Atharva Veda and the Brāhmaṇas, the Aryans were moving far into the heartland of India. From pastorals, they had become agriculturists. Political invasions, inter-marriage with the earlier inhabitants, etc., tended to change their outlook. Agriculture could have made the goddess cult attractive, and fertility rites could have helped the cult's resurgence.

The cult of the Mātṛs enabled innumerable village goddesses to enter the Big Tradition. Their fierce nature is given a gloss of benignity. Sanskritisation of the autochthonous goddesses starts in the epic and gets formalised in the Purāṇas. Kālī and Durgā are two sides of a coin, Kālī assisting Durgā in performing various onerous tasks. The folk-content in the make-up of Durgā, Kālī, and Cāmuṇḍā are undeniable, and are left as such in the epic and the Purāṇas.

Durgā is given form as the Great Goddess in the Devī Māhātmya, in her role as Mahiṣāsuramardinī. Even in the Kushana period stone icons depict this role of the Goddess. This further pre-dates this concept. The theme is simple and Devī is shown killing the demon with her bare hands. The full flowering of this theme is in the Gupta era, both in literature and iconography.

The word asura meant a chosen leader of exceptional capacity, in early literature. This word used in the plural, got a bad connotation, in later works. Both Durgā and Mahiṣa have a connection with agriculture and fertility. The folk origin of the Mahiṣāsuramardinī concept is seen in the various folk versions of the myth, and the status of Mahisa in the local cults of Maharashtra and the South.

The myth satisfies a psychological need in us. In traumatic situations, it lets the individual as well as the society come to terms with oneself without injuring one's psyche. This is the function of an eternal myth. But the cult's popularity is not on psychological grounds alone. It answers a need for balancing between continuity and change. In the traditionalist view this is the Kali age where there is corruption in moral and social values, and only a Goddess like Mahiṣāsuramardinī can combat the evil and give hope to the people. She satisfies the present needs, while remaining rooted in the mythical past. The stability of the creed in the face of transforming social values, progress and secularization, disproves the theory that Indian religious tradition is static or stagnant. India's traditionalism has an in-built mechanism which adapts itself to the changing values of its culture. It incorporates these new values by revalidating its own objectives. For many the symbol of the Goddess appears as an inner strength, advising them in day-to-day situations. For others the symbol appears only in crisis situations. Thus it acts in individual psyches also.

Folk myths were integrated into the Big Tradition, and thus people of the peripheral areas were brought into the caste system. This Sanskritisation process allowed movements in the castes. Thus, the tribal goddesses provided a channel for loosening and realigning the castes. Indian religious system assimilated foreign influences, enabling smoother changes in social and political movements.

Sacred symbols provide another dimension to which man aspires to rise, and refresh himself. By the individual transforming himself, society is able to change, and by adopting new ideas, it evolves. Female symbolism has been repressed in most other religions. (In Christianity, the exception is in Mariolatory). This may be due to the fact that religious symbols do not reflect social changes. India has not thrown away her ancient symbols for the few dubious advantages gained by modernisation. It would not be an exaggeration to state that the Goddess symbol has unified India, cutting across language and insularity. The Goddess is the major symbol in the centre, connecting various mini-symbols around her, of minor goddesses. She is a great integrating factor in Hinduism, because of the qualities found in her-life-giving, nourishing, protecting, and in the process punishing the errant. She stands at the centre of cosmic mythology, rich in archaic symbolism. She is as necessary and innate to man's psyche as breathing is to life. Her basic symbolism may not change, but the interpretation changes along with social and cultural changes. In spite of political and ideological onslaughts, Hinduism has remained integrated, entirely due to its religious symbolism, and its innate capacity for assimilating the variety. (cf. Pl. S 45 & 46).

The position of women as exemplified in the epics and the *Purāṇas* is accepted by and large by Indians. In the epics, the picture is of a woman who gives of herself to others, to her utmost capacity, uncomplainingly. The Indian woman is told to emulate the epic heroines, who worshipped their husbands, whether the latter were worthy of it or not. The myths of the Goddess offer another paradigm of a powerful Goddess. This might have provided the template for the vīrāṅganā type of heroines,[1] in the latter day literature. The evaluation of women as life-givers and nourishers is reinforced by the goddess worship. Both men and women adjudge feminine power in society in terms of the power of the Goddess.

Due to feminist movements in the West, goddess cult is receiving renewed interest. Similar movements in India are also afoot and are re-evaluating the cult and its symbolism.

The Hindu's myth-making propensity is far from extinct as seen in the sudden popularity of Santoshi Mā all over the North, in the recent years. There was a temporary emanation of the Goddess, named *'Śrama Devatā'*, goddess of hard work, but the cult folded up early in its career. There is a shrine of the goddess *Saṁkaṭā* in Banaras proper, receiving worship even now. She is the remover of obstacles of the devotees. The continuous popularity of the cult unbroken from the Palaeolithic period upto the present, shows that it is able to fulfil a psychological need of the people which science has not been able to do.

REFERENCE

1. Hansen, Katheryn, *The Virangana in North Indian History*, pp. 25-26.

BIBLIOGRAPHY

Original Texts and Translations

Agni Purāṇam
tr. Manmatha Nath Dutt Shastri,
Vol. I, The Chowkhamba Sanskrit Series Office
Varanasi-I. 1967.

Aitreya Brāhmaṇa
ed. by Vasudeva Sarma and Krishnambhatta Gore,
Nirnayasagar Press, Bombay, 1911.

Amarkośa
ed. by Krishnaji Govind Oka
Upāsanā Prakāshan
Delhi, 1981

Atharva Veda Saṁhitā
ed. by Shri Kanth Shastri, Parts I-IV.
Madhawa Pustakalayah, Delhi-(1975-79)

AtharvaVeda Saṁhitā
ed. by Shankar Pandurang Pandit,
Govt. Central Book Depot, Bombay, 1898

The Pariśiṣtaṣ of Atharvaveda
ed. by G. M. Bolling and J.V. Negelein, Vol. 1, Parts I-III
Leipzig, 1910.

The Harshacarita of Bāṇabhaṭṭa
with notes by P.V. Kane,
Motilal Banarasidass, 1973.

Bāṇa's Kādambarī
ed. by Kāśinātha Pāṇḍurang Parab
Nirnaya sagar Press, Bombay 8th ed. 1940.

The Baudāyana Śrauta Sūtra (belonging to the Taittirīya Saṁhitā)
ed. by W. Caland., Vol. I
Munshiram Manoharlal Publishers Pvt. Ltd., New Delhi. 2nd ed. 1982.

Śrīmad Bhāgavata Mahāpurāṇa (Parts I and II)

with English tr. by C.L. Goswami
Gita Press, Gorakhpur, Ist ed. 1971.

The Bhagavadgītā
with an introductory essay,
Sanskrit Text,
English tr. and notes
by S. Radhakrishnan

George Allen & Unwin Ltd., London, 6th ed. 1960.

Bhāsa's Two Plays
Avimāraka and Balacarita
with Eng. tr. by Bak Kunbae
Meharchand Lachhmandas

The Sanskrit Book Depot, Delhi-6, 1968.

The Cārudattam of Bhāsa
ed. with tr. by P.S. Sane and S.A. Upadhyaya
A.R.Seth & Co.
Educational Publishers and Booksellers,
Bombay-2. 2nd ed, 1967.
Bhavabhūti's Mālatīmādhava
ed. by M.R. Kale, Motilal Banarsidassm, 3rd ed, 1957.

The Bṛhadāraṇyaka Upaniṣad
tr. by Swami Mādhavānanda,
Advaita Ashrama, 5-Delhi Entally Road, Calcutta, 6th ed.

Bṛhat Saṁhitā
tr. and ed. by Baladevaprasad Misra,
Laksmi Venkatesvar Press, Kalyan, Bombay, 1897.

Chandogyopaniṣad
ed. by P.V. Ramanujaswami,
Tirumala Tirupati Devasthanam Press,
Tirupati, 1952.

Cilappatikaram
tr. with notes by V.R.R. Dikshitar,
The South India Saiva Siddhanta Works Publishing Society,
Tinnevelly, Ltd. Madras, 1978.

Dandin's Daśakumāracaritam
with Sanskrit and Hindi Translations
by Visvanath Jha and Subodhchandra Jha
Motilal Banarsidass, 1st ed, 1974.

Devī Bhāgavatam
ed, Kṣemarājā
Śrī Venkateśvar (Steam) Press, Bombay, 1840.

Studies in the Devī Bhāgavata
P.G. Lalye
Popular Prakashan, Bombay, 1st ed, 1973.

Śrī Devī Māhātmya
tr. (Tamil) and ed. by Aṇṇā
Sri Ramakrishna Math
11-Ramakrishna Math Road, Madras, 4th ed, 1977.

Śrī Devī Māhātmya
tr. (Tamil) and published by V. Raghavan, Madras, 1967.

Devīsūktāni Upaniṣadaśca
tr. (Tamil) and ed. by Aṇṇā
Sri Ramakrishna Math, Madras, 2nd ed, 1974.

Gobila Gṛihya-Sūtras
The Sacred Books of the East, Part II.
ed. by F. Max Müller, Motilal Banarsidass, 1973.

Gopatha Brāhmaṇam
ed. and published by Jīvānanda Vidyāsāgara Bhattācārya
Narayan Press, Calcutta, 1891.

The Mahābhārata critically

ed. by S. Sukthankar,
S.K. Belvalkar, and, P.L. Vaidya
Bhandarkar Oriental Research Institute, Poona.
Āraṇyaka Parvan 1942, Bhīsma Parvan 1947,
Śalya Parvan 1961, Harivaṁśa, Vol. I, 1969, Vol, II, Appendices, 1971

Śrī manmahābharataṁ
ed. by T. R. Krishnamachari and T.R. Vyasacharya

Niranayasagar Press, Bombay.

Suaptika Parva X. 1907; Virata Parva IV. 1908.
Maitrāyaṇī Saṁhitā
ed. by L.V. Schroeder
Leipzig, 1881.

Mānavagṛhyasūtra
Gaekwad Oriental Series No. XXXV, Central Library, Baroda, 1926.

Mānava Gṛhya Sūtra
ed. by Bhīmasena Śarma
Itawa.

Maṇimekalai
cr. ed. by U.V. Swaminathan Iyer
Dr. U.V. Swaminatha Iyer Library, Tiruvanmiyur, Madras, 7th ed.

The Matsyamahāpurāṇam
Foreword by H.H. Wilson, 2 Vols.
Nag Publishers, Delhi, Ist ed, 1983.

Matsya Purāṇam
ed. by Pañcānana Tarka Ratna Arunodaya Ray, Calcutta, 1890.

Matsya Purana—A Study.
Vasudeva S. Agrawala
All-India Kashiraj Trust, Ramnagar, Varanasi, 1963.

Manusmṛti
ed. by Vasudeva Sarma, Nirnayasagar Press, Bombay, 1920.

Śūdraka's Mṛcchakatikam
with Sanskrit commentary and tr. (Hindi) by
Ramasankar Tripati, Motilal Banarsidass, Delhi, 1975.

Two Plays of Ancient India
tr. by J.A.B. Van Buitenen
Motilal Banarsidass. Delhi, 1st ed, 1971.

Gṛihya-Sūtra by Paraskar

ed. by Mahādeva Gaṅgādhar Bākre, Munshiram Manoharlal Publishers Pvt. Ltd.
New Delhi, 2nd ed, 1982.

Śrī Harsha's Nāgānanda Nātakam
tr. (Hindi) by Pt. Sri Baladeva Upadhyay
The Chowkhamba Sanskrit Series Office, Banaras. 3rd ed, 1953.

Kāthakam
ed. L. Von Schroeder, Leipzig, 1910.

Kauṣītaka Gṛhya Sūtras
ed. by T.R. Chintamani
Panini, New Delhi, 1982.

Kuruntokai
ed. by B.M. Shanmukam Pillai
Tamil University,
Tanjavur, 1st ed, 1985.

Śrauta Sūtra of Lātyāyana
ed. by Ānandachandra Vedāntavagīśa,
Valmiki Press, Calcutta, 1872.
Bibliotheca Indica, Asiatic Society of Bengal.

Liṅgapurāṇam
ed. by Vīrasiṁhaśāstri
Calcutta, 1890.

Śrī Liṅga Purāṇam
tr. (Tamil) by Kartikeyan, Vasu Prasuram,
Madras, 2nd ed, 1977.

Pāṇinī's Aṣṭādhyāyī
The Siddhānta Kaumudi of Sri Bhattoji Deekshita, with the Commentary
Śrī Bālamanoramā of Śrī Vāsudeva Deekshita
ed. by S. Chandrasekhara Sastrigal, Teppakkulam,
Trichinopoly, 1910.

Pattuppāṭṭu
New Century Book House Pvt. Ltd.
Madras
ṚgVeda Saṁhitā
ed. by Śrīpāda Śarma
Svādhyāya maṇḍala, Paradi, Surat. 3rd ed., 1957.

ṚgVeda
tr. by H.H. Wilson,
Vol. I. The Bangalore Printing and Publishing Co.
Ltd, 2nd ed., 1946
Vols. II-VI Ashtekar & Co., Poona (1925-1928)

Sāmavidhānabrāhmaṇa
tr. by A.C. Burnell. Vol. I
Trubner & Co., London, 1873.

The Śatapatha Brāhmaṇa (according to text of the Mādyandina school)
tr. by Julius Eggling
Sacred Books of the East, Parts I & IV.
Motilal Banarsidass, 1978.

Śatapathabrāhmaṇam
Yajurvedamādhyāndinīyam
Vaidikayantralaya, Ajmer, 1959.

Śrīmadvālmīkirāmāyaṇam
Revised by Pandit K. Chinnaswamy Sastrigal, and Pandit V.H. Subrahmanya Sastri
Published by N. Ramaratnam, 2nd ed., 1958.

Taittirīya Āraṇyaka
Title page not available.

Śrī Vaikhānasa Gṛhyasūtram
ed. by R. Parthasarthi Bhattacharya, Vols. 1 & 2.
Tirumala Tirupati Devasthanams, 1967.

The Vājasaneyi-saṅhitā

ed. by Albrecht Weber
Williams and Norgate, 14-Henrietta Street, Covent Garden, 1849.

Vākpatirājā's Gauḍavaho
ed. by N.G. Suru, Poona
Prakrit Text Society, Ahmedabad-9, Varanasi-5, 1975.

The Vāmana Purāṇa
ed. by A.S. Gupta,
All-India Kashiraj Trust, Fort Ramnagar, Varanasi, 1968.

Varāha Purāṇa
ed by A.S. Gupta,
All India Kashiraj Trust, Fort Ramṅagar, Varanasi, 1981.

Vātsyāyana's Kāmasūtram
with commentary of Jayamaṅgala
Chowkhamba Series, Banaras.

Yājñavalkya Smṛti
with commentary by Viśvarūpācārya
ed. by T. Ganapati Sastri
Trivandrum Sanskrit Series LXXIV, 1922.

Taittirīya Brāhmaṇa of the Black Yajurveda
ed. by Rajendralāla Mitra., Vols. I-III.
Asiatic Society of Bengal.

Kṛṣṇa Yajurvedīya Taittirīya Saṁhitā
ed. by Sripadasarma
Bharat Press, Oundh Presidency, 1945.

Sukla Yajurveda Samhita
ed. by Shri Swami Govindanand ji Premacharya Shastri, Sadguru
Gangeshwar International Veda Mission
Bombay, 1st. ed.

Śuklayajurveda Saṁhitā
Vājasaneyi-Saṁhitā of the White Yajurved

ed. by Pandit Ram Sakala Misra
The Chowkhamba Sanskrit Book Depot, Banaras City, 1915.

Taittirīya Saṁhitā
ed. by Śrīpāda Śarma
Svādhyāya Maṇḍal, Oundh Presidency, 1945.

Taittirīya Saṁhitā, II Khāṇḍa Vol. II Part 1.
T. N. Dharmadhikari
Vaidika Sāṁśodhana Maṇḍala, Poona, 1981.

Secondary Sources

Agrawala, P.K. : *Goddesses in Ancient India*
Abhinav Publications,
New Delhi.

Agrawala, Vasudeva. S.: A Catalogue of the Brahmanical Images of Mathura Art,
U.P., Historical Society, Lucknow, 1951.
: *Ancient Indian Folk Cults*
Prithivi Prakashan, Varanasi-5, 1970.
: *Devī Māhātmyam, The Glorification of the Great Goddess*
All-India Kashiraj Trust, Ramnagar, Varanasi, 1963.

Allchin, Bridget and Raymond : *The Birth of Indian Civilization*
Penguin Books, 1968.

Altekar, A.S. : *The Position of Women in Hindu Civilization*
Motilal Banarsidass, Delhi, 1973.

Bachofen, J.J. : *Myth, Religion and Mother Right*
Bollingen Series LXXXIV, Princeton, 1967.

Balasubrahmanyam, S.R.: *Early Chola Temples*
Orient Longman Ltd., Bombay, Calcutta, New Delhi, Madras 1971.

Banerjea, J.N. : *Development of Hindu Iconography*
Munshiram Manoharlal Publishers Pvt. Ltd., New Delhi, 1974.
: *Paurāṇic and Tāntric Religion.*
University of Calcutta, 1966.

Bhandarkar, R.G. : *Vaiṣṇavism Śaivism and Minor Religious Systems*
Indological Book House, Varanasi, 1965.

Bhattacharji, Sukumari : *The Indian Theogony*
Firma KLM Pvt. Ltd., Calcutta, 1978.

Bhattacharyya, N.N. : *Ancient Indian Rituals and their Social Contents*
Manohar Book Service, New Delhi, 1975.

: *History of Indian Erotic Literature*
Munshiram Manoharlal Publishers Pvt. Ltd., *New Delhi, 1975.*
: *History of Śākta Religion*
Munshiram Manoharlal Publishers Pvt. Ltd., New Delhi, 1975.
: *The Indian Mother Goddess*
Manohar Book Service, 2 Ansari Road, New Delhi.
2nd ed., 1977.

Boner, Alice : *Principles of Composition in Hindu Sculpture*
Leiden, E.J. Brill, 1962.

Bosch, F.D.K. : *The Golden Germ (An Introduction to Indian Symbolism)*
Mouton & Co.

'S-Gravenhage, 1960.

Briffault, Robert : *The Mothers*, 3 Vols. George Allen and Unwin-London, 1927.

Brubaker, Richard : *Comments: The Goddess and the Polarity of the Sacred* in edd. John Stratton Hawley and Donna Marie Wulff, *The Divine Consort: Radha and the Goddesses of India*, Motilal Banarsidass, Ist ed, 1984.

Burridge, K.O.L. : *Lévi-Strauss and Myth*, in ed., Edmund Leach, 1968.

Bussagli, Mario : jt. ed with Sivaramamurti, *Calembus-5000 Years of the Art of India* Harry N. Abrams, Inc., New York-The Tulsi Shah Enterprises, Bombay, India.

Campbell, Joseph : *The Masks of God*, Vol. II, Oriental Mythology, Secker and Warburg, London, 1962.

Cassirer, Ernst : *An Essay on Man* Yale University Press, New Haven and London, 1972.

: *The Philosophy of Symbolic Forms*, 2 Vols. Tr. Ralph Manheim *Yale University Press. New Haven and London, 1955.*

Chakrabarti, Kunal : *Sychoanalytic Approaches to the Study of Ancient Indian Myths*, in edd. Sabyasachi Bhattacharya and Romila Thapar, *Situating Indian History for Sarvapalli*

Gopal, Oxford University Press, Delhi, 1986.

Chattopadhyaya, Dr. Sudhakar : *The Evolution of Theistic Sects in Ancient India* Progressive Publishers, Calcutta, 1962.

Childe, Gordon : *The Urban Revolution in Ancient Cities of the Indus* ed. Gregory Possehl, 1979.

Coburn, Thomas. B. : *Consort of None, Śakti of All: The Vision of the Devī-Māhātmya;* in, edd. J.S. Hawley and D.M. Wulff, 1984.

: *Devī Māhātmya: The Chrystallisation of the Goddess Tradition*, Motilal Banarsidass, 1984

Coomaraswamy, Ananda. K. : *The Transformation of Nature in Art.* Dover Publications, New York, 1956.

Dales, George. F. : *New Investigations at Mohenjo Daro,* in ed. Possehl, 1979.

Dange, A.S. : *Encyclopaedia of Puranic Beliefs and Practices*, Vol. III (H-N) Navrang, New Delhi. 1987.

Danielou, Alain : *Hindu Polytheism*, Rutledge and Kegan Paul, London, 1963.

Das, S.K. : *Śakti or Divine Power (A Historical Study Based on Original Sanskrit Texts)* University of Calcutta, 1934.

Desai, Nileshvari. Y. : *Ancient Indian Society, Religion and Mythology as Depicted in the*

Mārkaṇḍeya-Purāṇa (A Critical Study) Faculty of Arts, M.S. University of Baroda, Baroda, 1968.

Dhere, R.C. : *Lajjā Gaurī* (Marathi). Sri Vidya Prakasan, Poona, 1978.

Dikshit, S.K. : *The Mother Goddess (A Study Regarding the Origin of Hinduism)* The International Book Service, Deccan Gymkhana, Poona 4.

Dimmitt, Cornelia : *Sītā: Mother Goddess and Śakti.* In edd. J.S. Hawley and D.M. Wulff, 1984.

Dimcock, Edward. C. : *A Theology of the Repulsive: The Myth of the Goddess Sītalā,* in edd. J.S. Hawley & D.M. Wulff, 1984.

Douglas, Mary : *The Meaning of Myth with Special Reference to 'La Geste D'Asdiwal',* in ed. Edmund Leach, 1968.

Durkheim and Mauss : Jt. auths. *Primitive Classification.* Tr., with an Introduction by Rodney Needham London, Cohen and West, 1963.

Ehrenfels, Baron Omar : *Mother-Right in India* Osmania University Series Humphrey Milford, Oxford University Press, 1941.

Eliade, Mircea : *Patterns in Comparative Religion.* Tr. Rosemary Sheed, Sheed and Ward, London and New York, 1958.

: *Essays in Methodology.* The University of Chicago Press, 1959.

: *Myth, Dreams and Mysteries.* Tr. by Philip Mariet, Harvill Press, London, 1960.

: *Myth and Reality,* George Allen and Unwin Ltd., London, 1963

Eliade, Mircea : *The Two and the One.* Tr. J.M. Cohen, Harvill Press, London, 1965.

: *From Primitives to Zen (A Thematic Sourcebook of the History of Religions).* Collins, St. James Palace, London, 1967.

: *The Quest-History and Meaning in Religion,* The University of Chicago Press, Chicago and London, 1967

: *A History of Religious Ideas* Vol. I *(From Stone Age to the Eleusinian Mysteries).* Collins, St. James Palace, London, 1979.

Elmore, W.T. : *Dravidian Gods in Modern Hinduism,* C.L.S. Press, Madras, 1925.

: *Matriarchy, Art. In Encyclopaedia Brittanica,* Vol. 15, p. 92. ed. 1957.

Fair Service, Walter. A. : *The Origin, Character and Decline of an Early Civilization,* in ed. Possehl, 1979.

Farquhar, J.N. : *An Outline of the Religious Literature of India,* Motilal Banarsidass, 1967.

Farnell, L.R. : *The Attributes of God,* Clarendon Press Oxford, 1925.

Frankfort, H.& H.A. and others : *Before Philosophy,* Penguin Books, London, 1951.

Frazer, James. G. : *The Golden Bough, Avenel Books, USA,*

1981.

Gangoli, O.C. : *The Art of the Rashtrakutas.* Text and Descriptive Notes, Orient Longmans, 1958

Gatwood, Lynn : *Devi and the Spouse Goddess (Women, Sexuality and Marriage in India).* Manohar Publications, New Delhi, 1985.

Gaur, R.C. : *Mathura-Govardhana Region: An Archaeological Assessment in Historical Rerspective* in edd. S.K. Maity and Upendra Thakur, *Prof. D.C. Sircar Commemoration Volume,* Abhinav Publications 1st ed, 1987.

Griswold, H.D. : *The Religion of the Rig Vedam* in Jt. ed. with J.N. Farquhar, *The Religious Quest of India,* Humphrey Milford, Oxford University Press, Bombay, 1923.

Gonda, J. : *Change and Continuity in Indian Religion,* Mouton & Co., London, The Hague, Paris, 1965.

: *Aspects of Early Viṣṇuism,* Motilal Banarsidass, Delhi, 2nd, ed., 1969.

: *Notes on Names and the Name of God in Ancient India.* North-Holland Publishing Company, Amsterdam, London, 1970.

Gordon, D.H. : *The Pre-Historic Background of Indian Culture,* N.M. Tripathi (Pvt.) Ltd., Bombay, 1958.

Gupta, J.P. : *Seals and Statuettes of Kulli,* Zhob, Mohenjo Daro and Harappa Associated Publishing House, New Delhi, 1967.

Hale, Wash Edward : *Asura—In Early Vedic Religion,* Motilal Banarsidass, Delhi, 1986.

Hastings, James : *Encyclopaedia of Religion and Ethics,* Vol. V, Edinburgh: T & T Clark, 38-George Street. New York Charles Scribner's Sons, 597-Fifth Avenue, 1981.

Hawley, John Stratton edd. with Donna Marie Wulff, : *The Divine Consort: Radha and the Goddesses of India, Motilal Banarsidass* 1st ed., 1984.

Held, G.J. : *The Mahābhārata-An Ethnological Study.* Kegan Paul, Trench, Trubner & Co. Ltd., London, 1935.

Hillebrandt, Alfred : *Vedic Mythology,* Vols. I & II, tr. Sreeramula Rajeswara Sarma, Motilal Banarsidass, Delhi, 1980.

Hopkins, E.W. : *Epic Mythology,* Indological Book House, Delhi, 1972.

Hudson, Dennis : *Pinnai, Krishna's Cowherd Wife,* in edd. J.S. Hawley and D.M. Wulff, 1984.

Jacobi, Joland : *Complex/Archetype/Symbol in the Psychology of C.G. Jung.* Tr. by Ralph Manheim, Bollingen Series LVII, Princeton University Press, 1974.

Jaiswal, Suvira : *The Origin and Development of Vaiṣṇavism*. Munshiram Manoharlal, Delhi, 1967.

Jamkhedkar, A.P. : *The Buddhist Cave at Lonad*, in ed. M.S. Nagaraja Rao, Kusumāñjali, *New Interpretation of Indian Art and Culture*, C. Sivaramamurti Commemoration Volume, Vol. I, Agam Kala Prakashan, Delhi, 1987.

James, E.O. : *Primitive Ritual and Belief*, Methuen & Co. Ltd., London, 1917.

: *The Concept of Deity, A Comparative and Historical Study*, Hutchinson's University Library, London, 1950.

: *Myth and Ritual in the Ancient Near East*, Thames and Hudson, London, 1958.

: *Sacrifice and Sacrament*, Thames and Hudson, London, 1958.

: *The Cult of the Mother-Goddess, An Archaeological and Documentary Study*, Thames and Hudson, London, 1959.

Jayakar, Pupul : *The Earthern Drum, An Introduction to the Ritual Arts of Rural India*, National Museum, New Delhi.

Jung, C.G. & C. Kerenyi: *Introduction to a Science of Mythology* tr. by R.F.C. Hull, Routledge and Kegan Paul, Ltd., London, 1951.

Jung, C.G. : *Psychology of the Unconscious*, tr. Beatrice M. Hinkle, Kegan Paul, Trench, and Trubner and Co. Ltd. London, 1946.

: *The Archetypes and the Collective*

Unconscious, tr. R.F.C. Hull, Routledge and Kegan Paul, London, 1959.

: *Man and His Symbols*, Aldus Books Ltd., London, 1964.

: *Symbols of Transformation*, tr. by R.F.C. Hull, Bollingen Series XX, Princeton University Press, 1976.

Kane, P.V. : *History of Dharmaśāstra*, Vol. V, Part II, Bhandarkar Oriental Research Institute, Poona, 1962.

Kinsley, David : *The Sword and the Flute (Kālī and Kṛṣṇa)*, University of California Press, Berkley, Los Angeles. 1975.

: *Blood and Death Out of Place: Reflections on the Goddess Kali* in edd. J.S. Hawley and D.M. Wulff. MotilalBanarsidass, Delhi 1st ed, 1984.

: *Hindu Goddesses (Visions of the Divine Feminine in Hindu Religious Tradition)*, Archives Publishers, Distributors, New Delhi.

Kirk, G.S. : *Myth (Its Meaning and Functions in Ancient and Other Cultures)* Cambridge, University Press, 1970.

Kosambi, D.D. : *Myth and Reality*, Popular Prakashan, Bombay, 1962.

Kramer, Samuel. N. : *The Indus Civilization and Dilmun: The Sumerian Paradise Land*, in ed. Possehl, 1979.

Kuraishi, M.H. : *List of Ancient Monuments Protected Under Act VII of 1904, in the Province of Bihar and Orissa*, Govt. of India,

,Central Publication Branch, Calcutta, 1931.

Lalye, P.G. : *Studies in Devī Bhāgavata,* Popular Prakashan, Bombay, 1st ed. 1973.

Lang, Andrew : *Myth, Ritual and Religion,* Vols. I & II, Longmans, Green and Co., London, 1887. *Custom and Myth,* London-Longmans, Green and Co., 1893.

Langer, Susan : *Philosophy in a New Key,* Mentor Book, Published by the New American Library, 1951.

Larousse : *Mythology,* Encycopaedia of. Paul Hamlyn, London, 1964.

Leach, Edmund ed : *The Structural Study of Myth and Totemism.* Tavistock Publications, London, 1968.

: *Lévi-Strauss,* Fontana Paperbacks, William Collins Sons & Co. Ltd., Glasgow, 8th ed, 1982.

Leshnik, Lawrence S. : *The Harappan "Port" at Lothal: Another View,* in ed. Possehl, 1979.

Lévi-Strauss Claude : *The Scope of Anthropology.* Jonathan Cape, London, 1967.

: *Structural Anthropology,* tr. by Claire Jacobson and Brooke Grundfest Schoepf, Vol. I; Allen Lane, The Penguin Press, London, 1968.

: *The Story of Asdiwal,* in ed Leach, *The Structural Study of Myth and Totemism,* 1968.

: *Structural Anthropology* Vol. II tr. by Monique Layton, Allen Lane Penguin Books Ltd., London, 1977.

: *Myth and Meaning,* Routledge and Kegan Paul, London and Henley, 1978.

: *The Way of the Masks.* tr. Sylvia Modelski Jonathan Cape, *London, 1982.*

Maity, S.K. : edd. and Upendra Thakur, Indological Studies, Prof. D.C. Sircar Commemoration Volume, Abhinav Publications, 1st ed. 1987.

Mackay, Ernest : *Early Indus Civilization, Indological* Book Corporation, New Delhi, 1976.

Majumdar, R.C. : edd. with S.C. Altekar, *A New History of the Indian People,* Motilal Banarsidass, Lahore, 1st ed. 1946.

: Vol. III, *The Classical Age.* 3rd ed., 1970.

: *(Gen. ed.) The History and Culture of the Indian People,* Vol. II. *The Age of Imperial Unity, Bharatiya Vidya Bhavan, Bombay, 5th ed. 1980.*

Malinowski, Bronislaw : *Magic, Science and Religion and Other Essays.* The Free Press, Glencoe Illinois, 1948.

: *Sex, Culture and Myth,* Rupert Hart-Davis, Soho Square, London, 1963.

Mani, Vettam : *Purāṇic Encyclopaedia,* Motilal Banarsidass, Delhi, 1984

Marshall, Sir John : *Mohenjo-daro and the Indus Civilization,* Vol. I, Arthus Probsthain, Street, London, 1931.

Meister, Michael : edd. with Dhaky, M.A. -*Encyclopaedia of Indian Temple Architecture.* Vol. 1 text; Vol. I, Part 2, Plates and Text; American Institute of Indian Studies, Oxford University Press, Delhi, 1986.

Mitterwallner, Gritli Von: *The Kuṣāṇa Type of the Goddess Mahiṣāsuramardinī as Compared to the Gupta and Mediaeval Types,* Reprint from German Scholars on India, Contributions to Indian Studies, Vol. II, Nachiketa Publications Limited, *Bombay, 1976.*

Nuemann, Erich : *The Great Mother, An Analysis of the Archetype* by Ralph Manheim, Bollingen Series XLVII, 1954.

Nilakanta Sastri, K.A. : *Age of the Nandas and Mauryas.* Motilal Banarsidass, 2nd ed., 1967.

O' Flaherty, Wendy Doniger : *Asceticism and Eroticism in the Mythology of Śiva,* Oxford University Press, London, 1973.

: *Hindu Myths with an Introduction* Penguin Books, 1976.

: *The Origins of Evil in Hindu Mythology,* University of California Press, Berkley and Los Angeles London, 1976.

: *Sexual Metaphors and Animal Symbols in Indian Mythology,* Motilal Banarsidass, Delhi, 1981.

: *The Shifting, Balance of Power in the Marriage of Śiva and Pārvatī* in edd. J.S. Hawley and D.M. Wulff, 1984.

Oppert, Gustave : *The Original Inhabitants of India* Oriental Publishers, Delhi, 1972.

Pace, David : *Claude Lévi-Strauss, the Bearer of Ashes,* Ark Paperbacks, Great Britain 1986.

Pargiter, F.E. : *Markandey Purāṇa.* The Asiatic Society of Bengal, Calcutta. 1904.

Payne, Earnest.A. : The Śāktas. YMCA Publishing House, Calcutta, 1933.

Piggott, Stuart : *Prehistoric India to 1000 B.C.* Penguin Books Ltd., Harmondsworth, Middlesex, 1950.

Preston, James. J. : *Cult of the Goddess, Social and Religious Change in a Hindu Temple.* Vikas Publishing House Pvt. Ltd., New Delhi, 1980.

Przyluski, J. : Jt. Authors and Sylvan Lévi and Jules Bloch, *Pre-Aryan and Pre-Dravidian in India.* tr. P.C. Bagchi; University of Calcutta, 1929.

Possehl, Gregory : *Ancient Cities of the Indus,* Vikas Publishing House Pvt. Ltd., Bombay, 1979.

Pusalkar, A.D. : *Studies in the Epics and Purāṇas,* Bharatiya Vidya Bhavan, Bombay, 1955.

Quackenbos, George Payn: *The Sanskrit Poems of Mayūra,* Columbia University Press, New York, 1917.

Raikes, Robert. L. : *The End of the Ancient Cities of the Indus,* in ed. Possehl, 1979.

Ramaswamy, C. : *Monsoon Over the Indus Valley During the Harappan Period,* in ed. Possehl, 1979.

Raghavan. V. : *Śrī Devī Māhātmya (with Tamil tr.)*, Personal Publication Madras, 1967.

Rao, M. Rama : *Early Chalukyan Temples of Andhra Desa*, Andhra Pradesh Government Archaeological Series No. 20, The Government of Andhra Pradesh, Hyderabad, 1965.

Rao, M.S. Nagaraja : ed. *Kusumāñjali, New Interpretation of Indian Art and Culture*. C. Sivaramamurti Commemoration Volume. Vol. I. Agam Kala Prakashan, Delhi, 1987.

Rao, T.A. Gopinatha : *Elements of Hindu Iconography*. Vol. I, Part II, The Law Printing House, Madras, 1914.

Renou, Louis : *Religions of Ancient India*. University of London, The Athlone Press, 1953.

Sarma, I.K. : *Brahmanical Brick Temples and Cult Objects from Keesargutta*, in ed. M.S. Nagaraja Rao, 1987.

Schoff, Wilfred. H. : tr. and annotated, *The Periplus of the Erythraean Sea*. Oriental Book Reprint Corporation, New Delhi, 2nd ed. 1974.

Sharma, Pushpendra Kumar : *Śakti Cult in Ancient India*. Bharatiya Publishing House, Varanasi, 1974.

: *Śakti and Her Episodes on the Basis of Ancient Indian Tradition and Mythology*. Eastern Book Linkers, Indological Publishers and Booksellers, Delhi, 1981.

Sharma, Rajendra Nath : *Ancient India: According to Manu.* Nag Publishers, Delhi, 1st ed. 1980.

Shendge, Malati. J. : *The Civilized Demons: The Harappans in* Ṛgveda. Abhinav Publications, New Delhi, 1977.

Shivram, Pavetri Kumari: *Lajjā Gaurī Sculptures - With Special Reference to Gujarat.* Dissertation for M.A., M.S. University, Baroda,. April, 1987.

Singh, Gurdip : The Indus Valley Culture, in ed. Possehl, 1979.

Sinha, B.C. : *Hinduism and Symbol Worship.* Agam Kala Prakashan, Delhi, 1983.

Sircar, D.C. : *Studies in the Religious Life of Ancient and Medieval India.* Motilal Banarsidass, Delhi, 1st ed. 1971.

Slater, Gilbert : *The Dravidian Element in Indian Culture.* Asian Educational Services, New Delhi, Reprint, 1982.

Smith, Vincent.A. : *The Early History of India.* Oxford, At the Clarendon Press, 1967.

Spence, Lewis : *The Outlines of Mythology.* Watts & Co., London, 1944.

Spratt, P. : *Hindu Culture and Personality.* A.S. Manaktala & Sons Pvt. Ltd., Bombay, 1966.

Srivastava, M.C.P. : *Mother Goddess in Art, Archaeology, and Literature* Agam Kala Prakashan, Delhi, 1978.

Thapar, Romila : *Ancient Indian Social History (Some Interpretations)*, Orient Longman. 1978.

: *From Lineage to State.* Oxford University Press, Bombay, 1984.

Tiwari, J.N. : *Goddess Cults in Ancient India (with Special Reference to the first Seven Centuries A.D.).* Sundeep Prakashan, Delhi, 1985.

Thurston, Edgar : *Ethnographic Notes in Souther India, Part II.* Cosmo Publications, Delhi, Reprint, 1975.

Upadhya, Bhagwat Saran: *Women in RgVeda.* Nand Kishore and Bros., Banaras, 2nd ed., 1941.

Vaudeville, Charlotte : *Krishna Gopāla, Rādhā and the Great Goddess*, in edd. J.S. Hawley and D.M. Wulff, 1984.

Venkataraman, K.R. : *Devī Kāmākshī in Kāñcī.* R.A. Sattanathan, The Modern Stores, Tirunelveli, 2nd ed. 1973.

Wadley, Susan : *Women in the Hindu Tradition;* in jt auth. Jacobson, Doranne, *Women in India, Two Perspectives*, Manohar, 1977.

Weber, Max : *From: Essays in Sociology*, Tr. and ed. by H.H.Gerth and C.Wright Mills. Kegan Paul, Trench, Trubner & Co., Ltd., *London, 1947.*

: *The Religion of India.* Tr. and ed. by Hans H. Gerth and

Don Martindale. The Free Press, Glence, Illinois. 1958.
: *The Sociology of Religion.* tr. Ephraim Fishchoff, Methuen & Co. Ltd., London, 1965.

Wheeler, Sir Mortimer : *Harappan Chronology and the ṚgVeda,* in ed. Possehl, 1979.

Whitehead, Henry : *The Village Gods of South India,* Asian Educational Services, New Delhi, 2nd ed., 1983.

Woodroffe, Sir John : *Hymns to the Goddess,* Ganesh & Co., Madras, 1973.
: *Śakti and Śākta,* Ganesh & Co., Madras, 1975.

Wulff, David. M. : *Prolegomenon to a Psychology of the Goddess,* in edd. J.S. Hawley and D.M. Wulff, 1984.

Yalman, Nur : *'The Raw: the Cooked: Nature: Culturé-Observation on 'Le Cru et le cuit',* in ed. Edmund Leach, 1968.

Yocum, Glenn E. : *Comments: The Divine Consort in South India,* in edd. J.S. Hawley and D.M. Wulff, 1984.

Zimmer, Heinrich : *Myths and Symbols in Indian Art and Civilization.* Bollingen Series VI. 1972.
: *The Art of Indian Asia,* 2 Vols. Bollingen Series XXXIX, 1964.

Research Journals

Agrawala, Vasudeva S. : *Aditi and the Great Goddess,* IC. Vol.4 1937-38, pp. 401-409.

: Terracotta Figurines of Ahichchhatra, District Bareilly, U.P. Reprint from "*Ancient India*" No.4, July 1947-Jan. 1948.

Banerji-Sastri, A. : *Asura Expansion in India*. *JBROS*. XII. Part ii, June 1926. pp. 243-85

: *Asura Institutions, as above* pp. 503-39

Biardeau, Madeline : *Some More Considerations About Textual Criticism Purāṇa*, X.2, July 1968, pp. 115-23.

: *The Story of Arjuna Kārtavīrya without Reconstruction, Purāṇa*, XII. 2. July 1970, p.p. 286-303.

Bonazzoli, Giorgio : Devīliṅga-A Note, *Purāṇa* XX.1. Jan. 1978.

: *A Devī in the Form of Liṅga, Purāṇa*, XXII. 2. July 1980, pp. 220-31.

Boner, Alice : *The Symbolic Aspect of Form, JISOA*, XVII, 1949, pp. 42-50.

Brown, Norman : *Proselyting the Asuras (A note on RigVeda 10.124) JAOS*, 1919, pp. 100-103.

Chakraborty, Aparajita : *The Social Formation of Indus Society*, Economic and Political Weekly, *XVIII*, No. 50. Dec. 10, 1983, pp. 2132-36.

Chatterjee, Sunit Kumar: *Dravidian Origins and the Beginnings of* Indian civlization, *Mr. XXXVI*, nos. 1-6, July-Dec, 1924, pp. 665-79.

Chemburkar, Jaya : Umā Haimavatī Myth in the Devī Bhāgavata-A Study, *Purāṇa*, VIII.1, Jan, 1976, pp. 93-100.

Choudhuri, Narendra Nath : *Mother Goddess Durgā, The Poona Orientalist*, XV. nos. 1-4, 1950, pp. 32-38.

Coomaraswamy, A.K. : Angel and Titan-An Essay in Vedic Ontology, *JAOS*, 1935, pp. 373-419.

Dandekar, R.N. : Asura Varuna, *ABORI*, XXI. pp. 157-91.

Davane, G.V. : The Goddess Sarasvatī in Sanskrit Literature, *Journal of the University of Bombay, Arts and Social Sciences* Number, XXXVII, Oct. 1968, pp. 70-77, reprint.

Dhavalikar, M.K. : Śākambharī-The Headless Goddess, *ABORI*, LXVIII, 1987, pp. 281-93.

Dikshitar, V.R.R. : Migration of Legends, *ABORI*, XV., pp. 212-19.

Diskalkar, D.B. : A New Inscription of Chandragupta II of G.S. 61 found in Mathura, *ABORI*. XVIII, pp. 166-70.

Gangadharan, N. : Had Aparṇā (Pārvatī) Any Other Sisters? *Purāṇa*, XVIII.2, July 1976, pp. 153-61.

Gonda, J. : Pūṣan and Sarasvatī, *Book Review*, *JRAS*, 1986. no. 1. pp. 120-21.

Gupta, A.S. : Conception of Sarasvatī in the Purāṇas, *Purāṇa, IV. 1.* Jan, 1962, pp. 55-95.

Gupta, A.S. : Purāṇas and Their References, *Purāṇa*, VII. 2. July, 1965, pp. 321-51.

: Constitution of the Vāmana Purāṇa Text, *Purāṇa,* IX. 1, Jan. 1967, pp. 141-94.

: A Problem of Puraṇic Text Reconstruction, *Purāṇa* XII, 2. July, 1970, pp. 304-21.

: Eulogy of Devī by Mahādeva with Note, *Purāṇa,* XV.1, Feb. 1973, pp. 1-5

: Purāṇic Heritage, *Purāṇa,* XVIII. 1. Jan. 1976, pp. 39-55.

: Eulogy of Parāśakti by Gods, with Notes, *Purāṇa,* XIX, 1. Jan. 1977, pp. 1-7.

: Glorification of Goddess Rātri, With Notes, *Purāṇa,* XX. 1, Feb. 1978, pp. 1-6.

Hansen, Kathryn : The Virangana in North Indian History, Myth and Popular Culture, *Economic and Political Weekly,* XXIII, No. 18, Apl. 30, 1988, pp. 25-33.

Hazra, R.C. : The Upapurāṇas, *ABORI,* XXI, pp. 38-62.

Jamkhedkar, A.P. : Devī Worship, *AIRI Series XI,* Feb. 1981, pp. 92-95.

Kantawala : Asura in the ṚgVeda, *ABORI. LXIV,* Parts I-IV, 1983, pp. 119-28.

: Purūravas-Urvaśī Episode, *ABORI,* LVII, 1976, pp. 49-58.

Karmarkar, Anant P. : Fresh and Further Light on the Mohenjo Daro Riddle, *ABORI,* XXI, pp. 115-27.

Keith, Berriedale : The Aśvins and the Great Goddess, *IC,* Vol. 3, 1936-37, pp. 721-26.

Konow, Sten : Indo-European Religious Ideas in Ancient India, *ABORI*, VI, Part II, March 1925.

Kosambi, D.D. : Excerpt from-On the Origin of the Brahmin Gotras, *JBBRAS*, Vol. 26, Part I, 1950, pp. 20-80.

Law, B.C. : *Ancient Indian Tribes, ABORI*, XXI. pp. 203-12.

Mazumdar, B.C. : Durgā: Her Origin and History, *JRAS*, 1906, pp. 355-62.

Mukherji, Shyam Chand: The Cult of Ekānaṁśā, *IHQ*, XXXV. 1. pp. 189-208.

Przyluski, J : The Great Goddess of India and Iran, IHQ, X.3. Sept. 1934, pp. 405-30.

Pusalkar, A.D. : Authors of the Indus Culture, *ABORI*, XVIII, pp. 385-95.

Rai, Ganga Sagar : A Note on Kātyāyanī, *Purāṇa*, XXII. 1, Jan. 1980, pp. 102-103.

Rao, S.R. : Indus Script and Language, *ABORI*, LXI, Parts I-IV, pp. 157-88.

Sircar, D.C. : Śākta Pīthas, *JRASB*, Letters Vol. XIV, 1948, pp. 1-108.

Soifer, Deborah, A. : Towards an Understanding of Viṣṇu's Avatāras. *Purāṇa*, XVIII, 2, July 1976. pp. 128-48.

Smith, Daniel, H. : Vahanas in the Cultic Art of South Indian Temples, *AIRI Series*, No. X, Mar. 1980, pp. 12-29.

Srinivasan, Doris : Unhinging Śiva From the Indus

Civilization, *JRAS*, No. 1, 1984, pp. 77-87.

Swali, Haridas : Jyeṣṭhā—The Ambivalent Goddess, *JAŚOB*, Vol, 56-59, 1981-'84 (combined) pp. 326-34.

Vats, M.S. : Excavations at Harappa, reviewed by A.S. Altekar, *ABORI*, XXI, 1934-40, pp. 287-92.

Warner, Karel : Men, Gods and Powers in the Vedic Outlook, *JRAS*, No. 1, 1982, pp. 14-23.

Other Journals and Periodicals

Aryan, K.C. : The Little Goddess (Matrikas) reviewed by Kapila Vatsyayan, *Sunday Standard*, 10.8.1980.

Article : *Art: on French Cave Burials, The Economist, in Science and Technology Oct. 25-31, '86.*

Dhavalikar, M.K. : The First Farmers of Maharashtra, Art. in *Science Age*, Dec. 1987, pp. 12-18.

Eschmann, A. : Jt. Auth. with H. Kulke and G.C. Tripathy-The Cult of Jagannath and the Regional Tradition of Orissa. Book reviewed by Sitakant Mahapatra-Not a Cult But a Culture; *The Times of India*, 23.9.1979.

Goraya, B.S. : Mystic Monuments of Mandhata, *Indian Express*. 23.1.1988.

Kalaikkovan, R. : Viḍiyalin Veḷiccattil Varalāṟṟu Alundūr, Tamil Art. in *Kalaimagal*,

July, 1988.

Levathes, Louise, E. : Mysteries of the Bog, *National Geographic* Vol. 171, No. 3, Mar. 1987.

Nagaswamy, R. : Ninnayum Pakaḻuven Tāye, Tamil, Art. *Kalaimagal Deepavali Malar*, 1974, pp. 212-14 .

Padmanabhan, B.S. : Projections of Harappan Matrix, *The Hindu*, 24.7.1983.

Santini : Asuranai Aḻitta Eḻu Śaktikaḷ, Tamil Article in *Amuda Surabhi*, Dec. 1984.

Sankalia, H.D. : Prehistoric Europe, *The Illustrated Weekly of India, 26.6.1977.*

: The Rare Stuff, The Times of India, 28.8.86.

Singbal, G.R. : Image of Ancient Deity Found, *Indian Express, 23.7.1986.*

Report : *Mahishasuramardini Sculpture at* Chattisgarh Region, The Times of India Supplement, 21.4.1988.

Report : Oceanic Goddess Figure in Bulgaria, *The Times of India*, 2.3.1980.

Other Sources

Information on the Kathatiya Caves in Ch. II, from the personal notes of Shankar Aiyar.

INDEX

Shakti (Indus Valley)

Shakti Weapon (Indus Valley)

Mother Goddess, Mohenjodaro, Circa 2500 B.C

Yakshini, Maurya, 3rd Century B.C.

Mother Goddess, Adichanallur

Burial Urn, Adichanallur

Bronze Buffalo Figurine, Adichanallur

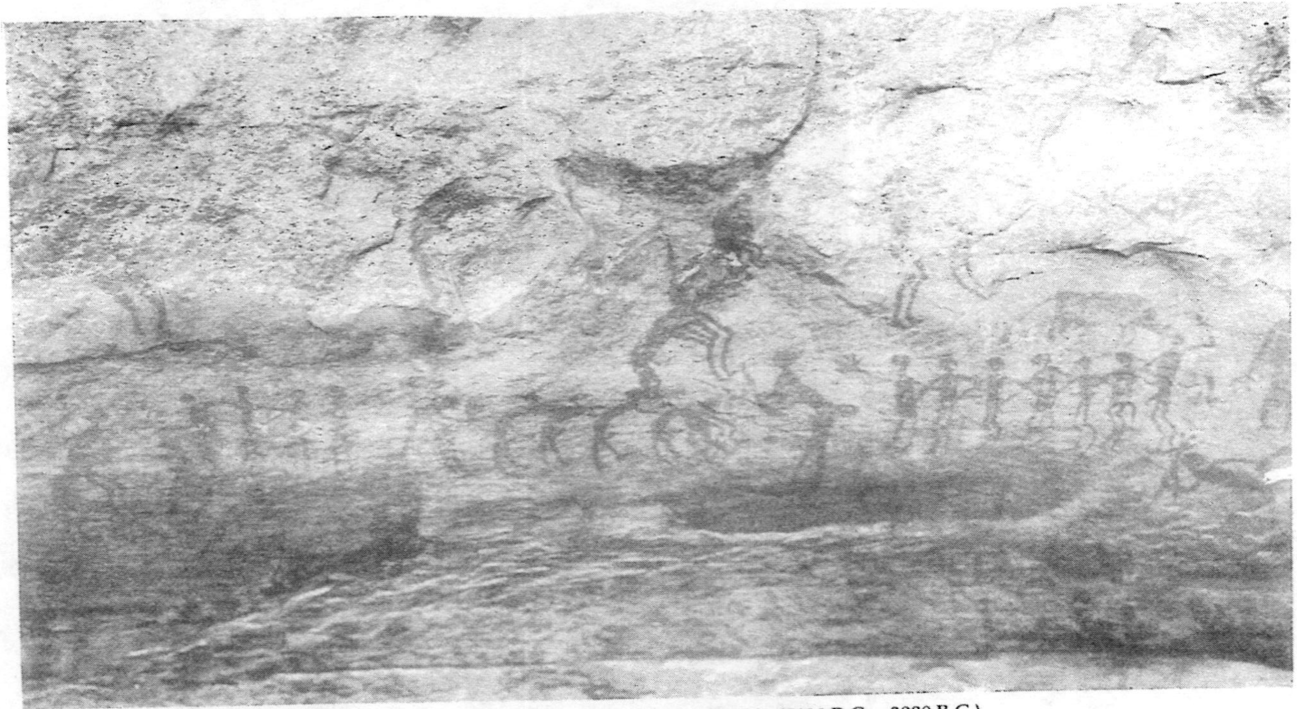

Kāthia Cave Painting of the Mother Goddess Worship (5000 B.C.—3000 B.C.), Bhopal

Vāhanas—Variety of Goddess Sarasvatī with Swan (Mathura)

Vāhanas—With Swan (Later Period)

Vāhanas—With Lion (1037 A.D.)

Vāhanas—With Ram (Chatingram 11th Century A.D.)

Vāhanas—With Peacock (12th Centurv A.D.) (Halebid)

Goddess—Laksmī—Kolhapur Lakṣmī with Elephant

Śrī-Lakṣmī—Brihadeśvara Temple, Raja Raja I (1010 A.D.)

Goddess Sarasvatī—Gaṅgaikoṇḍa Coḷapuram—Rajendra I (1030 A.D.)

Sapta-Mātṛs-Ravan-Ka-Khai, Cave 14, Ellora, Late 6th Century A.D.

Nārayaṇī Tiruvalancuḷi, Early Coḷa

Cāmuṇḍā-Tahākari, 11th Century A.D.

Kālī—Benign-Tillai Kālī Temple-Uḍaya-Parameśvarī, Bronze, Coḷa 11th Century A.D.

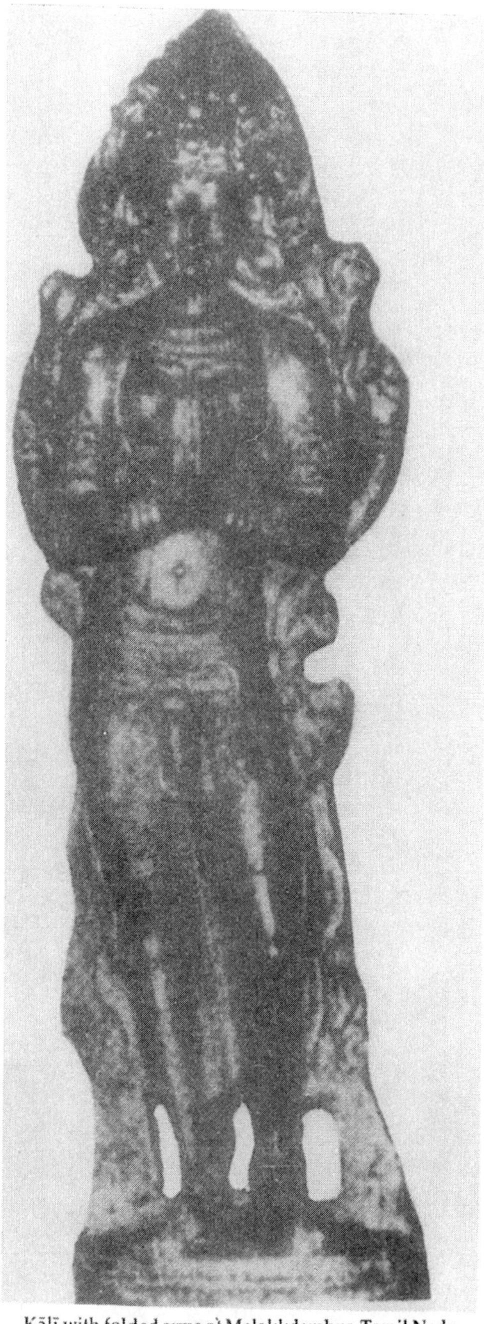

Kālī with folded arms at Melakkdambur, Tamil Nadu

Kālikā Devī

Kālī Stone Coḷa, Tiruvorriyur, 11th Century A.D

Dakṣineśvar Kālī

Lajjā Gourī, Bhitta-Terracotta, 1st Century A.D.

Ter. Maharashtra

Darasuram Tanjavur, Coḷa

Nevasa-Circa 1st-2nd Centuries A.D.

Bāvkā Dt., Panchmahals, C-10th-11th Centuries A.D.

Durgā as Mahiṣāsuramardinī, Alampur, Western Chalukya, 5th-6th Centuries A.D.

Durgā as Mahiṣāsuramardinī, Alampur, Western Chalukya, 5th-6th Centuries A.D.

Durgā as Mahiṣāsuramardinī, Alampur, Balabrahma Temple, Western Chalukya, 5th-6th Centuries A.D.

Durgā as Mahisāsuramardinī, Alampur, Western Chalukya, 5th-6th Centuries A.D.

Durgā as Mahiṣāsuramardinī—Aihole Śiva Cave, 6th Century A.D.

Benign Durgā, Gaṅgai Koṇḍa Coḷapuram, Rajendra I (1030 A.D.)

Durgā Mahiṣāsuramardinī, Kailasanatha Temple, Rayasimha Pallava, 700 A.D.

Durgā Mahisāsuramardinī, Ellora—Rāmeśvara Cave, 7th Century A.D.

Durgā Mahiṣāsuramardinī, Someśvara Temple, Mukhalingam, Eastern Ganga, 8th Century A.D.

Durgā Mahiṣāsuramardinī, Someśvara Temple, Mukhalingam, Eastern Ganga, 8th Century A.D.

Durgā Mahiṣāsuramardinī, Belūr, 12th Century A.D.

Goddess with Shivaji's Sword, Kolhapur Lakṣmī

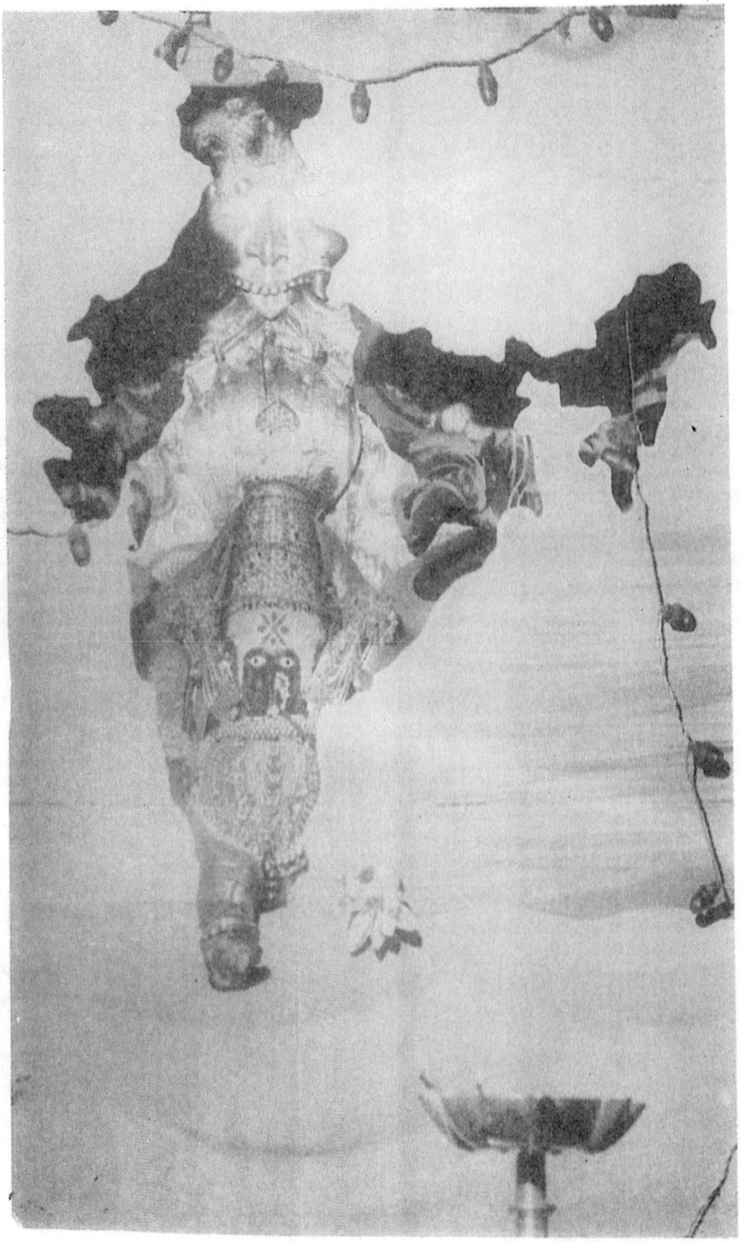

Kolhapur Lakṣmī as Bhārat Mātā.